D1607474

LATIN AMERICAN HORIZONS

A Symposium at Dumbarton Oaks
11TH AND 12TH OCTOBER 1986

Don Stephen Rice, *Editor*

Dumbarton Oaks Research Library and Collection
Washington, D.C.

Library of Congress Cataloging-in-Publication Data

Latin American horizons : a symposium at Dumbarton Oaks,
11th and 12th October 1986 / Don Stephen Rice, editor.
p.   cm.
Includes bibliographical references.
ISBN 0-88402-207-2
1. Indians—Antiquities—Congresses.   2. Latin America-
-Antiquities—Congresses.   3. Archaeology—Latin America-
-Congresses.   I. Rice, Don Stephen.   II. Dumbarton Oaks.
E65.L36 1986
980'.01—dc20   92-14833

Contents

PREFACE   vii

DON STEPHEN RICE
The Making of Latin American Horizons: An Introduction to
the Volume   1

REBECCA STONE-MILLER
An Overview of "Horizon" and "Horizon Style" in the Study
of Ancient American Objects   15

RICHARD L. BURGER
The Chavin Horizon: Stylistic Chimera or Socioeconomic
Metamorphosis?   41

DAVID C. GROVE
"Olmec" Horizons in Formative Period Mesoamerica:
Diffusion or Social Evolution?   83

ESTHER PASZTORY
An Image Is Worth a Thousand Words: Teotihuacan and the
Meanings of Style in Classic Mesoamerica   113

ARTHUR A. DEMAREST and ANTONIA E. FOIAS
Mesoamerican Horizons and the Cultural Transformations of
Maya Civilization   147

ALAN L. KOLATA
Understanding Tiwanaku: Conquest, Colonization, and
Clientage in the South Central Andes   193

Contents

RICHARD P. SCHAEDEL
Congruence of Horizon with Polity: Huari and the Middle
Horizon   225

RICHARD A. DIEHL
The Toltec Horizon in Mesoamerica: New Perspectives on an
Old Issue   263

EMILY UMBERGER and CECELIA F. KLEIN
Aztec Art and Imperial Expansion   295

JOHN HYSLOP
Factors Influencing the Transmission and Distribution of Inka
Cultural Materials throughout Tawantinsuyu   337

DON STEPHEN RICE
The Status of Latin American Horizons   357

INDEX   365

Preface

THIS VOLUME STEMS FROM a symposium held at Dumbarton Oaks in October 1986 to review and reassess the continued validity of the horizon concept in Pre-Columbian archaeology. Born in the 1940s, the familiar and now well-established horizon concept has held firm in Andean archaeology as the principal armature for organizing cultures in time and space. With the 1972 seminar on the Valley of Mexico held at the School of American Research, the horizon model seized a foothold in Meso-america as well. Because of its simplicity and relative neutrality, it is a strong model for structuring the past; but like all universalizing structures, it hides cultural variability and the nuances of the archaeological record, and it does carry its own message.

In organizing this conference, Don Rice wanted to see just how valid the horizon concept is as a structural tool for understanding Andean and Meso-american culture history and process. Does it still work in the Andes, and is it markedly better in Mesoamerica than the old Pre-Classic, Classic, and Post-Classic armatures?

This volume on Latin American horizons is therefore as much an episte-mological consideration as it is an anthropological and art historical analysis of Pre-Columbian cultures. It concerns itself not only with the Pre-Columbian past but also with how scholars view, categorize, and explain this past. Most of the individual authors in the volume have assessed the material remains of individual cultures to see whether and to what extent they conform to the horizon model. But many, as a first step, look at how the horizon concept was developed and applied to the culture in which they specialize, so that even within their anthropological analysis there is the recognition that such analyses are shaped by the model itself. Don Rice and Rebecca Stone-Miller address these epistemological questions directly.

In the end, the judgment is that the horizon concept is too broad and simple for the scholar, but that it is useful for the student. Although it fails upon specialized analysis, it does work as a general organizational scheme to arrange a large body of material in some logical manner. The organization of this volume itself is a case in point. The succession of the papers juxta-poses the "major" cultures of the Andes and Mesoamerica in pairs or clus-ters, thereby forcing comparisons and analogies—Chavin and Olmec,

Teotihuacan and Maya along with Huari and Tiahuanaco, Toltec and Aztec and Inca, which associate Pre-Classic and Early Horizon, Classic and Middle Horizon, Post-Classic and Late Horizon. The great differences between the cultures are there in the individual articles, but the overarching analogy is still implied.

A note on the orthography used in this volume: in Mesoamerica, the consensus among historians and archaeologists has been to spell Nahuatl words and proper names according to sixteenth-century Spanish pronunciation. Since the Aztec language was put into European alphabetic script soon after the conquest, the tradition of using the Spanish spelling is an old one; few have wanted to change it. One thus sees "Nahuatl" rather than "Nawatl." The exception is with works that focus on modern Nahuatl (and other indigenous languages), where modern linguistic orthography is commonly used.

In the Andes, however, the situation is more complicated. Many archaeologists and historians have abandoned the traditional Spanish spellings to adopt the orthography of modern Quechua, while others staunchly have not. A good many of these individuals feel strongly about their decisions. Some scholars feel that switching to the modern orthography would confuse Andean names and terms unnecessarily, while others see it as a convenient adoption of a new spelling authority; still others view it as a political statement—anti-Spanish and pro-Indian. Thus the field of Andean archaeology now uses both Inca and Inka, Huari and Wari, as well as Tiahuanaco and Tiwanaku. I debated whether to try to adopt a single orthography for this volume—and thus impose one view on all the authors—and in the end (after much discussion) decided not to do this. The field of Andean studies is composed of many perspectives and positions, and it seemed more important in a multi-authored work to keep the diversity that now exists. Therefore we have retained each author's spelling for these names, providing the alternative version in a parenthesis when it first appears. If the organization of the volume seems to draw different cultures together and compare them in terms of horizons, the orthography reveals the real diversity of present scholarship.

Elizabeth Hill Boone
Dumbarton Oaks

The Making of Latin American Horizons: An Introduction to the Volume

DON STEPHEN RICE

SOUTHERN ILLINOIS UNIVERSITY AT CARBONDALE

IN ARCHAEOLOGY, "HORIZON" IS A CLASSIFICATORY TERM originally intended to place a particular constellation of cultural traits in time and space. Philip Phillips and Gordon R. Willey have defined horizon as "a spatial continuum represented by the wide distribution of a recognizable art style" (1953: 625; see also Willey and Phillips 1958: 38, cited in Diehl, this volume). Under the assumption that styles are historically unique and that they change rapidly, Phillips and Willey have proposed that horizons are chronologically sensitive and "useful in equating in time phases of culture widely separated in space" (1953: 625). Breadth and rapidity of geographic disposition, then, are salient qualities of horizons; "the horizon is characterized by its relatively limited time dimension and its significant geographic spread" (Willey and Phillips 1955: 723).

As Rebecca Stone-Miller (this volume) indicates, a horizon is a unit of cultural space, but in many cases its creation rests on the definition and identification of style. A *horizon style* is the "aesthetic device" for the creation of horizons. Styles, often defined in terms of changes in the appearance of objects, exhibit a constancy of form and expression over measurable periods of time or geographic space (Schapiro 1953). For Willey, style was an encompassing category that could be broken down into three components for the purpose of analysis: technology, representation, and configuration (1951: 109). Technology includes materials and techniques of manufacture, representation is the subject matter or content of a style, and configuration is the manner in which a style's content is expressed. It is this last, configuration, that Willey considered unique to a specific style . . . "a matter of line, composition, and emphasis" (1951: 111).

Although Phillips and Willey equated horizon with horizon style in their initial discussion of the concepts (1953: 625; Willey 1951: 111), they later acknowledged that a horizon style "is one culturally determined means of establishing a horizon, but the latter must be defined in broader terms"

(Willey and Phillips 1958: 32). The horizon style concept presupposes an integrated, coherent pattern of elements and motives and a level of aesthetic development that is not necessarily demonstrated in all archaeologically identifiable societies. Nonetheless, other cultural data might serve to identify horizons in such instances. Potential "horizon markers" include components of Willey's style definition (1951)—materials or techniques, or specific representations—or widely traded specialized artifacts, unique artifact assemblages, or peculiar cultural practices (Phillips and Willey 1953: 626; see also Willey and Phillips 1958: 32, cited in Diehl, this volume).

These definitions and uses of the terms *horizon, horizon style,* and *horizon marker* serve a particular goal of archaeology, the identification of spatio-temporal boundaries. Material attributes are assessed and horizons defined that give insight into the relative contemporaneity of geographically defined cultural assemblages. Although horizon assemblages or styles are not necessarily emically significant to the producers of the artifacts and patterns, definitions of horizons by archaeologists assume some purposive human agency or mode for the spread of the defining styles or traits.

There is also a set of center-margin or core-periphery relations implicit in the construction of horizons. Centers of origin for particular artifacts, assemblages, or styles are assumed (centers of earliest occurrence and greatest elaboration), and these "move" from those centers to more peripheral regions. If that movement is widespread and rapid, then a horizon designation is warranted, and the horizon is useful for correlating the relative chronologies of "influenced" regions. If the distribution of defined traits is geographically constrained but temporally sustained, however, reflecting a localized trajectory of development, then the horizon concept does not apply, and the set of defining traits is less useful as an integrative chronological marker.

The most immediate and tangible result of such constructions is the "chronological chart," with the intersection of its vertical (time) and horizontal (space) axes creating "boxes" within which cultural or temporal designations are often given (see Stone-Miller, this volume, for a discussion of chronological charts and their implications). These charts make visible two prominent types of cultural relations: vertical progressions of development within localized regions, called "traditions" (Phillips and Willey 1953: 626–628; Willey and Phillips 1958: 35–40); and horizons of traits shared across space during temporally brief periods.

Several of this volume's contributors document that archaeology's preoccupation with spatial and temporal relationships, and the origin of the horizon concept itself, resulted from goals and needs that characterized the early history of the discipline. During the late nineteenth and early twentieth centuries, archaeologists in the Americas had to contend with considerable unprovenienced data, a lack of absolute dating for materials and sites, and a relative absence of historical analogs and contexts for the evaluation of artifacts and architecture. A first order of business was to establish spatial and chronological control over materials. This process involved the discovery of patterns of similarity and difference in horizontal space, the placement of these in vertical time, and the assessment of patterns in terms of historical continuities and disjunctions—the establishment of region-specific culture histories.

Critical to this cultural-historical approach was the identification of "stylistic types," classes of artifacts, architecture, or features whose chronological and spatial patterns could be measured and analyzed comparatively. Type definitions were based largely on portable objects that were ubiquitous in the archaeological record, in particular ceramics, and stylistic descriptions focused primarily on formal attributes, or homologous similarities, that were visible and easily measureable: form, physical properties of materials, surface treatment, and the structure and content of decoration. Although such attributes were often assumed to have been consciously manipulated by the original artisans, archaeologists rarely concerned themselves with original function or meaning in their creation of stylistic types (for a sense of early debate over the creation of types, and the problems of "empirical" versus "natural" or "cultural" types, see Ford 1954a, 1954b; Spaulding 1953, 1954).

The seriation of artifacts, or the collections or proveniences of which they are a part, allowed for creation of geographically bounded typologies that were considered time-sensitive. The archaeological record was thus describable in terms of these spatial and temporal "style units," sets of types that provided the bases for the definition of "cultures," chronological sequences of "culture periods," and cultural histories, where the term *culture* connotes artifacts, architecture, assemblages, and contexts that "recur repeatedly together" and "are assumed to be concrete expressions of the common social traditions that bind together a people" (Childe 1950: 2). Characteristic artifacts or markers became identified with social and historical realities, and the spatial and temporal variations in distributions of artifact assemblages were considered to reflect cultural change. While "no effort was made to explain why stylistic types displayed the distributions in time and space that proved so useful" (Dunnell 1986: 32), the processes invoked to explain the archaeological record as it had been conceptualized and described were those "that explained homologous similarities": acculturation, diffusion, migration, persistence, and trade (Dunnell 1978: 199; 1986: 31).

The development of the horizon concept, and debate over its utility to archaeology, is understandable within this context of cultural-historical goals and efforts. Discussions of the history of the horizon concept invariably begin with the work of Max Uhle at the turn of the century (e.g., Rowe 1962; Willey and Sabloff 1980: 71–73). In this volume, Stone-Miller describes how Uhle began his analysis of Central Andean materials while cataloging collections of the Royal Zoological and Anthropological Museum in Dresden in the 1880s, during which time he had to contend with a standing "prejudiced notion of generally regarding the various types of ancient culture as merely local styles, each being ascribed to a different geographic area and to a different tribe" (Uhle 1902: 754; also cited in Stone-Miller, this volume). Uhle was apparently influenced by W. M. Flinders Petrie's creation of a numbered sequence of relative periods constructed around seriated ceramic materials, by which to interpret archaeological data for Predynastic Egypt (Rowe 1962: 44–45), and he advocated that we "pay attention particularly to their [i.e., culture types] succession in time; for their importance as stylistic strata which succeeded and covered each other . . . is far beyond that which they may possess as local types" (Uhle 1902: 754; also cited in Stone-Miller, this volume).

Uhle organized the results of his museum work, and subsequent archaeological explorations in Bolivia and Peru accordingly. Applying the principles of seriation and stratigraphy, he proposed a four-period style-based sequence: early regional styles; Tiahuanaco-influenced styles; late regional styles; and Inca-related styles (Uhle 1903, 1910, 1913). Within this framework, local cultures are cross-dated and made understandable relative to one another by reference to the two horizons shared by all sampled regions, "the chronological horizon of the culture of Tiahuanaco" and "the chronological horizon of the Inca culture," under the assumption that the horizon styles had spread sufficiently rapidly that all occurrences, regardless of region, were contemporaneous (Rowe 1962: 45). In 1922, Alfred Kroeber and William Duncan Strong continued the cross-dating of regional sequences with stylistic time-markers in their analyses of Uhle's collections from Ica and Chincha, and they redefined Uhle's four periods as: Pre-Tiahuanaco, Tiahuanaco, Pre-Inca, and Inca (Kroeber and Strong 1924: 53).

The first formal definition of the horizon style concept was articulated some twenty years later by Kroeber in a summary of Peruvian archaeology as of 1942, wherein he discussed the nature of periodization and style in the context of known historical relations in the Andes. Here he characterized a horizon style as "showing definably distinct features some of which extend over a large area, so that its relations with other, more local styles serve to place these in relative time, according as the relations of priority, consociation, or subsequence" (Kroeber 1944: 108). Kroeber also added Chavin (see Middendorf 1893–95 and Tello 1929, cited in Burger, this volume; and Larco Hoyle 1938, 1941; Tello 1943, for early discussions of the status of Chavin as a wide-spread cultural phenomenon) to the two principal horizon styles proposed by Uhle, Tiahuanaco and Inca, as one of "three ancient cultures which were almost pan-Peruvian" (Kroeber 1944: 115).

One year later, Willey reviewed and reaffirmed the utility of Kroeber's horizon styles for Peruvian archaeology, calling them "the horizontal stringers by which the upright columns of specialized regional development are tied together in the time chart" (Willey 1945: 55). He noted, however, the possibility that "horizon styles were not absolutely coeval in all parts of Peru" because of the time that it would take stylistic traits to diffuse from regions of origin to more peripheral areas, and that "the time-chart device has been artificially arranged to place Inca, Tiahuanaco, and Chavin on horizontal levels, ignoring the factor of time lag" (1945: 55).

In the same year, John Rowe expressed similar concerns about the dating of horizons, pointing to the considerable stylistic variation that exists within the Inca horizon, and the impressive "vitality" of local styles (1945: 278). He also advocated the anchoring of relative chronologies, based on sequences of pottery types, in a more reasoned reading of the absolute chronology of the literature of the Inca period.

In Willey's 1945 assessment of Kroeber's arguments for several potential horizon indicators in Peru (Nazca B-Y, Negative, and White-on-Red), he also speculated on the existence of style-based "historical units of an order different from that of the horizon style" (Willey 1945: 53). Specifically, he proposed that within some geographic regions and culture areas "fundamental cultural unity justifies seeing ceramic developments in terms of long-time traditions as well as coeval phenomena" (1945: 53). The pottery tradition is not the integration of stylistic traits, diffused widely, that is characteristic of horizon styles. Rather, it consists of styles that arose and "remained strictly localized" (1945: 53).

Willey (1945) suggested that traditions and horizons are "opposable concepts in archaeological reconstruction," and he warned that efforts to use pottery traditions as style markers for time horizons can be a source of potential confusion in Peruvian studies. Acknowledging that "horizon styles have been interpreted functionally as well as having been used for historical reconstruction," however, Willey suggested that the study of the interplay between traditions and horizons "should explain more fully the various historical factors which have converged in time and space to produce the entity of style" (1945: 55). Herein lay the excitement of style as subject for cultural historical analysis, to search for the functional determinants underlying its origins, distribution, and persistence (Willey 1945: 56).

Willey pursued further a functional analysis of horizon styles in a paper in 1948, in which he attempted to "define and characterize as cultural forces on the level of social interaction what heretofore have been viewed chiefly as historical phenomena" (1948: 8). At the outset he assumed that "the functional significance of a horizontal diffusion and integration of a complex of cultural ideas, may, in part, be deduced from the structural types of culture with which these horizons are associated" (1948: 8), but the analysis appears to have been informed as much by implicit notions about style, and about the specific processes that shaped Andean history, as it was by a structural classification of cultural types.

In this study, the Chavin, Tiahuanaco, and Inca horizons were deemed to have "ingredients of true styles," as identified in "terms of specific designs and design combinations" (Willey 1948: 15). Styles were here considered symbols, or information, as indicated in Willey's suggestion that the period intervening between the Chavin and Tiahuanaco horizons "was an era of realization in terms of techniques already known, not a time of the ready borrowing of new ideas," and that "the local styles were in no sense experimental but crystallized symbols of the national consciousness" (1948: 12). Willey speculated that "foreign art symbolism" [the Tiahuanaco horizon style] would have been "unpopular," or represented a threat to local ruling castes during this period, and that there was social and political advantage to maintaining "a strong nationalism and attendant isolationism" (1948: 12).

Ultimately, the art symbolism of these expanding regional states "fell before a similar and more powerful aggressor," Tiahuanaco, an historical reconstruction consistent with the documented militaristic expansion of the later Inca empire (Willey 1948: 13). Religious symbols accompanied these "first great conquests," however, and it was suggested that "a revolutionary religious ideology might very well have been the catalytic agent through which several politically unrelated conquests were realized" (Willey 1948: 14). The Inca, on the other hand, had less effect on local styles, in part perhaps because of the brevity of their occupation, and in part because they were "no longer in need of a rich imperial symbolism" (1948: 14).

In 1949 Wendell Bennett and Junius Bird generalized from these extant definitions of horizons and interpretations of stylistic change to create a framework of developmental intervals within which Andean cultural units could be classified (Bennett and Bird 1949). Three ceramic-based horizon styles (White-on-Red, Negative, and Black-White-Red) were added to Chavin, Tiahuanaco, and Inca, each interrupted by a period of localized cultural developments, and these six together were categorized into a sequence of "stages" on the basis of presumed economic and political characteristics: Hunters, Early Farmers, Cultists, Experimenters, Master Craftsmen, Expansionists, City Builders, Imperialists, and Conquest. Here the term *stage* indicates a unit of cultural similarity, defined by a particular cultural pattern, and taken together as a series, these stages comprise a "historical-developmental" sequence (Willey and Phillips 1958: 64–72). When viewed as a time chart, the implication of this overarching unilineal structure is that the traits or behaviors assigned to each period are characteristic of the entire interval, and that the established trend of development is constant and uniform through time (see Stone-Miller's critique of similar time-chart characteristics and problems, this volume).

In 1956, Rowe responded to the use of such functional-developmental schemes with concern, pointing out that they erroneously conflate time and cultural process. He admonished that "cultural process should be a goal of our investigations, not something that we assume at the moment we try to put pottery styles in chronological order" (Rowe 1956: 627). Rowe advocated return to a terminology that distinguishes between the time span covered by a given style phase and the changes that took place in the style itself, and he recommended a chronological classification based on Kroeber's distinction of Early, Middle, and Late Periods. Expanding these to account for additions to the sequence since Kroeber's original analyses and formulation, he offered the now familiar terms: Initial Period, Early Horizon, Early Intermediate Period, Middle Horizon, Late Intermediate Period, and Late Horizon (Rowe 1956).

Rowe suggested that "as it becomes possible to make more precise correlations, we will have to equate this chronological scheme with the sequence in some particular Peruvian valley, so that it can be used to state time equivalences elsewhere" (1956: 628), and in 1962 he offered the Ica Valley as an appropriate point of reference because of the detailed chronology of pottery styles that had been developed there. Rowe felt that the establishment of such a master sequence would resolve some of the confusion between developmental stages, or "units of cultural similarity," and periods, "units of contemporaneity" (1962: 40). This confusion arises particularly when attempting to match local sequences over large areas, in that "[cultural] stages established on the basis of uniform criteria can be expected to give a different matching from periods, because of the effects of diffusion" (1962: 40).

With increased field work and control over the varied contexts for data, and the availability of absolute dates made possible by the introduction of radiocarbon dating techniques in 1950, greater and more precise subdivisions of sequences were being established. The behavior of materials and their stylistic attributes was making it increasingly apparent that traits by which horizons were defined may diffuse at different rates. This variability results from differences in points of origin and directions of spread, the nature of the agent(s) of dissemination, the density and distributions of populations and their centers, the definition of peripheries and boundaries, and so forth. Developmental stages, particularly stages defined on the basis of numbers of cultural traits which co-occur, cannot easily reveal these differences.

Although it was Rowe's belief that the "study of horizon styles and of their relationships to the local ones which separate them in time should provide us with some clues to the processes of cultural unification and diversification which the archaeological record reflects" (1956: 627), the data at hand suggested that "as the precision of our chronology increased beyond the point where the appearance of 'horizon styles' could be taken as a sufficient indication of contemporaneity, some new basis for defining the [temporal] periods had to be found" (1962: 48). The use of a master sequence to control a system of chronological intervals was Rowe's answer, where "relative dating can be put strictly on a basis of contemporaneity . . . without regard to whether there is any stylistic or technological resemblance between them [cultural units assigned to the same period]" (1962: 49).

Organizing archaeological data according to a system of temporal periods, rather than developmental stages, "permits the investigator to identify delays in the spread of cultural features and hence to determine the direction in which the spread took place and ultimately the area of origin of the feature studied" (Rowe 1962: 51). This control reinforces Rowe's point that the unit of contemporaneity is more important to cultural interpretation than the unit of cultural similarity. The ways in which contemporaneity can be established between the Ica Valley and another cultural unit include absolute dates, trade pieces, and stylistic influence [diffusion]. The latter risks the same problems of contemporaneity that Rowe was taking issue with. In the absence of absolute dates and/or well provenienced trade, the entire enterprise demands the assumption that the Ica Valley was culturally central or prominent throughout history, and that it participated in the total universe of significant (diagnostic) pan-Andean trade or influence.

As Rowe wrestled with problems attendant to a conflation of cultural and temporal classificatory units, and tried to establish the primacy of a neutral chronology, Willey was addressing further the functional role of style in Latin American horizons. In his 1961 Presidential Address to the annual meeting of the American Anthropological Association, Willey was concerned with what he termed the "great art styles" of the Chavin and Olmec, and with the role that these art styles, "or the motivations of which they are a symbol," played in the rise of "civilization" (1962). He was thus stepping beyond the issues of variability and contemporaneity that concerned Rowe and pursuing the equation of styles and horizons with particular historical or developmental constellations.

Willey referred specifically to art styles as they were expressed monumentally, in settings that were either sacred or secularly important to their makers (1962: 1). These he considered "fine arts" and their "greatness" was also evidenced by their pervasiveness in media and contexts, the skill with which they were rendered, their reflection of strict stylistic canons, their thematic subject matter, and their powerful or awe-inspiring visual impact (1962: 1). Willey felt that Chavin and Olmec art must have been the expressions of "two ecumenical religions" and that art was "in some way involved with the rise to the status of civilization in their respective areas" (1962: 7). As in his earlier discussions of horizon styles, Willey suggested that the Olmec and Chavin styles were "symbols of institutions, attitudes, beliefs," symbols of ideologies that served to unify the early farming societies of Mesoamerica and Peru (1962: 7–8). The sharing of a common ideology, and the resulting social, economic, and political coordination that such an ideology facilitated, "led to the threshold of civilization" (Willey 1962: 10).

Although this conclusion was speculative and did not resolve the issue of why Mesoamerica and Peru developed these ideologies and art styles, Willey's consideration of the problem focused attention on the functional analysis of style and horizonal phenomena at a time when original chronological utility of the horizon concept was being questioned. These divergent perspectives on style and horizons are symptomatic of problems both with the horizon concept and with changes that were taking place in the field of archaeology.

During the interval of archaeological field work and thinking glossed here, the archaeological record came to be described primarily in terms of styles, and the behavior of styles was the basis for periodization of culture history. The horizon concept served two functions in this context: as a chronological marker that served to integrate the local chronologies of disparate regions, and as an indication of cultural processes resulting in stylistic coherence over a broad region. The two are not necessarily mutually reinforcing; Rowe and others have discussed the difficulties attendant on equating horizons with cultural units, and ultimately with developmental stages, and the degree to which this tendency undermines both chronological function and fine-grained cultural interpretation.

Increasing complexity and detail of the archaeological record progressively called into question the chronological and cultural specificity of horizon definitions, and these were constantly being revised and subdivided, to the detriment of temporal and substantive schema. As George Kubler indicated, style as a relational concept is largely static, an idea best suited to description of synchronous events (1970: 137–138), and all but very short style-based periods fail to respond to, or reflect, what he called "differences in cultural time," the fact that change takes place at different rates in centers and peripheries, and temporal and developmental boundaries have variable rates of change (1970: 130–131). Unfortunately, style-based sequences also often suffer from "hardening of the periods"; once established, the diacritics and boundaries of sequences were hard to refute or overturn (Kubler 1970: 128). The same might be said for the style-based definitions of types themselves.

With respect to functional interpretations of stylistic units, periods or stages, Kubler also questioned the degree to which one could read history from pottery [writ style]. That is to say, how much information do styles carry (1970: 132)? The "quest for the meaning of the sherds has produced an incomparable history of pottery, but not a history of civilization, because pottery alone does not reveal much more than itself" (1970: 132). His point was that "information is not intrinsic to pottery," it is deduced from contexts and associations, where styles provide temporal control. Kubler noted that "culture history erected upon these foundations relies upon the indefinite integrals of intuition and analogy," and these bases for interpretation were largely implicit during the cultural historical period of archaeological research (1970: 133).

This is not the place to review the post-cultural-historical history of American archaeology; others provide that background in much greater detail and with more sophistication than I could achieve here (e.g., Lamberg-Karlovsky and Kohl 1988; Meltzer, Fowler, and Sabloff 1986; Trigger 1989; Willey and Sabloff 1974). Suffice it to say, however, that in the past several decades the discipline has moved away purposefully from a preoccupation with chronology and substantive histories and toward analyses of the cultural structures and processual dynamics of social units documented in those histories. One outcome of this change in perspective and goals has been debate over the bases for and logic of interpretation of the archaeological record (e.g., Binford 1983; Hodder 1986; Shanks and Tilley 1987; Spriggs 1984).

Despite the issues of data and dating that have caused some practitioners to question the utility of stylistically defined units of time and culture and despite the recent shifts of archaeological focus toward explanation of cultural configurations and change, the horizon framework remains in use in Andean and Mesoamerican archaeology. But what impact have a growing data base, refinements in the dating and sourcing of archaeological deposits, and ongoing methodological and theoretical arguments in archaeology, had on the substance and utility of the horizon concept as used by archaeologists and art historians? The contributors to this volume have sought to assess this question.

Following Stone-Miller's analysis of the horizon and horizon style concepts from an art historical perspective, each of the major horizons in Mesoamerica and South America is discussed, together with the horizonal status of the Mesoamerican groups, the Maya and the Toltec. In these chapters, the authors review the chronological and substantive data by which these horizons are currently defined, and they evaluate the analytical contexts within which horizons currently function. In so doing, they offer critical reevaluations of the material content and cultural coherence of these classifications and make important assessments of the viability of the horizon as a methodological and theoretical construct.

BIBLIOGRAPHY

BENNETT, WENDELL C., AND JUNIUS BIRD
   1949   *Andean Culture History.* American Museum of Natural History, Handbook Series, No. 15. New York.

BINFORD, LEWIS R.
   1983   *In Pursuit of the Past.* Thames and Hudson, London.

CHILDE, V. GORDON
   1950   *Prehistoric Migrations in Europe.* Institutet for Sammenlignende Kulturforskning, Ser. A. Foreslesninger, 20 (5). Oslo.

DUNNELL, ROBERT C.
   1978   Style and Function: A Fundamental Dichotomy. *American Antiquity* 43 (2): 192–202.
   1986   Five Decades of American Archaeology. In *American Archaeology Past and Future* (David J. Meltzer, Don Fowler, and Jeremy Sabloff, eds.): 23–49. Smithsonian Institution Press, Washington, D.C.

FORD, JAMES A.
   1954a   Comment on A. C. Spaulding: "Statistical Techniques for the Discovery of Artifact Types." *American Antiquity* 19: 390–391.
   1954b   The Type Concept Revisited. *American Anthropologist* 56: 42–54.

HODDER, D. IAN
   1986   *Reading the Past.* Cambridge University Press, Cambridge.

KROEBER, ALFRED
   1944   *Peruvian Archaeology in 1942.* Viking Fund Publications in Anthropology 4. New York.

KROEBER, ALFRED, AND WM. DUNCAN STRONG
   1924   *The Uhle Collections from Chincha.* University of California Publications in American Archaeology and Ethnology 28 (2). Berkeley.

KUBLER, GEORGE
   1970   Period, Style, and Meaning in Ancient American Art. *New Literary History* 1 (2): 127–144.

LAMBERG-KARLOVSKY, CARL, AND PHILIP L. KOHL (EDS.)
   1988   *Archaeological Thought in America.* Cambridge University Press, Cambridge.

LARCO HOYLE, RAFAEL
   1938   *Los Mochicas,* 1. Lima.
   1941   *Los Cupisniques.* Lima.

MELTZER, DAVID J., DON FOWLER, AND JEREMY SABLOFF (EDS.)
   1986   *American Archaeology Past and Future.* Smithsonian Institution Press, Washington, D.C.

Don Stephen Rice

MIDDENDORF, ERNST W.
  1893–95 *Peru: Beobachtungen und Studien über das Land und Seine Bewohner Wahrend Eines 25 Jahrigen Aufenthalts.* 3 vols., Robert Oppenheim, Berlin.

PHILLIPS, PHILIP, AND GORDON R. WILLEY
  1953 Method and Theory in American Archaeology: An Operational Basis for Culture-Historical Integration. *American Anthropologist* 55 (5,1): 615–631.

ROWE, JOHN H.
  1945 Absolute Chronology in the Andean Area. *American Antiquity* 10: 265–284.
  1956 Cultural Unity and Diversification in Peruvian Archaeology. In *Men and Cultures; Selected Papers of the Fifth International Congress of Anthropological and Ethnological Sciences:* 627–631. Philadelphia.
  1962 Stages and Periods in Archaeological Interpretation. *Southwestern Journal of Anthropology* 18 (1): 40–54.

SCHAPIRO, MEYER
  1953 Style. In *Anthropology Today: An Encyclopedic Inventory* (Alfred L. Kroeber, ed.): 287–312. University of Chicago Press, Chicago.

SHANKS, MICHAEL, AND CHRISTOPHER TILLEY
  1987 *Reconstructing Archaeology.* Cambridge University Press, Cambridge.

SPAULDING, ALBERT C.
  1953 Statistical Techniques for the Discovery of Artifact Types. *American Antiquity* 18: 305–313.
  1954 Reply to Ford. *American Antiquity* 19 (4): 391–393.

SPRIGGS, MATTHEW (ED.)
  1984 *Marxist Perspectives in Archaeology.* Cambridge University Press, Cambridge.

TELLO, JULIO C.
  1929 *Antiguo Peru: Primera Epoca.* Comision Organizadora del Segundo Congreso Sudamericano de Turismo, Lima.
  1943 Discovery of the Chavin Culture in Peru. *American Antiquity* 9: 135–160.

TRIGGER, BRUCE
  1989 *A History of Archaeological Thought.* Cambridge University Press, Cambridge.

UHLE, MAX
  1902 Types of Culture in Peru. *American Anthropologist* 4: 753–759.
  1903 Ancient South American Civilization. *Harper's Monthly Magazine,* 107 (October): 780–786.
  1910 Über die Frühkulturen in der Umgebung von Lima. *Sixteenth International Congress of Americanists:* 347–370. Vienna.
  1913 Die Ruinen von Moche. *Journal de la Société des Américanistes de Paris* 10: 95–117.

WILLEY, GORDON R.
  1945 Horizon Styles and Pottery Traditions in Peruvian Archaeology. *American Antiquity* 1: 49–56.

1948   A Functional Analysis of "Horizon Styles" in Peruvian Archaeology. In *A Reappraisal of Peruvian Archaeology* (W. C. Bennett, ed.), *Memoir*, no. 4: 8–15. Society for American Archaeology, Menasha, Wisc.

1951   The Chavin Problem: A Review and Critique. *Southwestern Journal of Anthropology* 7 (2): 103–144.

1962   The Early Great Styles and the Rise of the Pre-Columbian Civilizations. *American Anthropologist* 64: 1–14.

1971   *An Introduction to American Archaeology. Vol. 2: South America.* Prentice-Hall, Englewood Cliffs, N.J.

WILLEY, GORDON R., AND PHILIP PHILLIPS

1955   Method and Theory in American Archaeology II: Historical-Developmental Interpretation. *American Anthropologist* 57: 723–819.

1958   *Method and Theory in American Archaeology.* University of Chicago Press, Chicago.

WILLEY, GORDON R., AND JEREMY A. SABLOFF

1974   *A History of American Archaeology.* W. H. Freeman, San Francisco.

An Overview of "Horizon" and "Horizon Style" in the Study of Ancient American Objects

REBECCA STONE-MILLER

EMORY UNIVERSITY

T HE ALLIED CONCEPTS OF THE HORIZON and the horizon style bring up
a fundamental question upon which the fields of Pre-Columbian
art history and archaeology converge: simply, how does visual art
of the ancient Americas reveal cultural and aesthetic relationships in time
and across space? Despite the fact that time has "no intrinsic segmentation
of its own" (Kubler 1970: 128), there is a recurrent need to subdivide
history in order to study both long-term and short-term change and continuity. Material history is no exception. Subdivision has been the major
issue of twentieth-century inquiry into the ancient American past and has
typically proceeded from the initial identification of material remains to
subsequent grouping, ordering, and interrelating of art and artifacts. Therefore, at least basic chronologies now exist for all regions of the Americas,
however incomplete or arguable these may still be in some cases. The task
remains to interrelate fully the many sites, styles, chronologies, regions,
artists, and cultures that have been identified. In order to proceed with the
subtleties of historical reconstruction based on material remains, at this
stage it seems crucial to reexamine the assumptions upon which the basic
orderings were based. The horizon constitutes a prime focus for such a
reexamination.

The *horizon* is a concept that serves to group similar art and artifacts
across space, under the assumption that overall resemblance of objects indicates their general contemporaneity. From these categories of similar objects across wide expanses of space and short spans of time, an inference of
the existence of wider cultural unity is made. This grouping of peoples
through their surviving objects tends to rely heavily upon a component
concept of the *horizon style,* which pinpoints certain readily distinguishable
stylistic features or diagnostic formal configurations of the grouped pieces.
Thus, the two terms are closely interrelated; however, it is important to
stress that they are not interchangeable, because the *horizon* is a unit of

cultural space, while the *horizon style* is an aesthetic device for the formation of such units.

Neither remains merely a term; each can be said to perform the roles of a concept, a category, and a challenge. Firstly, a horizon is a spatial concept, under the hypothesis that periods of cultural similarity will be found to cut across the continuum of time in a materially recognizable fashion. The horizon style is also a concept, one that proposes to link the makers of art through the spread of a particular formal vocabulary. Secondly, the horizon concept creates a series of categories, the "boxes" created by the intersection of time and geography. These intersections are reified in the familiar chronological chart—constant companion to the horizon scheme—to be discussed below. Horizon style categories also function like boxes into which objects can be thrown mentally when their characteristics line up with those of the core styles. The historiographic basis for such an organizational need will be presented briefly. Thirdly, and perhaps most importantly for the present volume, horizon and horizon style concepts and categories together pose a scholarly challenge: to explore the particular significances of visual resemblance and difference over time. In order to chart the interrelation of similarity and change—in essence to develop a calculus of the visual past—one must have tools. The question will be raised, as it is throughout the present volume, whether the horizon/horizon style concepts still constitute such a tool.

To trace these three roles of the horizon and the horizon style, this paper will present first a brief historiography of the origin of these concepts. A formal analysis of several versions of the chronological chart then will highlight ways in which the space-time categories have been presented. Such a "stratigraphic" approach to the archaeologists' and art historians' prime, shared didactic device will demonstrate the underlying and overt messages encoded in graphic choices. Thirdly, some art historical challenges to the horizon style assumption that visual similarity bespeaks contemporaneity will be suggested.

ORIGIN AND DEVELOPMENT OF THE CONCEPTS

The concepts of the horizon/horizon style served as a bridge between nineteenth-century antiquarian thinking and twentieth-century "scientific" archaeological approaches. These ideas allowed the process of identification and ordering to begin before stratigraphic techniques enabled archaeologists to locate objects more precisely in space and time; however, they have persisted since such information has become more widely available. The horizon was formulated in Andean studies and has persisted explicitly in that terminology, while in Mesoamerican studies there has been slower and less universal acceptance (see Grove, this volume). Some clues to this situation may be found in historical circumstances.

The idea of a horizon as defined by stylistic unity implicitly underlay the pioneering scholarship of Max Uhle, who began his career cataloguing the collections of the Royal Zoological and Anthropological Museum in Dresden in the 1880s. Only after attempting to order a plethora of Andean pieces with a dearth of contextual information did Uhle proceed to the field to test his museological categories. His attempt to order in time was also in part a reaction to a point of view current in his time which he characterized as:

> the prejudiced notion of generally regarding the various types of ancient culture as merely local styles, each being ascribed to a different geographic area and to a different tribe. . . . In observing these types of culture we should pay attention particularly to their succession in time; for their importance as stylistic strata which succeeded and covered each other (and, for the greater part, covered a coëxtensive area), is far beyond that which they may possess as local types. (Uhle 1902: 754)

Rejecting the then-current astratigraphic view, Uhle established the first rough chronology of cultures for ancient America by distinguishing "Tiahuanaco"-style pieces from Inca-style examples. Subsequently he separated out objects that he felt belonged before and between the two known styles, thus establishing four relative periods: pre-Tiahuanaco, Tiahuanaco, post-Tiahuanaco, and Inca. The development of a rudimentary chronological horizon/horizon style concept thus can be seen as a response to a situation of undocumented works of art in museum collections. Although this predicament may have been particularly acute in the late nineteenth century, this unfortunate situation still holds true today. The Andean subfield originated, and has perpetuated, an aesthetic, object-based orientation at least partly in order to create order from an archaeological *cum* museological nightmare.

Yet, style was by no means discarded as a "second-best" analytical tool when stratigraphic archaeology was developed. In fact, it was the next scholarly generation—fully "entrenched" in stratigraphy—that codified these ideas. In 1944, Alfred Kroeber defined the concept when he wrote "by horizon style I mean one showing definably distinct features some of which extend over a large area, so that its relations with other, more local styles serve to place these in relative time, according as the relations are of priority, consociation, or subsequence" (Kroeber 1944: 108). Kroeber also studied objects before proceeding to field work; he first worked on the Uhle collections at the Lowie Museum of Anthropology at Berkeley. He explicitly applied the horizon/horizon style idea not only to pieces lacking provenance information, but also to those with a known site and those whose exact stratigraphic location within a site was documented. Thus, the horizon concept again served as a bridge.

Kroeber added "Chavin" to the Tiahuanaco and Inca horizons, thus setting up the tripartite division still in general use today. At the time, he also codified three other "horizons" based on ceramic decoration: the "Red-on-White," "Negative," and "Red-Black-White." These persisted for a time in the literature (see Bennett and Bird 1949) but were discarded soon after as a codification specific to ceramics rather than as a true horizon marker. This serves as an illustration that certain common features, especially technical ones, may have relevance within the history of a particular medium but fail to illuminate larger questions of culture history.[1]

Although the idea originated in Andean studies, horizons were proposed for Mesoamerican antiquity as early as 1942 at the Segunda Mesa Redonda held in Mexico City (Nicholson 1960). Horizon I was subtitled the "Archaic"; Horizons II and III divided up the Maya, Tajin, Teotihuacan, and Monte Alban sequences; and Horizon IV was subtitled "Mixteco-Puebla." However, the present tripartite Preclassic/Classic/Postclassic terminology that had taken hold by that time was maintained almost without exception from the 1940s onward. Barbara Price reintroduced the horizon terminology to Mesoamerican archaeology in 1976; however, the Classic scheme remains more common. Partly this may reflect the tenacity of known referents, such as the misnomer "Olmec" after all these years. The establishment of nomenclature emphasizing the period of Maya florescence, a Classic that other periods either precede or follow, certainly reflects the preponderance of Mayanists in Mesoamerican studies in the twentieth century. In a larger historiographic sense, "Mexico" was known much earlier and figured in larger philosophical arguments concerning the relative evolutionary status of Amerindians (Keen 1971). Thus, there may have been pressure to make Maya and Aztec art, already predominantly figural, directly comparable to European art. The value-laden term *Classic* serves this validating purpose, substituting its hierarchy of importance for the slightly more neutral horizonal scheme of alternating cultural unification and regionalism. Finally, in pointing up the differences between the two areas of research, Kroeber had suggested in 1942 that the greater numbers of "Mexicanist" scholars, with more funding and therefore more excavations, "struggle with an embarrassingly rich and complicating local diversity" (Kroeber 1944: 15). Kroeber may have suffered from a slight case of sour grapes, for an early abundance of more reliable information on Mesoamerica may have interfered with the codification of the sweeping unities implied by horizons.

---

[1] As George Kubler has pointed out, the change from Black-Figure to Red-Figure pottery painting in Classical Greece held no political or larger cultural significance, reflecting internal aesthetic choices within the ceramic medium alone. In fact, Kubler voices his doubts that ceramics in general hold the key to periodization (1970: 133). The case of the three additional ceramic "horizons" may serve as a cautionary tale for those who would reconstruct culture from single technical attributes of one type of art.

In post-1940s Andean studies the horizon idea and terminology has persisted full force. John Rowe (1945) in particular has been concerned with the issue, first establishing the currently accepted absolute chronology for the Inca, then introducing the current period names of Early, Middle, and Late "Horizons" alternating with corresponding "Intermediate Periods" (Rowe 1954). He placed the known local styles into these categories, where they have largely rested ever since. In 1962, Rowe fine-tuned the horizon concept by distinguishing between stages, "units of cultural similarity," and periods, "units of contemporaneity." (Rowe 1962: 40). He presented many of the recurrent assumptions underlying the transmission of associated cultural features, averring the relative rarity of independent invention; positing trade as "the best evidence of contemporaneity" (1962: 49); and stating that boundaries between stages "must be shown as a straight line on the chart of relationships" (1962: 41). (See section on chronological charts below.) He concluded, however, that the idea that the influence of a widespread set of stylistic features on local sequences indicates contemporaneity was past its usefulness as a chronological tool and proposed the use of the Ica Valley sequence as the master point of reference for cross-dating. Reliance on radiocarbon dates, repeated association of particular trade and local wares, and influence of one style on the local one(s) to establish contemporaneity all remained in the new Ica-related horizonal framework and thus the basic assumptions were retained.

The archaeological horizon/horizon style schema began to draw some criticism from both archaeologists and art historians in the 1950s. Irving Rouse in 1957 agreed that the correlation of phases, as non-temporal, non-spatial independent entities, must begin with the description of attributes. But he disagreed that such discovered similarities necessarily reflect contemporaneity or a genetic connection.

> To say that a phase in one area is contemporaneous with phases in other areas because they share a given horizon style . . . is on the genetic . . . level of interpretation, for it requires an assumption that the style has diffused from one phase to the others with little or no time lag. Too often an archaeologist who has made this assumption will proceed to draw the conclusion that the style must have diffused from one phase to the others simply because all the phases are contemporaneous, thereby involving himself in circular reasoning. (Rouse 1957: 718)

In 1962 George Kubler provided a new art historical proposal for a move away from all traditional historical time divisions made by contemporary "narrators" (1962a). He discussed stylistic similarity of objects in terms very different from those assumed in horizons: open and closed sequences, prime objects, replicas, and form classes, among others. His concepts link art produced in many times and places by stressing the formal exploration inherent in all creative production. Kubler thereby introduced a more dynamic view of "the history of things," one that stressed diachronic over synchronic relations. A *sequence,* in his terms, is a series of solutions to an artistic problem; sequences can be closed, that is, completed in the past; or open, that is, still producing new solutions today. Form classes consist of all the solutions to a particular problem. Prime objects, truly original works of art, spark series of replicas arrayed at no constant distance from the original in time or space. Such alternative concepts of stylistic influence and the movement of ideas in art are particularly useful when confronted by recurrent revivals and renascences, as are now becoming increasingly visible in ancient American art (see, for example, Umberger 1987). But Kubler's ideas also serve to remind us that art reveals the most about art itself, that the relationships between art objects may be to some degree atemporal, and that style is fluid, even irrational, in its spread over time and across space.

CATEGORIES: THE CHRONOLOGICAL CHART

The preceding brief historiographic remarks serve to introduce a consideration of how the categories set up by horizon and horizon style have been presented graphically. The horizon concept may have encouraged scholars to formulate the now-familiar chronological chart in order to present most clearly and succinctly the complex relationships between multiple time/space categories. In a static, two-dimensional chart these categories become patently visible as literal intersections of vertical and horizontal lines. Relative positions are easy to determine by following these lines in either direction. It seems that the clarity afforded by tabular presentation appeared necessary precisely when the relative positions of numerous identified cultures became an issue. Hence, it is no accident that Kroeber presented one of the first major chronological charts for ancient Andean studies at the same time as he explicitly laid out the horizon scheme in 1944 (Fig. 1). Despite the many blank spaces, representing gaps in knowledge at the time, the coherence of the vertical and horizontal format was well suited to reify the horizons Kroeber espoused. The chronological chart has continued in this role to the present day, illustrating in turn the various assumptions and historical positions of its various authors.

We have come to take these useful didactic devices for granted. In the archaeological and art historical literature they are found at the beginning of all summary publications and featured in articles in which a new chronological relationship is proposed. Tabular presentations are ubiquitous in ethnographic scholarship as well, which led Jack Goody to a very thought-provoking criticism of the table itself as inherently reductionist, arbitrary, and ethnocentric (Goody 1977).[2] However, their very ubiquity and useful-

---

[2] I am indebted to Diana Fane of the Brooklyn Museum of Art for this reference.

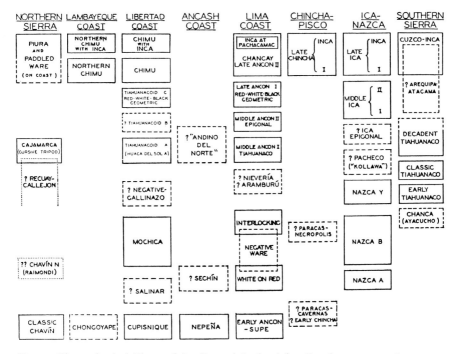

Fig. 1. Chronological Chart of the Central Andes (after Kroeber 1944: 112)

ness may have made us blind to the underlying assumptions they convey about the past.

Chronological charts do bear closer scrutiny as very persuasive and potentially misleading statements about the division of the historical continuum. They seek to translate ideas about physical reality into lines on a page; therefore, graphic design choices profoundly influence the messages conveyed. A diagram can convey statements dictated by the text, independent of it, or both. Five examples, two by archaeologists (Kroeber 1944 [Fig. 1] and Willey 1971 [Fig. 2]) and three by art historians (Sawyer 1968 [Fig. 3], Kubler 1975 [Fig. 4] and 1970 [Fig. 5]), will illustrate various presentations of horizon/horizon style categories. Distinctions between the archaeological and art historical charts will become apparent. For consistency, tabulations of Andean culture history in particular will be compared throughout this discussion.

Before turning to the examples, however, it is important to discuss the inherent tendency of the chronological chart to convey its own interpretation of the material it might appear to present neutrally. At base, a chart in and of itself sends the message that history can be subdivided into simple, often

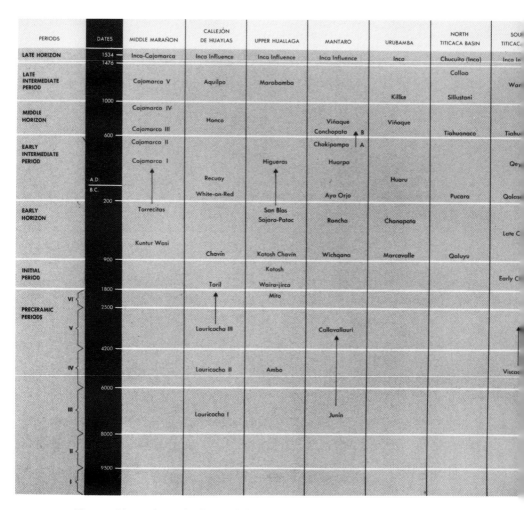

Fig. 2. Chronological Chart of the Central Andean Highlands (after Willey 1971: 85) (with permission of author)

symmetrically placed and "filled in" adjoining categories. History is thus automatically seen as discontinuous and as potentially known (despite its lack of "intrinsic segmentation" and the fact that we reconstruct history through a tiny extant proportion of the original evidence, not to mention through the veil of our own inescapable ethnocentricity). Blank spaces are to be filled in with a name, which encourages the proliferation of culture names and the stretching of a few facts into a distinct cultural entity. In addition, visual symmetry seems to influence unduly the placement of categories. Kroeber pointed out, for example, that the Middle Horizon may be placed at the

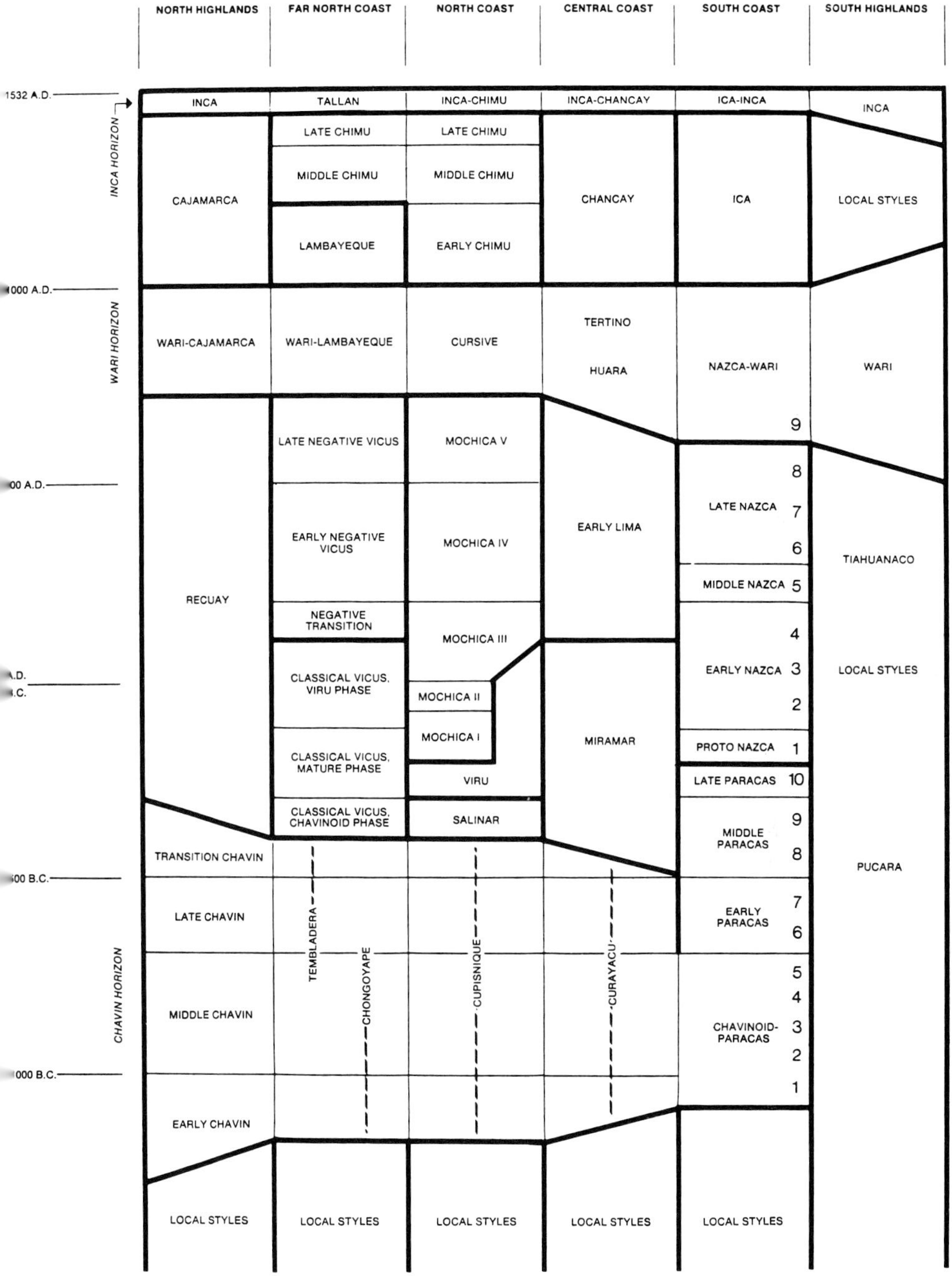

	NORTH HIGHLANDS	FAR NORTH COAST	NORTH COAST	CENTRAL COAST	SOUTH COAST	SOUTH HIGHLANDS
1532 A.D. (INCA HORIZON)	INCA	TALLAN	INCA-CHIMU	INCA-CHANCAY	ICA-INCA	INCA
	CAJAMARCA	LATE CHIMU	LATE CHIMU	CHANCAY	ICA	LOCAL STYLES
		MIDDLE CHIMU	MIDDLE CHIMU			
		LAMBAYEQUE	EARLY CHIMU			
1000 A.D. (WARI HORIZON)	WARI-CAJAMARCA	WARI-LAMBAYEQUE	CURSIVE	TERTINO / HUARA	NAZCA-WARI	WARI
600 A.D.	RECUAY	LATE NEGATIVE VICUS	MOCHICA V	EARLY LIMA	9 / 8 / LATE NAZCA 7 / 6 / MIDDLE NAZCA 5	TIAHUANACO
		EARLY NEGATIVE VICUS	MOCHICA IV		4	
		NEGATIVE TRANSITION	MOCHICA III		EARLY NAZCA 3	LOCAL STYLES
A.D. / B.C.		CLASSICAL VICUS, VIRU PHASE	MOCHICA II	MIRAMAR	2	
			MOCHICA I		PROTO NAZCA 1	
		CLASSICAL VICUS, MATURE PHASE	VIRU		LATE PARACAS 10	
		CLASSICAL VICUS, CHAVINOID PHASE	SALINAR		MIDDLE PARACAS 9 / 8	PUCARA
500 B.C. (CHAVIN HORIZON)	TRANSITION CHAVIN	TEMBLADERA	CUPISNIQUE	CURAYACU	EARLY PARACAS 7 / 6	
	LATE CHAVIN	CHONGOYAPE			5 / 4 / CHAVINOID-PARACAS 3 / 2	
	MIDDLE CHAVIN				1	
1000 B.C.	EARLY CHAVIN					
	LOCAL STYLES	LOCAL STYLES	LOCAL STYLES	LOCAL STYLES	LOCAL STYLES	

Fig. 3. Chronological Chart of the Central Andes (after Sawyer 1968: 105)

	NORTHERN ANDES		CENTRAL ANDES					
	Colombia	Ecuador	Northern Peru — coast / highland		Central Peru	Southern Peru and Bolivia — coast / highland		
1534 —	CHIBCHA Darién	INCA	INCA CHIMÚ LAMBAYEQUE		CHANCAY	ICA	CUZCO	Late Horizon
		Esmeraldas						
1000 ·	QUIMBAYA							Late Intermediate
	Tierradentro	Manabí	HUARI V MOCHICA		Pachacamac Huari	VIÑAQUE Tiahuanaco		
	San Agustín					NAZCA 9		
Integration 500 —					LIMA		8	Middle Horizon 500
	CALIMA		IV				QEYA 7	
	TOLIMA		III				6	
			II				5	
0 —			I				4	0
							3 Pucará 2	Early Intermediate
Regional Developmental 500 —		GUANGALA	Recuay SALINAR			PARACAS 10 Chiripa	1	500
							9 Chanapata	
							8	
			CUPISNIQUE				7	
			Moxeke Chavín				6	
1000			Cerro Sechín				5	Early Horizon 1000
							4	
							3	
							2	
Late Formative 1500		CHORRERA	Kotosh				1	1500
		MACHALILLA			Chuquitanta			Initial Period
2000								2000
2500								Pre-ceramic VI
Early Formative	Puerto Hormiga	Valdivia	Huaca Prieta					
3000								3000

Fig. 4. Chronological Chart of the Andes (after Kubler 1975: XLIII)

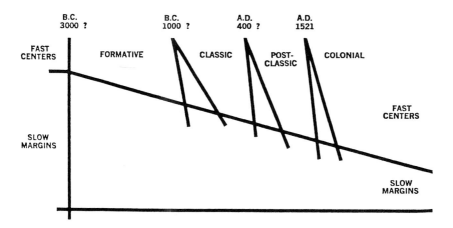

Fig. 5. Chart of "Regional Rates of Change and Period Boundaries" (after Kubler 1970: 130)

middle in diagrams rather than in its correct position relative to the span of known Andean history. A commonly employed six-part Andean system—with Early, Middle, and Late Horizons, organizing North, Central, and Southern areas—creates a particularly tidy picture, perhaps overly so.

The chart, with its adjoining category design, also limits presentation to two types of historical relationships: linear progressions within single geographical areas and general equivalences between different areas at the same time depth. In the case of the former, the diagram inherently illustrates Rouse's criticism that only genetic relationships are allowed to exist between cultures. In the case of the latter, the diagram reifies the horizon conceptual scheme particularly well using literally cross-cutting lines to forge equivalences in time and across space. Lost in two-dimensional renderings (and in a simplistic adoption of the horizon scheme itself, see below and elsewhere in this volume) are the more complex links, such as cross-fertilization between non-contiguous geographical areas, for example, Chavin and Paracas or Teotihuacan and the Maya. Certainly an overabundance of connecting lines and arrows would prohibit optimal visual clarity in a didactic table. Yet most charts eschew even the simple overlap of trends; single horizontal lines typically run straight across geographical subdivisions. The unbroken flat line also asserts that change always occurs across a region simultaneously and irrevocably, a characterization of historical change that is certainly disputable in the case of any well-known area or people. Rowe underlined the absoluteness with which charts' formats are regarded when he wrote "the stage boundary is the constant element which must be shown as a straight line on the chart of relationships" (Rowe 1962: 41). The secondary horizontal lines dividing the phases of a period also discourage the communication of gradual, irregular, or continuous style change within a tradition. The foremost danger of the chronological chart as a visual image lies in the fact that the power and limitations of the format itself may prevent us from seeing certain types of historical/aesthetic complexity.

Furthermore, the typical chart does not usually make explicit its exact subject group, that is, the "database" upon which its categories are determined. In archaeological charts elite culture is better represented, as a result of its more permanent material remains. But it is important to keep in mind that coexisting elite and non-elite cultures might tabulate very differently, not only in terms of types and rates of change, but even in basic cultural traits (as in the case of peasant culture that may change little as ruling groups replace one another). Thus, already several assumptions are encoded in the format of a chart regardless of its particular graphic appearance.

Kroeber was well aware of the effects and pitfalls of a visual representation of chronology. When he introduced his chart (Fig. 1) he wrote that it was

> at the cost of overcoming some internal resistances. . . . The reluctance is due to the knowledge of how a schematic presentation of this sort, tentative as its intended effect may be, quickly crystallizes into a dogma . . . of how it gives a sense of achievement approaching finality, and may end by being reproduced and persisting in manuals, compilations, textbooks, and educational charts long after it has been essentially modified by the labors of actively productive scholars. (Kroeber 1944: 111)

Kroeber's resulting diagram reflects the state of knowledge in the early 1940s: there are large gaps, including the entire Central Highlands, many question marks, and no absolute time scale suggested. The coastal areas predominate (comprising six of the eight geographical categories) and are comparatively more "complete," reflecting the fact that most excavations had taken place on the coast at that time. But more important than such historiographically understandable omissions is the relationship of the diagram as an image to the early archaeological presentation of cultures in time.

Kroeber's chart graphically conveys his written reservations in several, overlapping ways. Conventional question marks convey a lack of certainty about the placement of certain cultures in relation to others (for example, "?Paracas Cavernas" and "?Paracas Necropolis"). Doubled question marks, such as those preceding "??Chavin N," increase doubtfulness, as does the use of visually permeable dotted lines for these and other of the surrounding boxes. One partial box, "Recuay-Callejon," leaves the beginning of this period literally open-ended. Blank background spaces illustrate gaps in knowledge very succinctly. His overall choice of floating boxes rather than a tight grid to delineate cultural groupings communicates successfully that the proposed order remains in a state of flux. Inasmuch as no two boxes touch, Kroeber remains noncommital about the relationships between them and about transitions in general. Perceptually it is as if the viewer could detach, rearrange, or collapse a line of boxes at will, according to new information. The author, in fact, compared such tabulation to arranging the parts of a picture puzzle (Kroeber 1944: 114). These tentative graphic choices are congruent with the first summary of conclusions in a nascent field.

It is particularly surprising, however, that Kroeber did not seek to re-inforce the idea of horizons in his chart, although he boldly states the case for horizons in his text. No connecting lines or color-coding system visually link the boxes across space. Several boxes across the chart repeat the terms "Tiahuanaco" and "Inca," respectively, but these are not precisely adjacent, and it takes careful reading to see a trend. Chavin, despite the fact that Kroeber added it as "probably the most important" horizon in the text (1944: 111), has only one Northern Sierra box to represent it. Thus, the geographical expansion assumed for horizons is not depicted in the horizontal extension of the chart.

Kroeber was aware of certain discrepancies between text and picture that arise from graphic circumstances. He pointed out that he sought to communicate the sequence but not the duration of the individual cultural categories. Yet various boxes have different heights and so inevitably *do* convey duration: his "Mochica" box is taller than that of the "Chavin" and so inescapably asserts to the viewer that the Moche lasted longer. In addition, he also textually acknowledged the distortion that results from the fact that better-known periods necessitate expanded boxes in order to contain their more numerous subdivisions. Thus, in general, the later, shorter but better-documented periods—such as that of Inca domination—tend to be more weighted visually, while earlier ones are misleadingly truncated. This problem persists with the chronological chart whether boxes or subdivided columns are employed. In fact, it is highly impractical to communicate time on one standard scale; to illustrate the true ratio of periods, long "unfilled" early years, for example, the Lithic, would take up pages of space, while the later cultures would be squeezed—illegibly—at the top. A variable time scale, in which an inch represents thousands of years below and hundreds of years above the arbitrary B.C./A.D. line, is the only practical alternative. However, even if the scale shift is understood as it is read by a viewer, perceptually the chart communicates the equivalence of drastically non-equivalent passages of time. In sum, certain aspects of the flow of time are captured and others wildly distorted within the chart format.

Despite Kroeber's warnings, chronological tabulation has played a largely unexamined role in the continuing organization of diversity. Subdivided columns with their definite lines take over in subsequent archaeological charts as scholarly confidence grows. Visually, later charts present a static, increasingly regularized division of material history. Jack Goody (1977: 217) comments, "The complexity of tables generally lessens as the range of material widens. This lessening of complexity is accompanied by the attribution of increasing generality to the results." Perhaps the desire for graphic regularity grows with the amount and complexity of archaeological information in order to maintain a certain level of didactic clarity. Yet, paradoxically, as a simple communicative level is maintained in the face of new information, that information is effectively lost, and the remaining generalizations become increasingly uncommunicative.

An example of the fully developed chronological chart, one that Gordon Willey published in 1971, employs the familiar, regularized format (Fig. 2). Willey summarizes a more mature field in separate charts for the Andean coastal and highland sequences; the coast no longer predominates in scholarship as it did in Kroeber's time. In these presentations, the horizon terminology is asserted at left, generating horizontal lines that propel their subdivisions through the column of time and across the grey area of geography. Time is portrayed as absolute, its concreteness communicated through solid black column, like a monolith that can be etched by durations of varying lengths. Here, duration as well as sequence of the cultures is shown as set, and even estimated, rounded-off dates are averred. An extremely variable time scale is used before 900 B.C., but a general relationship of the longer earlier periods and shorter later ones is thereby preserved.

In fact, the Willey chart resembles the ideal stratigraphic cross-section. The regularization of unvarying horizontals allows only six phases to protrude from one stratum to the next via delicate black arrows; there is little "contamination" from one level to the next. The use of white for the horizontal demarcations serves to somewhat visually downplay their absoluteness—by contrast the vertical geographical divisions are more distinct in black—but the static effect of horizontals remains perceptually forceful. The overall message is that archaeologists have become confident of regular, uniform change with known dates as watersheds.

Art historical charts published around the time of Willey's archaeological example communicate certain contrasting ideas. That of Alan Sawyer (Fig. 3) is visually, and therefore conceptually, more complex. Perhaps the most immediately noticeable innovation is its utilization of boldface diagonal lines to show differential rates of change within areas. "Viru," for example, is shown to coexist with "Mochica I" and "Mochica II" then shade into "Mochica III" before it is terminated. The time scale is set at regularized 500-year intervals (relegating all early periods, of lesser art historical interest, to "Local Styles"). However, the thin horizontal lines generated by the estimated dates organize only partially the body of the chart: for example, the B.C./A.D. line—a concept totally unrelated to Andean history—never reappears, the 500 A.D. line penetrates only two phases, and the 1000 A.D. line does not apply to the South Highlands. Thus, the sureness of the Willey scheme in relation to absolute dating, the division of time, and the constancy of change is challenged by stylistic irregularities in a contemporaneous art historical chart.

With this graphic assertion of the peripheral nature of regular time divisions is added a similar message about period terminology and, hence, periodization itself. Archaeological horizon and intermediate period names are not used, while "Chavin," "Wari," and "Inca" Horizon labels are easily missed at the edge of the chart in upright italics. The bold lines within the chart, which might serve to separate horizons from intermediate periods, seem to delineate both horizons and traditions, plus, in the case of Vicus, different phases within a tradition as well. The absence of heavy black lines and use of the thinner vertical lines between geographical areas suggests, but certainly does not reinforce, the spread of the Chavin, Wari, and Inca polities that are here conflated with horizons (see Kolata, this volume). The predominance of local cultures between the horizons can only be inferred from the complex, and therefore somewhat confusing, presentation of darkly outlined and lightly subdivided areas. Thus, the relationships of thin and bold lines vertically, horizontally, and diagonally are too complex perceptually to illustrate a simple horizon/intermediate period alternation. The visual tabulation of the past becomes literally more difficult to read when more irregularity is acknowledged in knowledge, in rates of culture change, and in relationships between styles and areas. Sawyer, in an attempt to describe the complexity that had begun to be fathomed by scholars in both disciplines, sacrificed graphic clarity and its concomitant generalization of the facts; he went against the tendency described by Goody for a certain level of simplicity to be preserved. Perhaps this is because an art historian judging culture by art styles creates a more inescapably complex, even garbled, picture than does an archaeologist steeped in the order of stratigraphic levels.

George Kubler, more like Willey, presents a fairly traditional grid-like chart in his summary art historical volume (1962b, 1975 [Fig. 4]),[3] although it follows his text in graphically stressing diachronic relationships over synchronic ones. A nest of tall, self-contained boxes emphatically divides geographical tradition areas with double lines. Time is sectioned arbitrarily in 500-year increments whose lines cross-cut the chart to make a grid. Yet the names of styles, phases, cultures, and sites, differentiated by typeface,

[3] The present analysis concerns the diagram in the second edition, as the one in the first edition included color, which could not be reproduced here. Naturally it is not possible to discuss every chronological chart permutation; however, it may be suggested that the radical 1970 diagram discussed below may have influenced the 1975-edition chart to have reference to fewer set dates than the 1962b example.

float without lines to anchor them to these dates. A distrust of exactitude in dating is conveyed, and the cross-cutting lines of time must therefore be seen as merely an orientation device. The horizon names hover on the right, with the previously popular designations ("Formative," "Regional Development," and "Integration") on the left. This serves either for comparative purposes or to suggest that the various naming systems are interchangeable, that is, arbitrary. Neither cultural terminology determines the horizontal lines through time. Thus, the horizon concept is again met with visual skepticism, although it is included as a possibility.

Between the first and second editions of *The Art and Architecture of Ancient America,* Kubler eschewed the traditional diagram altogether (Fig. 5) to propose "an 'empty' chronology, filled only with the thin air of cultural theory" (1970: 129). His alternate chart contains just a few very general assertions about chronology itself. Rather than portraying change as constant or divisible geographically, he distinguishes only between "fast centers" and "slow margins." The chart delineates only "Formative," "Classic," "Post-Classic," and "Colonial" divisions, each with questioned beginning dates, undefined ends, and no internal subdivisions. In each case, changes take place quickly in the centers at the beginning of periods and fan out to penetrate slowly the marginal areas at the end of periods. Over time there are proportionately more "fast centers" and fewer "slow margins," and the changes are diffused more rapidly from one to the other (as indicated by the increasing steepness of the angled lines).

Graphically the chart is correspondingly radical; its abstraction, elegance (in mathematical terms), and inversion of usual categories remains cryptic and thought-provoking. All lines are diagonals, a choice that perceptually expresses Kubler's view of the dynamism of historical change. The time dimension runs across the top rather than the side, again giving diachronic relations priority. Because the barest of chronological assertions are all literally open-ended at base and questioned at the start, sequence and duration are concentrated to their essential relationships. The resulting viewer disorientation highlights how accustomed we have become to certain graphic conventions and thus to the dogmatic diagram. By changing the visual rules, Kubler (1970: 128) seeks to push inquiry away from the puzzle solving of marked-off phases and the arguing over "hardened" period dates and toward the basic mechanisms of culture dispersion in time. This "empty" chart comments on chronology itself, on the chart as its communicative device, and on the narrow views of historical reality that can be presented as a result.

Analysis of these five contrasting chronological charts shows how graphic choices encode different assumptions within the two disciplines as well as various authors' versions of the past (in part informed by their historiographic positions). As a result, graphic choices can be seen as far from neutral in their capacity to present distinct messages about the organization of the Andean, and naturally the Mesoamerican, past. Charts illustrate not only a range of views on the horizon/horizon style concepts, but also point up the tendency toward simplification inherent in the legible communication of complex and overlapping material histories. The more successful charts, in terms of clarity for the reader, are those that anchor a manageable number of culture names in a few ways to a static time/space framework. Yet such charts may thereby limit their vision to the point that subtle, complicated, or obscure passages of history are no longer described accurately. In addition, their construction may be based upon premises rendered incomplete or incorrect by new information, or upon logic flawed by tautological reasoning, as pointed out by Rouse. Reductionist tendencies, while understandable as reactions to rapidly expanding databases and interpretations, remain antithetical to the task of meaningful historical reconstruction.

ART HISTORICAL CHALLENGES

Art history can offer challenges to the two major assumptions of the horizon/horizon style schema, namely that stylistic similarity of works of art is the key to their contemporaneity and inevitably illustrates a wider cultural unity. First, the determination of stylistic congruence varies between disciplines and among individual scholars. Art historical discussion of the concept of style has taken place since the inception of the field in the mid-nineteenth century. The overused term *style* has numerous and varied definitions; however, it may be safe to characterize art historical inquiry into the notion of style as emphasizing *differences* (e.g., between one period and the next, between one country and another, between early and late works of a single artist). By contrast, especially the early archaeologists tended to seek out *similarities* preferentially, and thus ignore visual differences, in order to amass convincingly large corpora of like objects to substantiate horizon groupings (see Burger, this volume). In general, archaeologists have tended toward the use of a "trait list" approach to art, featuring lists of iconographic elements, techniques, and general style attributes (see Grove, this volume, on the Olmec trait list). Such lists serve to define style as static, while current art historical literature increasingly portrays style as intensely active and changing. In archaeological discussions objects that share a sufficient—and sometimes arbitrary—number of the listed traits are deemed similar, subsequently classified together, assumed to date from around the same time, and used to substantiate other conclusions (e.g., the Olmec "god clusters" postulated by Joralemon [1971]). Likewise, objects that do not share a substantial number of these features are seen as belonging to another class, as intrusive, or as from a different time period entirely.

Certainly such a methodology of establishing stylistic similarity was one of the few ordering tools available to the early scholars. It naturally maintains a strong "common sense" appeal. However, selective vision and a trait list approach employed together run a great risk of confusing pieces from markedly different time periods and places, ones whose relationships to each other and to the named horizon style may well be complicated and dissimilar. Given the many possibilities of stylistic and cultural relationships as explored in art history, it is important to note that a group of "similar" objects may not necessarily indicate the presence of a short-term, widely expansive cultural unity (i.e., horizon) nor does a group of pieces lacking surface similarity prove the absence thereof.

Given the many permutations of artistic, temporal, and spatial congruence, I would like to propose a stronger separation between horizon and horizon style. This does not invalidate the use of style itself as an analytical tool; in fact, it only seeks to redirect the endeavor away from a "cookbook" mentality and toward a multi-layered yet focused approach. As Esther Pasztory points out (this volume), style is uniquely suited to inform as to certain cultural arenas, such as ideology, but it does not necessarily shed light reliably on other aspects. Art, while eminently cultural, does not constitute an encyclopedia of culture, but contains its own powerful laws and tendencies that must be recognized if we are to succeed in completing a realistic chronology for the ancient Americas.

In the archaeological/anthropological literature, diffusion, trade, and conquest form the traditional mechanisms by which stylistically similar art works are thought to be disseminated over a wide geographical area. However, art historical theory raises questions about the explanatory power of these three mechanisms and offers several alternatives: revival, influence, medium-specific material and technical factors, and independent invention. Overall, individual artistic choice and the internal aesthetic processes (e.g., abstraction) are profoundly influential in the construction, evolution, and dissemination of any style. It is important here to envision an individual contribution not framed in terms of the European model—admittedly still prevalent in traditional art history—but to grant that art has makers in all cultures and that those makers are active agents capable of transmitting, transmuting, and transcending mainstream styles at any time. Including the concept of the individual artist may complicate the process of untangling art and culture, yet current studies of Pre-Columbian art have indicated that it is revealing as well as necessary (Reents-Budet 1987; Tate 1992).

Diffusion is the least explanatory, yet most widely applied term to account for widespread stylistic similarities in art. Diffusion creates the impression that ideas, objects, and practices flow from one area to another of their own accord, like honey on toast. Without indication of specific motives, means, and paths for such a movement, the concept is reduced to meaninglessness. (It is tempting to suggest that our own cultural milieu, in which news travels invisibly and rapidly through telecommunication networks, has distorted our conception of communication in other times and places.) Most importantly, any significant diffusion takes time and does not occur homogeneously across space; thus, a central premise of a horizon style becomes fundamentally untenable if diffusion alone is employed as the mechanism.

Trade is seen as an obvious candidate to clarify the issue of diffusion, and, of course, has been proven to exist in many cases. However, once again, too often the motives, means, and paths of trade are vague or unknown. Models from the later peoples are imposed upon earlier, culturally and temporally distinct situations (such as the hybrid term "Olmec *pochteca*"). New information may invalidate the conventional, and usually hypothetical, maps of trade routes (as in the case of jade sources), but the graphic persuasion of maps continues to sway, just as Kroeber warned regarding chronological charts. Given strong evidence for an established trading relationship, trade wares must then be distinguished from local versions of foreign products, which is often a difficult task. Further, limited interchange solely among elites must be separated from more broad-based and influential types of trade; the two are not interchangeable (see Pasztory, this volume). A direct relationship and congruence of values between widely separated, disparate peoples usually is assumed when trade can be substantiated through, for example, the unexpected presence of rarely occurring materials such as jade, *Spondylus* shell, or obsidian. However, a series of intermediaries may isolate the trading parties from one another, and/or the exact relationship(s) between principles and intermediaries may remain invisible in the material record. In addition, specific beliefs may or may not travel with specific high-status items; local conceptual traditions contribute to, if not supersede, foreign conceptual impositions. New elements introduced through trade may variously change the local material culture partially or completely, may serve to solidify local traditions through contrast, may coexist with local patterns, or may maintain their distinctness in order to reinforce elite prestige through exotic value (see Helms 1992). Thus, a uniform social fabric may *not* result from the trade of new ideas or objects. In addition, trade, like diffusion, takes time and the possibility of heirloom trade items sheds further doubt on the assumption of contemporaneity. Thus, the seemingly straightforward concept of trade cannot be employed loosely or haphazardly to explain horizonal spread or artistic contemporaneity.

Conquest shares with trade the appearance of a direct mechanism for the creation of a horizon and the broad extension of a particular style. Motive and means certainly can be fathomed more readily in the case of the relationship between conqueror and conquered. Yet Alan Kolata (this volume) strongly warns against the automatic conflation of polity with horizon. Such a conflation was deliberately avoided in the formation of the horizon concept (although it has often been adopted in subsequent literature and in certain chronological charts, such as Sawyer's [Fig. 3]). In addition, Cecelia

Klein and Emily Umberger as well as John Hyslop (this volume) point out that the two foremost, undisputed conquest states of the ancient Americas, the Aztec and the Inca, respectively, in fact may not display the expected monolithic character or uniform stylistic takeover. The unique centripetal structuring of states in the Pre-Columbian world, as well as the characteristic autonomy of the periphery, must be taken into account. The Aztec and—to a lesser extent—Inca empires resemble linked islands of selective control for which material evidence remains thin and spotty. Cross-pollination of state and local traditions is rampant. In a conquest situation, local and metropolitan versions first must be distinguished carefully. And, as in the case of diffusion and trade, conquests take place irregularly over time, and in the Aztec and Inca cases reconquests of many areas also took place generations apart. These considerations severely limit even conquest as a unifying force in the material realm. In sum, a case can be made that the three traditional mechanisms for the creation of a horizon do not constitute sufficient conditions on which to base such a construct.

Revival, medium-specific factors, and independent invention represent three readily apparent alternatives in which stylistic similarity neither implies contemporaneity nor accompanies a unified cultural system. The issue of revival has preoccupied European-centered art history for many years, particularly since the first publication of Erwin Panofsky's *Renaissance and Renascences in Western Art* in 1960. Panofsky explored the repeated renascences (rebirths, minor revivals) of Classical antiquity that preceded and led to "the Renaissance," which he defended as a horizon, in our terminology. Of relevance here, he warned " 'megaperiods' ["Classical," "Medieval," "Renaissance"] . . . must not be erected into 'explanatory principles' or even hypostatized into quasi-metaphysical entities. Their characterization must be carefully qualified according to time and place and must be constantly redefined according to the progress of scholarship" (1960: 3). During either a limited or a culture-wide revival, an already ancient art style is consciously resurrected in a later era for political, religious, or aesthetic reasons. Individual original and revival pieces may resemble one another closely on a superficial level, yet remain widely divergent in relation to temporal, spatial, and cultural context. Such a rebirth may signal an actual, perceived, or invented connection between reviver and revived. On closer examination, the reviving culture always chooses selectively from its model, changes structural relationships within compositions, varies combinations of elements, and irrevocably alters the context of the work it revives. Subtle visual distinctions notwithstanding, the intervening historical events and resultant divergent worldviews make a later piece conceptually estranged from its model (e.g., Christian Renaissance Europe's revival of the "pagan" world). Reviver and revived are by definition neither contemporaneous nor share a cultural unity.

Certainly such revival situations are not limited to Europe, as the well-known Moche revival of Chavin or the Mexica revival of Toltec and Teotihuacan art attest. Emily Umberger's (1987) work, "Antiques, Revivals and References to the Past in Aztec Art," stands as a pioneering model of art historical investigation into this difficult yet fertile subject. Regarding the Mexica, she introduces the various modes such revival takes: imitative, referential, reworked, and antiquarian. In many cases it is a difficult task to separate revival works from earlier idiosyncratic examples, one made more difficult, as Umberger points out, by the cyclical nature of Pre-Columbian thought in which past and present are inseparable concepts. However, art historical techniques can help distinguish later copies according to telltale anachronisms and/or the characteristic stylistic *gestalt* that betrays its makers. In these situations a trait-list approach does not tend to distinguish revivals, while a structuralistic analysis, in which the relationships between the parts provide primary evidence, has the ability to do so. In sum, visually similar works of art may result from various, considerably later interactions with a particular style; the real presence of revival stands as antithetical to the assumptions of the horizon style.

Medium-specific material and technical factors and independent invention also contribute to misleadingly analogous works of art created in widely disparate contexts. Without invoking a limited view of materials or technology, particularly the often-pejorative idea of technical determinism, it is important to acknowledge the very real interaction of artists with a medium, its inherent individual tendencies, and the finite world of visual forms. Some examples from the medium of textiles may be offered here. Indigo dyeing, a particularly obscure and indirect technique for producing blue and green coloring, has been independently developed all over the world—Mesoamerica, the Andes, Indonesia, and West Africa, among others—wherever the indigo plant exists (Sandberg 1989). By the same token, identical use of a variant technique of twining is found by around 2300 B.C. on the North Coast of Peru at Huaca Prieta and centuries later among the Eastern Woodland Native American peoples. Very complex techniques such as triple cloth also occur in various unrelated cultures. In general, the grid system of warp and weft in loom weaving encourages textiles from many eras and locations to share a rectilinear formal vocabulary. These occurrences of like techniques and patterns should not necessarily be taken for revivals or evidence of contact; different visual systems often come to isomorphic solutions to artistic problems (for example, the Northwest Coast, Olmec, and Chinese split-representations). These unrelated cases can only be categorized together as unicultural and contemporaneous if a simple, non-contextual study is conducted. Indeed, the field still entertains broad diffusionistic schemes—often outlandish and temporally impossible—to account for superficial congruences. As pointed out above, the motives, means, and direct evidence for contact are lacking in these broadly diffusionistic arguments. However, as Kubler (1962a) develops in detail in *The Shape of Time,* when one views objects as series of solutions to an artistic problem, atemporal and non-spatial visual commonalities are readily understood. Kubler's overall emphasis on the complexity and even irrationality of the creative realm highlights the need for non-simplistic assumptions about material history in general.

The element of individual artistic creation tends to disrupt sweeping assumptions about synchronic and diachronic patterns. A single Maya artist working in three distinct styles simultaneously is very strongly suggested by the material evidence uncovered by Ron Bishop and Dorie Reents-Budet (reported in Reents-Budet 1987). Such finds, based on close scientific as well as aesthetic analysis, emphasize the imposed nature of seriation in which sequential, regular change of one element at a time is postulated. Informed art historical analysis across cultures demonstrates how several styles simultaneously play out their variations at different systemic ages, to use a Kublerian term, rather than following one another in an orderly line. As in the case of the chronological chart, the idea of seriation may be influenced by the ideal succession of levels in archaeological stratification. It may also betray the aforementioned historiographic situation of abundant material evidence accompanied by relatively spotty information in which a seemingly straightforward, yet reductive categorization scheme helps create order.

In sum, images of unity give way to diversity as more is known of individual cultural components. As Esther Pasztory points out for Classic Mesoamerica (this volume), there can be many different centers whose traditions have, at once, independence, interdependence, and dependence upon one another. In most cases, there is no need to invoke a single dominant culture, and to do so disregards the autonomy and importance of a range of other cultures. Such exclusivity tends to distort scholarship rather than advance it. Rather, art styles simultaneously blend and distinguish peoples, change by internal mechanisms and in response to political and religious forces, determine and reflect culture, recur and fall away in a continuously discontinuous fashion, and show both individual and group contribution.

A fully realized calculus of Pre-Columbian art and culture remains to be formulated. It is hoped that the following papers on the issue of horizon and horizon style in Mesoamerica and the Central Andes will offer new, subtle views of the ancient American material past.

BIBLIOGRAPHY

BENNETT, WENDELL C.

    1948   The Peruvian Co-Tradition. In *A Reappraisal of Peruvian Archaeology. Memoirs of the Society for American Archaeology IV:* 1–7. Society for American Archaeology and Institute for Andean Research, Menasha, Wisc.

BENNETT, WENDELL C., AND JUNIUS B. BIRD

    1949   *Andean Culture History.* Lancaster Press, Lancaster, Penn.

BENNETT, WENDELL C., AND RENE HARNONCOURT

    1954   *Ancient Arts of the Andes.* The Museum of Modern Art, New York.

BLANTON, RICHARD, AND GARY FEINMAN

    1984   The Mesoamerican World System. *American Anthropologist* 86 (3): 673–682.

GOODY, JACK

    1977   Literacy and Classification: On Turning the Tables. In *Text and Context: the Social Anthropology of Tradition* (Ravindra K. Jain, ed.): 205–222. Institute for the Study of Human Issues, Philadelphia.

HELMS, MARY W.

    1992   Thoughts on Public Symbols and Distant Domains Relevant to the Chiefdoms of Lower Central America. In *Wealth and Hierarchy in the Intermediate Area* (Frederick W. Lange, ed.): 317–329. Dumbarton Oaks, Washington, D.C.

JORALEMON, PETER DAVID

    1971   *A Study of Olmec Iconography.* Studies in Pre-Columbian Art and Archaeology 7. Dumbarton Oaks, Washington, D.C.

KEEN, BENJAMIN

    1971   *The Aztec Image in Western Thought.* Rutgers University Press, New Brunswick, N.J.

KROEBER, ALFRED L.

    1944   *Peruvian Archaeology in 1942.* Viking Fund Publications in Anthropology 4. New York.

KUBLER, GEORGE

    1961   Rival Approaches to American Antiquity. In *Three Regions of Primitive Art:* 62–75. Museum of Primitive Art, New York.

    1962a   *The Shape of Time: Remarks on the History of Things.* Yale University Press, New Haven.

    1962b   *Art and Architecture of Ancient America: The Mexican, Maya and Andean People.* Penguin Books, Middlesex, England. (2nd ed., 1975)

    1970   Period, Style and Meaning in Ancient American Art. *New Literary History: A Journal of Theory and Interpretation* 1 (2): 127–144.

    1973   Science and Humanism among Americanists. In *The Iconography of*

Middle American Sculpture: 163–167. Metropolitan Museum of Art, New York.

1979 Towards a Reductive Theory of Visual Style. In *The Concept of Style* (Berel Lang, ed.): 118–127. University of Pennsylvania Press, Philadelphia.

MEANS, P.A.

1931 *Ancient Civilizations of the Andes.* Charles Scribner's Sons, New York.

NICHOLSON, H.B.

1960 The Mixteca-Puebla Concept in MesoAmerican Archaeology: A Re-Examination. In *Men and Cultures* (A. F. C. Wallace, ed.): 612–617. University of Pennsylvania Press, Philadelphia.

1981 The Mixteca-Puebla Concept Revisited. In *The Art and Iconography of Late Post-Classic Central Mexico.* (Elizabeth Boone, ed.): 227–254. Dumbarton Oaks, Washington, D.C.

PANOFSKY, ERWIN

1960 *Renaissance and Renascences in Western Art.* Almqvist and Wiksell, Stockholm.

PHILLIPS, PHILIP, AND GORDON WILLEY

1953 Method and Theory in American Archaeology: An Operational Basis for Culture-Historical Integration. *American Anthropologist* 55 (5, 1): 615–633.

PRICE, BARBARA J.

1976 A Chronological Framework for Cultural Development in Meso-america. In *The Valley of Mexico: Studies in Pre-Hispanic Ecology and Society* (Eric R. Wolf, ed.): 13–21. University of New Mexico Press, Albuquerque.

REENTS-BUDET, DORIE

1987 The Discovery of a Ceramic Artist and Royal Patron among the Classic Maya. *Mexicon* 9: 123–126.

ROUSE, IRVING

1954 On the Use of the Concept of Area Co-Tradition. *American Antiquity* 19 (3): 221–225.

1957 On the Correlation of Phases of Culture. *American Anthropologist* 57 (4): 713–722.

ROWE, JOHN

1945 Absolute Chronology in the Andean Area. *American Antiquity* 10: 265–284.

1954 *Max Uhle, 1856–1944: A Memoir of the Father of Peruvian Archaeology.* University of California Press, Berkeley.

1960 Cultural Unity and Diversification in Peruvian Archaeology. In *Selected Papers of the Fifth International Congress of Anthropological and Ethnological Sciences.* (Anthony F. C. Wallace, ed.): 627–631. University of Pennsylvania Press, Philadelphia.

1962 Stages and Periods in Archaeological Interpretation. *Southwestern Journal of Anthropology* 18: 40–54.

SANDBERG, GÖSTA
    1989   *Indigo Textiles: Technique and History.* Lark Books, Asheville, N.C.

SAWYER, ALAN
    1968   *Mastercraftsmen of Ancient Peru.* Solomon R. Guggenheim Foundation, New York.

SCHAPIRO, MEYER
    1953   Style. In *Anthropology Today: An Encyclopedic Inventory* (A. L. Kroeber, ed.): 287–312. University of Chicago Press, Chicago.

SOCIEDAD MEXICANA DE ANTROPOLOLOGIA
    1942   *Mayas y Olmecas, Segunda Reunión de Mesa Redonda sobre problemas antropológicos de México y Centro América.* Tuxtla, Gutierrez, Chiapas.

TATE, CAROLYN
    1992   *Yaxchilan: The Design of a Maya Ceremonial City.* University of Texas Press, Austin.

TAYLOR, R. E., AND CLEMENT W. MEIGHAN
    1978   *Chronologies in New World Archaeology.* Academic Press, New York.

TUFTE, EDWARD R.
    1983   *The Visual Display of Quantitative Information.* Graphics Press, Cheshire, Conn.

UBBELOHDE-DOERING, HEINRICH
    1967   *On the Royal Highways of the Inca.* Praeger, New York.

UHLE, MAX
    1902   Types of Culture in Peru. *American Anthropologist* n.s. 4: 753–759.

UMBERGER, EMILY
    1987   Antiques, Revivals and References to the Past in Aztec Art. *RES: Anthropology and Aesthetics* 13: 63–106.

WILLEY, GORDON
    1945   Horizon Styles and Pottery Traditions in Peruvian Archaeology. *American Antiquity* 11: 49–56.
    1948   Functional Analysis of "Horizon Styles" in Peruvian Archaeology. In *A Reappraisal of Peruvian Archaeology. Memoirs of the Society for American Archaeology IV:* 8–15. Society for American Archaeology and Institute for Andean Research, Menasha, Wisc.
    1971   *An Introduction to American Archaeology. Vol. 2: South America.* Prentice-Hall, Englewood Cliffs, N.J.

WILLEY, GORDON, AND PHILIP PHILLIPS
    1958   *Method and Theory in American Archaeology.* University of Chicago Press, Chicago.

WILLEY, GORDON, AND JEREMY SABLOFF
    1974   *A History of American Archaeology.* W.H. Freeman and Co., San Francisco.

The Chavin Horizon: Stylistic Chimera or Socioeconomic Metamorphosis?

RICHARD L. BURGER

YALE UNIVERSITY

I T IS PROBABLY FAIR TO SAY that the concept of horizon style has fallen out of fashion in North American archaeology. Its explicitly chronological intent is out of step with the interests of processual and post-processual archaeologists who make up the rank and file of the profession, and its value as a chronological tool has long been overshadowed by competing methods of establishing contemporaneity between regions. At the same time, the pan-regional frame of reference implicit in the horizon style concept is at odds with the contemporary focus by Andeanists on smaller, more manageable spatial units, especially single valleys. In the current intellectual climate, any claim for a prehistoric horizon in Peru is likely to be considered with skepticism, no matter how well established it seems to be in the archaeological literature.

How then are we to view the putative Chavin horizon, the worst documented of the three accepted Peruvian horizons? In order to answer this question, the intellectual history of this term will be reviewed, and recent controversy concerning its current status in light of recent discoveries will be summarized and critiqued. It will be argued that there is still sufficient evidence to justify the concept of a Chavin horizon, and an interpretation will be offered of the socioeconomic causes and significance of this unprecedented cultural phenomenon.

HISTORICAL BACKGROUND

The idea of a pan-regional Chavin culture was first proposed by the German physician Ernst Middendorf (1893–95) just before Max Uhle initiated scientific archaeological research in Peru at the site of Pachacamac. Middendorf's affirmation of a pre-Inca Chavin empire with its capital at Chavin de Huantar was prophetic rather than scientific inasmuch as the evidence upon which it was based was almost nonexistent. The idea was ignored in archaeological circles until three decades later, when Julio C. Tello suddenly revived it without explicit reference to Middendorf's work.

As early as 1921, Tello's writings refer to the spread of the Chavin culture through the northern highlands and coast. Unlike Middendorf, Tello based his hypothesis on archaeological evidence, a fraction of which was published in his books and articles. Tello (1921, 1922: 244) linked the style of the sculptures at Chavin de Huantar with feline motifs on a distinctive type of dark monochrome pottery widespread in Peru, and he recognized examples of the Chavin-style ceramics in Victor Larco Herrera's private collections from the Chicama Valley of the North Coast (Tello 1922: pls. VIII, X, XVII). He also claimed that this Chavin-style pottery was found to the south of Chavin de Huantar in highland areas like Cajabamba, Tupe, Huarochiri, and Canta, although none of these cases has ever been substantiated (Tello 1929: 96). With the identification of the ceramics excavated by Uhle on the central coast at Ancon and Supe as expressions of Chavin style and the documentation of Chavin elements on the newly discovered Paracas Cavernas pottery of the South Coast, Tello was able to make a plausible argument for the pan-regional distribution of the Chavin culture in his 1928 paper for the XXIII International Congress of Americanists. A tomb containing Chavin-style pottery and gold was unearthed at the North Coast site of Chongoyape in Lambayeque shortly before the publication of the volume, and it provided crucial confirmation of his argument for the "irradiation" of the highland Chavin style throughout the coast (Tello 1929, 1930).

Over the next two decades, Tello continued his prolific field work and gradually broadened his definition of Chavin to incorporate new discoveries without taking the time to publish the materials originally used to formulate his argument for a pan-regional Chavin culture or to analyze this new material. The additional finds were uncritically absorbed in his growing list of Chavin sites, and at the 1939 International Congress of Americanists, Tello (1942) ennumerated more than fifty Chavin sites. He described sites like Cerro Narrio in Ecuador, Pucara in the Peruvian altiplano, and even sites of the Barreal culture of Argentina as Chavin-related (Fig. 1). Despite the striking differences between these assemblages, Tello affirmed:

> It is noteworthy that this Chavín art is so uniform and typical in style in its multiple and various manifestations at sites far from its centers of greatest development, maintaining the characteristics of a mature production, elaborated on the basis of fixed norms without the substantial modifications so common in other arts that have been propagated far from their center of origin. Considered rigorously, there are no fundamental differences between one piece of pottery found in Chavín and another found on the coast, along the Huallaga or in the south of Ecuador. (1942: 91, my translation)

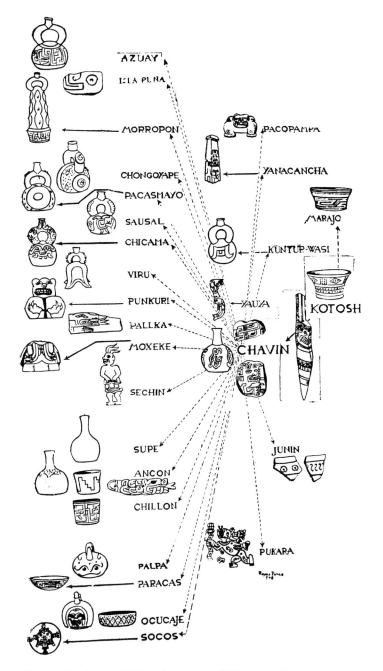

Fig. 1. Tello's irradiation model for the spread of Chavin civilization as represented by Rebeca Carrión Cachot (after Carrión Cachot 1948: lám. xxxvi)

Alfred Kroeber tried to evaluate Tello's claims critically but he complained that, although it appeared to contain a kernel of validity, the concept of Chavin still proved difficult to use. "Seeming always more interested in a likeness than in a discrimination," Kroeber (1944: 82) wrote in frustration, "Tello has weakened his own excellent case by treating remote or doubtful similarities on a par with overwhelmingly strong ones." He recommended a more careful definition of what was meant by Chavin through a study of the Chavin culture at Chavin de Huantar and its systematic comparison with the materials from other areas identified as Chavin. Kroeber concluded:

> "Chavín," having by now become quite Protean, is an unsatisfactory descriptive label for any particular and distinctive culture, other than at Chavín itself. Chavín properly designates a horizon or an influence found in a number of cultures. This is obviously the sense in which Tello, the developer of the concept, uses the term. (1944: 43)

Rafael Larco Hoyle was one of the few contemporaries of Tello actually to undertake a comparison of one group of "coastal Chavin" materials with those of Chavin de Huantar. In 1939, he initiated excavations at the cemeteries of Barbacoá and Palenque in the Chicama Valley and encountered dozens of tombs; on the basis of the artifacts found with these burials, Larco concluded that they were roughly coeval with Chavin de Huantar (Larco 1941). However, he also argued that this material represented a local culture, rather than merely constituting an irradiation of Chavin. He referred to this culture as Cupisnique and used this case study to raise doubts about Tello's entire framework. Larco wrote:

> if we carefully analyze the different cultures that are supposed to be included with the so-called Chavín Civilization, we arrive at the conclusion that if they do indeed have cultural elements in common, they have others in even greater quantity that permit us to differentiate one culture from another. . . . The characteristics in common are due to the exchange of cultural elements that existed without signifying that the peoples abandoned their own cultural mode. (Larco 1948: 16, my translation)

Larco and Tello defined the two extremes between which interpretations fluctuated for the next three decades. Tello claimed that the Chavin cultural traits identified throughout Peru were virtually the same as those at Chavin de Huantar, with minor cultural variations primarily due to differences in local environments and their resources. Larco, in contrast, argued that this time period was characterized by local cultures and that the diffusion of a few conspicuous traits should not obscure this fact. In some respects, the difference between these two positions is a matter of emphasis: both scholars agreed that features were shared over a broad area and that these ele-

ments indicated contemporaneity. Tello's conception mirrored the diffusionist model of Old World development espoused by Gordon Childe,
while Larco's emphasis on in situ cultural processes paralleled Julian Stew-
ard's writings on multilinear evolution.

The contrasting interpretations also reflected political and personal differences too complex to consider here in detail. For Tello (1930: 263), the study
of Peruvian prehistory had revealed "a great variety of cultures and styles
corresponding to the development and differentiation of only one civilization nurtured in the Andes, the Andean civilization," and the Chavin culture
was the civilizational matrix out of which this *one* civilization grew. Thus,
Chavin provided a very ancient basis for the fundamental unity of the
diverse cultures occupying the Central Andes; as such, the idea of a Chavin
culture served to naturalize and legitimate the modern Peruvian nation state
which, like Tello's Chavin, was supposed to link the ecologically and culturally disparate groups living in the highlands, coast, and tropical forest.

The naturalness and legitimacy of the Peruvian nation is by no means self-
evident. Mario Vargas Llosa, Peruvian novelist and recent presidential candi-
date, recently summarized his thinking on his nation's past and present as
follows:

> Our country . . . [is] in a deep sense more a fiction than a real-
> ity. . . . It never was, at least for the majority of its inhabitants that
> fabulous country of legends and fictions, but rather an artificial
> gathering of men from different languages, customs, and traditions
> whose only common denominator was having been condemned by
> history to live together without knowing or loving one another.
> (1990: 51–52)

This is precisely the vision that Tello attempted to undermine through his
writings concerning the ancient development of *one* Andean civilization.

In contrast, Larco's arguments in support of the purely local character of
the Cupisnique culture may have consciously or unconsciously reflected the
powerful currents of North Coast regionalism that were and continue to be
a feature of Peruvian political and cultural life. As a member of Peru's
coastal oligarchy, Larco preferred to interpret the coastal Cupisnique culture
as a product of local creativity, rather than highland genius. Moreover,
Larco highlighted those elements in the Cupisnique culture that could be
interpreted as antecedents for later North Coast cultures like Moche and
Chimu, and thereby constructed a past in which the peoples of the North
Coast shaped their own destiny, except in brief moments, like the Inca
conquest, when alien groups curbed local self-determination through the
use of brute force.

By 1942, archaeologists from the United States had come to accept
Tello's claims that the Chavin materials were of considerable antiquity and

that the new evidence warranted adding a third pan-Peruvian horizon to the Uhle sequence (Bennett 1943: 326; Kroeber 1944: 43). But it was not until Gordon Willey's (1951) article, "The Chavin Problem: A Review and Critique," that a systematic evaluation of the full range of Tello's claims was undertaken in order to delineate this horizon. The Chavin horizon style was defined by Willey on the basis of the stone sculpture of Chavin de Huantar, but the scarcity of evidence frequently led Willey to make comparisons using the non-iconographic aspects of other artifact classes, particularly ceramic style. Not surprisingly, most of Tello's cases did not measure up to Willey's definition, and the majority of fifty-odd cases was viewed as not necessarily contemporaneous or having any intimate historical relation with Chavin de Huantar (Willey 1951: 135).

Yet even setting these aside, seventeen sites or regions were still considered by Willey to display undeniable evidence of the Chavin style. Willey recognized the uneven quality and patchy distribution of these cases, but he believed that the evidence was sufficient to reaffirm the heuristic value of the concept of a Chavin horizon and its value as an effective time marker (Willey 1951: 124). With Kroeber, Bennett, Strong, Rowe, and Willey in agreement with the modified version of Tello's formulation, a consensus had been achieved in Peruvian archaeology. Eventually, the concept of a Chavin horizon was incorporated not only into descriptive syntheses of Peruvian cultural history, but also into the chronological frameworks used to organize and talk about Peruvian prehistory. The acceptance of a Chavin horizon is implicit in John Rowe's definition of the Early Horizon, and in Lumbreras' threefold division of the Formative (Burger 1988: 106–111; Lumbreras 1969, 1974; Rowe 1962b).

The integral role of the Chavin horizon in structuring these terminologies may be seen as testimony to the utility of the Chavin horizon as a chronological tool during the 1950s and early 1960s before the full impact of the radiocarbon revolution. Nevertheless, Rowe's system of relative chronology recognizes that a horizon style is not in itself a sufficiently precise temporal marker for the analysis of culture change. In the Rowe framework, the Chavin horizon and the other two Peruvian horizons are subdivided into a number of sequential epochs or phases on the basis of pottery style. These smaller units of "relative" time can then be used to trace the development, spread, and transformation of the horizon style and associated cultural phenomena. Alternatively, the increasing number and accuracy of radiocarbon dates make it theoretically possible to subdivide a horizon into units of absolute or chronometric time. Thus, the use of a horizon style as a temporal index seems increasingly redundant and outmoded. However, once freed from its function as a chronological tool, the horizon phenomenon can itself become the object of investigation.

Though emphasizing the utility of horizons for the formulation of chronologies, Gordon Willey, like Tello, recognized that the spread of a unified Chavin art style over much of Peru was an extraordinary and unprecedented occurrence whose functional significance ultimately had to be understood in terms of cultural processes (Willey 1948, 1962). Willey followed Larco (1941) and Carrión Cachot (1948) in arguing that the degree of stylistic homogeneity characteristic of the Chavin horizon was due to the spread of a shared system of beliefs to culturally distinct populations. As Willey put it:

> the diffusion of the Chavin art style can most easily be explained as the peaceful spread of religious concepts. Perhaps these Chavin concepts were the sanctions, on a spiritual plane, of the life-giving agriculture and sedentary arts that had only recently been adopted by Formative populations. (Willey 1948: 10)

Although this has continued to be the dominant position in the following decades (e.g., Keatinge 1981; Lanning 1967: 98; Moseley 1978: 520; Patterson 1971) there have been dissenters. Donald Lathrap, for example, argued that the Chavin cult was spread by a tightly integrated and authoritarian state that could demand and achieve the rendering of their religious and state art in the most durable material possible (1974: 149–150).[1]

Regardless of functional interpretations, there remained almost unanimous agreement concerning the heuristic value of the Chavin horizon concept, despite differences in opinion about whether specific sites should be considered as part of this horizon (e.g., Bischof 1985, Burger 1981, Daggett 1987). Recently, however, Thomas and Shelia Pozorski (1987) have denied the very existence of a Chavin horizon and even argued that Rowe's chronological framework should be modified by changing the term Early Horizon to the Early Period. They interpret recent research on the Cotton Preceramic and the Initial Periods as having demonstrated that related symbol systems on the coast existed for close to 2,000 years and that the iconography of Chavin de Huantar is simply one of many variants of these other long-lived systems. They contest both the stylistic uniqueness and panregional integrity of the Chavin style and, by implication, deny the rapid spread of any pre-Middle Horizon style over a broad geographical area. If we accept their conclusions, the concept of the Chavin horizon would meet the same fate as the "Negative horizon" and the "White-on-Red horizon" four decades ago (Kroeber 1944: 108–110; Willey 1948: 10–12). Exploration of the significance of the Chavin horizon would be pointless if such a phenomenon never existed, so before proceeding further, we will address this fundamental question.

---

[1] John Rowe offered a similar interpretation in a 1966 lecture presented at the University of Cuzco and published more than a decade later (Rowe 1977: 10), but he no longer believes that the spread of the style through military expansion is consistent with the available evidence (personal communication, 1991).

THE CHAVIN HORIZON: A STYLISTIC CHIMERA?

Is the Chavin horizon an illusion produced by conflating styles of differ-ing ages and origins? Is there a real need for positing a Chavin horizon? Once again, we find ourselves confronting the same question that Kroeber faced in 1942 and Willey attempted to resolve in 1951.

In trying to carve out a meaningful horizon marker from the broader, richer and more ambiguous Chavin concept of Tello, Willey defined the Chavin horizon style as being identical to, or closely resembling, the designs on stone carvings from Chavin de Huantar. Though he decided to err on the side of conservative hesitancy rather than uncritical acceptance, many of the seventeen sites or regions judged as acceptable do not have any direct ana-logues with specific Chavin de Huantar sculptures, even with the greatly amplified inventory of carvings now available. One looks to Chavin de Huantar in vain for close parallels to the feline-crab incised on the bone snuff tablet from Puerto de Supe, the spear-wielding agnatic skeletal supernatural from Kuntur Wasi, and the almost abstract "plant or fruit" motif on the stirrup-spouted bottle from Morropon. The Chavin de Huantar sculptures differ from these pieces as much in their style as in thematic content.

Five of the seventeen examples of the Chavin horizon accepted by Willey are not archaeological sites or even regions; instead, they are isolated arti-facts without archaeologically established provenience. There is a lone small stone vessel from Lives Farm in the Province of Hualgayoc, Cajamarca (Tello 1943: pl. XVIIIb)[2]; a unique ceramic bottle from Morropon in Piura (Larco 1941: fig. 209); the engraved "Pickman Strombus" trumpet from the airforce base in Chiclayo (Larco 1941: fig. 174); a carved bone spatula from the Hacienda Huamaya in Huaura (Lothrop 1951: fig. 74); and the stone sculpture from Yauya in the Callejon de Conchucos (Tello 1960: lám. xxxa).[3] The Moche (or Mochica) culture was also included in Willey's list because of the Moche bottles with Chavin archaistic elements (Rowe 1971). When these insubstantial cases are set aside, only ten examples of the Chavin horizon remain from Willey's original list besides Chavin de Huantar itself.

At these ten sites, stylistic configurations on a small number of crucial sculptures or portable objects were used to establish contemporaneity by way of the horizon-marker concept. Although there was little alternative to this approach in 1951, subsequent excavations and the introduction of radio-

---

[2] Unlike the stone bowl from Lives Farm, the carved monolith and "megalithic mausole-ums" from Yanacancha in the Province of Hualgayoc discussed by Tello are not related to the Chavin horizon style (Willey 1951: 113).

[3] Yauya is sometimes referred to as a Chavin site (e.g., Willey 1951: 113), but it is actually a modern town in the Callejon de Conchucos. A large classic Chavin-style sculpture of a cayman kept in its church was recorded by Tello's 1919 expedition. A 1973 visit by the author failed to elicit the archaeological site provenience of the stone carving, despite numerous interviews of older residents and surface reconnaissance of the town and surrounding area.

carbon dating make it possible now in some cases to evaluate independently whether these remaining "indisputable" examples of the Chavin horizon are contemporaneous with the sculptures from Chavin de Huantar.

Research at Chavin de Huantar succeeded in establishing a three-phase ceramic sequence tied to a series of radiocarbon measurements (Burger 1981, 1984: 277–281), which consists of the Urabarriu Phase (890–490 B.C.), the Chakinani Phase (460–390 B.C.), and the Janabarriu Phase (390–200 B.C.). This chronology is significantly later than many scholars had believed (e.g., Lumbreras and Amat 1969). Several of the first radiocarbon measurements available for Chavin de Huantar were made on bone samples from the floor of the Rocas Canal that had been soaked for millennia in water draining from the limestone-rich temple buildings (Burger 1981: 596). Whether due to the limitations of collagen analysis twenty years ago, to carbonate contamination, or a combination of these and other factors, the tests yielded results that were 500–900 years too old. Chavin de Huantar does not appear to have been occupied prior to the Urabarriu Phase and consequently the Lanzon and the sculpture adorning the Old Temple was probably not carved until the ninth century B.C. Many of the classic Chavin sculptures were actually produced in the fourth and third centuries B.C. during the Janabarriu Phase, which corresponds to Phase D/EF in the Rowe sculptural sequence, when the highland center reached its zenith (Burger 1981, 1984).

Of the remaining ten sites from Willey's list, many can now be shown to have occupations coeval with the Chakinani and/or Janabarriu Phases and thus the use of the horizon concept in Willey's hands was often successful as a chronological tool. Nevertheless, recent excavations at Moxeke, one of the sites with "indisputable Chavin influence," revealed that it was built and abandoned long before Chavin de Huantar was founded. Tello excavated Moxeke in 1937, and he used the results to substantiate the pan-regional distribution of Chavin civilization (Tello 1943, 1956). Until recently, this large site in the Casma Valley continued to figure prominently in discussions of the Chavin horizon in general syntheses (e.g., Kauffmann Doig 1978; Lumbreras 1974: 68). Moxeke was originally accepted by Willey (1951: 118–119) as Chavin on the basis of the "strong Chavin cast" of the polychrome clay sculptures decorating the third terrace of the stepped platform mound (Fig. 2a,b). In 1974 Peter Roe dated these friezes on seriational grounds to Phase C of the Chavin de Huantar sculptural sequence (Roe 1974: 33–34, chart VI) and concluded that Moxeke was constructed somewhat later than the Old Temple at Chavin de Huantar.

Tom and Shelia Pozorski's recent investigations at Moxeke confirmed that Pampa de las Llamas and Moxeke constituted a single center covering an area of 220 hectares, and the mixture of twined and woven textiles suggested an early Initial Period dating for the site. Twenty-three radiocarbon samples from these excavations now indicate that the site was occupied

Fig. 2. (a) Polychrome clay sculptures decorating Moxeke's third terrace as seen from the west; (b) detail of anthropomorphic figure with snake, in process of being revealed by Tello's excavations at Moxeke (photos: courtesy of Donald Collier)

between 1600 and 1200 B.C. (S. Pozorski 1987; Pozorski and Pozorski 1986, 1990). Consequently, Moxeke cannot be marshalled as evidence of a Chavin horizon, because it is not coeval with the sculpture that was used to define it. In retrospect, the public art of Moxeke is quite different in style and content from the Chavin de Huantar sculpture, although there are some general similarities and shared elements (Tello 1956: 60–66). The only stone sculpture known from Moxeke was found in the final construction phase at Huaca A (approx. 1300–1200 B.C.). A human hand and a double-bodied snake are depicted, and the carving does not strongly resemble any of the sculptures at Chavin de Huantar (Burger 1989; Pozorski and Pozorski 1988). Not surprisingly, the Moxeke findings have reinforced doubts concerning the utility of the Chavin horizon concept. It is likely that when new investigations are carried out at Punkuri in Nepeña (Proulx 1985: 35–41), another of the sites on Willey's list, they will reveal that this site also dates to the Initial Period.

The Moxeke results surprised few of the scholars actively involved with questions of early Peruvian civilization. Independent evidence from excavations, ceramic analysis, and radiocarbon measurements had already shown that many of the themes, stylistic elements, and conventions of the Chavin style had precursors long before Chavin de Huantar sculptures were carved. The assertion (Lathrap 1974: 145–146) that the Chavin style arose suddenly and without precedent became increasingly untenable as these new results were published (Bischof 1986; Burger 1981, 1985; T. Pozorski 1983).

Many of the Chavin themes have their roots in the textile images of the late Preceramic Period. The textiles at Huaca Prieta and La Galgada depict (a) frontal anthropomorphic supernaturals with flowing hair or snakes hanging from their bodies (Fig. 3,c,d,e) (Bird, Hyslop, and Skinner 1985: fig. 130; Grieder, Bueno, Smith, and Malina 1988: fig. 150) (b) raptorial birds with wings outstretched and head turned sideways (Fig. 3a,b) (Bird et al. 1985: fig. 111; Grieder et al. 1988: fig. 136), and (c) profile felines (Bird et al. 1985: 125; Grieder et al. 1988). More sophisticated renditions of analogous images appeared more than 1,000 years later on the Chavin de Huantar sculpture.

Over a decade ago, Chiaki Kano (1979) demonstrated that representations of the feline, snake, eagle, and anthropomorphic beings appeared on the early Initial Period Wairajirca ceramics from Shillacoto. Thus, some of the first known figurative representations from the highlands of Huanuco depict the themes found a millennium later at Chavin de Huantar. Daniel Morales (1980) reached a similar conclusion in his analysis of the iconography of the Initial Period pottery from Pacopampa in the northern highlands. He found that many of the themes and elements associated with Chavin de Huantar had a long history in the Pacopampa area before the Chavin horizon. In both Huanuco and Pacopampa, the style employed in depicting these motifs was unlike that of Chavin de Huantar.

In recent years, renewed large-scale excavations at early monumental complexes on the North and Central Coasts have unearthed new clay murals and

Richard L. Burger

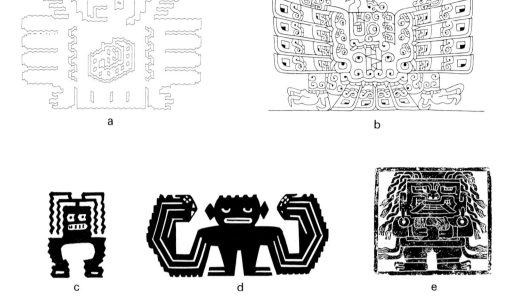

a
b
c
d
e

Fig. 3. Some late Preceramic antecedents for classic Chavin art: (a) late preceramic representation of condor with wings outstretched from a twined cotton textile found at Huaca Prieta, Chicama valley (after Bird 1963: fig. 6); (b) late Initial Period representation of crested eagle with wings outstretched from a granite sculpture found at Chavin de Huantar, Mosna valley (after Rowe 1967: fig. 12); (c) late Preceramic frontal representation of an anthropomorphic figure with flowing hair from a twined cotton fabric found at Huaca Prieta (redrawn after Bird, Hyslop, and Skinner 1985: 184); (d) late Preceramic frontal representation of an anthropomorphic figure with pendant snakes from a looped cotton bag found at La Galgada (redrawn after Grieder, Bueno, Smith, and Malina 1988: 179); (e) the principal deity of Chavin de Huantar represented on a mid-Early Horizon granite sculpture from the New Temple (after a rubbing illustrated in Rowe 1962a: 15, fig. 11)

sculptures that suggest the existence of several regional traditions of religious art prior to the emergence of the Chavin style (Moseley and Watanabe 1974; T. Pozorski 1976; Pozorski and Pozorski 1988). Often, the themes these public sculptures represent, like the supernatural arachnids of Garagay (Fig. 4) or the stylized wave motif of Cardal, have no analogue at Chavin de Huantar (Burger and Salazar-Burger 1991; Ravines and Isbell 1976; Scheele n.d.: fig. 8a), but many of the stylistic conventions, specific elements, and general subjects were appropriated to form the "great art style" known as Chavin (Burger 1988; Ravines 1984).

Styles that were direct precursors of Chavin and those that were not

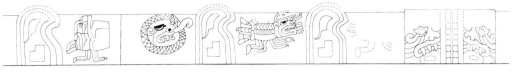

Fig. 4. Late Initial Period polychrome clay frieze decorating the atrium of the Middle Temple at Garagay, Rimac valley (redrawn from Ravines and Isbell 1976: lám. Elevacion de Murales)

Fig. 5. Early Initial Period cache from La Galgada consisting of shell and stone discs and crystal beads attached to a cotton cloth, including a *Spondylus* disk in a style reminiscent of late Chavin art (photo: courtesy of Terence Grieder)

coexisted during the Initial Period. A cache discovered by Terence Grieder and Alberto Bueno at La Galgada illustrates the artistic diversity that gave rise to the Chavin style. A *Spondylus* shell disk (Fig. 5) carved in a style reminiscent of later Chavin art was found attached to a cotton cloth along with two other shell disks that were carved in a style more closely related to that found on the late Preceramic textiles. A radiocarbon analysis of the textiles yielded a date of 1370 B.C. (TX-5606; Grieder et al. 1988: tab. 2).

A growing awareness of the richness of Initial Period iconography has been paralleled by the realization that the scale and complexity of Initial Period architecture far exceeds earlier expectations. As in the art, many architectural features associated with the Chavin horizon had antecedents in the late Preceramic and the Initial Periods (Burger 1985; Williams 1980). In fact, several sites identified as Chavin on the basis of architectural features, like the U-shaped layout and the sunken circular courtyard, have proven to be pre-Chavin by many centuries (e.g., Patterson 1985b).

It would be a mistake, however, to conceptualize the Chavin horizon on the basis of these findings as a passive and mechanical mixing of "influences" from older traditions; a more productive approach (Hobsbawm 1983) would be to think of it as the intentional construction of a new tradition by the highland builders of Chavin de Huantar. Through the creative recombination and juxtaposition of selected elements with rich and complex histories, the artists and designers of the Old Temple automatically implied continuity with these older coastal traditions, while at the same time using these ancient traditions to help establish and legitimize what was, in reality, a new social order in the Mosna Valley.

Does the new evidence briefly reviewed here destroy the heuristic value of a Chavin horizon? In my judgment it does not. The revelation that antecedents exist for the sculptural, architectural, and technological style of Chavin de Huantar does not in itself undermine the applicability of the horizon style concept any more than the discovery that the Roman Imperial style had roots in the Etruscan and Hellenistic world would preclude the possibility of a Roman horizon style. The fact that sites like Moxeke, Cerro Sechin, Garagay, and Huaca de los Reyes were identified incorrectly as belonging to the Chavin horizon is unfortunate from a historical perspective but not really relevant to evaluating the value of the Chavin horizon for contemporary archaeologists. Viewed in retrospect, the themes and style of these clay friezes are different from that of the Chavin de Huantar sculpture and from each other. Their misidentification does not logically require the rejection of the Chavin horizon but simply modifies the list of candidates to be included in it.

The fundamental question is whether or not something remains to be explained after the various pre-Chavin and non-Chavin cases have been stricken from the hypothetical Chavin horizon. In my opinion, there still are numerous instances of the Chavin style distributed widely across the coast and highlands of central and northern Peru, which appear to constitute a true horizon in terms of stylistic uniqueness and coherence, pan-regional extent, and relatively short temporal duration (Willey and Phillips 1958).[4] If

[4] Rowe's use of the term *Early Horizon* is frequently misinterpreted as being synonymous with the term *Chavin horizon* despite its definition as a block of time between the appearance of Chavin influence in Ica and the beginning of Nazca pottery in Ica (Rowe 1962b). The Chavin horizon style is presumed to have begun during the final epochs of the Initial Period and continued during the first five or six epochs of the Early Horizon, if we follow the Ocucaje sequence. The final epochs of the Early Horizon post-date the Chavin horizon. Consequently, Thomas and Shelia Pozorski's recent criticism (1987) that the Early Horizon cannot be a horizon because its duration is too long, misses its mark. Rowe never claimed that the Early Horizon was a horizon in the Willey and Phillips sense.

a strict application of the Willey definition of the Chavin style is applied, most of the cases of the horizon style outside Chavin de Huantar relate to the D/EF sculpture of Chavin de Huantar and can therefore be tentatively dated to two or three centuries of the Early Horizon (i.e., 490–200 B.C.).

The New Temple at Chavin de Huantar is the most likely source of this horizon style, since the D/EF images introduced in different regions of Peru can be shown to have evolved directly out of the local AB phase sculptures of Chavin de Huantar's Old Temple (Fig. 6). In contrast, other centers coeval with the Old Temple, like Pacopampa, Kotosh, or even Garagay, were executing religious art in regional styles that can be distinguished from that of Chavin de Huantar. Because the Chavin sculptural style was originally inspired primarily by Initial Period sources on the Central and North Coasts, its adoption in these zones during the Early Horizon has an almost *déjà vu* sense to it as it reintroduces older coastal elements in a transformed state. In contrast, the penetration of the Chavin horizon style into the Central Highlands and South Coast is more conspicuously intrusive because the Initial Period art styles of these areas were apparently not sources of inspiration for the Chavin style.

One of the problems of using a "great art style" as a horizon marker is the difficulty of recovering examples of it in situ. This problem was not immediately apparent because the Chavin horizon was defined on the basis of stone sculpture, which is conspicuous, resistant to the elements, and often heavy enough to be left near its original location. Unfortunately, stone carving is rare outside the Chavin de Huantar area during the Initial Period and Early Horizon (Burger 1988: 125–128) and painted and/or sculpted clay murals were a more common means for decorating public architecture throughout Peruvian prehistory (Bonavia 1985). This was certainly the case on the coast during the Initial Period and Early Horizon, and recent investigations by the Japanese Scientific Expedition at Huacaloma in Cajamarca and Cerro Blanco and Kuntur Wasi in the headwaters of the Jequetepeque drainage have demonstrated for the first time that this also was true for northern highland centers (Terada and Onuki 1985, 1988; Terada and Onuki, personal communication, 1990). Unfortunately, these murals were poorly suited to resist the highland fluctuations in temperature and precipitation and, thus far, only fragments of them have been found intact. Even on the coast where conditions are more favorable, large-scale excavations are needed to unearth the fragile painted and sculpted facades of public buildings, and, since Tello's time, few investigators have attempted such enterprises.

As a consequence, the sample of early public art available for comparison with the Chavin de Huantar sculpture is really quite limited, especially considering the large number of public centers documented for the Initial Period and Early Horizon. The Chavin horizon style also appears on portable artifacts of gold, bone, pottery, and textiles, but all of these items were

Richard L. Burger

Fig. 6. (a) A Chavin-style image of the crested eag
represented on a mid-Early Horizon stirrup-spout
vessel from the North Coast (photo: courtesy Ped
Rojas Ponce); (b) crested eagle represented on a mi
Early Horizon granite sculpture from the New Ter
ple of Chavin de Huantar (note its derivation fro
earlier local sculptures, as seen in Fig. 3b)

highly curated in antiquity and are rarely recovered except in caches or burials. Because they have a high value in the modern art market, they are more frequently sought after and encountered by looters than by archaeologists. Climate is also a factor. Decorated cloth with motifs related to the Chavin style is only known from the Central and South Coasts, probably due to poorer organic preservation on the moister North Coast and Highland regions. In summary, depositional and post-depositional factors have sharply diminished the number of well-documented cases of the Chavin horizon style available for study as well as strongly influencing where such examples have been found.

One of the clearest expressions of the Chavin horizon style occurs on the Peruvian South Coast, approximately 500 km from Chavin de Huantar. The Early Horizon ceramic style in this region features figurative decoration, and it has long been recognized that pottery (i.e., Ocucaje 3–5) and pyroengraved gourds in the early Paracas style show images related to the Chavin de Huantar sculpture, both in content and style (Kroeber 1953; Menzel, Rowe, and Dawson 1964; Rowe 1962b: figs. 18,55; Sawyer 1966; Willey 1951). These representations appear on locally produced ceramics so that there is no question that this complex symbolic system was actively reproduced by peoples living in an area previously unconnected with Chavin de Huantar and distinct from it in terms of ecology and cultural traditions. The themes shown on the Ocucaje 3–5 pottery and gourds include felines, the "staff gods," fanged mouth bands, and rows of repeating Chavin symbols (S's, concentric circles, circle dots). The full range of religious themes has not yet been encountered and may not have been represented on Paracas style pottery.

The presence on the South Coast of the Chavin horizon style in all of its complexity became apparent only with the publication of painted cotton textiles said to have been looted from Callango in the Ica Valley (Rowe 1962b: figs. 29–30), Chincha (Conklin 1971), and the site of Karwa (or Carhua) located on the littoral of the Paracas Peninsula (Cordy-Collins n.d.). Fragments discarded on Karwa's surface by the looters confirm this poorly known site as the source of the textiles now found in museums and private collections throughout the world (Burger 1988: 117–120). More than 200 decorated textile fragments are said to have been found in a large rectangular tomb at Karwa, and many of these bear the supernatural images familiar from the Chavin de Huantar sculptures: the cayman, the anthropomorphic deity with staffs, the crested eagle, the jaguar, and the serpent. The figures are executed using the traditional Chavin stylistic conventions. As Fig. 7 illustrates, the images on the Karwa textiles and Chavin de Huantar sculpture are variants of the same iconographic system, the same "great art style" that is the marker of the Chavin horizon. The size and structure of some of these textiles suggest that they may have once decorated the walls

Richard L. Burger

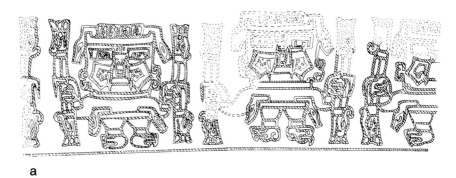

a

b

d

c

e

Fig. 7. Painted Chavin-style representations on cotton textiles reported to be from the Karwa tomb, Paracas peninsula: (a) supernatural figure with staffs (redrawn after Roe 1974: 49); (b) supernatural with cayman attributes (composite reconstruction based on Roe 1974: 47 and slides of an additional Karwa textile fragment); (c) jaguar (after Sawyer and Maitland 1983); (d) crested eagle (after Sawyer and Maitland 1983); (e) snake (after Sawyer and Maitland 1983)

of temples in a manner analogous to the sculptures at Chavin de Huantar itself. Recently, two new painted Chavin textiles have been found at another site in the lower Ica Valley (Jose Pinilla, personal communication). It should be emphasized that classic Chavin textiles are rare at Karwa and other coeval sites of the Paracas culture, and that it is the extensive destruction of these sites by *huaqueros* that has brought the Chavin style textiles to light. Small-scale archaeological field work might never encounter similar materials, even if work was carried out at these sites.

The Karwa find is, in some respects, analogous to the discovery of two caches of Chavin gold in Chongoyape, Lambayeque, located 900 km north of Paracas (Lothrop 1941). The Chongoyape gold bore classic Chavin motifs, and the iconography and the pottery associated with one of the lots indicates contemporaneity with the New Temple. Like the Karwa textiles, these gold crowns, earspools, and gorgets show classic Chavin stylistic conventions. Until recently, nothing was known of the Early Horizon culture in Lambayeque, which was responsible for the burials in which these pieces were found. After their discovery, they remained an isolated testimony to the northern extent of the Chavin horizon. Work at the early sites of Huaca Lucia and Huaca Cholope did not provide additional evidence of the Chavin horizon (Shimada, Elera, and Shimada 1983) because both sites date to the late Initial Period and were abandoned several centuries prior to the Chavin horizon phenomenon.[5] Only in 1979, when excavations were carried out at Morro de Eten at the mouth of the Lambayeque drainage, did archaeologists finally encounter Early Horizon refuse and burials, including bottles decorated with classic Chavin renditions of crested eagles (Elera 1983).

Similar Early Horizon pottery with classic Chavin representations had long been known from looted tombs from Chicama, Zaña, and Jequetepeque Valleys (e.g., Alva 1986: figs. 329, 346; Roe 1974: fig. 36b, 1982). These valleys composed the heartland of the Cupisnique culture, and the unprovenienced Chavin style pieces (Fig. 6a) were anomalous when compared with those recovered by Larco (1941) at the cemeteries at Barbacoa and Palenque. Indeed, if a strict definition of Chavin is adhered to, Larco's Cupisnique materials cannot be included in a Chavin horizon. This, however, is understandable in light of the excavations at Chavin de Huantar that have encountered Cupisnique-style vessels resembling those of Barbacoa in the Ofrendas Gallery and with Urabarriu refuse (Burger 1985: 79–80, 175–177; Lumbreras 1973). These associations at Chavin de Huantar

---

[5] Shimada refers to Huaca Lucia and Huaca Cholope as Early Horizon sites, but radiocarbon dates and ceramics place them at the end of the Initial Period (certainly before the introduction of Chavin motifs in Ica, which is the definition of the beginning of the Early Horizon). Huaca Lucia is not contemporary with Chongoyape and Moro de Eten, two authentically Early Horizon sites in the Lambayeque drainage. Another source of similar confusion in the literature is the characterization of the late Initial Period complex of Huaca de los Reyes at the site of Caballo Muerto as Early Horizon (T. Pozorski 1976). An Early Horizon component does exist at Caballo Muerto and has been documented by T. Pozorski and Watanabe for Huaca Guavalito and Huaca Herederos Chica. The ceramics from both mounds are Janabarriu-related and have much in common with the Morro de Eten assemblage. A radiocarbon measurement of 440 ± 70 B.C. (Tx1939) has been published for Huaca Guavalito.

demonstrate that this "classic" phase of the Cupisnique style is partially contemporary with the Urabarriu Phase and Old Temple, and consequently predates the Chavin horizon.

In contrast, the testing at Huaca Guavalito and Huaca Herederos Chica at Caballo Muerto in the lower Moche valley and site reconnaissance at Huaca de los Chinos in the upper Moche Valley have revealed an Early Horizon component similar to the Janabarriu Phase materials at Chavin de Huantar (T. Pozorski 1983; Watanabe n.d.), and Tello encountered coeval assemblages at Mokan in Chicama and Pallka in Casma. With the exception of Cerro Blanco (Tello 1943: XIIa), the religious iconography of Early Horizon centers on the North Coast is unknown at the present time.

This is not the appropriate place to review each individual instance of the Chavin horizon style, but the indisputable instances of Chavin style in Paracas on the South Coast and Lambayeque on the far North Coast separated by nearly a thousand km should suffice to demonstrate that the dismissal of the Chavin horizon by the Pozorskis (T. Pozorski and S. Pozorski 1987) is unjustified. Their ill-considered conclusion seems due both to an inadequate differentiation between evidence from the late Initial Period and Early Horizon and to the presumption that the situation in Casma, with which they are most familiar, is representative of Peru as a whole.

Although the definition of the Chavin horizon solely on the basis of the Chavin de Huantar sculptural style is feasible, it is not the only approach available. It will be recalled that horizons, in the abstract, can be based on any phenomenon that is easily identifiable and spreads rapidly over a broad area. Over the past two decades it has become apparent that the Chavin horizon is not merely marked by a "great art style." It is also characterized by the spread of a suite of ceramic attributes and a series of technological innovations in metallurgy and textiles (Burger 1988; Conklin 1978; Lechtman 1980).

The incorporation of ceramic criteria in the definition of the Chavin horizon is helpful because of the ubiquity of pottery as compared to complex iconography, and it is useful from a functional perspective because pottery reflects dimensions of social behavior different from those expressed in religious art. The ceramic traits associated with the Chavin horizon are best documented for the Janabarriu Phase (Lumbreras' Rocas Phase) at Chavin de Huantar (Burger 1985: 107–158), and their incorporation into assemblages throughout central and northern Peru during the Chavin horizon has been summarized elsewhere (Burger 1978: 329–391, 1988: 133–139). The intrusion of these traits into local ceramic traditions has been observed by other investigators, who have signalled the heavy influence of these Chavin elements by descriptive terms like Pacopampa Chavin or Kotosh Chavin. Some of the intrusive elements are conventionalized symbols like the concentric circle and *S*, which also occur as elements in more

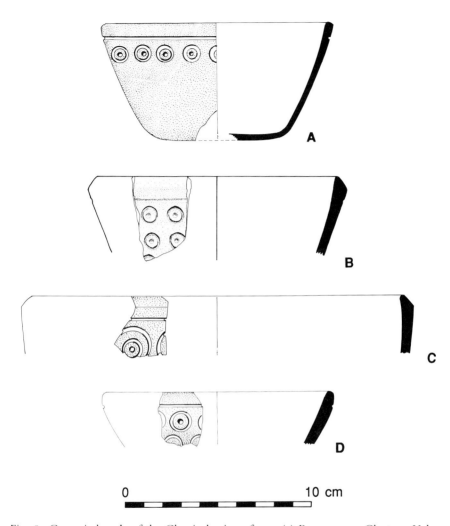

Fig. 8. Ceramic bowls of the Chavin horizon from: (a) Pacopampa, Chotano Valley, Cajamarca (redrawn after Fung 1976: fig. 54); (b) Chavin de Huantar, Mosna valley; (c) Ancon, Chillon valley; (d) Atalla, Huancavelica

complex Chavin iconography, but there is also the spread of particular vessel forms, like the stirrup-spouted bottle, and techniques of decoration, like dentate rocker stamping (Fig. 8). These new elements were combined with earlier local elements to produce distinctively local styles.

Because most of these Early Horizon styles retain numerous elements from the preceding styles, some investigators select descriptive terms that emphasize the local features of the assemblage. For example, Daniel Morales refers to the Early Horizon pottery as Pacopampa Expansivo rather than Pacopampa Chavin as Rosas and Shady had done. Similarly, Carlos Elera (1983) advocates the term *Cupisnique Tardío* for the Chavin-influenced style of pottery produced on the North Coast. The differences in the nomenclature utilized are less significant than the widespread acknowledgement by these and other investigators that all of these ceramic styles share numerous attributes of form and decoration with each other and with Chavin de Huantar.

The distribution of the Janabarriu traits associated with the Chavin horizon is more extensive than the known distribution of the Chavin art style. No examples of classic Chavin iconography have been reported for the central highlands, but at Atalla in Huancavelica, the pottery assemblage is remarkably similar to that of Janabarriu Phase ceramics from Chavin de Huantar (Burger and Matos n.d.). Even further to the south, work in the Ayacucho area revealed a Janabarriu-related style called Kichka Pata (Lumbreras 1974), defined on the basis of bowls and other utilitarian ware from refuse deposits. In 1983, tombs were found at the Ayacucho site of Jargam Pata de Huamanga that contained bottles resembling the Janabarriu-related pottery from the Chongoyape tomb, located 900 km to the north (Ochatoma n.d.).

The appearance of the Chavin horizon was unprecedented in Peruvian prehistory. Initial Period ceramic styles, like post-Chavin pottery styles, were highly variable, with distinctive styles characterizing single valleys or, in some cases, small portions of valleys. For example, recent excavations at the late Initial Period site of Cardal in the lower Lurin Valley has documented a characteristic ceramic assemblage distinct from that being utilized at the shoreline community of Curayacu, located only 20 km away at the southern edge of the Lurin delta. Before the Chavin horizon, the pottery of distant regions like Lambayeque, the Callejon de Huaylas, Rimac, Huanuco, Huancavelica, Ayacucho, and Ica had virtually nothing in common, and they again shared almost nothing during the seven centuries following it.

Unfortunately, there has been almost no work on coastal sites that might be assigned to the Chavin horizon, and even in the highlands, emphasis has been directed to the study of the pre-Early Horizon components at most sites. We are faced with a data base of uneven quality, but with all of its limitations there is still ample reason to retain the concept of a pan-regional phenomenon that can be called the Chavin horizon.

The Chavin horizon reflects a short-lived moment in Peruvian prehistory in which disparate, unrelated societies were somehow brought together in a single system. The horizon concept helps us step out of the provincial realm of the valley or site study and confront this broader phenomenon. But because *horizon* is merely a formal descriptive term of our own making, it does not explain this pattern. There are many differences between this horizon, as presently understood, and that of the Incas. For instance, there is no specialized administrative architecture characteristic of the Chavin horizon, nor do we know of intrusive enclaves, like Huanuco Pampa, in which a pure expression of the horizon style is found surrounded by continuing local traditions. The Chavin horizon style does not appear to be the propaganda tool of an expansive imperial state, and there is little evidence that would support the hypothesis that it was spread by conquest. The Chavin phenomenon fits the formal definition of a horizon, but it would seem to be a different kind of horizon, one whose causes may have little in common with those of the other two Peruvian cases.

MODELING THE CHAVIN HORIZON

What does the Chavin horizon represent? As we noted earlier, Peruvianists traditionally have interpreted it as the material manifestation of a set of religious beliefs. The representation of the Chavin pantheon on the painted textiles from the Karwa tomb in Paracas have lent weight to this conclusion (Fig. 7a–e). There is no question either of the intrusive nature of the symbols or of the detailed knowledge they imply of Chavin ideology. At the same time, the cotton fiber, the weaving techniques, and the unique features of the iconography suggest that these cloths were produced on the coast, rather than the highlands. A technical analysis of the Karwa painted textiles by Dwight Wallace indicates that, although some of the cotton cloth was woven locally, part of it was produced on the Central Coast, and possibly the North Coast. Significantly, there is no significant difference in the iconography on the different kinds of cloth (Dwight Wallace 1979; personal communication, 1990).

But how should we conceptualize the spread of the Chavin religious ideology to these distant areas during the Early Horizon? Until recently, most scholars had not given much thought to this problem, but those who did often relied on the pattern of religious expansion most familiar to us. Thus, analogies have been drawn to the spread of Christianity under the Romans (Patterson 1971), and the Karwa textiles have been analyzed as a catechism brought by Chavin missionaries (Cordy-Collins n.d.).

Some scholars associate expansive religious movements so closely with Christianity and other modern world religions that they find it difficult to conceive of comparable processes occurring in the pre-Hispanic world, particularly in early times (Sanders 1978: 40). This position is unjustified on both theoretical and empirical grounds. Expansive religions, known in the ethnographic literature as regional cults or revitalization movements, have been documented for a wide range of state and non-state societies in a variety of cultural milieux (A. Wallace 1956; Werbner 1977). Regional cults can be shown to have existed in pre-Hispanic Peru on the basis of sixteenth century historical records, and one of these, Pachacamac, was described in some detail because its independent wealth aroused the special interest of the Spanish conquerors (Jimenez Borja and Bueno 1970; Patterson 1985a; Rostworowski 1972). The evidence available indicates that this regional cult had flourished for centuries before it was incorporated into Tawantinsuyu. Moreover, other regional cults existed in Peru in the early sixteenth century, which resembled the Pachacamac cult in organization (Spaulding 1984: 61–71).

The religious network centered at Pachacamac provides a useful model of how pre-Hispanic Peruvian regional cults were organized and how their ideas were disseminated. Unlike most Old World religions, the expansive Pachacamac cult spread without proselytizing missionaries or the drama of personal conversion. Instead, it was based on the establishment of branch oracles in areas that differed in ethnic affiliation, language, and economic base from the center of the cult. Each branch had its own identity and myths, while at the same time recognizing the authority of and paying tribute to the cult center at Pachacamac. The relationship of the branch shrines to the main center was expressed in kinship terms, with the supernatural petitioned at the local shrines being considered the brother, sister, daughter, son, or wife of the supernatural responsible for the power of the main oracle.

The cult activities were supervised by religious specialists, and branch shrines were provided with representatives by the principal center. The branch shrines were supported by produce derived by community labor on lands allocated to the cult and thus, the cult activity was thoroughly embedded in local systems of social organization and communal production. It is consistent, therefore, that adoption of the cult, like the maintenance of its oracle, was based on community decisions, rather than individual conversion. The center of the Pachacamac cult received gifts from all of its branch oracles, and it was said that tribute came from as far away as Ecuador. It should be noted that although Pachacamac also served as the political and economic center of a small polity called Ychma, its influence over more distant communities was limited to its religious authority reinforced by pilgrimages to Pachacamac by community representatives bearing gifts and/or requesting guidance from the oracle.

This Andean pattern of regional cults differs from Judaeo-Christian patterns of expansive religions in several significant ways. First, the regional cult was an addition to, rather than a substitute for, older local cults. Andean peoples accepted the notion of hierarchically arrayed supernatural powers, each associated with particular objects or elements of sacred geography. Thus, a non-local supernatural could be accepted as having greater power to assist the community in some aspects of life without denying the need to continue to propitiate supernatural forces embedded in the local landscape or represented by the community temple. Local religious traditions could continue alongside the newly established branches of the re-

Fig. 9. Painted image from a Karwa textile of a female supernatural figure with staffs (redrawn after Roe 1974: 48)

gional cult. Second, because reciprocity was the idiom of these cults, tribute in the form of gifts to both the local and regional centers was necessary for its participation in the religious network, since the prestation of these goods initiated and maintained reciprocal obligations with the supernatural forces in question. Third, branch oracles were only established upon acceptance by the principal center of petitions from local communities. Judging from the evidence on Pachacamac, this process produced a pattern of non-contiguous cult activity. This pattern might be described as a religious archipelago spanning the Andean landscape both vertically and laterally (Rostworowski 1972). Some communities or even regions may not have participated in the religious network due to local conditions or because of rejection from the principal center. As a consequence of this, the absence of the regional cult in a particular valley or site should not be interpreted as constituting disproof of the pan-regional extent of a particular cult. Finally, each branch of the cult had a unique identity, symbolized by its own mythical character.

In our opinion, the Pachacamac model helps to explain the nature and distribution of Chavin horizon markers, particularly those determined by the presence of images similar to the Chavin sculptural style. It suggests that we should not expect the principal supernaturals to be identical at the center and branches of the Chavin cult, even if they were all participating in the same religious cult. The explicitly female characteristics of the principal supernaturals at Karwa (Fig. 9) and Pacopampa may signal wives, sisters, or daughters of the deity shown on the Raimondi Stone at Chavin de Huantar, and the plants growing from the Karwa staff goddess (Cordy-Collins 1979) may represent her particular mythic attributes. Similarly, some particularly

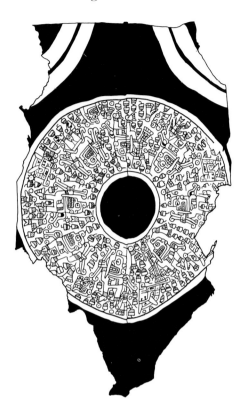

Fig. 10. Painted image of a procession scene with fish and hummingbirds from a cotton textile said to have been found by looters at Samaca, a site in the lower Ica valley (redrawn after a photograph, courtesy of Jose Pinilla Blenke)

elaborate painted textiles from Ica and Paracas depict elaborate scenes unknown from Chavin de Huantar, perhaps narrating critical events in the individual myths that validated each branch of the cult (Fig. 10).

The Pachacamac model also suggests the likelihood of peaceful coexistence of the regional cult with earlier local religious institutions. During the Late Horizon, Pachacamac had an Inca temple to the solar deity alongside the still-functioning shrine of ancient oracle. This pattern helps to explain Early Horizon sites like Huaricoto in the Callejon de Huaylas where, during the Late Capilla phase, Chavin-style ritual paraphernalia is found alongside ceremonial chambers where offerings were burnt as part of the ongoing Kotosh Religious Tradition (Burger and Salazar Burger 1980). Similarly, non-Chavin mythical events in the Cupisnique Tradition continued to be produced during the Early Horizon along the North Coast (Alva 1986: fig. 349), and local deities appear on some stone sculptures at Kuntur Wasi (Carrión Cachot 1948: lám. xx).

It is likely that some communities or areas did not participate at all in the Chavin religious network, and one would not expect them to exhibit the

Chavin horizon style nor adopt the Janabarriu-related ceramic traits. Negative evidence is rarely compelling in archaeology, but several regions show comparatively little evidence of the Chavin horizon despite considerable investigation. Conspicuous among these is the highland area between Quiruvilca and Cajamarca (Terada and Onuki 1985; Kryzanowski 1986), which has yet to yield Chavin-related materials despite strong Chavin components to the north, south, and west. Similarly, the Early Horizon occupation of the lower Casma at sites San Diego and Pampa Rosario show little imprint of the Chavin phenomenon (S. Pozorski 1987; S. Pozorski and T. Pozorski 1987), despite the fact that Chavin influence on iconography and ceramics (Tello 1956; Burger 1978) is strong only a short distance upstream at Pallka (900 m above sea level).[6] Such a situation is puzzling only if we make the unjustified assumption that a horizon, like most modern nation states, must cover an unbroken geographic expanse.

But, how does the spread of Janabarriu-related ceramic attributes relate to the foregoing interpretation of the Chavin horizon as an expansive religious cult? William Adams (1979) observed, on the basis of his work on Nubian pottery, that religious conversion or subjugation by an outside group need not manifest itself directly in locally produced ceramics; in fact, such pressures may have the reverse effect, as the Inca conquest of Huanuco illustrates. All the more significant, then, that the pottery produced and consumed on the household level between the fifth and third centuries B.C. incorporated Janabarriu-related features. These stylistic attributes were shared with neighboring and distant societies, breaking the long-standing pattern whereby pottery represented distinctive cultural identity and separateness from other groups. Simple diffusion of traits does not explain this change because there is ample evidence of contact between these groups during the Initial Period without significant blurring of stylistic divisions.

The decision to produce and use pottery similar to that of the other alien communities can be interpreted as a powerful symbolic statement of a broadened social identity, presumably stimulated by the adoption of shared religious ideology and the associated participation in a broadened network of economic activity (Burger 1988). The representation of Chavin symbols on this locally produced pottery suggests the importance that the shared religious beliefs provided by the Chavin cult played in this process. In the Classical world, the term *oecumenos* (derived from the Greek for "inhabited

---

[6] The weak relationship of the societies in the lower Casma Valley to the Chavin horizon is inferred from the architecture of San Diego and Pampa Rosario. Although the published ceramics from these sites (Pozorski and Pozorski 1987) share fewer features with Chavin de Huantar than Pallka, in Casma's mid-valley, they do have elements of form and decoration that emulate nearby Janabarriu-related styles (e.g., the form of the stirrup spouts on the bottles). More extensive excavation of these or other Early Horizon sites in lower Casma may require a reevaluation of these centers with those neighboring groups in the Chavin horizon.

Richard L. Burger

world") was sometimes used to express a general sense of shared cultural identity among a plethora of ethnic groups and nations. It was essentially an emic category designed to distinguish the "civilized we" from the "barbaric other" without implying cultural homogeneity or political unity. Although this term, occasionally employed by New World archaeologists (e.g., Gordon Willey), has limited analytical value, one wonders whether some analogous general sense of shared identity might not have existed among the diverse groups that together comprised the Chavin horizon.

THE CHAVIN HORIZON: SOCIOECONOMIC METAMORPHOSIS

The foregoing discussion has attempted to show that a Chavin horizon existed and to provide a plausible interpretation of what it represents. Having explored the nature of this particular example of the horizon phenomenon, it is difficult not to wonder what caused it. Why, at this particular moment in Peruvian prehistory, was it possible for the Chavin cult to achieve pan-regional acceptance and support? The answer is bound to be complex. It will be no easier to determine than why Christianity or Islam spread when and how they did—issues that continue to be debated by Old World historians despite an abundance of documentation and a relatively detailed knowledge of the societies in question. In the case of the Chavin horizon, for which archaeological data is scarce and difficult to interpret, it would be unrealistic to expect any definitive answers in the near future.

Nevertheless, the question is worth raising in order to stimulate debate and additional research. Initial Period societies, particularly on the coast, were extremely conservative. For more than 1,000 years, one finds few radical changes in the settlement patterns, diet, and architectural styles. The societies in question appear to be largely unstratified agricultural communities governed by some form of corporate leadership closely associated with sacred knowledge. The stability and continuity of these societies is remarkable until the end of the Initial Period, when major public sites throughout the Central and North Coasts are suddenly abandoned (Burger 1981, 1985; S. Pozorski 1987).

The Chavin horizon appears on the heels of this upheaval, and judging from the chronological information available, it is more likely to be a function of the conditions produced by this disruption than the cause. At Cardal in the Lurin Valley and at Sechin Bajo and Taukachi-Konkan in Casma, portions of the public architecture were left unfinished, and at Haldas, the paralyzation of corporate labor activities was so sudden that the surveyor's stakes and cord were left in place, witnesses to the demise of the social system responsible for these monumental undertakings (Grieder 1975: 102–103; S. Pozorski 1987: 22). Thus far, few major public works are known to have been initiated in any of the lower coastal valleys following these abandonments, and it would appear that the long-standing ability of coastal

68

societies to mobilize collective labor for public ends was declining rather than increasing at the time when the Chavin cult was spreading; the adoption of the cult does not appear to have reversed this trend. However, the disruption on the coast was not total. Many fishing villages, like Ancon and Curayacu, continued as before and some major sites prospered in mid or upper valleys, like Pallka and Kuntur Wasi.

The evidence we have from Early Horizon coastal sites reveals significant cultural changes. In lower Casma, the Early Horizon sites lack major pyramid mounds and bear little resemblance to immediately antecedent Initial Period centers (S. Pozorski 1987). Analysis of Early Horizon refuse on the South, Central, and North Coasts point to an increase in the consumption of llamas. In fact, this highland meat source may displace marine resources as the principal source of animal protein at inland sites in some coastal valleys. The latter shift suggests a greater dependency on adjacent highland areas, and a formidable increase in exotics is characteristic of many coastal and highland Early Horizon occupations. It is tempting to see the decline of Initial Period polities as producing a breakdown in the small self-sufficient socioeconomic systems that had sustained them, and leading in the Early Horizon to the emergence of a larger interaction sphere in which exchange of goods and ideas became increasingly common (cf. Browman 1975). These trends should not be interpreted as "progress," but rather as alternative strategies for struggling societies.

Thomas Patterson (1983) has argued that the innate ability of large lineages to produce a surplus and gradually constitute separate classes was neutralized in the Initial Period by channeling excess production and labor into public endeavors, like the pyramid complexes. Similarly, the corporate group charged with coordinating religious and public activities also had the potential of accumulating wealth but likewise must have been stopped from doing so by ideological sanctions preventing the conversion of ideological power into personal wealth. Clearly, these Initial Period societies were replete with contradictions, and by the end of the Initial Period they may no longer have been capable of resolving the difficulties confronting their members using the traditional economic system and its associated ideology.

The uncontrollable forces of nature may have exacerbated their difficulties. Michael Moseley believes that one of the worst El Niño events in Peruvian history occurred on the North Coast around 500 B.C. and caused massive flooding (Nials et al. 1979: 6). Robert Bird (1987) argues that a major tidal wave disrupted the northern coastline at the beginning of the Early Horizon. Besides these natural disasters, there may have also been steady climatic deterioration along the coastline beginning around 500 B.C., which lasted several centuries (Moseley, Feldman, and Ortloff 1981: 248). Other scholars believe that between 800–580 B.C. and 420–300 B.C. there was a marked cooling in the highlands, which would have shifted the lower limits of the *puna* grasslands downward, reducing the lands available for cultivation (Cardich 1985).

A cross-cultural review of successful religious movements concluded that their spread usually occurs when the expectations of a group concerning its overall well-being remain basically unchanged but its perceived capabilities for realizing these expectations decline; situations like this have been called decremental deprivation (Barkun 1974: 35). Other scholars have suggested that new religious beliefs are adopted to alleviate the stress produced by the contrast between reality experienced under unfavorable circumstances and the explanations and claims offered by the traditional ideology (A. Wallace 1956). Consequently, disasters produced by social and/or natural causes have often acted as catalysts for the rapid diffusion of regional cults (Barkun 1974). The limited data available for the Early Horizon suggest that such conditions may have existed, and we can speculate that the Chavin cult might have provided a new ideological message suited to explaining the new conditions under which people were living.

We know little about the content of the Chavin ideology, but it was certainly eclectic and synthetic. From its inception, the Chavin de Huantar temple absorbed alien ideas, synthesized them, and transformed them into new composite configurations, thereby transcending the limitations of individual local systems. Consequently, the ideology of the Chavin cult was consistent with the broadening of economic and social relations and the corresponding redefinition of cultural identity by these groups.

Unfortunately, our current understanding of the Early Horizon is so poor that it is frequently difficult to determine whether a particular factor is the partial cause or the consequence of the Chavin horizon. Expanding trade networks, for example, encouraged the spread of Christianity in South America, but in other instances trade developed as a by-product of the improved social relations resulting from the adoption of shared beliefs. The expansion of trade in the Early Horizon is often assumed to be an example of the latter process, but this presumption has never been rigorously tested.

Social change may produce disturbances more profound than those resulting from economic or environmental factors, and thereby encourage revitalization movements. The emergence of marked social stratification radically transformed the nature of Andean society. The first clear-cut evidence of this process appears at the beginning of the Early Horizon and it seems unlikely that its contemporaneity with the Chavin horizon could be simply happenstance.

There appear to be marked differences in the distribution of wealth in the settlement contemporary with the New Temple of Chavin de Huantar. Differential presence of imported pottery, coastal fish and shell, and rare items like gold were the original basis for this conclusion (Burger 1984). Contrasts in the quality of domestic architecture were consistent with this position, and

Fig. 11. Gold pectoral said to come from Chavin de Huantar (Dumbarton Oaks collection)

the types of tools and craft by-products suggested that differences in consumption of exotics were correlated with different productive activities.

Recent research on the faunal materials has lent independent support to this conclusion (Miller and Burger n.d.). Both the hypothetical high-status and low-status areas of Chavin de Huantar depended on llama meat as the principal source of animal protein during the Janabarriu Phase, but a comparison of the ages of the animals being consumed reveals that the upper-status area was consuming younger, more tender animals than the nearby lower-status workers. Moreover, an analysis of selective representation of camelid bones from both sectors of the site indicates that these animals were not being slaughtered at Chavin de Huantar, but instead were being butchered elsewhere, presumably in the contemporary villages like Pojoc and Waman Wain near the high pasture land. It is interesting in this light that a large cache of Chavin gold described by Lothrop (1951) was probably looted from a Janabarriu tomb in the Chavin de Huantar area (Fig. 11).[7] We

[7] Sometime prior to 1941, a large group of gold objects in the Chavin style were purchased in Recuay. Their first owner, Juan Dalmau, told Rafael Larco Hoyle that they had been found at Chavin de Huantar (Larco 1941: fig. 204; Lothrop 1951). This ascription is plausible because Recuay served as a major outlet for produce from Chavin intended for the Callejon de Huaylas and coast prior to 1941. It is the first town on the trail leading over the Cordillera Blanca from Chavin de Huantar. There are no known Chavin style sites in or around Recuay. Prior to 1941, Chavin de Huantar received few visitors, and it would have been difficult to market looted antiquities there. Objects of this type from Chavin de Huantar could have been sent to Recuay for sale there or for eventual transport to the coast. On the other hand, it is difficult to think of a rationale for bringing looted antiquities to a small highland town, like Recuay, if they had been found on the North Coast. The discovery of a gold fragment in Janabarriu refuse at Chavin de Huantar (Burger 1984: 35) confirms that gold jewelry was used at this site.

Fig. 12. Gold crown (a) and earplugs (b) from Chongoyape tomb in Lambayeque (photos: courtesy of the National Museum of the American Indian, Smithsonian Institution, New York)

may speculate that one of the features of Chavin ideology may have been its rationalization of the hierarchically arrayed social statuses that were emerging and the conflicts they must have produced.

This process of incipient class formation was apparently not limited to Chavin de Huantar. At Kuntur Wasi, in the upper reaches of the Jequetepeque Valley, Pablo Carrera discovered an intact tomb on the southern slopes of the temple, which, judging from the contents, suggests the existence of an elite class. Alongside the body was a "classic Chavin" vessel, a necklace, and six gold discs decorated with repoussé snakes. The necklace included "turquoise" beads, a small gold sphere, thirty-two rectangular sheets of gold foil, four of which were in the form of a strombus shell (Carrión Cachot 1948: 63).

In the 1970s, grave robbing at the site of Cerro Corbacho in the Cayalti area of the lower Zaña Valley unearthed a new cache of Chavin-style gold objects similar to and coeval with those found three decades earlier at Chongoyape in Lambayeque (Fig. 12) (Kauffmann Doig 1981: 37–38, 130, 142, 143, 147). Recent excavations on the summit of Kuntur Wasi by the

Fig. 13. Gold crown from Kuntur Wasi, upper Jequetepeque drainage. Discovered in Tomb 2 by the University of Tokyo Archaeological Mission (photo: courtesy of Yoshio Onuki)

University of Tokyo Expedition under the direction of Yoshio Onuki uncovered Early Horizon shaft tombs with even richer grave goods than those found by Carrera (Fig. 13) (Yoshio Onuki, personal communication). These finds on the summit of Kuntur Wasi parallel the Chavin horizon tombs looted at Chongoyape and Cayalti, all of which yielded considerable quantities of Chavin gold, including crowns, disc-like gorgets, pins, nose ornaments, and earspools. On the South Coast, the Karwa tomb showed a comparable concentration of wealth but in the form of fine textiles rather than precious metals. In all of these interments, the elite individuals were personally associated with the iconography of the Chavin cult. Moreover, these sacred images are executed utilizing technological innovations introduced during the Chavin horizon. It should be emphasized that no Initial Period tombs with offerings comparable to these Early Horizon tombs are known to exist. The sharp decline in public construction during the Chavin horizon may be due, in part, to the appropriation of labor by the elite for their own benefit rather than for public goals (Patterson 1983).

The increase in the scale of procurement and distribution of exotic pottery, cinnabar, and Huancavelica obsidian in central and northern Peru by cultures participating in the Chavin horizon is probably a pale reflection of the intensification of networks of exchange and the interdependency between regions that these new relationships may imply. The degree to which local elites were able to control this new pattern of exchange and manipulate the goods being moved for their own benefit merits further study. The exchange of goods between the different groups of the Chavin horizon reinforced and, in some cases, probably underlay the social and ideological linkages touched upon earlier. Many of the interactions may have been between elites of roughly equivalent regional centers like Chavin de Huantar, Pacopampa, and Kuntur Wasi. Referred to as "peer polity interaction" by Colin Renfrew (1982), the dynamics of these relationships may have played an important role in the emergence of early civilization in the Central Andes as they did in the Mediterranean. Yet, the concept of peer-polity interaction does not address equally important socioeconomic contacts between these regional centers of power and less developed groups, possibly including some that lack centralized political authority. In such instances, the newly formed relationships, often initiated to acquire exotic raw materials, produce sharp changes in the organization of the less developed societies (Kohl 1987). Such a situation appears to have occurred in areas like Huancavelica, Ayacucho, and perhaps even the South Coast during the Chavin horizon (Burger and Matos n.d.).

In summary, the information available suggests that much of Peru was going through a socioeconomic metamorphosis between the fifth and third centuries B.C. This brief period appears to correspond to a transition between the largely unstratified societies of the Initial Period and the militaristic class-based polities of the early Early Horizon and Early Intermediate Period. The concept of the Chavin horizon remains useful because it helps us to isolate this critical episode in Peruvian prehistory and to focus our attention on the pan-regional context of prehistoric socioeconomic change in Peru. The Chavin horizon is not a stylistic chimera as some have contended, but a real pattern whose explanation is intertwined with the difficult problems of class formation, the emergence of the coercive state, and the development of a pan-regional sphere of economic interaction and interdependency.

BIBLIOGRAPHY

ADAMS, WILLIAM
1979   On the Argument from Ceramics to History: A Challenge Based on Evidence from Medieval Nubia. *Current Anthropology* 20: 727–734.

ALVA, WALTER L.
1986   Cerámica temprana en el valle de Jequetepeque, norte del Perú. *Materialien zur Allgemeinen und Vergleichenden Archäologie* 32. Munich.

BARKUN, MICHAEL
1974   *Disaster and the Millennium.* Yale University Press, New Haven.

BENNETT, WENDELL
1943   The Position of Chavin in Andean Sequences. *Proceedings of the American Philosophical Society* (1942) 86: 323–327. Philadelphia.

BIRD, JUNIUS
1963   Pre-ceramic Art from the Huaca Prieta, Chicama Valley. *Ñawpa Pacha* 1: 29–34.

BIRD, JUNIUS, JOHN HYSLOP, AND MILICA SKINNER
1985   The Preceramic Excavations at the Huaca Prieta, Chicama Valley, Peru. *Anthropological Papers of the American Museum of Natural History* 62 (1). New York.

BIRD, ROBERT
1987   A Tsunami in the Peruvian Early Horizon. *American Antiquity* 52 (2): 285–303.

BISCHOF, HENNING
1985   Zur Entstehung des Chavin-Stils in Alt-Peru. *Beiträge zur Allgemeinen und Vergleichenden Archäologie* 6 (1984): 355–452.

BONAVIA, DUCCIO
1985   *Mural Painting in Ancient Peru* (P. J. Lyon, trans.). University of Indiana Press, Bloomington.

BROWMAN, DAVID
1975   Trade Patterns in the Central Highlands of Peru in the First Millennium B.C. *World Archaeology* 6 (7): 322–329.

BURGER, RICHARD L.
1978   *The Occupation of Chavin, Ancash, during the Initial Period and Early Horizon.* University of California, Berkeley. University Microfilms, Ann Arbor.
1981   The Radiocarbon Evidence for the Temporal Priority of Chavin de Huantar. *American Antiquity* 46 (3): 592–602.
1984   *The Prehistoric Occupation of Chavin de Huantar, Peru.* University of California Press Publications in Anthropology 14. University of California, Berkeley.
1985   Concluding Remarks: Early Peruvian Civilization and Its Relation to

Richard L. Burger

the Chavin Horizon. In *Early Ceremonial Architecture in the Andes* (Christopher Donnan, ed.): 269–289. Dumbarton Oaks, Washington, D.C.

1988   Unity and Heterogeneity within the Chavin Horizon. In *Peruvian Prehistory* (Richard Keatinge, ed.): 99–144. Cambridge University Press, Cambridge.

1989   The Pre-Chavin Stone Sculpture of Casma and Pacopampa. *Journal of Field Archaeology* 16: 478–485.

BURGER, RICHARD L., AND RAMIRO MATOS MENDIETA

n.d.   Core/Periphery Relations in the Chavin Horizon: An Example from Atalla, Huancavelica. Paper presented at the American Anthropological Association, Washington, D.C., November 1989.

BURGER, RICHARD, AND LUCY SALAZAR-BURGER

1980   Ritual and Religion at Huaricoto. *Archaeology* 33: 26–32.

1991   The Second Season of Investigations at the Initial Period Center of Cardal, Peru. *Journal of Field Archaeology* 18 (3): 275–296.

CARDICH, AUGUSTO

1985   The Fluctuating Upper Limits of Cultivation in the Central Andes and Their Impact on Peruvian Prehistory. *Advances in World Archaeology* 4: 293–333.

CARRIÓN CACHOT, REBECA

1948   La cultura Chavín: Dos nuevas colonias Kuntur Wasi y Ancón. *Revista del Museo Nacional de Antropología y Arqueología* 2 (1): 99–172.

CONKLIN, WILLIAM J

1971   Chavin Textiles and the Origins of Peruvian Weaving. *Textile Museum Journal* 3 (2): 13–19.

1978   The Revolutionary Weaving Inventions of the Early Horizon. *Ñawpa Pacha* 16: 1–12.

CORDY-COLLINS, ALANA

1979   Cotton and the Staff God: Analysis of an Ancient Chavín Textile. In *The Junius B. Bird Pre-Columbian Textile Conference* (A. Pollard Rowe, E. P. Benson, and A.-L. Schaffer, eds.): 51–60. The Textile Museum and Dumbarton Oaks, Washington, D.C.

n.d.   *An Iconographic Study of Chavin Textiles from the South Coast of Peru: The Discovery of a Pre-Columbian Catechism.* Ph.D. dissertation, University of California, Los Angeles, 1976.

DAGGETT, RICHARD

1987   Reconstructing the Evidence for Cerro Blanco and Punkuri. *Andean Past* 1: 111–163.

ELERA, CARLOS

1983   Morro de Eten, Valle de Lambayeque. *Boletín* 8: 25–26. Museo Nacional de Antropología y Arqueología, Lima.

FUNG, ROSA

1976   Excavaciones en Pacopampa, Cajamarca. *Revista del Museo Nacional* 41 (1974): 129–210.

GRIEDER, TERENCE

    1975   A Dated Sequence for Building and Pottery at Las Haldas. *Ñawpa Pacha* 13: 99–112.

GRIEDER, TERENCE, ALBERTO BUENO, C. EARLE SMITH, JR., AND ROBERT MALINA

    1988   *La Galgada, Peru: A Preceramic Culture in Transition.* University of Texas Press, Austin.

HOBSBAWM, ERIC

    1983   Introduction: Inventing Traditions. In *The Invention of Traditions* (Eric Hobsbawm and Terence Ranger, eds.): 1–14. Cambridge University Press, Cambridge.

JIMENEZ BORJA, ARTURO, AND ALBERTO BUENO

    1970   Breves notas acerca de Pachacamac. *Arqueología y Sociedad* 4: 13–25.

KANO, CHIAKI

    1979   *The Origins of the Chavin Culture.* Studies in Pre-Columbian Art and Archaeology 22. Dumbarton Oaks, Washington, D.C.

KAUFFMANN DOIG, FEDERICO

    1978   *Manual de arqueología Peruana.* Ediciones PEISA, Lima.

    1981   Introducción a la cultura Chavín. In *Chavin Formativo* (Jose de Lavalle and Werner Lang, eds.): 9–44. Banco de Crédito del Perú en la Cultura, Lima.

KEATINGE, RICHARD

    1981   The Nature and Role of Religious Diffusion in the Early Stages of State Formation: An Example from Peruvian Prehistory. In *The Transition to Statehood in the New World* (G. D. Jones and R. R. Kautz, eds.): 172–187. Cambridge University Press, New York.

KOHL, PHILIP

    1987   The Use and Abuse of World Systems Theory: The Case of the Pristine West Asian State. *Advances in Archaeological Method and Theory* 11: 1–35.

KROEBER, ALFRED

    1944   *Peruvian Archaeology in 1942.* Viking Fund Publications in Anthropology 4. New York.

    1953   Paracas Cavernas and Chavin. *University of California Publications in American Archaeology and Ethnology* 40 (8): 313–348. Berkeley.

KRYZANOWSKI, ANDRZEJ

    1986   The Cultural Chronology of Northern Andes of Peru (the Huamachuco-Quiruvilca-Otuzco Region). *Acta Archaeologica Carpathica* 25: 231–264.

KUBLER, GEORGE

    1975   *The Art and Architecture of Ancient America: The Mexican/Maya and Andean Peoples.* Penguin Books, Harmondsworth, Middlesex.

LANNING, EDWARD

    1967   *Peru before the Incas.* Prentice-Hall, Englewood Cliffs, N.J.

LARCO HOYLE, RAFAEL

    1941   *Los Cupisniques.* Casa Editora La Crónica y Variedades, Lima.

Richard L. Burger

1948   *Cronología arqueológica del norte del Perú.* Biblioteca del Museo de Arqueología Rafael Larco Herrera, Hacienda Chiclin, Trujillo.

LATHRAP, DONALD

1974   The Moist Tropics, the Arid Lands, and the Appearance of Great Art Styles in the New World. In *Art and Environment in Native America* (Mary Elizabeth King and Idris Traylor, eds.): 115–158. The Museum Special Publication 7. Texas Tech University, Lubbock, Texas.

LECHTMAN, HEATHER

1980   The Central Andes: Metallurgy without Iron. In *The Coming of the Age of Iron* (T. Wertime and J. Muhly, eds.): 267–334. Yale University Press, New Haven.

LOTHROP, SAMUEL K.

1941   Gold Ornaments of Chavin Style from Chongoyape, Peru. *American Antiquity* 6 (2): 250–262.

1951   Gold Artifacts of Chavin. *American Antiquity* 16 (3): 226–240.

LUMBRERAS, LUIS

1969   *De los pueblos, las culturas y las artes en el antiguo Perú.* Moncloa-Campodonico Editores, Lima.

1973   Los estudios sobre Chavín. *Revista del Museo Nacional* 38: 73–92. Lima.

1974   *The Peoples and Cultures of Ancient Peru.* Smithsonian Institution Press, Washington, D.C.

LUMBRERAS, LUIS G., AND HERNÁN AMAT

1969   Informe preliminar sobre las galerías interiores de Chavín (Primera temporada de trabajos). *Revista del Museo Nacional* 34 (1965–66): 143–197. Lima.

MENZEL, DOROTHY, JOHN ROWE, AND LAWRENCE DAWSON

1964   *The Paracas Pottery of Ica: A Study in Style and Time.* University of California Publications in American Archaeology and Ethnology 50. Berkeley.

MIDDENDORF, ERNST W.

1893–95   *Perú: Beobachtungen und Studien über das Land und seine Bewohner wahrend eines 25 jährigen Aufenthalts,* 3 vols. Robert Oppenheim, Berlin.

MILLER, GEORGE, AND RICHARD L. BURGER

n.d.   We Don't Eat Caymans Here: An Exploration of the Ideoeconomic Universe of Chavin de Huantar. Manuscript in possession of the authors.

MORALES, DANIEL

1980   *El Dios Felino en Pacopampa.* Seminario de Historia Rural Andina. Universidad Nacional Mayor de San Marcos, Lima.

MOSELEY, MICHAEL E.

1978   The Evolution of Andean Civilization. In *Ancient Native Americans* (J. D. Jennings, ed.): 491–541. W. H. Freeman, San Francisco.

MOSELEY, MICHAEL, AND LUIS WATANABE

1974   The Adobe Sculpture of Huaca de los Reyes. *Archaeology* 27: 154–161.

Moseley, Michael, Robert Feldman, and Charles Ortloff

  1981   Living with Crisis: Human Perception of Process and Time. In *Biotic Crises in Ecological and Evolutionary Time* (M. Nitecki, ed.): 231–267. Academic Press, New York.

Nials, Fred, Eric Deeds, Michael Moseley, Shelia Pozorski, Thomas Pozorski, and Robert Feldman

  1979   El Niño: The Catastrophic Flooding of Coastal Peru, Part 2. *Field Museum of Natural History Bulletin* 50 (8): 4–10.

Ochatoma, Jose A.

  n.d.   *Acerca del Formativo en la Sierra Centro-Sur.* Thesis for Licenciado en Arqueología, Universidad Nacional de San Cristobal de Huamanga, Ayacucho, 1985.

Patterson, Thomas C.

  1971   Chavín: An Interpretation of Its Spread and Influence. In *Dumbarton Oaks Conference on Chavín* (Elizabeth Benson, ed.): 29–48. Dumbarton Oaks, Washington, D.C.

  1983   The Historical Development of a Coastal Andean Social Formation in Central Peru, 6000–500 B.C. In *Investigations of the Andean Past* (D. Sandweiss, ed.): 21–37. Cornell University Latin American Studies Program, Ithaca.

  1985a   Pachacamac—an Andean Oracle under Inca Rule. In *Recent Studies in Andean Prehistory and Protohistory* (A. P. Kvietok and D. Sandweiss, eds.): 159–176. Ithaca.

  1985b   The Huaca La Florida, Rimac Valley, Peru. In *Early Ceremonial Architecture in the Andes* (Christopher Donnan, ed.): 59–69. Dumbarton Oaks, Washington, D.C.

Pozorski, Shelia

  1987   Theocracy vs. Militarism: The Significance of the Casma Valley in Understanding Early State Formation. In *The Origins and Development of the Andean State* (Jonathan Haas, Shelia Pozorski, and Thomas Pozorski, eds.): 15–30. Cambridge University Press, Cambridge.

Pozorski, Thomas

  1976   El complejo de Caballo Muerto y los frizos de barro de la Huaca de los Reyes. *Revista del Museo Nacional* 41: 211–252. Lima.

  1983   The Caballo Muerto Complex and Its Place in the Andean Chronological Sequence. *Annals of the Carnegie Museum of Natural History* 52: 1–40.

Pozorski, Shelia, and Thomas Pozorski

  1986   Recent Excavations at Pampa de las Llamas-Moxeke, a Complex Initial Period Site in Peru. *Journal of Field Archaeology* 13: 381–401.

  1987   *Early Settlement and Subsistence in the Casma Valley, Peru.* University of Iowa Press, Iowa City.

Pozorski, Thomas, and Shelia Pozorski

  1987   Chavin, the Early Horizon and the Initial Period. In *The Origins and Development of the Andean State* (Jonathan Haas, Shelia Pozorski, and

Thomas Pozorski, eds.): 36–46. Cambridge University Press, Cambridge.

1988 An Early Stone Carving from Pampa de las Llamas-Moxeke, Casma Valley, Peru. *Journal of Field Archaeology* 15: 114–119.

1990 Reply to "The Pre-Chavin Stone Sculpture of Casma and Pacopampa." *Journal of Field Archaeology* 17: 110–111.

PROULX, DONALD A.

1985 An Analysis of the Early Cultural Sequence in the Nepeña Valley, Peru. *Research Report Number 25,* Department of Anthropology, University of Massachusetts, Amherst.

RAVINES, ROGGER

1984 Sobre la formación de Chavín: Imágenes y símbolos. *Boletín de Lima* 35: 27–45.

RAVINES, ROGGER, AND WILLIAM ISBELL

1976 Garagay: Sitio ceremonial temprano en el valle de Lima. *Revista del Museo Nacional* 41: 254–275. Lima.

RENFREW, COLIN

1982 Polity and Power: Interaction, Intensification and Exploitation. In *An Island Polity: The Archaeology of Exploitation in Melos:* 264–290. Cambridge University Press, Cambridge.

ROE, PETER

1974 *A Further Exploration of the Rowe Chavin Seriation and Its Implications for North Central Coast Chronology.* Studies in Pre-Columbian Art and Archaeology 13. Dumbarton Oaks, Washington, D.C.

1978 Recent Discoveries in Chavin Art. Some Speculations on Methodology and Significance in the Analysis of Figural Style. *El Dorado* 3 (1): 1–41.

1982 Cupisnique Pottery: A Cache from Tembladera. In *Precolumbian Art History* (Alana Cordy-Collins, ed.): 231–253. Peek Publications, Palo Alto.

ROSTWOROWSKI, MARÍA

1972 Breve ensayo sobre el señorio de Ychma o Ychima. *Boletín del Seminario de Arqueología* 13: 37–51. Lima.

ROWE, JOHN H.

1962a *Chavin Art. An Inquiry into its Form and Meaning.* The Museum of Primitive Art, New York.

1962b Stages and Periods in Archaeological Interpretation. *Southwestern Journal of Anthropology* 18 (1): 40–54.

1967 Form and Meaning in Chavin Art. In *Peruvian Archaeology: Selected Readings* (John H. Rowe and Dorothy Menzel, eds.): 72–103. Peek Publications, Palo Alto.

1971 The Influence of Chavín Art on Later Styles. In *Dumbarton Oaks Conference on Chavín* (Elizabeth Benson, ed.): 101–124. Dumbarton Oaks, Washington, D.C.

1977 Religión e imperio en el Perú antiguo. *Antropología Andina* 1–2: 5–12. Cuzco.

SALAZAR-BURGER, LUCY, AND RICHARD BURGER
    1983   La araña en la iconografía del horizonte temprano en la costa norte del Perú. *Beiträge zur Allgemeinen und Vergleichenden Archäologie* 4: 213–253.

SANDERS, WILLIAM
    1978   Ethnographic Analogy and the Teotihuacan Horizon Style. In *Middle Classic Mesoamerica: A.D. 400–700* (Esther Pasztory, ed.): 33–44. Columbia University Press, New York.

SAWYER, ALAN
    1966   *Ancient Peruvian Ceramics. The Nathan Cummings Collection.* The Metropolitan Museum of Art, New York.

SAWYER, ALAN, AND MAUREEN MAITLAND
    1983   A Reappraisal of Chavin. In *Art of the Andes* (Lois Katz, ed.): 47–67. The Arthur M. Sackler Foundation, Washington, D.C.

SCHEELE, HARRY
    n.d.   The Chavin Occupation of the Central Coast of Peru. Ph.D. dissertation, Department of Anthropology, Harvard University, 1970.

SHIMADA, IZUMI, CARLOS ELERA, AND MELODY SHIMADA
    1983   Excavaciones efectuadas en el Centro de Huaca Lucía-Chólope del horizonte temprano, Batan Grande, Costa Norte del Peru: 1979–1981. *Arqueológicas* 19: 109–298. Lima.

SPAULDING, KAREN
    1984   *Huarochiri: An Andean Society under Inca and Spanish Rule.* Stanford University Press, Stanford.

TELLO, JULIO C.
    1921   *Introducción a la historia antigua del Perú.* Lima.
    1922   *Prehistoric Peru.* Reprinted from April volume of Inter-America: 238–250. Doubleday, Page and Company, New York.
    1929   *Antiguo Perú: Primera época.* Comisión Organizadora del Segundo Congreso Sudamericano de Turismo, Lima.
    1930   Andean Civilization: Some Problems of Peruvian Archaeology. *Proceedings of the 23rd International Congress of Americanists:* 259–290. New York.
    1942   Origen y desarrollo de las civilizaciones prehistóricas. *Actas del XXVII Congreso de Americanistas (1939).* Librería e Imprenta Gil, Lima.
    1943   Discovery of the Chavin Culture in Peru. *American Antiquity* 9 (1): 135–160.
    1956   *Arqueología del valle de Casma: Cultura Chavin, Santa o Huaylas Yunga, y Sub-Chimu.* Publicación Antropológica del Archivo Julio C. Tello de la Universidad Nacional Mayor de San Marcos 1. Lima.
    1960   *Chavín Cultura Matriz de la Civilización Andina.* Publicación Antropológica del Archivo Julio C. Tello de la Universidad Nacional Mayor de San Marcos 2. Lima.

TERADA, KAZUO, AND YOSHIO ONUKI
    1985   *The Formative Period in the Cajamarca Basin, Peru: Excavations at Huaca-*

Richard L. Burger

loma and Layzon, 1982. Report of the Japanese Scientific Expedition to
Nuclear America, 3. University of Tokyo Press, Tokyo.

1988   Las Excavaciones en Cerro Blanco y Huacaloma, Cajamarca, Peru, 1985.
University of Tokyo Press, Tokyo.

VARGAS LLOSA, MARIO
1990   Questions of Conquest. Harper's Magazine (December): 45–51.

WALLACE, ANTHONY
1956   Revitalization Movements. American Anthropologist 58: 264–281.

WALLACE, DWIGHT T.
1979   The Process of Weaving Development on the Peruvian Coast. In The
Junius B. Bird Pre-Columbian Textile Conference (A. Pollard Rowe, E. P.
Benson, and A. L. Schaffer, eds.): 27–50. The Textile Museum and
Dumbarton Oaks, Washington, D.C.

WATANABE, LUIS
n.d.   Sitios Tempranos en el Valle de Moche (Costa Norte del Perú). Ph.D.
dissertation, Programa de Ciencias Histórico-Sociales, Especialidad
Arqueología, Universidad Nacional Mayor de San Marcos, Lima,
1976.

WERBNER, R. P. (ED.)
1977   Regional Cults. Academic Press, New York.

WILLEY, GORDON
1948   Functional Analysis of "Horizon Styles" in Peruvian Archaeology. In
A Reappraisal of Peruvian Archaeology (Wendell Bennett, ed.): 8–15.
Memoirs of the Society for American Archaeology 4. Menasha, Wisc.

1951   The Chavin Problem: A Review and Critique. Southwestern Journal of
Anthropology 7 (2): 103–144.

1962   The Early Great Styles and the Rise of the Pre-Columbian Civilizations. American Anthropologist 64 (1): 1–14.

WILLEY, GORDON, AND PHILLIP PHILLIPS
1958   Method and Theory in American Archaeology. University of Chicago
Press, Chicago.

WILLIAMS, CARLOS
1980   Arquitectura y urbanismo en el antiguo Perú. In Historia del Perú 8:
369–585. Editorial Juan Mejia Baca, Lima.

"Olmec" Horizons in Formative Period Mesoamerica: Diffusion or Social Evolution?

DAVID C. GROVE

UNIVERSITY OF ILLINOIS

OLMEC HORIZONS: A BACKGROUND

IN MESOAMERICA THE TRANSITION from simple farming villages to complex proto-state level societies took place within the time span of the Early and Middle Formative (Preclassic) periods, ca. 1600–500 B.C. It was then that many of the cultural foundations for Mesoamerica's later civilizations were laid, and thus an understanding of the developments during those periods is of great importance.

The literature on the Formative period is dominated by discussions of the Olmec, the archaeological culture of Mexico's southern Gulf Coast, which is often credited with being Mesoamerica's "mother culture" (e.g., Caso 1942: 46; Stirling 1968: 6). Within the span of their existence, the Olmec created Mesoamerica's first stone monuments, built impressive earthen public architecture at their political-ceremonial centers, utilized fabulously crafted jade and greenstone objects, and decorated their pottery and portable objects with some of Mesoamerica's earliest iconographic motifs. However, it has been recognized for decades that except for the monumental art, many of the artifacts and iconographic symbols found at Gulf Coast Olmec sites occur at Formative period villages and hamlets in other parts of Mesoamerica as well. Over the years many of those same non–Gulf Coast objects and motifs have become labeled as "Olmec," or "Olmec style," even though they may have first been discovered at sites outside of the Gulf Coast or might even occur in equal or greater quantities at non–Gulf Coast sites.

Because the "Olmec-style" artifacts are so widely distributed across Mesoamerica during portions of the Formative period, they have sometimes been used by scholars to distinguish archaeological horizons. This chapter focuses on three of those horizons, one during the Early Formative (Early Olmec), and two during the Middle Formative (Late Olmec, and Modified Olmec;

83

after Lowe 1977: 212–228)[1] and examines whether our perception of those horizons remains feasible in the light of current data. Although archaeological understanding is always constrained by the vagaries of the archaeological record, it is also captive to the manner by which that record has been interpreted. Thus, because an Olmec-centric view has pervaded Formative period prehistory for nearly half a century, it is neither coincidental nor surprising that those Formative period horizons now bear Olmec-related names, nor that they are often presumed to be significantly associated with the Gulf Coast Olmec in some manner. It can also be argued that because of their inferred association with the Olmec, the horizons have become "interpretive models" to some extent. In this chapter I review the horizons and the attributes that define them, but from a different point of view, by suggesting that the social dynamics responsible for the horizons had little to do specifically with the Gulf Coast Olmec.

WHAT IS OLMEC?

A review of Olmec horizons must begin by acknowledging the confusion raised by the fact that the name Olmec carries two meanings. *Olmec* is the term used to denote the archaeological culture of southern Veracruz and Tabasco between ca. 1150–500 B.C., and is also used to name a widely spread "art style" during that same time period. A prevalent assumption is that the archaeological culture gave birth to the art style. However, that presumption is seriously questioned in the following pages, and thus it is worthwhile to begin by considering the significant difference between Olmec as an archaeological culture and Olmec as an art style.

An archaeological culture is one distinguished by a characteristic set or assemblage of artifacts that recur repeatedly within a specific geographic area (after Childe 1950: 2). The archaeological culture called Olmec is known primarily from excavations at just two centers, La Venta, Tabasco (Drucker 1952; Drucker, Heizer, and Squier 1959; Lowe 1989), and San Lorenzo Tenochtitlan, Veracruz (Stirling 1955; Coe and Diehl 1980). The region of the Gulf Coast occupied by the archaeological Olmec is not in question and is relatively consistently defined on maps (Fig. 1). It extends from the Papaloapan River in the west to somewhat beyond the Tonala River and the site of La Venta in the east and fundamentally is defined by sites yielding stone monumental art similar to that found at San Lorenzo and

---

[1] The "Early Olmec horizon" is not Mesoamerica's earliest ceramic horizon. Lowe (1977: 207–212) identified an Ocos horizon in the Isthmian region, and recent research by John Clark, Michael Blake, and others has revised the coastal Formative period sequence for Chiapas (Clark, Blake, Guzzy, Cuevas, and Salcedo n.d.: 79–90) and separated an early Ocos component (ca. 1450–1300 B.C.), which they call the Locona phase. Clark (1991: 12) has defined a Locona horizon in southern Mesoamerica (n.d.: fig. 8), and he suggests a complementary Red-on-Buff horizon for central Mexico.

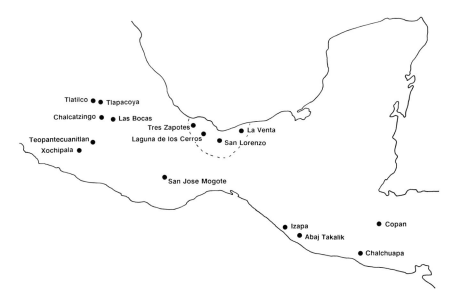

Fig. 1. Map of Mesoamerica showing major sites mentioned in the text. The dashed line delimits the Olmec region

La Venta. The "origins" of Olmec culture have been speculative at times. Because the early La Venta explorations were confined to a mound-plaza complex (Complex A) now known to be relatively late in Olmec prehistory, no antecedents to the artifacts recovered there were readily apparent, and thus a notion began that perhaps Olmec culture was intrusive and that it had not originated on the Gulf Coast (see below also). However, the stratigraphic data later retrieved by Michael Coe and Richard Diehl from San Lorenzo clearly demonstrate that Olmec culture is indeed indigenous to the Gulf Coast (Coe 1970; Coe and Diehl 1980; Grove 1981a: 376–378).

Surprisingly, it is actually quite difficult to define a viable set of *distinctive* archaeological traits for Gulf Coast Olmec culture, because so many of the artifact categories recovered at San Lorenzo and La Venta also co-occur at sites elsewhere in Mesoamerica. A strict archaeological definition of Gulf Coast Olmec using those co-occurring *non-distinctive* attributes would therefore be imprudent. Nevertheless, it is usually those very attributes that are given the greatest attention in published excavation reports, while traits possibly idiosyncratic to Gulf Coast sites remain to be identified. Therefore, although certain utilitarian pottery types and vessel forms may in time serve as viable markers, today what best sets the Gulf Coast Olmec apart from their immediate neighbors and contemporaneous societies elsewhere in Mesoamerica—and thereby makes them unique—is the production of stone monuments and the use of stone for various ritual or functional purposes (e.g., stone drain systems, tombs, massive offerings) at major Olmec centers.

The conception of Olmec as an art style contrasts markedly with the definition of the archaeological Olmec, for the style is based entirely upon a series of motifs and objects and therefore is not restricted to one area or a particular society. Furthermore, although the "Olmec style" has been loosely defined (e.g., Coe 1965b; Covarrubias 1943, 1946; Joralemon 1971), the identification of motifs and objects as "stylistically Olmec" is often intuitive and subjective rather than definable and objective. Olmec has thus become an easy *descriptive* term to denote a particular attribute, a set of attributes, or a "feeling" or *geist* in Formative period art or artifacts, no matter where they are found. The use of the term *Olmec* is frequently quite casual, and the user often may not intend to imply any association between the artifact or attribute described as Olmec and the archaeological culture called Olmec. Some scholars believe the art style is fundamentally associated with the Gulf Coast archaeological culture, and others do not (see below), but both use the term *Olmec,* although with very different connotations. Thus, misunderstandings abound: which meaning is to be inferred or understood when the word *Olmec* is used—archaeological culture or art style? The double usage, in fact, continues to lead many scholars and students to the assumption that the "Olmec art style" originated with the archaeological Olmec on the Gulf Coast, and that "Olmec style" artifacts and motifs in other regions of Mesoamerica are indeed somehow significantly related to the Olmec archaeological culture through diffusion, borrowing, or even some form of direct contacts or control. In the light of the confusion between art style and archaeological culture, what are we to understand of the Formative period's "Olmec" horizons?

HISTORY OF FORMATIVE PERIOD HORIZONS

The explicit notion that one or more (Olmec) horizons could be defined within the Formative period archaeological record developed slowly but was predicated on viewing Olmec as an art style, because the concept of a horizon was itself based upon "the wide distribution of a recognizable art style" (Willey and Phillips 1958: 32). Although in the first major La Venta report Philip Drucker wrote of a "La Venta horizon" (1952: 204,232), his use of the term was restricted to the Gulf Coast and had the intended meaning of what today would be termed a regional phase. In their influential book *Method and Theory in American Archaeology,* Gordon Willey and Philip Phillips spoke of an "Olmec style" but not of a horizon (1958: 55). Slightly later, Willey (1962) wrote of Olmec as an "early great style," but again without horizon connotations. In fact, in his definitive article on the "Olmec style" in *The Handbook of Middle American Indians,* Michael Coe

(1965b: 771–772) argued that Olmec was not a horizon style, for he felt it did not meet the criteria of a horizon as defined earlier by Willey (1948: 8). Nevertheless, Coe believed the style originated with the archaeological Olmec and had been diffused to societies outside of the Gulf Coast by the Olmec (1965b: 771–772). At the time Coe wrote that important article, Formative period chronology was not well understood, and Olmec culture and Olmec art were thought to date to the "Middle Preclassic" time period. All "Olmec" objects, portable (e.g., greenstone or ceramic) or monumental, were viewed as essentially contemporaneous.

Following Coe's major archaeological research project at the Gulf Coast Olmec center of San Lorenzo Tenochtitlan, it was recognized that both the style and the archaeological culture spanned portions of the Early and Middle Formative periods (e.g., Coe 1968, 1970). Traits comprising the widespread style were not all contemporaneous but exhibited change over time. Armed with those new data, Coe began to utilize the concept of Olmec horizons, identifying an Early Formative "San Lorenzo horizon," 1150–900 B.C., and a subsequent Middle Formative "La Venta horizon," ca. 900–400 B.C. (Coe 1977: 184–185). The San Lorenzo horizon was characterized by "boldly carved vessels" and white-slipped baby-faced figurines (traits of his San Lorenzo phase), and the La Venta horizon by white wares decorated with the "double-line-break" rim motif, jade, and bas-relief carvings with narrative scenes (Coe 1977: 184–185).

The idea of "Olmec horizons" began to find wider use in the literature. John Henderson (1979) employed the concept of an "Olmec Blackware horizon" (Early Formative) and an "Olmec Whiteware horizon" (Middle Formative) in writing on the archaeology of Guerrero. Even earlier, however, "Early Olmec" and "Late Olmec" sub-horizons were identified in the Isthmian region by Dee Green and Gareth Lowe (1967: 65). The "Early Olmec" horizon on the Pacific Coast of Chiapas was correlated with Coe's "San Lorenzo horizon," and the "Later Olmec" horizon with his "La Venta horizon" (Lowe 1971: 222–224; 1977: 219). Lowe also defined an additional "Modified Olmec" horizon, which matched the "drastically modified ceramic complex" of Phases 3 and 4 of La Venta's Complex A (1977: 212–226). He has continued to use those horizon categories in more recent publications, as have some of his colleagues in Chiapas (e.g., Agrinier 1984; Lee 1989; Lowe 1981, 1989). Although the "Later" and "Modified Olmec" horizons presented some problems of correlation with the broadly but vaguely defined "La Venta Horizon," Lowe (1989) has recently written more explicit definitions of the Gulf Coast components of those horizons and has slightly revised their names: Initial Olmec (Early Olmec or San Lorenzo horizon), Intermediate Olmec (Later Olmec: the initial portion of the La Venta horizon), and Terminal Olmec (Modified Olmec: the latter portion of the La Venta horizon).

A different system of periods and horizons for Mesoamerica was proposed by Barbara Price (1976) at approximately the same time. Her suggested framework was a modification of the period concept that was created by Andean archaeologists for the purpose of providing non-cultural names for horizons and periods. In Price's system, the 1300–800 B.C. time period became the Early Horizon (with subdivisions 1–4) and the 800–200 B.C. time span became the First Intermediate (with 11 subdivisions). For various reasons, this horizon system has not been widely adopted, and its supporters have primarily been archaeologists working in the Basin of Mexico (e.g., Sanders, Parsons, and Santley 1979; Tolstoy 1978, 1989b).

Both explicitly and implicitly, the horizon concept's use seems to be twofold for the Formative period. First, following the Willey and Phillips (1958: 33) definition of horizons, that "the archaeological units linked by a horizon are . . . assumed to be *approximately* contemporaneous," horizon attributes are heavily used for cross-dating and correlating sequences across a wide area of western Mesoamerica. Secondly, because the horizons and their attributes are given Olmec-associated names, the discovery of such attributes at any site frequently leads otherwise cautious scholars to assume incautiously that the horizon attributes are indicative of "Olmec" influence or "interaction." Although most Formative period researchers do not write explicitly of Olmec horizons in their publications, I believe that a great many do implicitly accept the "Olmecness" of the horizons.

Archaeological knowledge of the Mesoamerican Formative period has, of course, significantly improved over the past several decades, and as more data became available another interpretive position emerged. This perspective is that Formative period regional developments must be studied independently, without prejudged notions of external factors (i.e., Olmec influences) affecting cultural developments. The artifacts normally labeled as "Olmec style" should be studied for how they functioned within the local societies. Most archaeologists working from that standpoint view the co-occurring "Olmec" artifacts and motifs as a "pan-Mesoamerican" and "multi-ethnic" phenomenon and attempt to divorce those objects from connotations of Gulf Coast ties or origins (e.g., Demarest 1989; Flannery 1968; Grove 1989b; Marcus 1989; Niederberger 1987: 745–750). That perspective underlies this chapter. The question to be addressed is, if those horizons are not the result of an Olmec-related phenomenon, what alternative sociocultural actions can be posited to explain them?

THE EARLY OLMEC HORIZON

The earliest and perhaps the most misinterpreted "Olmec horizon" occurs during the Early Formative period, or ca. 1150–900 B.C. Called "Early Olmec" by Lowe, the "San Lorenzo horizon" by Coe, and the "Olmec Blackware horizon" by Henderson, its principal diagnostics are pottery

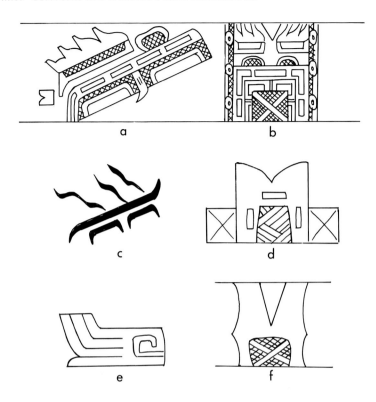

Fig. 2. Common Early Formative period vessel motifs. (a, c) earth caiman, profile and abstraction ("fire serpent"); (b, d, f) earth caiman frontal view and abstractions ("were-jaguar"); (e) wing version of "paw-wing" motif; a–b is a design incised on a vessel from Tlapacoya

vessels (frequently black wares) decorated with incised iconographic motifs, and clay figurines of humans with bald, pear-shaped heads (so called "baby-face" figures). The incised motifs comprise a relatively limited set of designs, including the "were-jaguar," "fire-serpent," and "paw-wing" symbols (Fig. 2). Such motifs are commonly called "Olmec motifs" (e.g., Coe 1965a, 1965b; Joralemon 1971). The motifs and figurines mark a horizon that is distributed across much of central Mexico and extends southward to the Gulf Coast and the Pacific Coast of Chiapas and Guatemala. A few pottery vessels decorated with the "standard" motifs have also been found in Honduras (Healey 1974; Schele and Miller 1986: 119).

This motif and figurine complex is greatly misunderstood. If indeed I am correct, then the causes underlying the horizon are likewise misunderstood. Contrary to popular belief, the motif complex is not the same everywhere it appears but actually manifests distinctive regional variations in both iconographic content and execution (Grove 1989b). For instance, pottery vessels found at central Mexican sites include motifs that never appear on ceramics in Oaxaca, Chiapas, or the Gulf Coast, and vice-versa. Motifs that do co-occur frequently exhibit regional variation in their execution. Significantly, the vessel forms upon which the motifs were placed are also often regionally distinctive. Motifs that are incised on flat-bottom flaring-wall bowls in one region may occur in another region on jars with cylindrical necks, and in a third area on cylindrical bowls. In fact, some notable form and motif differences even occur between site assemblages within the same region, as Paul Tolstoy and co-workers (Tolstoy, Boksenbaum, Vaughn, and Smith 1977: tab. 5) have shown in comparing pottery motifs found at Tlatilco and Tlapacoya in the Basin of Mexico.

Some of the most famous "Olmec" pottery in museums and private collections comes from central Mexican sites such as Tlatilco (Covarrubias 1943, 1950; M. Porter 1953; Piña Chan 1958), Las Bocas, near Izucar de Matamoros, Puebla (Coe 1965a), and Xochipala, in central Guerrero (Gay 1972b). Yet, there is every reason to believe that its creators were ethnically and linguistically distinct from the peoples inhabiting the Gulf Coast Olmec sites and had little if any contact with the latter. Thus, some of those highland societies created comparatively more elaborate and aesthetically sophisticated pottery than any yet known from Gulf Coast Olmec sites, and therefore in stylistic terms those highland vessels are subjectively more "Olmec" than actual Gulf Coast Olmec ceramics. It is that very same pottery which defines the "Early Olmec horizon." Consequently, the horizon designated "Early Olmec" is only "Olmec" in the stylistic sense meant by Covarrubias (1946) and Willey (1962), and not in an ethnic, cultural sense. However, nearly everyone infers an ethnic, Gulf Coast association with the pottery and motifs and ascribes their presence to Gulf Coast influences.

The important regional differences that occur in the vessel forms (and colors) upon which the motifs are executed and in the actual motifs depicted, suggest that the widespread motif and figurine complex reflects a shared belief system that was manipulated, elaborated upon, and contributed to by many Formative period societies over its history, including the Olmec (Grove 1989b). The style and its motifs (and the ideas they symbolized) were apparently of multiple origins, rather than the creation of a single society or region. In that light, it is significant to note that during the past fifty years of Olmec research, scholars have repeatedly observed that some of the attributes of the "Olmec style" seem to appear earlier outside of the Gulf Coast, in regions such as Guerrero or Morelos (Covarrubias 1957: 76, 110; Gay 1972b; Paradis 1978, 1981: 204; Piña Chan 1955a: 26–27, 1955b: 106–107). Although such observations were often followed by hypotheses that assumed the attributes were Olmec and suggested that the ultimate origin of *all* of Gulf Coast Olmec culture also lay in those other regions, the assertions serve to draw attention to the probable contribution and input of many Early Formative societies into the symbol set. The totality of the Early Formative symbol set called "Olmec style" may be no more Gulf Coast Olmec than it is Oaxacan, Central Mexican, or any other single region. Unfortunately, unlike the Chavin case discussed by Burger for Peru (this volume), we lack any precise region-by-region dating of the appearance of the symbol set or its individual motifs in Mesoamerica. Instead, the "horizon" has become a self-dating and self-validating system.

The underlying roots of some of the symbols discussed above may, in fact, lie deep in antiquity. Certain concepts, such as the earth caiman (represented in the so-called fire-serpent and were-jaguar motifs[2]; Fig. 2a–d,f), are shared not only across Mesoamerica but are fundamental to the early art of South America as well (e.g., Lathrap 1974; Stocker, Meltzoff, and Armsey 1980; Burger, this volume). Donald Lathrap (1974) has effectively argued that those shared symbols reflect the presence of a more ancient belief system common to early agricultural societies across nuclear America. From that viewpoint, it is possible that when those symbols begin to appear in the Formative period archaeological record across Mesoamerica that they do not represent the creation of a new ideology or the borrowing or intrusion of a new religion, but perhaps signify instead (a) the placement on *nonperishable* media of symbols reflecting long-held beliefs, and (b) the rapid adoption by many societies of certain visual or material symbols to express concepts they already held in common. In one sense the horizon can be said to reflect the moment when a widely shared belief system was made visually manifest.

Whatever the roots of the symbol set, an important question must be asked: what social reasons underlay the adoption and utilization of the symbol set by diverse societies over a wide area of Mesoamerica? In other words, what did the motifs communicate that made them acceptable/desirable to the developing agricultural societies of Central Mexico, Oaxaca, Chiapas, and the Soconusco Coast, the Gulf Coast, and even tropical lowland areas of Honduras? Nanette Pyne (1976), and Kent Flannery and Joyce Marcus (1976b: 380–382) were among the first scholars to address the motif problem by asking that question. Their data from the Early Formative settlement of San José Mogote, Oaxaca, suggest that at least two major motifs have distinctive distributions within that ancient village. The east

---

[2] Although named separately as the "fire-serpent" and "were-jaguar" motifs, a vessel from Tlapacoya (Fig. 2a–b; Joralemon 1971: fig. 120; 1976: fig. 6c; Stocker, Meltzoff, and Armsey 1980: fig. 4b) demonstrates that those are the profile and frontal views, respectively, of the same supernatural creature. Each view seems to have carried a different symbolic meaning (e.g., Marcus 1989: 169–173). Several scholars have established that the supernatural being depicted is neither a serpent nor a jaguar, but is a saurian with caiman characteristics (e.g., Joralemon 1976; Stocker, Meltzoff and Armsey 1980).

and west quadrants of the village seem to have significantly greater amounts of black or grey pottery decorated with the stylized caiman profile (fire-serpent) motif, while in the settlement's north and south quadrants there are more white or yellow potsherds bearing the caiman frontal (were-jaguar) motif. Flannery and Marcus go on to indicate that smaller villages and hamlets in the valley used either one motif or the other, but not both. Their interpretation is that the supernaturals represented by the motifs functioned in the valley as patrons or lineage ancestors in the local society and have nothing to do with external influences. Their social interpretation represented a radical and refreshing departure from the standard diffusionist "Olmec as donor" explanations. It suggests that the symbol set served Early Formative peoples in Oaxaca as a means of expressing and classifying internal social divisions. Available data from other regions of Mesoamerica seem to indicate that the motifs there served a similar function (e.g., Tolstoy et al. 1977: tab. 5).

Although there has never been a rigorous non-subjective test to ascertain whether the pottery motif set and bald-headed figurines indeed have Gulf Coast origins, many scholars still continue to credit the Olmec for them (e.g., Coe 1989; Tolstoy 1989b: 294–301). There are at least two underlying reasons why that is so. The first is the continuing usage of the term *Olmec* for both the archaeological culture and the art style, and inferences incorrectly drawn from that fact, as noted above. The second is related to what is considered to be "Olmec precocity" in creating Mesoamerica's first stone monuments. The size and magnificence of those creations have served to elevate the Olmec above their contemporaries *in the minds of scholars*.

For decades now the creation of monumental art has all too frequently been mistaken as a sign of Olmec "cultural superiority," and that perception underlies the belief that the "superior" Olmec must have been responsible for *all* early Mesoamerican innovations—including the Early Formative symbol set. A corollary to this presumption is the notion that if the Olmec originated it, then they also must have been responsible for its diffusion to other societies. It is that thinking which forms the basis of the idea that the Olmec were Mesoamerica's "mother culture." Over the years, most scholars have accepted those assumptions and have not raised some fundamental questions: is the presence or absence of monumental art a reflection of "superiority" and "inferiority," or are there other social explanations for this phenomenon that should be explored? Why did Gulf Coast Olmec society carve monuments while other societies did not? What did the Gulf Coast monuments display and communicate? If societies were borrowing Gulf Coast ideas such as pottery motifs, why were they not also borrowing the concept of monumental art?

The dominant theme in Olmec monumental art was rulership, and carvings such as the magnificent colossal heads portray specific identified rulers

(Coe 1977: 186; Grove 1981b: 65–67). The rulership theme in monumental art continued over another 2,000 years of Mesoamerican prehistory and essentially distinguishes western Mesoamerica (where it is virtually lacking) from southern/eastern (Maya) Mesoamerica (where it was very important). With few exceptions,[3] the importance or non-importance of identified rulership within the political ideology generally accounts for the presence or near absence of stone monumental art at major Mesoamerican centers until the Postclassic period. During the Classic period, monumental art carrying a rulership theme was prevalent throughout the Maya realm but was unimportant at the great central Mexican centers such as Teotihuacan, Cholula, and Monte Alban. Interestingly, the same scholars who accept an Olmec "superiority" because of monumental art at Olmec centers do not judge Maya centers such as Tikal to have been somehow superior to central Mexican cities like Teotihuacan, because they realize that the difference is plainly the reflection of two extremely different Classic period ideological systems. However, exactly the same rationale should be applied to the Formative period. In the Gulf Coast Olmec sociopolitical and ideological system, as with the Maya a millennium later, rulership was personalized and reified through monumental art, while the ideological structure of societies in western Mesoamerica had different foci—foci in which monumental portraits of rulers were unimportant because rulership was structured quite differently (Grove and Gillespie n.d.). That regional dichotomy continued essentially unchanged through the Classic period.

What are we to make, therefore, of the so-called Early Olmec horizon? The Early Formative period appears to have been a time when societies across much of Mesoamerica reached a level of population and social development such that the differentiation of social groups via readily accessible material symbols became important (e.g., Flannery and Marcus 1976b; Marcus 1989: 154–155). In basic terms, the horizon seems to reflect that social need, although clearly there are many nuances begging for future explanation. This viewpoint also both accepts and expects precocious, independent developments by all societies, and not merely the Olmec. For example, Early Formative public architecture at sites such as San José Mogote, Oaxaca (Flannery and Marcus 1976a), Chalcatzingo, Morelos (Prindiville and Grove 1987), and Teopantecuanitlan, Guerrero (Martínez Donjuán 1982, 1985, 1986), may well be independent of any Gulf Coast developments and must first be studied in terms of the local and regional social contexts in which such architecture appears, rather than by an a priori explanation immediately linking such constructions to some form of external influences or stimuli.

---

[3] A major exception is found in Oaxaca, where a conquest and militarism theme dominates the publicly displayed stone monuments (Marcus 1976).

THE EARLY TO INTERMEDIATE OLMEC HORIZON TRANSITION

About 900 B.C. a major change in the non-utilitarian artifact assemblages took place across much of Mesoamerica. It marks the end of the Early Formative period and Early Olmec horizon and the beginning of the Middle Formative period and Intermediate Olmec horizon. At Gulf Coast Olmec sites that transition has sometimes been interpreted as relatively abrupt, indeed, the result of a violent revolutionary action hypothesized to have taken place in that region about 900 B.C. (e.g., Coe 1968: 63; Coe and Diehl 1980: 188). The "evidence" for such a revolution appears to be the marked change in archaeological assemblages between the Early and Middle Formative periods, the occurrence of a great number of undated mutilated Olmec monuments, and the fact that some monument mutilation is known to have taken place about 900 B.C. (Coe 1967, 1968: 47–54; Coe and Diehl 1980: 298). Within that scenario, the "Intermediate Olmec" horizon of the Middle Formative period witnessed a "post-revolution" Olmec resurgence in which a new wave of Olmec influences swept across Mesoamerica; those "new influences" included greenstone objects and ceramics incised with the double-line-break motif. That hypothesis essentially implies that a revolution on the Gulf Coast resulted in significant changes there and that renewed Gulf Coast influences across Mesoamerica were the foundation for a new and materially different Olmec horizon. But, the evidence for those two assumptions needs to be examined. Did a major revolution really separate the "Early Olmec" horizon from the "Intermediate Olmec" horizon, and if so, was that Gulf Coast revolution also indirectly responsible for the changes elsewhere in Mesoamerica after 900 B.C.?

As I argued a decade ago (Grove 1981b), a revolution need not be hypothesized to explain monument mutilation, nor is a revolution about 900 B.C. supported by the archaeological data. Rather than representing a single revolutionary event, monument mutilation appears to have been an ongoing phenomenon for centuries. For example, the earliest evidence of any carved Olmec monument is actually a monument fragment from a "pre-Olmec" Chicharras phase (1250–1150 B.C.) deposit at San Lorenzo (Coe 1970: 26; Coe and Diehl 1980: 294, fig. 259a). That "pre-Olmec" fragment may very well represent the first evidence of monument destruction. Mutilation was carried out on Early Formative period monuments at San Lorenzo and also on Middle Formative period monuments at La Venta. Even some Late Formative (post-Olmec) monuments at the site of Tres Zapotes are mutilated (see Stirling 1943b: 4–26; Porter n.d.), as are some Late Formative carvings at Izapa on the Pacific Coast (see Norman 1976). Classic Maya monuments also occasionally suffered mutilation (Schele and Miller 1986: 43–44). The evidence indicates that monumental carvings were destroyed across the course of Olmec history and long afterwards as well.

Mutilation can alternatively be explained as due to peaceful social acts that would have had little, if any, impact beyond the Olmec center at which they took place. As already mentioned, most Olmec monuments appear to be portrait representations of specific rulers, and the vast majority have been mutilated by decapitation or a few other standard patterned ways (see Grove 1981b). A decapitated monument head found interred in a Middle Formative period elite crypt grave at the non-Gulf Coast site of Chalcatzingo (discussed below; Grove 1981b: 58, fig. 7; Merry de Morales 1987: 103, fig. 8.8) provided a valuable insight into the reason for mutilation, that is, that it was a "termination ritual" by which a ruler's monuments were "neutralized" at death (Grove 1981b: 63–65). Just as there were many rulers across the Olmec region during its nearly 700 years of history, so too were there many termination rituals to neutralize monuments at their death.[4]

THE INTERMEDIATE OLMEC HORIZON

Although there is no evidence for any revolutionary act either causing or separating the pre-900 B.C. and post-900 B.C. horizons, significant changes did occur in the Formative period artifact assemblages after 900 B.C. Those changes are not merely a Gulf Coast phenomenon but are virtually a pan-Mesoamerican transformation. Michael Coe's apt description of the transition at the Olmec site of San Lorenzo thus applies to other regions equally as well:

> Gone are the large, white-slipped, baby-faced figures. The boldly carved vessels of the San Lorenzo horizon are replaced by hard, white pottery incised with the double-line-break and similar abstract motifs . . . [and] . . . Jade appears for the first time. (Coe 1977: 184)

The double-line-break motifs on pottery and the appearance of jade (greenstone) artifacts are used to define the "Intermediate Olmec" horizon (also known as "Later Olmec horizon," Lowe 1971: 222–224, 1977: 219; "La Venta horizon," Coe 1977: 184; or "Olmec Whiteware" horizon, Henderson 1979). However, it is a horizon in only the loosest sense, for it spans nearly 400 years and is based upon a few limited and generalized attributes—one stylistic (the double-line-break motif, usually executed on white vessels) and the other a medium (greenstone) worked into a variety of objects. Both the pottery motif and greenstone use underwent changes during that span of time.

Although the details of the Early to Middle Formative transition are

---

[4] A recent observation by James Porter (1989) suggests that some monuments were even recarved into other forms. He noted that at least two of the Olmec colossal heads from San Lorenzo had been recarved from stone table-top altars and suggests that altar "mutilation" (the removal of the corners) may merely represent the first step in that recarving process.

unclear in the Gulf Coast archaeological record (e.g., Lowe 1989: 55) and may appear abrupt there, the Basin of Mexico data of Christine Niederberger (1976, 1987) and Paul Tolstoy (1978, 1979: fig. 1) demonstrate that there the changes were not sudden but gradual. (They merely look particularly abrupt and dramatic in time charts created by archaeologists). During the transformation, the complex of design motifs ("boldly carved vessels") defining the Early Formative period horizon faded into disuse and were slowly "replaced" across western Mesoamerica by white-slipped shallow bowls decorated with double-line-break motifs (and variations) on their rims (e.g., Coe 1961: 61; Niederberger 1987: fig. 474–476; Plog 1976). Both the hollow and solid clay figurines of bald-headed humans ceased to be made and new figurine types appeared, although none of those latter actually seems to have had pan-regional importance. Unfortunately, some of those Middle Formative clay figurines are modeled with facial features that include broad cheeks and large lips. They are therefore sometimes misnamed "baby-face," thus implying they are morphologically (and symbolically) similar to Early Formative bald-headed figurines. This assumption is unproven and probably also unwarranted.

Perhaps the more significant change is the increasing presence of greenstone artifacts in Middle Formative period archaeological assemblages. Although a few late Early Formative greenstone objects have been found at San Lorenzo (Coe 1970: 28; Coe and Diehl 1980: 241–242), with burials at San José Mogote (Flannery, Marcus, and Kowalewski 1981: 73–74; Marcus 1989: 184), Tlatilco (e.g., Tolstoy 1989a: 109–111), and Copan, Honduras (Fash n.d.; Schele and Miller 1986: 80, pl. 17), greenstone use did not become significant until the Middle Formative period. Middle Formative greenstone objects are varied and include jewelry (beads, pendants, pectorals, earspools), celts (either plain or engraved with iconographic motifs), stiletto-like "perforators," and anthropomorphic figures with bald, pear-shaped heads. Greenstone artifacts have perhaps a wider general distribution across Mesoamerica than did the decorated pottery and clay bald-headed anthropomorphic figurines marking the early Olmec horizon, but they occur regionally in much fewer numbers and lack the social ubiquity of that earlier pottery.

It appears to be a common scholarly assumption that jade and greenstone use is a distinctively "Olmec" trait that was diffused by the Olmec to other Mesoamerican societies. That belief has exactly the same weaknesses as the identification of Early Formative pottery motifs as "Olmec," and should be treated with equally great skepticism. The assumed one-to-one correlation between the Olmec and jade use almost certainly has its foundations in the abundant and dazzling discoveries of jade and other greenstone artifacts recovered during the excavation of Complex A at the Olmec center of La Venta in the 1940s and 1950s (Drucker 1952; Drucker, Heizer, and Squier

1959; Stirling 1941, 1943a; Stirling and Stirling 1942). That research represented the first major Olmec excavations, and the fact that it yielded some of the most magnificent Olmec treasures ever found clearly established in scholars' minds from that day forward the conception of Olmec grandeur. Jade and quality greenstone objects became synonymous with Olmec. Rightly or wrongly, the early La Venta discoveries stereotyped the Olmec achievement and have biased interpretations of the archaeological record.

The wide distribution of greenstone objects and the general similarities in forms and decorative motifs found interregionally on greenstone are explainable with the same general model of a shared symbol set proposed above for the Early Formative period, but for slightly different reasons. In fact, several regional styles can be differentiated within the known corpus of greenstone artifacts, including a "Pacific Coast Chiapas-Guatemala style."[5] Following the view in this chapter that shared symbol sets were operative in Mesoamerica during both the Early and Middle Formative periods (Early and Intermediate Olmec horizons), a great deal can be learned by examining the modifications in the symbol system over time and particularly the social implications of greenstone usage.

With the Middle Formative period there is clear and unambiguous evidence for a rapidly emerging elite within Mesoamerican societies. Just as during the Early Formative period social groups marked their identity with pottery motifs, the Middle Formative period elite chose a variety of visual ways to distinguish themselves and their social rank. One such method involved the acquisition and personal display of exotic paraphernalia. Exotics were valued for their very rarity and were clearly a medium restricted to and controlled by the elite. Greenstone was the Middle Formative period's non-perishable exotic of choice, both on the Gulf Coast and elsewhere, and the rise in greenstone use across Mesoamerica can be attributed to the demand for that commodity by the burgeoning elite, who shared common conceptions as to how their rank should be displayed.

The manner by which elite members of any society acquired those exotics has yet to be fully explored. At any settlement most elite probably had little or nothing to do with the procurement of exotics. It was the regional chiefs who would have obtained the greenstone, iron ore mirrors, and similar materials through long-distance, chiefly exchange networks (e.g., Helms 1979), and lower-ranked elite likely acquired such exotics via their position within chiefly lineages or through their clientele relationships with regional chiefs. But whether greenstone objects took the form of jade beads or anthropomorphic figurines, their wide use in the Middle Formative period, if loosely used to define a "horizon," can primarily be explained as a desire

[5] This is based upon on-going and as yet unpublished research by myself, Kent Reilly (University of Texas), and Perry Draper (University of Illinois). Some of my observations will appear in a forthcoming book on Pre-Columbian jade edited by Frederick W. Lange.

by elite members of numerous societies to display and thus communicate (local) social differentiation. That the chiefs at La Venta carried greenstone acquisition and use to a high level may say a great deal about the power controlled by those late Middle Formative period Olmec rulers but should not be used as a measure by which to evaluate or interpret greenstone use elsewhere or to infer an Olmec origin to the horizon.

An important, but often neglected, difference between the Early and Middle Formative periods is the *disappearance* of the shared symbol system from pottery vessels. The rise in greenstone use by elites does not at first glance seem to be related to that change, yet on closer inspection the two are closely linked. Pottery is a non-exotic medium. It is easily manufactured, abundant, and, at least in terms of both production and "cost," a medium theoretically accessible to most or all members of a society, whether as vessels or figurines. Although the symbolism *in that medium* began declining ca. 900 B.C., and ultimately disappeared, neither the motifs nor the concepts they represented actually disappeared. Instead, the majority reappear executed on greenstone objects, the medium restricted to the elite. There are even greenstone figures of bald-headed babies to replace those in clay. Thus, over the period of a century or so, a transformation occurred in which the system of iconographic expression passed into the control of regional elites. Those elites expanded upon it and manipulated it for their own ends, and as noted above, regional styles developed within the motif set (Grove and Gillespie 1992).

Ceramics, of course, remained the accessible medium to the vast non-elite population across Mesoamerica after ca. 900 B.C. Middle Formative pottery appears plainer when compared to the "boldly carved" motifs of the Early Formative, for interior rims on bowls were often decorated only with the double-line-break motif or its variations, and interior bases were incised with other simple motifs. However, those motifs and their execution on pottery (usually white) exhibit generalized similarities over much of Mesoamerica, which can again be explained within the model of a shared symbol system. And, although I am arguing here that the elite gained control of the iconographic system during the Middle Formative period, the double-line-break motif in its most basic form (Fig. 3) maintains one clear link to the Early Formative motif set.

Both Flannery (cited in Plog 1976: 272) and Lathrap (personal communication; Grove 1987b: 430) observed long ago that the basic double-line-break motif was identical to the caiman ("fire serpent) jaw row motif (with inverted-U bracket teeth) common on Early Formative pottery. That motif also decorates the upper ledge of some Olmec altars (e.g., La Venta Altar 4, Potrero Nuevo Monument 2), and there clearly symbolizes the earth's surface. Thus, although the elite took control and manipulated the symbol system for their own purposes, one basic motif related to the earth (and

Fig. 3. Basic double-line-break
motif decorating the interior rim
of a bowl

presumably to earthly fertility) remained expressed (albeit in a very ab-
stracted manner) on ceramic vessels. In other words, there was an elite/non-
elite division of motifs, with the earth motif remaining with the common-
ers, as it did throughout Mesoamerican prehistory.[6]

MODIFIED (OR TERMINAL) OLMEC HORIZON

The Modified (Terminal) Olmec horizon (Lowe 1977: 222–228; 1989: 56–
64) may be a phenomenon of southern Mesoamerica and therefore of very
limited regional extent. Lowe uses the horizon only to discuss the archaeology of Chiapas, and there he correlates it with phases III and IV of Complex
A at La Venta, or post-600 B.C. (Lowe 1989: tab. 4.1). The primary defining
traits are an undecorated "highly polished red-to-orange-brown ceramic
ware," greenstone, public architecture, and some monumental art (Lowe
1977: 222–223). Two of these horizon traits, greenstone and public architecture, frequently predate the horizon in many areas of Mesoamerica and are
therefore of limited utility.[7] The remaining two, "highly polished red-to-
orange-brown ceramic ware" and monumental art, are lacking at most sites
in western Mesoamerica.

[6] Many later complex linear rim motifs diverge so markedly from the basic double-line-
break that it is probable they no longer carry the same symbolic meaning (see e.g., Cyphers
Guillén 1987: figs. 13.26, 13.27; Plog 1976: figs. 9.2, 9.3).

[7] Public architecture was present at both Chalcatzingo and Teopantecuanitlan during the
Early Formative period (Martínez Donjuán 1982, 1986; Prindiville and Grove 1987), and
greenstone during the Middle Formative (Niederberger 1986: 96; Thomson 1987). There is no
evidence that in public architecture there is anything other than local innovation, particularly in
the case of Teopantecuanitlan's sunken patio, which may date to as early as 1400 B.C. (Martínez
Donjuán 1986).

David C. Grove

Although a broad horizon may not be definable during this time period, monumental art, one of Lowe's Modified Olmec horizon traits, does occur at a few sites in central Mexico and on the Pacific Coast of southern Mesoamerica[8] and is therefore worthy of a brief discussion. Two such sites in central Mexico—Chalcatzingo, Morelos, and Teopantecuanitlan, Guerrero—will serve a focus for the discussion.

The presence of monumental art at Chalcatzingo has been known for more than fifty years (Guzmán 1934); Teopantecuanitlan, on the other hand, is a recent discovery (Martínez Donjuán 1982, 1985, 1986). Like other non-Gulf Coast sites with monumental art, Chalcatzingo and Teopantecuanitlan are each unique within their region. To date, thirty carvings have been discovered at Chalcatzingo (Grove and Angulo 1987), and most follow the canons and themes of Gulf Coast style monumental art (including termination by mutilation). From both contextual evidence and their stylistic similarities to La Venta's late monuments, the Chalcatzingo carvings seem to date between ca. 700 and 500 B.C. (Grove 1987b: 426, 430; 1989a: 132–136; Grove and Angulo 1987: 125; Prindiville and Grove 1987: 78; cf., Tolstoy 1989b: 279–281). Teopantecuanitlan, 60 mi. southwest of Chalcatzingo, has only five carvings, four nearly identical bas-relief faces inset into a walled sunken patio, and one carved (but not colossal) stone head (Martínez Donjuán 1985: figs. 7–10, 13). Those carvings also seem to date to the 700–500 B.C. time period (Martínez Donjuán 1986; Grove 1989a: 142–144).

Although the wide distribution of the ceramic motifs and greenstone objects characterizing the previous horizons can be explained by social developments independent of Gulf Coast actions, the appearance of monumental art at a limited number of sites such as Chalcatzingo and Teopantecuanitlan implies a very different phenomenon. Monumental art in Mesoamerica *was* an Olmec innovation and has no antecedents at sites on the Pacific Coast or in central Mexico, where it seems to arrive fully developed and executed according to general Gulf Coast stylistic principles (see below).[9] However, although the monumental art suggests that more pronounced and direct interaction took place between Gulf Coast leaders and chiefs at a few distant sites (e.g., Grove 1987c: 436–441), the exact nature of that new phenomenon requires much further clarification on a site-by-site basis and should be approached with caution.

That need for caution is exemplified by both the Chalcatzingo and

---

[8] Those sites include Chalcatzingo, Morelos (Guzmán 1934; Piña Chan 1955a; Gay 1972a; Grove 1984, 1987a), Juxtlahuaca, Oxtotitlan, San Miguel Amuco, and Teopantecuanitlan, Guerrero (Gay 1967; Grove 1970; Grove and Paradis 1971; Martínez Donjuán 1982, 1986), Padre Piedra, Pijijiapan, Tzutzuculi, and Xoc in Chiapas (Ekholm 1973; Lee 1989; McDonald 1983; Navarette 1969, 1974), Abaj Takalik, Guatemala (Graham 1982, 1989), and Chalchuapa, El Salvador (Boggs 1950; Anderson 1978).

[9] From his research at Abaj Takalik, Guatemala, John Graham suggests instead that the style originates on the Pacific Coast (Graham 1982; 1989).

Fig. 4. One of four nearly identical monoliths from the walled sunken patio at Teopantecuanitlan, Guerrero (drawn after Martínez Donjuán 1985: fig. 7)

Teopantecuanitlan carvings. At Chalcatzingo, for example, although many monuments display Gulf Coast themes and are carved following Gulf Coast canons, they often express those themes slightly differently, and some depictions have no Gulf Coast counterparts.[10] Those differences must be considered with the same care and seriousness given to Gulf Coast similarities, for they may reflect significant independence and innovation. At Teopantecuanitlan, the faces depicted on the four monoliths in the walls of the sunken patio are quite familiar to everyone acquainted with the "Olmec style" (Fig. 4), yet their significance can easily be misconstrued. It is important to realize that as familiar as those faces may be, they do not occur on *any* known Gulf Coast Olmec monuments. They are readily recognizable, however, because they appear engraved on Middle Formative greenstone objects (see e.g., Joralemon 1971, 1976: figs. 12, 13). Thus, rather than being images that might imply some form of significant direct interaction between Teopantecuanitlan and one or more Gulf Coast Olmec centers, they instead suggest a derivation from portable greenstone objects obtained via elite exchange networks.[11] Interestingly, Guadalupe Martínez Donjuán (1986: 70) has

[10] Because some monuments at Chalcatzingo and other Middle Formative sites with Gulf Coast-like carvings share certain stylistic features not found on Gulf Coast Olmec monuments, Veronica Kann and I have applied the term *frontier style* to the art at those sites (Grove and Kann n.d.; Grove 1984: 57–59, 1987c: 436).

[11] Interestingly, one major trait of those four Teopantecuanitlan faces, a headband with 4 "celts," is also found on a La Venta celt (Drucker 1952: fig. 47a), a Dumbarton Oaks figure and a celt, which may both be from Arroyo Pesquero (Benson 1971; Joralemon 1976: fig. 8d), the

David C. Grove

noted that Teopantecuanitlan's large carved stone head has its closest similarities to monuments in Chiapas and Gautemala, and not the Gulf Coast.

The Guatemala-Chiapas connection is not limited to Teopantecuanitlan. Possible interaction with southern Mesoamerica's Pacific Coast has also been suggested for Chalcatzingo (Grove 1987c: 436–437, 1989a: 141–142). Significantly, trait similarities there include ceramics comparable to the "highly polished red-to-orange-brown" pottery described by Lowe for Chiapas and La Venta (Chalcatzingo's Peralta Orange; Cyphers Guillén 1987: 234, 249). From such data it is becoming evident that patterns of long-distance interaction between late Middle Formative period chiefdoms were far more complex than we have previously realized.

CONCLUDING COMMENTS

The horizon concept dates to a period in American archaeology when gathering basic chronological and classificatory information and elucidating general regional developments ("culture history") were the major goals (e.g., Willey and Sabloff 1974: 160). At that time, the cultural processes underlying the traits selected as horizon markers ("archaeology as anthropology") were not well understood at any level (interregional, regional, or local); this is merely an observation and not a retrospective criticism. Today, however, such basic data have been recovered, and scholars should now begin to reexamine and reevaluate the interpretations that have endured over the years.

This chapter has attempted to reevaluate the so-called Olmec horizons of Formative period Mesoamerica. Underlying those horizons is a long-standing belief that they represent Olmec superiority and diffusion. The premise for that belief is largely impressionistic and based upon the exceptional stone monuments created by the Olmec, as well as the magnificent greenstone offerings and other spectacular discoveries at Complex A, La Venta. Elsewhere in Mesoamerica, archaeological objects that "look Olmec," for one reason or another, have been construed as representing some form of Olmec contact or influence, and thus the horizons represented by those same artifacts have been similarly interpreted.

The Early Olmec horizon is primarily identified through a set of iconographic motifs incised on pottery. This shared symbol set functioned to differentiate segments of society in agricultural villages across large areas of Mesoamerica. The origin of this iconographic system remains unresolved

Las Limas figure (Joralemon 1971: fig. 10), and a celt from Los Tuxtlas, Veracruz (Joralemon 1971: fig. 177). As noted above, several regional styles can be defined among greenstone artifacts, and this headband motif may be a Gulf Coast "regional trait." If so, it would suggest the Teopantecuanitlan images may have been copied or adapted from a portable object of actual Gulf Coast derivation.

but is more likely multiple rather than unique. However, if in time the symbol system is shown by valid archaeological data to have Gulf Coast origins, scholars will still need to develop more sophisticated explanations to account for the system's widespread adoption and regional manipulation. Once a motif was adopted, its continued use in a region can only be understood in the context of that particular society, and it would not reflect external "influences" of any sort.

I see nothing "Olmec" in the transformation to the Intermediate Olmec horizon and believe instead that the changing archaeological record indicates on-going and gradual social evolution across much of Mesoamerica. That horizon reveals an increasing importance of the elite groups and their concomitant desire to communicate their elevated social position through greenstone objects. The transformation also reflects the elite's control and utilization on greenstone of the iconographic system previously executed on pottery.

The Modified Olmec horizon may be primarily a phenomenon of southern Mesoamerica. The "highly polished red-to-orange-brown" pottery found at La Venta and in Chiapas suggests increasing Gulf Coast interaction with the Maya region. Unlike pottery motifs and greenstone, the presence of monumental art at Chalcatzingo and a few other sites outside of the Gulf Coast may for the first time indicate significant relationships between those sites and the Olmec. However, that interaction was almost site-specific, was relatively short-lived, and does not represent a horizon.

A serious problem with the horizon concept today is the manner in which horizons are misunderstood and the inferences scholars draw through their misunderstanding. Horizons are modern archaeological constructs based upon a few general traits chosen by scholars. Those traits are unrepresentative archaeological end-products of various complicated social phenomena, and as horizon markers they are divorced from their social contexts. Therefore, by their very structure, horizons can never provide easy answers to complex questions on past societies. The practice of naming some Formative period horizons "Olmec" gives them a social identity they should not carry. They should be renamed, and while Henderson's (1979) "Blackware" and "Whiteware" horizons are not perfect terms, they would be preferable alternatives. Regardless of the name, however, any usefulness once served by the horizon concept will rapidly fade as regional chronologies and typologies are refined and as social processes become better understood.

Acknowledgments I am indebted to Susan Gillespie, Don Rice, and Elizabeth Boone for their valuable criticisms of various drafts of the manuscript.

BIBLIOGRAPHY

AGRINIER, PIERRE
 1984 *The Early Olmec Horizon at Mirador, Chiapas, Mexico.* Papers of the New World Archaeological Foundation 48. Brigham Young University, Provo, Utah.

ANDERSON, DANA
 1978 Monuments. In *The Prehistory of Chalchuapa, El Salvador* (Robert J. Sharer, ed.) 1: 155–180. University of Pennsylvania Press, Philadelphia.

BENSON, ELIZABETH P.
 1971 *An Olmec Figure at Dumbarton Oaks.* Studies in Pre-Columbian Art and Archaeology 8. Dumbarton Oaks, Washington, D.C.

BOGGS, STANLEY
 1950 *"Olmec" Pictographs from the Las Victorias Groups, Chalchuapa Archaeological Zone.* Notes on Middle American Archaeology and Ethnology 99. Carnegie Institution, Washington, D.C.

CASO, ALFONSO
 1942 Definición y extensión del complejo "Olmec." In *Maya y Olmecas, Segunda Reunión de Mesa Redonda:* 43–46. Sociedad Mexicana de Antropología, Mexico.

CHILDE, V. GORDON
 1950 *Prehistoric Migrations in Europe.* Harvard University Press, Cambridge, Mass.

CLARK, JOHN E.
 1991 The Beginning of Mesoamerica: *Apologia* for the Soconusco Early Formative. In *The Formation of Complex Society in Southeastern Mesoamerica* (William R. Fowler, ed.): 13–26. CRC Press, Boca Raton, Fla.

CLARK, JOHN E., MICHAEL BLAKE, PEDRO GUZZY, MARTA CUEVAS, AND TAMARA SALCEDO
 n.d. *Final Report to the Instituto Nacional de Antropología e Historia of the Early Preclassic Pacific Coastal Project.* New World Archaeological Foundation, 1987. Mimeographed.

COE, MICHAEL D.
 1961 *La Victoria, an Early Site on the Pacific Coast of Guatemala.* Papers of the Peabody Museum of Archaeology and Ethnology 53. Harvard University, Cambridge, Mass.
 1965a *The Jaguar's Children: Pre-Classic Central Mexico.* The Museum of Primitive Art, New York.
 1965b The Olmec Style and Its Distribution. In *The Handbook of Middle American Indians* (Robert Wauchope, ed.) 3: 739–775. University of Texas Press, Austin.
 1967 Solving a Monumental Mystery. *Discovery* 3 (1): 21–26. New Haven.
 1968 San Lorenzo and the Olmec civilization. In *Dumbarton Oaks Conference*

on the Olmec (Elizabeth P. Benson, ed.): 41–71. Dumbarton Oaks, Washington, D.C.

1970   The Archaeological Sequence at San Lorenzo Tenochtitlán, Veracruz, Mexico. *Contributions of the University of California Archaeological Research Facility* 8: 21–34. Berkeley.

1977   Olmec and Maya: A Study in Relationships. In *The Origins of Maya Civilization* (Richard E. W. Adams, ed.): 183–195. School of American Research Advanced Seminar Series, University of New Mexico Press, Albuquerque.

1989   The Olmec Heartland: Evolution of Ideology. In *Regional Perspectives on the Olmec* (Robert J. Sharer and David C. Grove, eds.): 68–82. School of American Research Advanced Seminar Series, Cambridge University Press, Cambridge.

COE, MICHAEL D., AND RICHARD A. DIEHL

1980   *In the Land of the Olmec,* 1. The Archaeology of San Lorenzo Tenochtitlán. University of Texas Press, Austin.

COVARRUBIAS, MIGUEL

1943   Tlatilco, Archaic Mexican Art and Culture. *Dyn* 4–5: 40–46. Mexico.

1946   El arte "olmeca" o de La Venta. *Cuadernos Americanos* 28 (4): 153–179. Mexico.

1950   Tlatilco, el arte y la cultura Preclásica del Valle de México. *Cuadernos Americanos* 51 (3): 149–162. Mexico.

1957   *Indian Art of Mexico and Central America.* Alfred A. Knopf, New York.

CYPHERS GUILLÉN, ANN

1987   Ceramics. In *Ancient Chalcatzingo* (David C. Grove, ed.): 200–251. University of Texas Press, Austin.

DEMAREST, ARTHUR A.

1989   The Olmec and the Rise of Civilization in Eastern Mesoamerica. In *Regional Perspectives on the Olmec* (Robert J. Sharer and David C. Grove, eds.): 303–344. School of American Research Advanced Seminar Series, Cambridge University Press, Cambridge.

DRUCKER, PHILIP

1952   *La Venta, Tabasco, a Study of Olmec Ceramics and Art.* Bureau of American Ethnology Bulletin 153. Smithsonian Institution, Washington, D.C.

DRUCKER, PHILIP, ROBERT F. HEIZER, AND ROBERT J. SQUIER

1959   *Excavations at La Venta, Tabasco, 1955.* Bureau of American Ethnology Bulletin 170. Smithsonian Institution, Washington, D.C.

EKHOLM, SUSANNA M.

1973   *The Olmec Rock Carving at Xoc, Chiapas.* Papers of the New World Archaeological Foundation 32. Brigham Young University, Provo, Utah.

FASH, WILLIAM L., JR.

n.d.   A Middle Formative Cemetery from Copan, Honduras. Paper presented at the 81st Annual Meeting of the American Anthropological Association, Washington, D.C., 1982.

FLANNERY, KENT V.
>   1968   The Olmec and the Valley of Oaxaca: A Model for Interregional Inter-
>   action in Formative Times. In *Dumbarton Oaks Conference on the Olmec*
>   (Elizabeth P. Benson, ed.): 79–110. Dumbarton Oaks, Washington,
>   D.C.

FLANNERY, KENT V., AND JOYCE MARCUS
>   1976a Evolution of the Public Building in Formative Oaxaca. In *Cultural
>   Change and Continuity: Essays in Honor of James Bennett Griffin* (Charles
>   E. Cleland, ed.): 205–221. Academic Press, New York.
>   1976b Formative Oaxaca and the Zapotec Cosmos. *American Scientist* 64 (4):
>   374–383.

FLANNERY, KENT V., JOYCE MARCUS, AND STEPHEN A. KOWALEWSKI
>   1981   The Preceramic and Formative of the Valley of Oaxaca. In *The Hand-
>   book of Middle American Indians, Supplement 1, Archaeology* (Jeremy A.
>   Sabloff, ed.): 48–93. University of Texas Press, Austin.

GAY, CARLO T.A.
>   1967   Oldest Paintings of the New World. *Natural History* 76 (4): 28–35.
>   1972a *Chalcacingo.* International Scholarly Book Service. Portland, Ore.
>   1972b *Xochipala: The Beginnings of Olmec Art.* The Art Museum, Princeton
>   University.

GRAHAM, JOHN A.
>   1982   Antecedents of Olmec Sculpture at Abaj Takalik. In *Ancient Mesoamer-
>   ica: Selected Readings* (John A. Graham, ed.): 163–176. Peek Publica-
>   tions, Palo Alto, Calif.
>   1989   Olmec Diffusion: A Sculptural View from Pacific Guatemala. In *Re-
>   gional Perspectives on the Olmec* (Robert J. Sharer and David C. Grove,
>   eds.): 227–246. School of American Research Advanced Seminar Se-
>   ries, Cambridge University Press, Cambridge.

GREEN, DEE F., AND GARETH W. LOWE
>   1967   *Altamira and Padre Piedra, Early Preclassic Sites in Chiapas, Mexico.* Pa-
>   pers of the New World Archaeological Foundation 20. Brigham
>   Young University, Provo, Utah.

GROVE, DAVID C.
>   1970   *The Olmec Paintings of Oxtotitlan Cave, Guerrero, Mexico.* Studies in Pre-
>   Columbian Art and Archaeology 6. Dumbarton Oaks, Washington,
>   D.C.
>   1981a The Formative Period and the Evolution of Complex Culture. In
>   *The Handbook of Middle American Indians, Supplement 1, Archaeology*
>   (Jeremy A. Sabloff, ed.): 373–391. University of Texas Press,
>   Austin.
>   1981b Olmec Monuments: Mutilation as a Clue to Meaning. In *The Olmec and
>   Their Neighbors* (Elizabeth P. Benson, ed.): 49–68. Dumbarton Oaks,
>   Washington, D.C.
>   1984   *Chalcatzingo: Excavations on the Olmec Frontier.* Thames and Hudson,
>   New York.

1987a   *Ancient Chalcatzingo* (David C. Grove, ed.). University of Texas Press, Austin.

1987b   Comments on the Site and Its Organization. In *Ancient Chalcatzingo* (David C. Grove, ed.): 420–433. University of Texas Press, Austin.

1987c   Chalcatzingo in a Broader Perspective. In *Ancient Chalcatzingo* (David C. Grove, ed.): 434–442. University of Texas Press, Austin.

1989a   Chalcatzingo and Its Olmec Connection. In *Regional Perspectives on the Olmec* (Robert J. Sharer and David C. Grove, eds.): 122–147. School of American Research Advanced Seminar Series, Cambridge University Press, Cambridge.

1989b   Olmec, What's in a Name? In *Regional Perspectives on the Olmec* (Robert J. Sharer and David C. Grove, eds.): 8–14. School of American Research Advanced Seminar Series, Cambridge University Press, Cambridge.

GROVE, DAVID C., AND JORGE ANGULO V.

1987   A Catalog and Description of Chalcatzingo's Monuments. In *Ancient Chalcatzingo* (David C. Grove, ed.): 114–131. University of Texas Press, Austin.

GROVE, DAVID C., AND SUSAN D. GILLESPIE

1992   Ideology and Evolution at the Pre-State Level: Formative Period Mesoamerica. In *Ideology and Pre-Columbian Civilizations* (Arthur Demarest and Geoffrey Conrad, eds.). School of American Research Advanced Seminar Series, School of American Research, Santa Fe.

GROVE, DAVID C., AND VERONICA KANN

n.d.   Olmec Monumental Art: Heartland and Frontier. Paper presented at the 79th Annual Meeting of the American Anthropological Association, Washington, D.C., 1980.

GROVE, DAVID C., AND LOUISE I. PARADIS

1971   An Olmec Stela from San Miguel Amuco, Guerrero. *American Antiquity* 36: 95–102.

GUZMÁN, EULALIA

1934   Los relieves de las rocas del Cerro de la Cantera, Jonacatepec, Morelos. *Anales del Museo Nacional de Arqueología, Historia, y Etnografía,* Época 5, 1 (2): 237–251. Mexico.

HEALEY, PAUL F.

1974   The Cayumel Caves: Preclassic Sites in Northeast Honduras. *American Antiquity* 39: 435–447.

HELMS, MARY W.

1979   *Ancient Panama: Chiefs in Search of Power.* University of Texas Press, Austin.

HENDERSON, JOHN S.

1979   *Atopula, Guerrero, and Olmec Horizons in Mesoamerica.* Yale University Publications in Anthropology 77. New Haven.

JORALEMON, PETER DAVID

1971   *A Study of Olmec Iconography.* Studies in Pre-Columbian Art and Archaeology 7. Dumbarton Oaks, Washington, D.C.

David C. Grove

1976   The Olmec Dragon: A Study in Pre-Columbian Iconography. In *Origins of Religious Art and Iconography in Preclassic Mesoamerica* (Henry B. Nicholson, ed.): 27–71. Latin American Studies Series 31. UCLA Latin American Center, Los Angeles.

LATHRAP, DONALD W.
1974   The Moist Tropics, the Arid Lands, and the Appearance of Great Art Styles in the New World. In *Art and Environment in Native America* (Mary Elizabeth King and Idris R. Traylor, Jr., eds.): 115–158. Special Publications 77, The Museum, Texas Tech University, Lubbock.

LEE, THOMAS A., JR.
1989   Chiapas and the Olmec. In *Regional Perspectives on the Olmec* (Robert J. Sharer and David C. Grove, eds.): 198–226. School of American Research Advanced Seminar Series, Cambridge University Press, Cambridge.

LOWE, GARETH W.
1971   The Civilizational Consequences of Varying Degrees of Agricultural Dependency within the Basic Ecosystems of Mesoamerica. *Contributions of the University of California Archaeological Facility* 11: 212–248. Berkeley.
1977   The Mixe-Zoque as Competing Neighbors of the Lowland Maya. In *The Origins of Maya Civilization* (Richard E. W. Adams, ed.): 183–195. School of American Research Advanced Seminar Series, University of New Mexico Press, Albuquerque.
1981   Olmec Horizons Defined in Mound 20, San Isidro, Chiapas. In *The Olmec and Their Neighbors* (Elizabeth P. Benson, ed.): 231–255. Dumbarton Oaks, Washington, D.C.
1989   The Heartland Olmec: Evolution of Material Culture. In *Regional Perspectives on the Olmec* (Robert J. Sharer and David C. Grove, eds.): 33–67. School of American Research Advanced Seminar Series, Cambridge University Press, Cambridge.

McDONALD, ANDREW J.
1983   *Tzutzuculi: A Middle Preclassic Site on the Pacific Coast of Chiapas.* Papers of the New World Archaeological Foundation 47. Brigham Young University, Provo, Utah.

MARCUS, JOYCE
1976   The Iconography of Militarism at Monte Alban and Neighboring Sites in the Valley of Oaxaca. In *Origins of Religious Art and Iconography in Preclassic Mesoamerica* (Henry B. Nicholson, ed.): 123–139. Latin American Studies Series 31. UCLA Latin American Center, Los Angeles.
1989   Zapotec Chiefdoms and the Nature of Formative Religions. In *Regional Perspectives on the Olmec* (Robert J. Sharer and David C. Grove, eds.): 148–197. School of American Research Advanced Seminar Series, Cambridge University Press, Cambridge.

MARTÍNEZ DONJUÁN, GUADALUPE
1982   Teopantecuanitlán, Guerrero: Un sitio olmeca. *Revista Mexicana de*

Estudios Antropológicos 28: 128–133. Sociedad Mexicana de Antropología, Mexico.

1985   El sitio Olmeca de Teopantecuanitlan en Guerrero. *Anales de Antropología:* 215–226. Universidad Nacional Autónoma de México, Mexico.

1986   Teopantecuanitlan. In *Primer coloquio de arqueología y etnohistoria del estado de Guerrero:* 55–80. Instituto Nacional de Antropología e Historia y Gobierno del Estado de Guerrero, Mexico.

MERRY DE MORALES, MARCIA

1987   Chalcatzingo Burials as Indicators of Social Ranking. In *Ancient Chalcatzingo* (David C. Grove, ed.): 95–113. University of Texas Press, Austin.

NAVARRETE, CARLOS

1969   Los relieves olmecas de Pijijiapan, Chiapas. *Anales de Antropología* 6: 183–185. Universidad Nacional Autónoma de México, Mexico.

1974   *The Olmec Rock Carvings at Pijijiapan, Chiapas, Mexico and Other Olmec Pieces from Chiapas and Guatemala.* Papers of the New World Archaeological Foundation 35. Brigham Young University, Provo, Utah.

NIEDERBERGER, CHRISTINE B.

1976   *Zohapilco, cinco milenios de ocupación humana en un sitio lacustre de la cuenca de México.* Colección Científica 30. Instituto Nacional de Antropología e Historia, Mexico City.

1986   Excavación de un área de habitación doméstica en la capital "Olmeca" de Tlacozotitlan: Reporte preliminar. In *Primer coloquio de arqueología y etnohistoria del estado de Guerrero:* 83–103. Instituto Nacional de Antropología e Historia y Gobierno del Estado de Guerrero, Mexico.

1987   *Paléopaysages et archéologie pré-urbaine du bassin de Mexico.* Collection Études Mésoaméricaines 11. Centre d'Études Mexicaines et Centraméricaines, Mexico.

NORMAN, GARTH V.

1976   *Izapa Sculpture.* Paper of the New World Archaeological Foundation 30. Brigham Young University, Provo, Utah.

PARADIS, LOUISE I.

1978   Early Dates for Olmec-Related Artifacts in Guerrero, Mexico. *Journal of Field Archaeology* 5: 110–116.

1981   Guerrero and the Olmec. In *The Olmec and Their Neighbors* (Elizabeth P. Benson, ed.): 195–208. Dumbarton Oaks, Washington, D.C.

PIÑA CHAN, ROMAN

1955a   *Chalcatzingo, Morelos.* Informes 4. Instituto Nacional de Antropología e Historia, Mexico.

1955b   *Las culturas preclásicas de la Cuenca de México.* Fonda de Cultura Económica, Mexico.

1958   *Tlatilco.* Serie Investigaciones 1–2. Instituto Nacional de Antropología e Historia, Mexico.

PLOG, STEPHEN

1976   Measurement of Prehistoric Interaction between Communities. In *The*

Early Mesoamerican Village (Kent V. Flannery, ed.): 255–271. Academic Press, New York.

PORTER, JAMES B.
  1989 Olmec Colossal Heads as Recarved Thrones: "Mutilation," Revolution and Recarving. *Res: Anthropology and Aesthetics* 17–18: 23–29. Cambridge, Mass.
  n.d. *The Monuments and Hieroglyphs of Tres Zapotes, Veracruz, Mexico.* Ph.D. dissertation, Department of Anthropology, University of California, Berkeley, 1989.

PORTER, MURIEL NOÉ
  1953 *Tlatilco and the Pre-Classic Cultures of the New World.* Viking Fund Publications in Anthropology 19. New York.

PRICE, BARBARA
  1976 A Chronological Framework for Cultural Development in Mesoamerica. In *The Valley of Mexico: Studies in Pre-Hispanic Ecology and Society* (Eric R. Wolf, ed.): 13–21. School of American Research Advanced Seminar Series, University of New Mexico Press, Albuquerque.

PRINDIVILLE, MARY, AND DAVID C. GROVE
  1987 The Settlement and Its Architecture. In *Ancient Chalcatzingo* (David C. Grove, ed.): 63–81. University of Texas Press, Austin.

PYNE, NANETTE
  1976 The Fire-Serpent and Were-Jaguar in Formative Oaxaca: A Contingency Table Analysis. In *The Early Mesoamerican Village* (Kent V. Flannery, ed.): 272–282. Academic Press, New York.

SANDERS, WILLIAM T., JEFFREY R. PARSONS, AND ROBERT S. SANTLEY
  1979 *The Basin of Mexico: Ecological Processes in the Evolution of a Civilization.* Academic Press, New York.

SCHELE, LINDA, AND MARY ELLEN MILLER
  1986 *The Blood of Kings: Dynasty and Ritual in Maya Art.* Kimbell Art Museum, Fort Worth.

STIRLING, MATTHEW W.
  1941 Expedition Unearths Buried Masterpieces of Carved Jade. *National Geographic Magazine* 80 (3): 277–302.
  1943a La Venta's Green Stone Tigers. *National Geographic Magazine* 80 (3): 321–332.
  1943b *Stone Monuments of Southern Mexico.* Bureau of American Ethnology Bulletin 138. Smithsonian Institution, Washington, D.C.
  1955 *Stone Monuments of the Rio Chiquito, Veracruz.* Bureau of American Ethnology Bulletin 157: 1–23. Smithsonian Institution, Washington, D.C.
  1968 Early History of the Olmec Problem. In *Dumbarton Oaks Conference on the Olmec* (Elizabeth P. Benson, ed.): 1–8. Dumbarton Oaks, Washington, D.C.

STIRLING, MATTHEW W., AND MARION STIRLING
  1942 Finding Jewels of Jade in a Mexican Swamp. *National Geographic Magazine* 82 (5): 635–661.

STOCKER, TERRY, SARAH MELTZOFF, AND STEVE ARMSEY
1980   Crocodilians and Olmecs: Further Interpretations of Formative Period Iconography. *American Antiquity* 45: 740–758.

THOMSON, CHARLOTTE W.
1987   Chalcatzingo Jade and Fine Stone Objects. In *Ancient Chalcatzingo* (David C. Grove, ed.): 295–304. University of Texas Press, Austin.

TOLSTOY, PAUL
1978   Western Mesoamerica before A.D. 900. In *Chronologies in New World Archaeology* (Robert E. Taylor and Clement W. Meighan, eds.): 241–284. Academic Press, New York.
1979   The Olmec in the Central Highlands: A Non-Quintessential Approach. *American Antiquity* 44: 333–337.
1989a   Coapexco and Tlatilco: Sites With Olmec Materials in the Basin of Mexico. In *Regional Perspectives on the Olmec* (Robert J. Sharer and David C. Grove, eds.): 85–121. School of American Research Advanced Seminar Series, Cambridge University Press, Cambridge.
1989b   Western Mesoamerica and the Olmec. In *Regional Perspectives on the Olmec* (Robert J. Sharer and David C. Grove, eds.): 275–302. School of American Research Advanced Seminar Series, Cambridge University Press, Cambridge.

TOLSTOY, PAUL, MARTIN W. BOKSENBAUM, KATHRYN BLAIR VAUGHAN, AND C. EARLE SMITH, JR.
1977   The Earliest Sedentary Communities of the Basin of Mexico: A Summary of Recent Investigations. *Journal of Field Archaeology* 4: 92–106.

WILLEY, GORDON R.
1948   A Functional Analysis of "Horizon Styles" in Peruvian Archaeology. In *A Reappraisal of Peruvian Archaeology* (W. C. Bennett, ed.): 8–15. Memoirs of the Society for American Archaeology 4. Menasha, Wisc.
1962   The Early Great Styles and the Rise of Pre-Columbian Civilizations. *American Anthropologist* 64: 1–14.

WILLEY, GORDON R., AND PHILIP PHILLIPS
1958   *Method and Theory in American Archaeology.* University of Chicago Press, Chicago.

WILLEY, GORDON R., AND JEREMY A. SABLOFF
1974   *A History of American Archaeology.* W. H. Freeman and Company, San Francisco.

An Image is Worth a Thousand Words: Teotihuacan and the Meanings of Style in Classic Mesoamerica

ESTHER PASZTORY

COLUMBIA UNIVERSITY

HISTORICAL PERSPECTIVE

IF THIS VOLUME had been published at the turn of the century, the horizon discussed in the Classic period would have been that of the Maya, because Teotihuacan as a culture and art style had not yet been formulated. Even now, Teotihuacan exists only in the mind of scholars. Everyone else thinks of it as Aztec.

By the turn of the century the calendrical portion of Maya glyphs were deciphered, and Maya studies were undertaken by scholars who came to be thought of as "Mayanists," separate from other "Mexicanists." A polarity had been created between the intellectual Maya, compared with the Greeks, and the empire-building Aztecs, compared with the Romans. Once defined, Teotihuacan was treated as an earlier version of the Aztecs, and this polarity was projected into Classic times. Even at present, books by the same publisher divide Mesoamerica into "Maya" and "Mexicans."[1]

By mid-century, Mesoamerican history was divided into Preclassic, Classic, and Postclassic periods based on the best known and artistically most impressive body of material, the dated Maya stelae, A.D. 300–900. The period corresponding to the stelae was called "Classic," anything before it was called "Formative" or "Preclassic" and believed to lead up to the florescence of the Classic, and the period following it was viewed as a decline and called Postclassic.

Until 1941, Teotihuacan was believed to be a Toltec site that the Aztec texts referred to as "Tollan." It was believed to date just prior to the Aztecs who came to power about A.D. 1300. To the Aztecs, Teotihuacan was at once the place where the gods created the world, the burial place of the

---

[1] See, for example, the books written by Henri Stierlin (1964, 1968) for several publishers of popular books such as Rizzoli, Grosset and Dunlap, and MacDonald and Co. These books divide Mexico into "Mayan" and "Mexican" or "Maya" and "Aztec," the Aztec being the equivalent of "Mexican."

rulers of a great ancient kingdom, and a contemporary shrine embodying the precepts of civilization to barbarian newcomers (Pasztory 1976: 16). The Nahuatl word *Teotihuacan* means "the place of the gods," and the notion implies an Aztec awareness of the antiquity of the site. At the same time, the Aztecs did not distinguish between Teotihuacan and the Toltecs but appear to have lumped them together in a golden age of antiquity and called several cities by the name of "Tollan."

The Aztec confusion between Teotihuacan and the Toltecs lasted until 1941, when Wigberto Jimenez Moreno showed conclusively that the Toltec "Tollan" was a group of ruins near the modern city of Tula in Hidalgo (Jimenez Moreno 1941). Earlier stratigraphic excavations by Manuel Gamio (1920, 1922) and George Vaillant (1935a, 1935b) demonstrated the chronological position of Teotihuacan after the so-called archaic cultures and before the rise of Tula in A.D. 900. This placed Teotihuacan in the "Classic" period, and Pedro Armillas (1950) summarized this revised history of central Mexico and what was known about Teotihuacan until 1950 in an important article.

In 1946 Alfred Kidder, Jessie Jennings, and Edwin Shook excavated the early Classic Maya site of Kaminaljuyu in the Guatemala highlands and found Teotihuacan-style architecture and burial offerings next to Maya-style artifacts. This was further proof of the Classic date of Teotihuacan and the beginning of the discussion of Teotihuacan influence in southern Mesoamerica. However, in 1946, the paramount question was still the dating of Teotihuacan in the Classic period (Kidder, Jennings, and Shook 1946: 241–260).

As more Teotihuacan-style artifacts were noted throughout Mesoamerica, they were explained by the movements of people, following the model of the sixteenth-century historical accounts in which the migration of people accounts for cultural and historical changes. Kaminaljuyu came to be seen as a "colony" settled by Teotihuacan individuals during the lifetime of the site, or a place of refuge after the collapse of Teotihuacan. This Teotihuacan "diaspora" was related to the distribution of the Nahuatl Pipil language in the sixteenth century by several scholars (Jimenez Moreno 1966; Borhegyi 1965) (Fig. 1).

As recently as Miguel Covarrubias' 1957 *Indian Art of Mexico and Central America,* Teotihuacan was described as a ceremonial center:

> Teotihuacan was not a city in the proper sense of the word, not a dwelling place, but an enormous civic and religious center. It is full of palaces, but there is no trace of houses for the common people. (Covarrubias 1957: 122, note 1)

In 1962, Renè Millon began directing a mapping survey of Teotihuacan that demonstrated that the "palaces" were in fact the "houses of the common

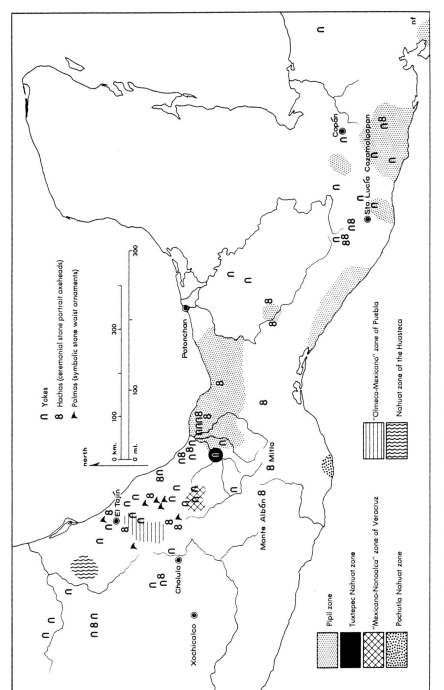

Fig. 1. Map of the Pipil migrations (after Paddock 1966: 66)

Legend (map):

∩ Yokes
8 Hachas (ceremonial stone portrait axeheads)
▲ Palmas (symbolic stone waist ornaments)

Pipil zone
Tuxtepec Nahuat zone
"Mexicano-Nonoalca" zone of Veracruz
Pochutla Nahuat zone

"Olmeca-Mexicano" zone of Puebla
Nahuat zone of the Huasteca

Labeled places: Xochicalco, Cholula, El Tajín, Monte Albán, Mitla, Potonchan, Copán, Sta. Lucía Cozcacualapan

Scale: 0 km. 100 300 / 0 mi. 100 300

north

people" of Teotihuacan (R. Millon 1973, 1981). The project showed that the great pyramids were in the center of an urban city planned on a grid with a population estimated to be 100,000 to 200,000 at its height. In Millon's view, the city was a great religious, craft, and market center. The craft for which there was the most abundant evidence was obsidian manufacture. Nearly 400 workshops were located by Michael Spence (1967).

At the same time, William Sanders was directing a mapping survey of the basin of Mexico as a whole from Preclassic times to the Conquest (Sanders, Parsons, and Santley 1979). This demonstrated that in Classic times outside the huge city of Teotihuacan there were very few small towns and villages in the basin of Mexico, indicating a great deal of centralized control over the population by the state. Earlier, Sanders and Price (1968) argued that Teotihuacan grew into a state as a result of the development of irrigation agriculture. They contrasted the urban, mercantile, centrally organized state of Teotihuacan with the smaller, more scattered Maya cities and defined them developmentally as chiefdoms. The linchpin in this comparison was that of the plan of Teotihuacan with the plan of Tikal, whose population at its height was estimated as no more than 40,000. (The demotion of the Maya states to chiefdoms has, of course, been hotly debated by Mayanists.)

The artifacts outside of Teotihuacan showing Teotihuacan influence were seen as the manifestations of state-sponsored commerce and empire building. Kaminaljuyu (Sanders and Michels 1977) and more recently Matacapan (Santley 1989) have been seen as Teotihuacan colonies occupied by long-distance traders on the Aztec model of the *pochteca*. The *pochteca* were independent traders as well as agents of the Aztec state. They frequently traded goods along their way that were not necessarily brought back to the capital. In imperial expansion they performed the role of spies and agents provocateurs. In this view, the Teotihuacan empire was seen as a smaller version of the Aztec empire. Because the emphasis was on the processual development of cultures and state building, Teotihuacan became the central problem of the Classic period, replacing the previous emphasis on the Maya.

In 1972, at a symposium in Santa Fe, a group of archaeologists with few Mayanists or Mexican scholars among them, decided to abandon the Preclassic, Classic, Postclassic periodization that was customary and switch to the system based on that used by Andeanists, in which periods are divided on the basis of regional isolation or interaction (Wolf 1976). Short periods with widespread ceramic and other material indications that relate to a single point of origin were called "horizons." According to this view, the time between A.D. 200 and 750, roughly but not entirely coeval with the Classic period, would be a Middle Horizon based on the power and influence of the recently defined state of Teotihuacan. Ultimately, even the growth of the Maya centers were attributed to the stimulus of the Teotihuacan state and of its traders (Rathje 1971; Sanders and Price 1968).

Teotihuacan was seen to have had an obsidian monopoly, which was the basis of its empire (Santley 1983).

The earlier period terminology was based on the biological metaphor of growth, florescence, and decline. The new terminology was based on regionalism and the rise and fall of empires within social evolution. The terminology based on growth and quality was Maya centered, the one based on size and quantity of diffused items was Teotihuacan centered. The Maya were given credit for their intellectual and artistic achievements and Teotihuacan for its political and economic successes. Thus, we returned to a new version of the "Greeks" and "Romans."

The "Classic" terminology has been rightly criticized for being value-laden and subjective. The horizon-period terminology appears more neutral but has other difficulties. Because the horizon concept is based on the diffusion of style from one area to another and concepts such as "empires" or "trade" in practical terms, making the distinctions on the basis of material evidence is very difficult. As Cecelia Klein and Emily Umberger show in this volume, our knowledge of the Aztec empire is largely based on sixteenth century documents, and it is by no means clear that we would know its extent purely in terms of excavated artifacts in Aztec style.

A major problem of the horizon terminology is that it is linked to content that may change with new research. For example, recent research suggests that the empire of Teotihuacan may be shrinking. The bottom is falling out of the obsidian market. John Clark (n.d.) has reevaluated the obsidian evidence and suggests that Teotihuacan might have had only 100 workshops and made tools primarily for internal use and not for export. It is evident that changes in the notion of the Teotihuacan state will affect the interpretations of "influences" and of the presence or absence of horizon markers.

THE "INFLUENCE" OF TEOTIHUACAN

The influence of Teotihuacan has been extensively charted by both archaeologists and art historians on the basis of style and iconography in art and architecture (Berlo n.d.; Hellmuth n.d.; Miller 1983; R. Millon 1988; Pasztory 1978). Initially, most of these studies showed that Teotihuacan-style objects are found in almost all areas of Mesoamerica, and the material did indeed look comparable to what was later defined as a horizon style. What was always puzzling, however, is that this Teotihuacan presence was extremely variable. Only a few sites, such as Matacapan, Kaminaljuyu, and Dzibilchaltun have Teotihuacan-style architecture, which has led to the theory that these sites might have been "colonies" or dominated for a period by persons of Teotihuacan origin. What more intensive research has demonstrated is that almost everywhere the items that look Teotihuacan in form are actually locally made imitations of Teotihuacan objects, and the imported pieces are few. Matacapan is the only site with Teotihuacan-style figurines, indicating that the people residing there followed the Teotihuacan household cults, but even these figurines are made locally, in molds much larger than the normal Teotihuacan molds (Santley 1989; Warren Barbour, personal communication, 1986).

The attempt to chart the influence of Teotihuacan is complicated by the fact that one of the most distinctive ceramic markers of the period is Thin Orange, a ware that was not manufactured at Teotihuacan but at Puebla and is presumed to have been traded by Teotihuacan merchants (Rattray 1981). Sigvald Linné purchased this Thin Orange tripod vessel ornamented with Classic Veracruz scroll designs (Fig. 2) while he was excavating Tlamimi-lolpa at Teotihuacan in the 1930s. The cylindrical tripod vessel is generally associated with Teotihuacan as a type, but Evelyn Rattray has shown that it is most likely of Veracruz origin and is found locally in several areas of Mesoamerica not necessarily indicating a specific relationship with Teotihu-acan (Rattray n.d.). In 1934, Linné excavated Maya and Teotihuacan-style cylinder tripods in the same grave (Linné 1934: 59–63) (Fig. 3). If a horizon style is determined by the wide spread of an art style, another good candi-date might be Veracruz. Works with Veracruz-style interlace have been found in great numbers outside Veracruz: at Teotihuacan, significantly in relatively early times, at Kaminaljuyu, at Cholula, and in the Maya area.

Recently, René Millon (1988) summarized the present state of the evi-dence for the external relationships of Teotihuacan. It is significant that his is the first study to attempt to define spatially these contacts on a map. What he suggests is the presence of various "corridors" connecting Teotihuacan with other centers in interaction spheres, without Teotihuacan influence fanning out from the center like an ink drop in water. Should the large-scale obsidian trade model collapse, the picture that emerges is one of trade or some other form of exchange between the elites of various centers, rather than a trading empire throughout the region.

The problem in discussing the "influence" of Teotihuacan is the way in which the question is phrased. The word *influence* suggests something oozing out of Teotihuacan-style objects that affects the arts of other areas rather like the physical process of osmosis. As Michael Baxandall has shown (1985: 58–60), this is looking the wrong way at a situation, confus-ing the agent with the patient. Influence, in fact, works the other way around. What we have to examine is how and why someone draws upon, adapts, reinterprets, or appropriates another style or subject. Tikal stela 31 represents the Maya ruler Stormy Sky flanked by two individuals dressed in Teotihuacan costume. This is not a situation in which a Tikal artist was "influenced" by Teotihuacan, but a situation in which a conscious choice was made to represent an individual carrying a Teotihuacan-style shield with a Teotihuacan deity on it for a specific purpose by a Maya artist and patron (Fig. 4).

Fig. 2. Thin Orange vessel, Teotihuacan. Etnografiska Museum Stockholm

Fig. 3. Maya and Teotihuacan-style vessels. Etnografiska Museum Stockholm

Fig. 4. Stela 31, Tikal, Guatemala (after W. Coe 1970: 49)

THE IDEOLOGICAL ASPECTS OF STYLE

One of the most problematic aspects of archaeology is the interpretation of artistic objects. In archaeology, art styles are interpreted to recover cultural information, an approach I will characterize as "materialistic." Because art styles are sensitive indicators of change, stylistic changes are traditionally used as chronological markers. Because art styles are usually local in nature, they are interpreted to reveal sources of origin. When an object in one style is found in a place where another style reigns, some form of contact between their makers is assumed. Traditionally, cultural history—time, space, interaction—is created out of the data of artistic style. Art works are further used to provide ethnographic content: if the art shows war, the people were warlike. Such materialistic interpretations of art are not wrong so much as incomplete. Art styles do provide such information, as long as we recognize that this was never their primary purpose and that they might provide it indirectly or as through a distorting mirror. The larger questions this chapter addresses is what purposes did art fulfill in these societies, and what were the societies' attitudes towards art and style as it can be reconstructed from the works they left behind.

In this chapter I examine the ideological meanings of style in Classic Mesoamerica. I suggest that style is not a culturally constant concept but a historically defined one and that the Mesoamerican concept of style and the Western one, on which the usual scientific interpretations are based, are different. I discuss style juxtaposition, style as ethnic identifier, style as a symbol of conquest, and style as symbolic polarity, to indicate the ideological aspects of the nature of the meaning of style in Mesoamerica. I hope that this discussion will indicate that one has to be very careful in the direct interpretation of cultural evidence from styles and some of the difficulties inherent in the horizon style concept. Subsequently, I will discuss more specifically the Teotihuacan style and its possible associated meanings.

THE JUXTAPOSITION OF STYLISTIC CONVENTIONS

The notion that stylistic conventions may have culturally determined meanings was first suggested to me in the presence of several works in which the conventions from two areas are juxtaposed in one monument.[2] Tikal stela 31 and the Bazan slab from Monte Alban embody how Classic Mesoamerica understood the interrelationship of culture, history, warfare, writing, art, and style, and my discussion will unravel only a small part of that message.

On Tikal stela 31 (see Fig. 4), the ruler Stormy Sky is flanked by an individual dressed in Teotihuacan costume and carrying a spearthrower (atl-atl) and a shield with a Teotihuacan deity depicted on it. It is generally assumed that the two flanking figures represent the same individual seen from two sides. The identity of this personage is not yet clear. He was first described as an "ambassador" from Teotihuacan, and more recently as the deceased father of Stormy Sky in Teotihuacan garb (Jones and Satterthwaite 1982: 73). For this discussion what is important is the evident affiliation with Teotihuacan in the costume, and the Teotihuacan style of the shield. The style of the figure is Maya in outline and proportion, although the simple rendering of the body and the few encumbering ornaments are unlike the figure of Stormy Sky. Moreover the emphasis on clear vertical and horizontal lines in the design of the figure are also Teotihuacan in approach (Pasztory 1978: 116–117).

On the Bazan slab, a Monte Alban anthropomorphic jaguar stands in front of the Teotihuacan-style human dressed as a priest (Fig. 5). The jaguar/human is named 3 Turquoise on the platform on which he stands, and the Teotihuacan figure is named 13 Turquoise (Marcus 1980: 162).

---

[2] I first discussed style juxtapositions in a paper entitled "From Mythic Tollan to Horizon Style: The Role of Teotihuacan in Mesoamerica," which was presented at a symposium entitled "The Position of the Teotihuacan Civilization in America" at Colgate University in 1977.

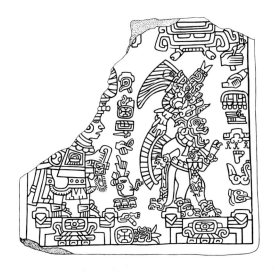

Fig. 5. Bazan slab, Monte Alban, Oaxaca (after Covarrubias 1957: 153)

They are preceded by rows of glyphs, and the tassel headdress glyph in front of 13 Turquoise is the same as the headdress in the shield of the figure on Stela 31 (C. Millon 1973). Tikal stela 31 is dated A.D. 445. The precise date of the Bazan slab is unknown, but is of the Classic period.

The style similarities are easy to see. Stormy Sky and 3 Turquoise are represented with flowing, curvilinear lines, ornamented with mask personifications. The Teotihuacan deity with the tassel headdress and 13 Turquoise are rendered in angular lines and shapes that approximate geometric forms such as squares, circles, triangles, and trapezoids. Although there are many differences between the Maya and Monte Alban styles, as Flora Clancy (1983) has shown, there are similarities too. The Bazan slab and Tikal stela 31 share a similar artistic heritage in which figures in ritual regalia that emphasize masks and scrolls are related to texts that have historical and calendrical meanings.

The Teotihuacan images closest to these are known to us from an incised pottery vessel in the Diego Rivera Museum (Pasztory 1974: fig. 18), and mural paintings in the San Francisco De Young Museum (Fig. 6). On the incised pottery, a hand holding a shield with crossed spears is below a frontal face with a tassel headdress. The entire image reads not so much as a figure but as a complex emblem. Such frontal composite images are characteristic of Teotihuacan deity representations. On the mural fragment, a human figure in profile wears the tassel headdress and walks towards a goggled image with claws also wearing a tassel headdress. The human figure is not represented as an individual, for all the other figures from this mural are identical. The emblems in front of them, however, are different,

Fig. 6. Mural with Figure Wearing Tassel Headdress, Teotihuacan. DeYoung Museum, San Francisco (after Berrin 1988: pl. 39)

and Clara Millon (1988a) has suggested recently that they may be the name glyphs of these personages. However, these names could be those of places or lineages and need not necessarily be the names of individual people. Nor are these emblems comparable to the dated texts found in Maya stelae.

The figure on the Teotihuacan mural carries an incense bag common in profile figure representations, which suggests an office or ritual activity. A speech scroll in front of his mouth has a series of signs that may refer to language, such as a chant, or an invocation, but its variable structure suggests that it is not a true text (Barthel 1982; Kubler 1967; Pasztory 1989). Teotihuacan stylistic conventions are characterized by the geometrization and angularity of forms. Teotihuacan iconography normally consists of heraldic emblems that range from composite signs to deity images. Profile individuals appear to represent priestly and/or governmental officials who may have had titles, something along the lines of our "senator" or "bishop." The differences from the Maya and Monte Alban works are therefore not only stylistic in nature but iconographic as well, and suggest that these northern and southern traditions were very different.

Stylistic juxtapositions comparable to the Bazan slab are also found at Teotihuacan but rarely noted. In one apartment in the compound of Tetitla, the lower wall was painted with an anthropomorphic jaguar approaching a temple in Teotihuacan style, while small-scale figures with Mayoid features

Fig. 7. (a) Fragment of Pinturas Realistas, Tetitla, 1970;

(b) Glyphs from mural (after Villagra 1952: 72, 78)

wearing Maya costumes were painted on the upper wall above them (Fig. 7a). Unfortunately, the mural is too fragmentary for the interpretation of the meaning of this juxtaposition. Some fragments indicate the presence of glyphs, but not enough remains to provide an entire text (Villagra 1952) (Fig. 7b). As of this writing we have a number of isolated glyphs, but as yet no text in Teotihuacan art.

Such style juxtapositions are rare in art. How rare we can see if we try to find a parallel in the art of another time and place. Can we imagine a pot

Fig. 8. Gentile Bellini, *A Turkish Artist* (pen and gouache on parchment, 7¼ × 5½″). Isabella Stuart Gardner Museum, Boston

Fig. 9. (right) Gentile Bellini, *Mahomet II* (70 × 50 cm) National Gallery of Art, London

from the Andes with a Moche-style figure on one side and a Nazca-style figure on the other? In my search I have come across a few examples, only partially similar. Between 1479 and 1480 the Venetian painter Gentile Bellini painted the portrait of a Turkish artist in which he imitates a Turkish miniature (Fig. 8), thus relating his subject to the style of his country in a work that has always been an art historical curiosity. During the fifteenth century, Venice had extensive political and trade contacts, including long periods of war, with the Ottoman empire. In 1470 Venice signed a peace treaty that ended sixteen years of warfare, and the sultan, Mohammed II, asked the Doge, accompanied by a portrait painter, to come to his court in Constantinople. The actual occasion was the wedding of his daughter. The Doge did not go on this mission of good will, but Bellini was sent as a cultural ambassador. While there, he painted a large, realistic, Venetian-style oil painting of the sultan (Fig. 9) and the Turkish miniature-style portrait of the artist. The miniature is on parchment, painted with pen and gouache, and both its small size (7″ × 5″) and the Arabic inscription give it an authentic Middle-Eastern look (Bottari: 1960 447–450; Collins n.d.: 12–14).

Bellini's portrait of the sultan is very interesting in that the ruler sought to represent himself in the style of an alien culture, presumably because of the prestige of the art and city of Venice and perhaps due to a personal predilection. The miniature must have a different explanation—surely Bellini was not invited to Constantinople to paint in Turkish style! We must also note that the miniature may be a private rather than a public work of art. Though these two paintings show Bellini's ability to understand and work in different styles, they are not a single work of art.

The Mesoamerican style juxtapositions discussed above are, however, single monuments and works of public art. I will try to show that these juxtapositions are rare but very much at home in the art of Classic Mesoamerica and that they hold the key to the Mesoamerican meaning of style.

STYLE AS ETHNIC IDENTITY

I tried to find situations in European art and history that might be parallel to the horizon style concept but did not get very far. Are the Middle Ages isolationist periods or is there a "Gothic horizon"? Is there a Renaissance horizon? Are we currently living in an American horizon? What is more striking in European art history is that there are larger period styles that override local traditions. For example, the art of Italy and Holland are very different traditions, but in the seventeenth century both share a series of general stylistic conventions that we call Baroque. The horizon concept may have been useful when a certain quantity of material needed organizing, but once there is more complex and contradictory material available it is too simple. We may eventually find that Mesoamerica as a whole participates in shared ideas and styles like Europe in the Renaissance and Baroque periods.

Mesoamerica is not unlike Europe in consisting of several separate cultural, linguistic, and ethnic regions related to each other in trade, dynastic alliance, war, religion, calendar, and ideology. Both Mesoamerica and Europe constituted at one time what Fernand Braudel (1984) has called the "known world" surrounded by cultures of very different traditions (such as the Islamic Middle East for Europe) or by tribal groups (such as the Chichimecs of the Aztecs). In Classic Mesoamerica the number and boundaries of the regions are far from clear. In order to discuss the concept rather than its details, I shall refer to Covarrubias' famous map, and list merely the regions of Oaxaca, Veracruz, Maya highlands, Maya lowlands, Yucatan, in addition to Teotihuacan, as the loci of a variety of polities (Fig. 10). What is significant in the Classic period is that there is no one major power like the Aztec empire in the Postclassic, despite various attempts to turn Teotihuacan into a mini-Aztec empire. As there is no one dominant political power there is also no one dominant art style that originates in a single center.

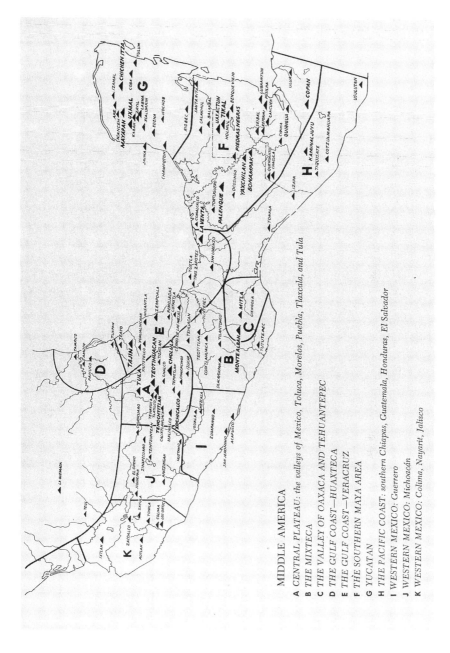

Fig. 10. Map of Mesoamerican culture areas (after Covarrubias 1957: 2)

MIDDLE AMERICA

A *CENTRAL PLATEAU: the valleys of Mexico, Toluca, Morelos, Puebla, Tlaxcala, and Tula*
B *THE MIXTECA*
C *THE VALLEY OF OAXACA AND TEHUANTEPEC*
D *THE GULF COAST—HUAXTECA*
E *THE GULF COAST—VERACRUZ*
F *THE SOUTHERN MAYA AREA*
G *YUCATAN*
H *THE PACIFIC COAST: southern Chiapas, Guatemala, Honduras, El Salvador*
I *WESTERN MEXICO: Guerrero*
J *WESTERN MEXICO: Michoacán*
K *WESTERN MEXICO: Colima, Nayarit, Jalisco*

The second major fact of the Classic period is that these various cultures and polities are in intensive and extensive contact with one another. The evidence for this is the find of foreign objects, which indicate at least gift exchange on the elite level if not actually "trade." Moreover, the representation of foreigners and/or some foreign stylistic traits occur at nearly every center. One of the issues to be examined is what other types of processes, besides the empire/trade model stipulated, could have resulted in so much interaction. I am going to suggest that in Classic Mesoamerica the various polities were extremely conscious of their separateness and independence from one another and that they did their best to advertise this in their works of public art.

George Kubler (1973) analyzed the architectural profiles characteristic of temple platforms and the highly standardized forms these take in the Classic period (Fig. 11). In Teotihuacan there is the two-part talud-tablero, with a rectangular panel over a sloping base. In Oaxaca, the rectangular panel is given square projections at the ends and at rhythmic intervals in the center. In Veracruz a flaring cornice is added to the tablero. Among the Maya, instead of the tablero, a variety of apron moldings are added to the sloping base. Kubler compared these architectural profiles to the Classical orders, and insofar as the Ionic and Doric orders are believed to have come from different places, that is an interesting parallel. However, in Classical antiquity Doric and Ionic acquired different meanings and were used for different temples at the same precinct. The Mesoamerican pyramid profiles are never used that way, because they appear to be ethnic or polity identifiers. These profiles appear to have been devised to differentiate pyramids from the pyramids of other groups, and their very consistency suggests that they maintained this function for a considerable time. Such a use of architectural

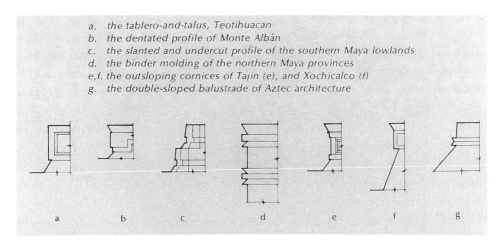

a. the tablero-and-talus, Teotihuacan
b. the dentated profile of Monte Albán
c. the slanted and undercut profile of the southern Maya lowlands
d. the binder molding of the northern Maya provinces
e,f. the outsloping cornices of Tajin (e), and Xochicalco (f)
g. the double-sloped balustrade of Aztec architecture

a   b   c   d   e   f   g

Fig. 11. Mesoamerican architectural profiles (after Kubler 1973: 34)

articulation is comparable to the ways peasants in traditional villages have their own village style of dress and consider the making of such visual distinctions essential.

In fact, Classic Mesoamerica appears to have had a most rigid idea of the relationship of a people or group to a style. The style juxtaposition of the Bazan slab illustrates that they did not merely think of their neighbors as the same type of individuals wearing different dress, but they thought of them literally as being made differently. Judging from the examples of style juxtaposition and from the presence of pyramid articulation, Classic Mesoamerica was extremely concerned with boundaries and the maintenance of separations. Such a preoccupation with boundaries is relevant only if the actual situation is one of a great deal of contact and even a kind of cosmopolitanism.

STYLE AS A SYMBOL OF CONQUEST

The tendency in Mesoamerican culture of the Classic period was to try to control things and events through the appearance of things or events. This preoccupation with appearances is one of the many reasons for the important development of the visual arts. This is quantifiable perhaps only in the realm of architecture. Richard Blanton et al. (1981: 159–164) have noted the great disparity in the quantity of ceremonial architecture built in the Classic period in comparison to that of the Postclassic. Evidently, in the Classic period art was an instrument consciously used for non-artistic ends, while in the Postclassic period more practical measures were taken. The Classic period was more art and style conscious and was more concerned with the manipulation of images than was the Postclassic.

This can be best demonstrated by a few extreme, and therefore dramatic, illustrations. When the Palenque ruler Kan Xul was captured and killed at Tonina, a monument was erected to commemorate this in the style of Palenque, at Tonina (Fig. 12). We do not know how this was done, whether

Fig. 12. Monument 122, showing Kan Xul of Palenque as a Captive, Tonina, Guatemala (after Becquelin and Baudez 1982, 3: 1355)

a Tonina artist imitated Palenque style, or whether a Palenque artist was sent for to carve it (Becquelin and Baudez 1982). The latter interpretation is possible in view of some Postclassic practices. The Mexica, after defeating the Chalca, required that as part of their tribute they build a causeway to Tenochtitlan (Pasztory 1983: 52). As Linda Schele and Mary Ellen Miller (1986:219) have suggested, Piedras Negras Stela 12 is very likely a monument carved by a Pomona artist to represent the Piedras Negras conquest of Pomona and to increase thereby the humiliation of Pomona (Fig. 13). A foreign art style in this context is the symbol of conquest rather than "influence." Mesoamericans did not merely capture prisoners, they captured styles as well. This complicates greatly what we consider the "normal" pattern in which styles are diffused and interact.

How are we to interpret the eclectic style of Xochicalco and Cacaxtla? Do the strong Maya elements suggest a Maya "influence"—by which we mean a military or an intellectual or aesthetic conquest—in Central Mexico? Or, is the imitation of Maya style really a humiliating conquest over the Maya by Central Mexicans who required art works as tribute from their victims? In other words, who captured whom and who depicted whom?

"Style juxtaposition" and "style as a symbol of conquest" are really two sides of the same coin. In both the basic assumption is that the style of a group is as inalienable a part of their existence and reality as is their costume or language. Style is not relatively neutral and cannot move separately from this cultural baggage. This is unlike our own concepts of style, which are more neutral. For example, during the sixteenth century, artists in Northern Europe imitated the style of the Italian Renaissance, without concern that the Catholic traditions of the South might be an aspect of the style and inappropriate to the Protestant North.

STYLE AS SYMBOLIC POLARITY

A curious aspect of stylistic juxtapositions in Classic period art is the fact that Teotihuacan is generally one of the figures represented. Since no Maya/Oaxaca or Oaxaca/Veracruz images are known to me, I assume that these are either non-existent or very few, and perhaps readers will bring them to my attention. This fact can be variously interpreted. It might indeed argue for the power and prestige of Teotihuacan. Strangely enough, this polarity continued to exist even after effective contact with Teotihuacan apparently ceased. On structure 5D-57 at the Central Acropolis at Tikal, the Maya Ruler A is shown as a severely rectilinear figure with Teotihuacan symbols holding a captive in Maya style by a rope (Fig. 14). Because both of these figures are Maya, and by this time in the early eighth century active contact between the Maya and Teotihuacan had ceased, the stylistic reference to Teotihuacan must have an ideological rather than a literal meaning.

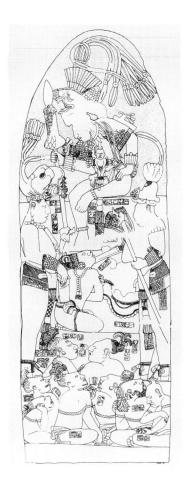

Fig. 13. Stela 12, Piedras Negras
(after Greene, Rands, and Graham
1972: pl. 43)

Fig. 14. Relief from Structure 5D–57, Central Acropolis, Tikal, Guatemala (after
Miller 1978: 66)

Marvin Cohodas (1989) has suggested that in the Classic period Meso-america was symbolically divided into a northern, Teotihuacan half and a southern, Maya half. These two halves functioned as an ideological polarity, somewhat like a moiety system, but between rather than within polities. Cohodas suggests that the ideological polarity in Mesoamerica is geo-graphic and contrasts the people of the cold highlands and the warm low-lands. It can operate in a small area, so the nearby state of Morelos could be the lowland "tierra caliente" for Tenochtitlan in the Basin of Mexico, or on the "known world" scale, so the province of Soconusco on the Pacific Slope of Guatemala could take on that role. In Classic Mesoamerica Teotihuacan was the culture primarily associated with the highlands, and the various Maya city-states, foremost among them Tikal, were associated with the lowlands. In this view, for a Mesoamerican, objects representing Teoti-huacan and the Maya could represent the totality of their known world (i.e., Mesoamerica). The Becan cache in which a Teotihuacan host figure contain-ing ten little figurines was found in a Maya-style cylinder tripod has been much discussed as an example of Teotihuacan "influence" (Fig. 15) (Ball 1974). It is possible to see this cache not just politically but symbolically. A Teotihuacan host figure within a Maya vessel could represent the totality of

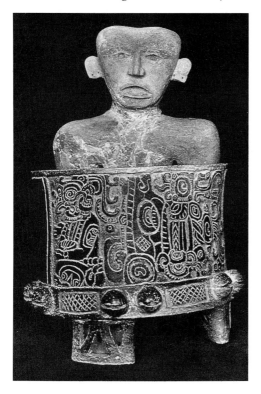

Fig. 15. Becan cache consisting of a Teotihuacan-style "host" figu-rine placed within a Maya-style vessel (after Ball 1974: cover)

the known world in terms of this geographic polarity made visually distinct through style.

Returning to the Tikal Palace representation (Fig. 14), if the two Maya figures shown represent a ritual rather than an actual division into Maya and Teotihuacan, why are they represented as conqueror and victim in the context of battle? Is the battle shown a real battle disguised as a symbolic battle, or a symbolic battle disguised as a real battle? A number of the little figures in the Becan cache are military individuals. Warren Barbour (n.d.) has suggested that the Teotihuacan host figures with little figurines inside them may represent the totality of the body politic at Teotihuacan. The hosts may be deities, while the figurines are the male and female inhabitants and functionaries (Fig. 16). Could the placement of such a host figure in a Maya vessel represent a symbolic "conquest" at Becan? It is worth noting that the tributes that found their way into the Templo Mayor offerings may have been seen as conquered gods and objects by the Mexica (Nagao 1985). In Mesoamerica tribute may have been seen as the conquest of things, some

Fig. 16. "Host" figurine with smaller interior figurines, Teotihuacan style. American Museum of Natural History New York collection. Neg./Trans. No. 332943 (photo: courtesy Dept. Library Services AMNH)

of which were intended for cached offerings in the temples. Conquered things from a place that was symbolically the opposite may have been greatly desired to represent the totality of the world. Some rituals and representations therefore juxtapose highland and lowland styles to refer to the world as a whole.

Styles could represent identity and conquest only if they remained different and distinct. The ideological forces against a territorial empire in Mesoamerica are well known. There were similar forces against the wide spread of art styles. Stylistic difference was a major value in Mesoamerica, and in the Classic period these differences were played up rather than down. These factors oppose the relatively easy spread of an art style, and a horizon style is not likely to emerge. It is worth noting that the horizon style concept grows out of Andean studies, and in the New World it is in the Andes that we find examples of systematically integrated states and conquest empires. A closer examination of the nature of style in the Andes might result in interesting differences from those of Mesoamerica.

TEOTIHUACAN STYLE AND ITS ASSOCIATED MEANINGS

The symbolic polarity I have discussed is created in large part by the entry of the style of Teotihuacan on the Mesoamerican artistic map, and therefore we must turn to the origins of the Teotihuacan style to understand its significance.

How and why is a new style created? It is created to express multiple needs, which might include a new political power, social reality, or understanding of religion. A new tradition is created when an old one is found to be inadequate. The creation of a new stylistic tradition is neither easy nor casual. Note how the eclectic mix of the styles found at Xochicalco and Cacaxtla does not quite result in the creation of a new style. These styles remind me of a recipe: take one cup of Teotihuacan, one cup of Classic Maya, a half-cup of Veracruz, a spoonful of Monte Alban, and stir. The result is something like a fruitcake with the ingredients—nuts and fruits—clearly visible. At Cacaxtla and Xochicalco we are always too much aware of the sources of the different elements. Whereas the Teotihuacan style, once it is developed, is quintessentially itself and does not consist predominantly of borrowed elements. In the case of Cacaxtla and Xochicalco what really needs to be asked is why did these centers develop such eclectic arts when the cultural tendency in Classic Mesoamerica was for centers to create their own individual profile in style.

Where does one get a new style? When the Mexica Aztec came to power, one of their major aims in creating an imperial art was to publicize their legitimate descent from the earlier dynasties and cultures in the Valley of Mexico. This, of course, was largely a lie. The Mexica began by imitating the arts of Tula, Teotihuacan, and Xochicalco and slowly transformed this eclectic mixture to make it their own. As Emily Umberger (1987) has shown, their innovation was through archaism and the fiction of continuity.

One of the striking features of the art of Teotihuacan is that it does not imitate or relate to the earlier monumental arts in Mesoamerica. Mesoamerica had had impressive monumental arts for more than a thousand years prior to Teotihuacan in the Olmec, Monte Alban, Izapan, and other related styles. Olmec monuments are as close to the Valley of Mexico as Chalcatzingo in Morelos. In fact, very much later, the Aztecs built stairways at Chalcatzingo and saw it clearly as an ancient sacred center to be venerated. Recent excavations show that during the late phases of Teotihuacan (III and IV) the nearby site of Las Pilas had Teotihuacan-style architecture and offerings (Martin Arana 1987: 387). Teotihuacan did have access to Olmec-style lapidary art, and Olmecoid figures in greenstone have come to light in recent excavations (Cabrera, Rodriguez and Morelos 1982). However, most of its art is inherently different in character from Olmec art.

For southern Mesoamerica in the Classic period, the Olmec and Izapan traditions fulfill the role that Classical antiquity plays in Europe. These styles survive through various transformations, and aspects of them are sometimes revived. These southern styles are curvilinear and naturalistic. They were created to glorify individual rulers and their specific conquest, or to humiliate their captives. They are thus primarily historical within a context of sacred justifications. They are often associated with glyphs and texts. The victims that are the Danzantes of Monte Alban and the ruler on the El Baul Herrera stela are examples of this southern tradition (Figs. 17–18).

In Teotihuacan art, not only individuality, but often the entire anthropomorphic reality of the body is deleted. Faces are turned into mask-like panels overlooking the flat costume planes, as in the colossal goddess (Fig. 19), or facial features may be entirely missing with a face implied by headdress, nosebar, and earplugs, as on a relief found near the Palace of the Butterflies (Fig. 20). Except in a few late works, glyphs are rare, and texts are entirely absent. Although there is plenty of evidence for human sacrifice, it is usually indirect; there are no representations of human captors and captives as individuals. All these traits indicate an emphatic opposition to the historical, dynastic cult of southern Mesoamerica.

The art of Teotihuacan was, in my opinion, created in part through denial—by a conscious opposition to the art and traditions of their southern neighbors. The reason for this negation probably has to do with the nature of the Teotihuacan state and the creation of a new language of forms to express it visually. Teotihuacan appears to have been organized as a corporate state led by officials who combined sacred and secular functions and kept a low personal profile. George Cowgill (1983) has suggested a parallel to the Vatican State. René Millon (1981: 231–235) has suggested that the urban concentration of the Teotihuacan population may have taken place

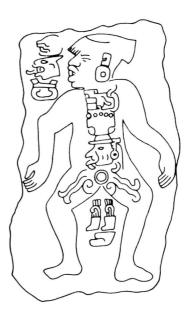

Fig. 17. Danzante 55, Monte Alban, Oaxaca (after Flannery and Marcus 1983: 95)

Fig. 18. Herrera stela, El Baul, Guatemala (after Covarrubias 1957: 242)

Fig. 19. (left) Colossal goddess, Teotihuacan. Museo Nacional de Antropología, Mexico

Fig. 20. (above) Face panel, Teotihuacan. Site Museum

initially to build the great pyramids and that therefore the state was integrated around religion and the gods rather than around sacred rulers. The individual on the Bazan slab is probably there in terms of his office, such as "senator" or "bishop," as suggested earlier. Previous work on Teotihuacan has stressed the power and bureaucratic organization of the state. I feel that one of the ways in which the state maintained allegiance in its population was through some form of ritualistic participation in the process of government (Pasztory 1989). Another was through the emphasis on gods rather than human rulers. The elite are always represented in the guise of priests, thus putting them into the position of servants in relation to the gods. As Barbour has suggested, the Teotihuacan host figures may represent structurally the nature of the Teotihuacan state—the outer deity image, sometimes male, sometimes female, contains a representative selection of the men, women, and hierarchy of officials that made up the Teotihuacan state. In these images the gods have literally taken humanity hostage in themselves.

The point I am trying to emphasize is that had Teotihuacan wanted to express its relationship to Olmec- and Izapan-related polities, styles, and dynasties, it could have done so. The fact that its artists developed a new style that was, in many ways, the opposite of the southern styles was probably a way of expressing visually their sense of social, political, and religious difference. The entry of Teotihuacan art and culture on the Mesoamerican scene around the time of Christ resulted literally in a polarity, which the subsequent symbolic polarities in art strove to represent. The differences between southern Mesoamerica and Teotihuacan are as great as the cultural and political differences between the U.S. and the U.S.S.R. in the twentieth century. Though I do not mean to suggest that they are otherwise similar, the situation is comparable in the presence of a political and cultural opposition that has been exaggerated, rather than being scaled down or merged.

Why then is Teotihuacan style so often associated with military imagery, with shields and spears and other military accoutrements outside of Teotihuacan? Why does the figure on Tikal stela 31 carry a Teotihuacan-style shield, and why is the Teotihuacan-style figure on Yaxha Stela 11 also dressed in military garb? (Greene et al. 1972: 163). These facts had previously been used as evidence in creating a conquest-empire model for the role of Teotihuacan in Mesoamerica. I do not have the answer to this question, only a different hypothesis.

War in southern Mesoamerica was commemorated on monuments as a dynastic and historical event, beginning with monuments such as Altar 4 at La Venta with the ruler holding a prisoner by the rope, and the Danzante and conquest glyph panels at Monte Alban. My hypothesis is that Teotihuacan may have developed a type of warfare that was played in more of a ritual guise appropriate to the less personal and more corporate traditions created at Teotihuacan. Such a ritualized war may have been the antecedent of the Aztec Flowery War between Tenochtitlan and Tlaxcala, which was played between relative equals with the aim of taking prisoners for the altars of the gods, and perhaps as a continuous testing of the status quo. Such ritual wars may have been one of the processes of interaction between different areas in Mesoamerica, perhaps originally initiated by Teotihuacan. Another possible form of interaction may have been the ball game, which, in my view, could have been played not just within states but between states (Pasztory 1989). It is evident that between the various polities of Classic Mesoamerica there was a high degree of hostility and conflict, although no one power tried (?) or could conquer the area as a whole. It may have been international institutions such as the ball game and ritual war that helped to channel and contain these hostilities so that the cosmopolitan exchange of goods and ideas continued to flow without breakdown.

This postulated ritual war may have been associated with Teotihuacan paraphernalia, perhaps in featherwork (Pasztory 1989). Schele and Miller (1986:213) have suggested that Teotihuacan paraphernalia remained in use among the Maya even after the collapse of Teotihuacan in A.D. 750, and that that explains the many instances in which Teotihuacan symbolic elements continue to occur in Maya art. If the symbolic polarity of Mesoamerican thought was dramatized in ritual battles, the actual existence of Teotihuacan as a polity need not have been a requirement, but the insignia, images, and the concept of a highland power was. If this polarity was to continue after the collapse of Teotihuacan, other Central Mexican powers, such as the Toltecs or the Aztecs, could fulfill that role.

CONCLUSIONS

The horizon concept can be applied to Classic Mesoamerica only with difficulty because of the nature of both politics and art style. At this time Mesoamerica is not dominated by any one culture, despite the importance of Teotihuacan. Rather than the spread of some kind of cultural uniformity, the Classic period sees the development and florescence of several individual regional cultures. Two processes appear to be evident: the regional cultures seek to emphasize their uniqueness and differentness, while at the same time the monuments and elite goods indicate extensive interaction between them. This is not necessarily a peaceful era; there are many indications of competitiveness, hostility, and conflict, but they appear to be of a small enough scale so that none of the major regional cultures is conquered or destroyed by any other.

In the Andes, where the horizon concept originated, each horizon is associated with a horizon style, which is an art style disseminated by a conquering empire. In Classic Mesoamerica there is no one art style that is found throughout the area suggesting such a "horizon." Teotihuacan-style figures and artifacts are widespread, but then so are Veracruz objects. It is misleading to model the history of Mesoamerica on that of the Andes, with periods of regional isolation alternating with unifying horizon-empires. Although there are periods of regional isolation or Balkanism in Mesoamerica, they alternate not with empires but with periods of long-distance elite interaction between several regions. The regions may not be equal in status and power, but their independence appears to be maintained. Even the Aztec empire has many features of such a system and accounts for those elements that never made sense in a territorial empire.

The concept of the horizon style does not help to explain the nature of art and style in Classic Mesoamerica. I have tried to show that a horizon style was unlikely to be found because in Classic Mesoamerica a great emphasis was placed on the creation of clearly recognizable styles in art and architecture that signified ethnic and/or polity affiliation. This emphasis on the difference between centers rather than on their similarities results in unusual representations, such as style juxtaposition, in which the figures from two centers are shown in their own style, and in conquest monuments in which the downfall of an enemy is represented in the home style of the enemy. From these types of representations it is evident that for Mesoamericans there was no such thing as a neutral artistic style, because style always had an ideological content.

It was further suggested that some references to other styles are not necessarily due to factual reasons but could be ideological in nature. Some representations may refer to a lowland–highland polarity that can be in the guise of Maya or Teotihuacan figures. It was postulated that some of the long-distance interaction between groups may have been in the form of ritual war or ball games that dramatized such polarities. The origin of the highland-lowland polarity is seen from the emergence of Teotihuacan, whose style and institutions were in dramatic opposition to those of the south.

Information taken from art works and art style does not necessarily give us a one-to-one access to culture and history, however much we should like to be able to reconstruct those. What we do get, however, is an insight into the ideologies of the time. From their use of styles, we can reconstruct how they saw style in general; how they related it to their polities and to their neighbors. Though we cannot reconstruct what they did, the monuments show us how they wanted to appear both to themselves and to others.

BIBLIOGRAPHY

ARMILLAS, PEDRO
    1950   Teotihuacan, Tula, y los Toltecas, culturas post-arcaicas y pre-aztecas del Centro de Mexico. *Runa: Archivo para las Ciencias del Hombre:* 37–70, Buenos Aires.

BALL, JOSEPH W.
    1974   A Teotihuacan Style Cache from the Maya Lowlands. *Archaeology* 27: 2–9.

BARBOUR, WARREN D.
    n.d.   Shadow and Substance: The Iconography of Host Figurines Associated with Ancient Teotihuacan Mexico. Paper presented at the meeting of the Society for American Archaeology in New Orleans, 1986.

BARTHEL, THOMAS S.
    1982   Veritable "Texts" in Teotihuacan Art? *The Masterkey* 56: 1: 4–12.

BAXANDALL, MICHAEL
    1985   *Patterns of Intention.* Yale University Press, New Haven.

BECQUELIN, PIERRE, AND CLAUDE F. BAUDEZ
    1982   *Tonina, une cité Maya du Chiapas, Mexico.* Mission Archéologique au Mexique, Mexico.

BERLO, JANET C.
    n.d.   The Teotihuacan Trapeze and Ray Sign: A Study of the Diffusion of Symbols. M.A. thesis, Department of Art History, Yale University, 1976.

BERRIN, KATHLEEN (ED.)
    1988   *Feathered Serpents and Flowering Trees: Reconstructing the Murals of Teotihuacan.* The Fine Arts Museums of San Francisco.

BLANTON, RICHARD E., STEPHEN KOWALEWSKI, GARY FEINMAN, AND JILL APPEL
    1981   *Ancient Mesoamerica, A Comparison of Change in Three Regions.* Cambridge University Press, Cambridge.

BORHEGYI, STEPHAN F.
    1965   Archaeological Synthesis of the Guatemala Highlands. In *Handbook of Middle American Indians, vol. 2: Archaeology of Southern Mesoamerica* (Gordon R. Willey, ed.): Part 1, 3–58.

BOTTARI, STEFANO
    1960   Gentile Bellini. *Encyclopaedia of World Art* 2: 447–450, McGraw-Hill, New York.

BRAUDEL, FERNAND
    1984   *The Perspective of the World.* Harper and Row, New York.

CABRERA CASTRO, RUBEN, IGNACIO RODRIGUEZ, AND NOEL MORELOS (EDS.)
    1982   *Teotihuacan 80–82. Primeros resultados.* Instituto Nacional de Antropología e Historia, Mexico.

CLANCY, FLORA S.

    1983   A Comparison of Highland Zapotec and Lowland Maya Graphic Styles. In *Highland-Lowland Interaction in Mesoamerica: Interdisciplinary Approaches* (A. G. Miller, ed.): 223–240. Dumbarton Oaks, Washington, D.C.

CLARK, JOHN E.

    n.d.   From Mountains to Molehills: A Critical Review of Teotihuacan's Obsidian Industry. *Research in Economic Anthropology* 8 (in press).

COE, WILLIAM

    1970   *Tikal, a Handbook of the Ancient Maya Ruins.* University Museum, University of Pennsylvania, Philadelphia.

COHODAS, MARVIN

    1989   The Epiclassic Problem: A Review and Alternative Model. In *Mesoamerica after the Decline of Teotihuacan, A.D. 700–900* (R. A. Diehl and J. C. Berlo, eds.): 219–240. Dumbarton Oaks, Washington, D.C.

COLLINS, HOWARD F.

    n.d.   Gentile Bellini: A Monograph and Catalogue of Works. Ph.D. dissertation, University of Pittsburgh, Dept. of Art History, 1970.

COVARRUBIAS, MIGUEL

    1957   *Indian Art of Mexico and Central America.* Alfred A. Knopf, New York.

COWGILL, GEORGE

    1983   Rulership and the Ciudadela: Political Inference from Teotihuacan Architecture. In *Civilization in the Ancient Americas: Essays in Honor of Gordon R. Willey* (R. M. Leventhal and A. L. Kolata, eds.): 313–343. University of New Mexico Press and Peabody Museum, Cambridge, Mass.

EKHOLM, GORDON F.

    1971   *Ancient Mexico and Central America.* American Museum of Natural History, New York.

FLANNERY, KENT V., AND JOYCE MARCUS

    1983   *The Cloud People: Divergent Evolution of the Zapotec and Mixtec Civilizations.* Academic Press, New York.

GAMIO, MANUEL

    1920   Las excavaciones del Pedregal de San Angel y la cultura arcaica del Valle de Mexico. *American Anthropologist* n.s. 22 (2): 127–143.

    1922   *La población del Valle de Teotihuacán.* 5 vols. Dirección de Talleres Gráficos, Mexico.

GREENE, MERLE, ROBERT L. RANDS, AND JOHN GRAHAM

    1972   *Maya Sculpture from the Southern Lowlands.* Lederer Street and Zeus, Berkeley, Calif.

HELLMUTH, NICHOLAS M.

    n.d.   Mexican Symbols in the Classic Art of the Southern Maya Lowlands. M.A. thesis, Department of Anthropology, Brown University, 1969.

JIMENEZ MORENO, WIGBERTO
 1941   Tula y los Toltccas segun las fuentes historicas. *Revista Mexicana de Estudios Antropológicos* 5 (2–3). Mexico.
 1966   Mesoamerica Before the Toltecs. In *Ancient Oaxaca* (J. Paddock, ed.): 1–82. Stanford University Press.

JONES, CHRISTOPHER, AND LINTON SATTERTHWAITE
 1982   The Monuments and Inscriptions of Tikal: The Carved Monuments. In *Tikal Report 33*, part A. The University Museum, Philadelphia.

KIDDER, ALFRED V., JESSIE D. JENNINGS, AND EDWIN M. SHOOK
 1946   *Excavations at Kaminaljuyu, Guatemala.* Carnegie Institution of Washington, Pub. 561. Washington, D.C.

KUBLER, GEORGE
 1967   *The Iconography of the Art of Teotihuacan.* Studies in Pre-Columbian Art and Archaeology 4. Dumbarton Oaks, Washington, D.C.
 1973   Iconographic Aspects of Architectural Profiles at Teotihuacan and in Mesoamerica. In *The Iconography of Middle American Sculpture:* 24–39. The Metropolitan Museum of Art, New York.

LINNÉ, SIGVALD
 1934   Archaeological Researches at Teotihuacan. *The Ethnographical Museum of Sweden,* n.s. Pub. 1. Stockholm.
 1942   Mexican Highland Cultures. *The Ethnographical Museum of Sweden,* n.s. Pub. 7. Stockholm.

MARCUS, JOYCE
 1980   Teotihuacan Visitors on Monte Alban Monuments and Murals. In *The Cloud People* (K. V. Flannery and J. Marcus, eds.): 175–181. Academic Press, New York.

MARTIN ARANA, RAUL
 1987   Classic and Postclassic Chalcatzingo. In *Ancient Chalcatzingo* (D. C. Grove, ed.): 387–399. University of Texas Press, Austin.

MILLER, ARTHUR G.
 1978   A Brief Outline of the Artistic Evidence for Classic Period Cultural Contact between the Maya Lowlands and the Central Mexican Highlands. In *Middle Classic Mesoamerica: A.D. 400–700* (E. Pasztory, ed.): 63–70. Columbia University Press, New York.
 1983   (Ed.) *Highland-Lowland Interaction in Mesoamerica: Interdisciplinary Approaches.* Dumbarton Oaks, Washington, D.C.

MILLON, CLARA HALL
 1973   Painting, Writing, and Polity in Teotihuacan, Mexico. *American Antiquity* 38: 294–314.
 1988a A Reexamination of the Teotihuacan Tassel Headdress Insignia. In *Feathered Serpents and Flowering Trees: Reconstructing the Murals of Teotihuacan* (Kathleen Berrin, ed.): 114–134. The Fine Arts Museums of San Francisco.

1988b   Maguey Bloodletting Ritual. In *Feathered Serpents and Flowering Trees: Reconstructing the Murals of Teotihuacan* (Kathleen Berrin, ed.): 195–205. The Fine Arts Museums of San Francisco.

MILLON, RENÉ

1973   *The Teotihuacan Map, Urbanization at Teotihuacan, Mexico,* 1. University of Texas Press, Austin.

1981   Teotihuacan: City, State, and Civilization. In *Supplement to the Handbook of Middle American Indians* (V. R. Bricker and J. A. Sabloff, eds.): 198–243. University of Texas, Austin.

1988   The Last Years of Teotihuacan Dominance. In *The Collapse of Ancient States and Civilizations* (N. Yoffee and G. Cowgill, eds.): 104–164. University of Arizona Press, Tucson.

NAGAO, DEBRA

1985   *Mexica Buried Offerings. A Historical and Contextual Analysis.* BAR International Series 235. Oxford.

PADDOCK, JOHN (ED.)

1966   *Ancient Oaxaca.* Stanford University Press, Stanford, Calif.

PASZTORY, ESTHER

1974   The Iconography of the Teotihuacan Tlaloc. In *Studies in Pre-Columbian Art and Archaeology* 15. Dumbarton Oaks, Washington, D.C.

1976   *The Murals of Tepantitla, Teotihuacan.* Garland Publications, New York.

1978   (Ed.) *Middle Classic Mesoamerica: A.D. 400–700.* Columbia University Press, New York.

1983   *Aztec Art.* Harry N. Abrams, New York.

1988   A Reinterpretation of Teotihuacan and its Mural Painting Tradition. In *Feathered Serpents and Flowering Trees* (K. Berrin, ed.): 45–77. The Fine Arts Museums of San Francisco.

1989   Identity and Difference: The Uses and Meanings of Ethnic Styles. In *Cultural Differentiation and Cultural Identity in the Visual Arts* (Susan J. Barnes and Walter S. Melion, eds.): 15–38. National Gallery of Art, Center for the Advanced Study in the Visual Arts, Washington, D.C.

RATHJE, WILLIAM L.

1971   The Origin and Development of the Lowland Classic Maya Civilization. *American Antiquity* 36: 275–285.

RATTRAY, EVELYN C.

1981   Anaranjado delgado: Cerámica de comercio de Teotihuacan. In *Interacción cultural en Mexico Central* (E. C. Rattray, Jaime Litvak King, and Clara Diaz O., eds.): 55–80. Universidad Nacional Autónoma de México, Mexico.

n.d.   Gulf Coast Influences at Teotihuacan. Paper presented at the symposium Art and the Rise of the Teotihuacan State, 1983. UCLA, Los Angeles, Calif.

SANDERS, WILLIAM J., AND JOSEPH W. MICHELS (EDS.)

1977   *Teotihuacan and Kaminaljuyu: A Study in Prehistoric Culture Contact.* The Pennsylvania State University Press, University Park, Pa.

SANDERS, WILLIAM J., AND BARBARA J. PRICE
  1968 *Mesoamerica: The Evolution of a Civilization.* Random House, New York.

SANDERS, WILLIAM J., JEFFREY R. PARSONS, AND ROBERT S. SANTLEY
  1979 *The Basin of Mexico: Ecological Processes in the Evolution of a Civilization.* Academic Press, New York.

SANTLEY, ROBERT S.
  1983 Obsidian Trade and Teotihuacan Influence in Mesoamerica. In *Highland-Lowland Interaction in Mesoamerica: Interdisciplinary Approaches* (A. G.. Miller, ed.): 69–124. Dumbarton Oaks, Washington, D.C.

SANTLEY, ROBERT S.
  1989 Obsidian Working, Long-Distance Exchange, and the Teotihuacan Presence on the South Gulf Coast. In *Mesoamerica after the Decline of Teotihuacan, A.D. 700–900* (R. A. Diehl and J. C. Berlo, eds.): 131–151. Dumbarton Oaks, Washington, D.C.

SCHELE, LINDA, AND MARY ELLEN MILLER
  1986 *The Blood of Kings: Dynasty and Ritual in Maya Art.* Kimbell Art Museum, Fort Worth, Texas.

SPENCE, MICHAEL
  1967 The Obsidian Industry of Teotihuacan. *American Antiquity* 32: 507–514.

STIERLIN, HENRI
  1964 *Living Architecture: Mayan.* Grosset and Dunlap, New York.
  1968 *Living Architecture: Ancient Mexican.* MacDonald and Co., London.

UMBERGER, EMILY G.
  1987 Antiques, Revivals, and References to the Past in Aztec Art. *RES* 13: 62–105. Cambridge, Mass.

VAILLANT, GEORGE C.
  1935a Excavations at El Arbolillo. *Anthropological Papers, American Museum of Natural History* 35 (2).
  1935b Early Cultures of the Valley of Mexico. *Anthropological Papers, American Museum of Natural History* 35 (3).

VILLAGRA, AGUSTIN C.
  1952 Trabajos realizados en Teotihuacan, 1952. *Instituto Nacional de Antropología e Historia, Anales* 6: 69–78. Mexico.

WOLF, ERIC R. (ED.)
  1976 *The Valley of Mexico.* University of New Mexico Press, Albuquerque.

Mesoamerican Horizons and the Cultural Transformations of Maya Civilization

ARTHUR A. DEMAREST
and
ANTONIA E. FOIAS
VANDERBILT UNIVERSITY

T HE ARCHAEOLOGY OF EASTERN MESOAMERICA, especially the Maya area, has provided fertile ground for the application of the horizon concept. The great stylistic horizons, especially the "Olmec" and "Teotihuacan," have been seen as archaeological traces of interregional contacts that carried ideas, economic change, and political influences. The Maya culture has supposedly been a receiver of foreign influences that have helped it climb each step of the evolutionary ladder, from origins to statehood and beyond. Such applications of the horizon concept have forced Mayanists to look beyond their often parochial focus on the elite culture and to consider Maya social evolution in the broader context of Mesoamerica as a whole. The question remains, however, as to whether the horizon concept has also encouraged artificial chronological alignments, overemphasis on external forces, and other problems in the interpretation of Maya cultural evolution.

THE "EARLY HORIZON" AND THE RISE OF CIVILIZATION IN EASTERN MESOAMERICA

The Early and Middle Preclassic periods (ca. 2000–400 B.C.) are the most poorly understood phases of Maya prehistory, yet at the end of this span, Maya culture and social evolution had largely taken shape. The paucity of data has not inhibited interpretation of the role of horizons in this initial stage of civilization in eastern Mesoamerica. The origins of many aspects of Maya culture have been traced indirectly to a proposed "Early Horizon" of influence from the Olmec centers of the Gulf Coast. The later civilizations of the lowlands, highlands, and coasts of eastern Mesoamerica sometimes have been seen as descendants of a "mother-culture" in the Olmec heartland of Veracruz and Tabasco.

Eastern and southeastern Mesoamerica, especially the highland Maya region, have been viewed as prime areas of impact of this "Early Horizon" of "Olmec" influence. Olmec or "Olmecoid" monumental sculptures have been found along the Pacific Coast and highlands of Guatemala and El Salvador, and are especially prominent at Abaj Takalik, Kaminaljuyu, and Chalchuapa. This same area is generally believed to be the region of the development of much of Maya elite culture, including the stela-altar complex, hieroglyphic writing, and calendrics. These "Olmecoid" cultures in the highlands and on the Pacific Coast have been seen as an intermediary between the Olmec and the incipient lowland Maya civilization, inspiring many aspects of Maya elite culture.

A recent School of American Research Advanced Seminar (Sharer and Grove 1989) specifically addressed the issue of Olmec diffusion and its role in cultural evolution throughout Mesoamerica. A majority of the scholars disagreed with Olmec-centric perspectives and called for more complex interactional models for the period (e.g., Demarest 1989; Grove 1989; Marcus 1989; Sharer 1989). However, several scholars (Tolstoy 1989; M. Coe 1989; Lee 1989; Lowe 1989) held that Olmec heartland culture was precocious and that it dominated the evolution of the Early and early Middle Formative culture of Mesoamerica.

Turning to the actual evidence, though, examples of "Olmec influence" in the highlands and coast of Guatemala are scattered, poorly defined, and not chronologically consistent. Olmec motifs on ceramics are found on the far western Pacific Coast of Guatemala in the late Middle Formative and occasionally appeared in scattered finds in the highlands (Demarest 1989; Sharer and Grove 1989). Olmec-style monumental bas-reliefs are found in a few sites along the coast and highlands as far southeast as El Salvador (Sharer 1989). At Abaj Takalik, a cluster of such monuments suggests the probable presence of a significant chiefdom at this center in the Middle Formative period (Graham 1989). The presence of Olmec iconography in this area certainly demonstrates that some of the coastal and highland chiefdoms participated in the international elite iconographic system of that period. They do not, however, indicate dominance by the Olmec heartland in Veracruz, since ceramics and artifacts are of local styles (Grove 1989; Sharer and Grove 1989).

Areas with well-dated, complete Middle Formative sequences, and associated ecological and settlement data, clearly show a rise of regional chiefdoms through local ecological processes—not through Olmec intrusions. Interregional interaction did play an important role in the evolution of these southern highland and coastal polities. But most critical was the interaction *between* these coastal areas and the adjacent evolving highland systems in Guatemala (rather than long-distance contact) (see especially Bove 1989;

Demarest 1986; Sharer 1978; Sharer and Sedat 1987; Hatch 1987b; Michels 1979).

When we turn to evaluate the Olmec horizon in the Maya lowlands of the Peten and the Yucatan peninsula, we find a different, rather stark, picture: a nearly complete lack of evidence. Few sites have significant deposits of Middle Formative materials. Those that have been found show almost no evidence of participation in any aspect of the Olmec symbolic system. The absence of the Olmec horizon is even more conspicuous given the proposed derivations of many later Maya iconographic elements and even conceptual themes from Olmec or "Olmecoid" antecedents (e.g., M. Coe 1977; Quirarte 1977; Grove, this volume). Nonetheless, hard evidence of Olmec contact is limited to a few jade caches and scattered finds of "Olmecoid" portable objects.

A cache dated at Seibal to 660 B.C. ± 75 (Smith 1982: 118, 243; Willey 1978: 88–89) was a cruciform La Venta-style arrangement of jade celts, a jade bloodletter, and local ceramics. Copan, actually a site of highland cultural affiliation during the Preclassic period, has a Middle Formative cemetery containing many jade objects together with vessels bearing paw-wing and flame-eyebrow motifs (Fig. 1). However, these motifs are diagnostic of the proposed Early Formative or early Olmec horizon, despite the Middle Formative date of the Copan cemetery and other vessels in its deposits (Fash n.d.). Again, this chronological misalignment underscores the complexity and lack of coherence of "Olmec" finds in eastern Mesoamerica. At Chacsinkin, Yucatan, E. Wyllys Andrews V reported the most recent Olmec find—a cache of seventeen jades, many incised or carved in full La Venta Olmec style (Andrews 1986). Andrews would date the cache from its general nature to the late Middle Formative period.

Other than these caches, Olmec evidence is limited to scattered finds of jade pendants, figurines, or pectorals in later contexts or without true provenience (e.g., Proskouriakoff 1962: 352; M. Coe 1966; Rathje, Sabloff, and Gregory 1973). Direct influences on Maya ceramics from the Olmec area have been proposed (e.g., Joesink-Mandeville 1977; Velásquez 1980), but these proposals have not withstood subsequent scrutiny. Indeed, it appears that the Maya lowland ceramic traditions are notable for their lack of stylistic similarity to the related Olmec, isthmian, and coastal complexes (Lowe 1977, 1978; Andrews 1986, 1991). Exceptions appear to include possible limited ceramic trade between Yucatan and La Venta, as well as Chiapan influence on the early Middle Formative Xe ceramics of Seibal and Altar (Andrews 1986, 1991).

All things considered, the Olmec presence in the Maya lowlands is surprisingly weak. To a certain extent this negative evidence probably reflects our tiny and erratic sample of Middle Formative remains. It also may reflect the

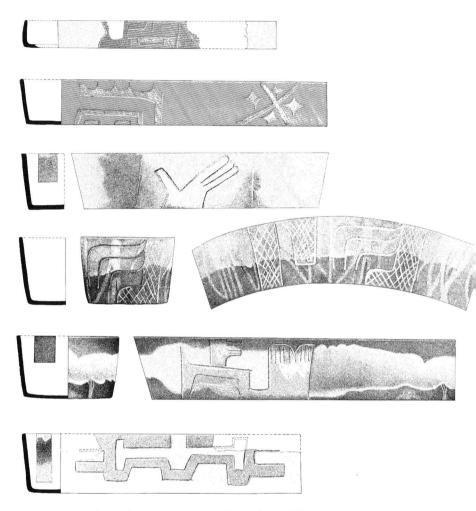

Fig. 1. Olmec designs on ceramics from the Middle Formative cemetery at Copan, Honduras (after Fash 1991)

relatively late dating now given to most of the earliest lowland ceramic phases (Andrews 1991). The implication is that the Olmec-derived features and themes present in Classic Maya art incorporated influences from epi-Olmec and Late Formative styles from the highlands, where there was greater participation in the Middle Formative symbolic system. Again, we emphasize that this "Olmec" symbolic system should be characterized as a network of Mesoamerican chiefdoms with multiple origin points for the symbolic elements involved (even if the heartland centers were the most precocious of these chiefdoms). Thus, the "Olmec" elements in lowland Maya art and culture may actually be traced back to a general and varied Middle Formative Mesoamerican symbolic system, rather than to any direct heartland contact or specific Olmec horizon.

TEOTIHUACAN AND THE EMERGENCE OF THE MAYA STATE

The next Mesoamerican horizon is, of course, the epoch in which the great Mexican urban center of Teotihuacan radiated influences throughout the Mesoamerican world. A long-standing question in Maya studies has been the degree to which contact with Teotihuacan was responsible for the rise of the Maya states. A decade ago, it was possible for archaeologists to suggest that both Kaminaljuyu and the Maya lowland polities were "secondary" state formations. Specific models proposed that the transition from the chiefdom level of social organization to the state was stimulated by the presence of Teotihuacan enclaves at Kaminaljuyu and Tikal and the subsequent influence from these two centers on developments elsewhere (Sanders and Price 1968; Cheek 1977a; Santley 1983; Sanders 1974; Price 1978).

These models of secondary state formation also proposed specific mechanisms of diffusion and dominance driven by Teotihuacan's commercial needs. Obsidian and cacao were the raw materials involved in Teotihuacan's presence in the Maya area (e.g., Santley 1983; Parsons 1969, 1978; Brown 1977a; Sanders and Michels 1977). Teotihuacan-style caches and the discovery of a grid-planned Early Classic center at Balberta supported analogies to Aztec conquest or commercial dominance of the chocolate coast (Hellmuth 1975, 1978; Pasztory 1978b). In the Maya highlands at Kaminaljuyu, talud-tablero structures and Teotihuacan-style artifacts were found in mounds A and B and in the Palangana architectural complex, while similar structures were found at Solano a bit further south (Kidder, Jennings, and Shook 1946; Sanders and Michels 1977; Cheek 1977a, 1977b; Brown 1977b). In the lowlands at Tikal, talud-tablero architecture and Teotihuacan-style artifacts appeared to be coeval with a historically identified dynastic crisis and realignment apparently involving foreigners from Teotihuacan or Kaminaljuyu (Coggins n.d, 1979; Jones 1977). By the end of the 1970s, it appeared that an overwhelming body of evidence proved Teotihuacan's role in stimulating a secondary state formation on the South Coast, in the Maya highlands, and in the Peten (Sanders and Michels 1977; Sanders 1974; Price 1978; Santley 1983).

The fundamental problem with all of these interpretations is that recent evidence from the Maya area indicates a chronological misalignment between this epoch of Teotihuacan influence and the burst of development that probably marks the transition to the state in the Maya lowlands. Excavations at Cerros (Freidel 1979, 1986b), Lamanai (Pendergast 1981), Edzna (Matheny et al. 1983), Nohmul (Hammond 1985; Hammond et al. 1987), the "Mundo Perdido" area of Tikal (Laporte n.d.a, n.d.b; Laporte and

Fialko 1987), and El Mirador (Matheny 1980, 1986; Dahlin 1984; Demarest 1984) have pushed back our datings for the rise of the Maya state to a period coeval with, if not earlier than Teotihuacan. The scale and complexity of monumental architecture and settlement at these sites indicate that by A.D. 0 they had achieved control over power and corporate labor greater than that of even most centers of the Late Classic Maya apogee.

For example, at El Mirador much of the residential occupation and monumental architecture appears to date from the first and second centuries B.C. to the second century A.D. The two largest ceremonial structures, the Tigre pyramid and Danta complex, were both built before A.D. 300. Furthermore, large, monumental architecture has recently been found at the site of Nakbe, dating to at least as early as 500–300 B.C. Late Formative monumental architecture at such other sites as Lamanai, Edzna, and the Mundo Perdido sector of Tikal were on the scale of Late Classic period architecture of a millenium later. The relatively short period in which some of these constructions were built indicates great control over corporate labor (Hansen n.d.; Freidel 1981; Matheny 1986). All of these impressive developments occurred in a period in which Teotihuacan was itself only a developing local center.

Of equal importance to the scale of construction and presumed control over labor is the complexity of specific features at Preclassic lowland Maya sites. Elizabeth Chambers has explored a wall and ditch at El Mirador of more than 1,600 m in length (Matheny 1980). Although its function remains uncertain due to its unusual positioning, it indicates, at the very least, complex social divisions within the city itself. A massive central acropolis at El Mirador demonstrates the existence of a specialized elite with early palace constructions (Matheny 1986). Excavations of domestic architecture have revealed a variety of plaza group forms and artifactual material suggesting differential wealth (Demarest et al. 1984). Meanwhile, neutron-activation and compositional studies have revealed patterns of regional and interregional trade in lithics, ash, and some ceramics (Bishop 1984; Fowler et al. 1989).

Such internal complexity was also apparent at other Preclassic centers. At Cerros (Robertson and Freidel 1986; Freidel 1979, 1986b) ceremonial constructions were found in a site also having a probable port facility, moat, complex elite residences, and raised fields. Matheny's excavations at Edzna (Matheny 1987) revealed not only complex public architecture, residences, and earthworks, but an elaborate water control system encompassing over 22 km of canals, moats, and artificial ponds. At Lamanai a massive Late Preclassic construction was found in addition to evidence of tremendous concentrations of wealth (Pendergast 1981), predating any contact with Teotihuacan (Pring 1977). At Nohmul, Norman Hammond has excavated what appears to be a Preclassic palace structure (Hammond et al. 1987). As Matheny (1987) has pointed out, these Preclassic Maya centers all fulfill the lists of criteria (internal stratification, nucleation of power, control over corporate labor, economic complexity, etc.) compiled by Henri Claessen, Peter Skalnik, and others to define archaic states (e.g., Claessen and Skalnik 1978; Claessen 1984).

Meanwhile, at Cerros (Freidel 1979, 1981, 1986b; Freidel and Schele 1988), Lamanai (Pendergast 1981), and El Mirador (Hansen n.d.), similar imagery in stucco plaster gives a more detailed view of elite symbol systems in the Late Preclassic period. In a recent study of the masks and architecture of the Preclassic sites, Freidel and Schele (1988) have identified most of the specific features and general themes characteristic of the dynastic ideology of the Classic Maya. This ideology legitimated the power of Maya kings in their role as mediators of a cosmogram involving both solar elements and ancestor worship. Evidently, this state ideology was fully in place before 100 B.C. Together with the preponderance of architectural and excavation evidence, the iconography demonstrates the existence of city-states centuries before Teotihuacan contact with the Maya lowlands.

But what of the better documented examples of Teotihuacan stimulated secondary state formation of the South Coast and at the highland center of Kaminaljuyu? At Kaminaljuyu, Teotihuacan contact and the establishment of a Mexican enclave was believed to be a critical stimulus for the formation of a secondary state (Sanders 1977; Price 1978; Santley 1983). Meanwhile, on the South Coast of Guatemala, analogies to later Aztec conquest of the coastal cacao sources were inspired by the discovery of caches of Teotihuacan-style vessels and artifacts (Hellmuth 1975; Berlo 1984; Shook 1965), and the discovery of a gridded, possibly fortified, center at Balberta (Bove n.d.a).

However, as in the lowlands, new evidence in the past few years has contradicted the "secondary state formation" models with the same simple, but irrefutable fact: state formation seems to *predate* Teotihuacan contact. For both the coast and highlands the process of cultural evolution, now far better understood, appears to be primarily driven by local ecological adaptations combined with regional trade patterns. New evidence on these regions includes Bove's (n.d.a, n.d.b) settlement studies in Escuintla and the continuing excavations at Kaminaljuyu (Hatch 1987b, personal communications, 1984–88).

The projects at Kaminaljuyu have demonstrated that the Late Preclassic center was far larger, economically more diverse, and organizationally more complex than previously believed. Hatch has discovered a large irrigation system in one area of the center and an extensive specialized food-processing area, where cacao imported from the South Coast was probably prepared. Furthermore, the Late Preclassic at Kaminaljuyu is a period of intense interaction with the South Coast as identified in ceramic ties and trade (Hatch 1987b, personal communications, 1984–88). It now seems probable that the process of state formation at this site/center involved a combination of local agricultural intensification together with regional trade in cacao and obsidian. Highland-to-coast trade, rather than long-distance exchange, appears most critical in this process. These developments appear to predate identified Teotihuacan contacts.

The recent excavations at Balberta on the Central South Coast of Guatemala (Bove n.d.a., 1989) set out to document the nature of the transition from the Terminal Formative to the Early Classic on the Pacific Coast. A radical shift in Escuintla regional settlement patterns and a nucleation of population was demonstrated to be contemporary with the construction of massive architecture at the major regional center of Balberta (Bove n.d.a). However, the radical transformation of Balberta is now known to have been carried out by local populations using an evolved version of the coastal ceramic tradition (Medrano n.d.b) and local burial practices (Arroyo 1990). Frederick Bove (1989: 13) has recently summarized this new evidence on coastal evolution, and rejected Teotihuacan domination over this process:

> I have rejected this model and now believe that almost all the changes are due to local evolutionary processes. The indigenous cultures probably incorporated Teotihuacan imagery from the relatively few Teotihuacan merchants (pochteca type agents) entering the region during the transitional phase. I now believe that, similar to the situation at Tikal, the Teotihuacan-Mexican symbols were borrowed/introduced over a period of time and incorporated differently into the local societies.

Thus, the most recent evidence has shown that by the fourth to fifth centuries, when significant Teotihuacan influence appears, the state was probably in place in the Maya lowlands, in the southern highlands, and on the Pacific Coast. Local ecological processes alone do not explain the emergence of these states since exchange systems probably played a major role. However, these primarily involved regional, not long-distance, trade.

Still, the later Teotihuacan contacts are certainly well documented and may have been critical to aspects of later Classic Maya culture. This observation shifts our focus to the precise nature of the proposed "Middle Classic Horizon."

TEOTIHUACAN INFLUENCE IN THE MAYA AREA: A REEVALUATION OF THE "MIDDLE HORIZON"

In the past two decades, Teotihuacan-Maya contact has been much discussed, and a number of specific models have been presented to explain this "Middle Horizon" interaction (Pasztory 1978c; Miller 1978; Sanders and Michels 1977; Santley 1983). In the Maya lowlands, Clemency Coggins, Christopher Jones, and others have documented the fourth- and fifth-century dynastic history at Tikal and have correlated it with new features of architecture, burial practices, iconography, and even calendrics (Coggins n.d., 1979, 1980; Jones and Satterthwaite 1982; W. Coe 1965, 1967). Coggins has suggested that Mexican elites introduced the celebration of *katuns* to the lowlands, emphasizing quadripartition and the Teotihuacan rain deity, Tlaloc (Coggins 1980). All of these shifts were seen to be related to a Kaminaljuyu-mediated Teotihuacan contact at Tikal, a political and economic connection that was believed to explain Tikal's rise to Classic period preeminence in the Peten.

Based principally on grave goods and the iconography of Stela 31 and Stela 4, Coggins proposed that the fourth-century Tikal ruler, Curl-Snout, was a foreigner—probably of Teotihuacan descent from Kaminaljuyu (Coggins n.d., 1979). According to this reconstruction, the reign of Curl-Snout and of his successor, the great Stormy Sky, saw the introduction of highland ritual practices to Tikal and Uaxactun. The proposed events at Tikal seemed to align with other evidence of Teotihuacan contact at Becan, Altun Ha, Dzibilchaltun, Rio Azul, and elsewhere. It has also been proposed that Tikal and Kaminaljuyu were nodes in Teotihuacan's monopolistic obsidian control system (Santley 1983). Thus, in the Middle Classic period, it has seemed that at least one pan-Mesoamerican horizon penetrated the Maya world and had a transforming effect—even if archaic states had already taken form there earlier. What was most intriguing about these interpretations was that specific contacts and interactions had been identified, moving beyond vague notions of "diffusion" or "influence" previously inherent in the horizon concept.

More recent studies, however, have begun to reassess this Middle Classic horizon in the lowlands, raising questions about many of the previously proposed scenarios for Teotihuacan-Maya contact. Four sources of data have been used to demonstrate Teotihuacan influence in the Maya area: Teotihuacanoid ceramics, Pachuca green obsidian, Teotihuacan architecture, and Teotihuacan iconography. A closer look at the current evidence in each of these categories should allow us to judge the alternative reconstructions of Teotihuacan influence in the Maya region.

Teotihuacan Ceramics

Cylindrical tripods, *candeleros,* copa-shaped vases or cream pitchers, *floreros, incensarios,* Thin Orange ceramics, and Teotihuacanoid figurines have all been mentioned as proof of either the presence of Teotihuacan enclaves or of strong trade relationships with Teotihuacan (Fig. 2). At the outset, it is worth noting that the designation of these ceramics as Teotihuacan markers is not beyond dispute. Evelyn Rattray (1977, personal communication, 1986) has questioned whether the cylindrical tripod represents a local Teotihuacan development or an adoption of a Gulf Coast shape. It has also been suggested that the few Miraflores tripods found at Kaminaljuyu

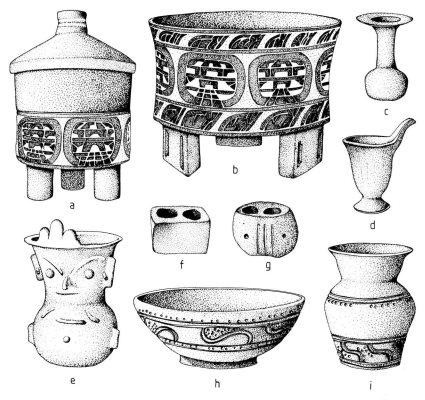

Fig. 2. Teotihuacan diagnostics (examples from Early Classic burials at Teotihuacan): (a–b) cylindrical tripods; (c) *florero;* (d) cream pitcher; (e) jar with face of Tlaloc; (f–g) *candeleros;* (h–i) Thin Orange ware (drawn after M. D. Coe 1982: fig. 69)

may indicate that there the Early Classic and Middle Classic cylindrical tripod is a local variant, rather than an import from Teotihuacan (Foias n.d.). It also appears that the *candeleros* found at some sites like Copan may be distinct from Teotihuacan influence. At Copan, *candeleros* were present in all periods of the site's occupation and appear to represent a local evolution of this artifactual type (Willey et al. n.d.).

Putting aside these doubts for a moment, we can review the specific relevant ceramic evidence at a number of important Maya sites. Kaminaljuyu has been identified as a Teotihuacan colony or a site with a Teotihuacan enclave. This interpretation relies especially on the rich burials in Mounds A and B containing numerous Teotihuacanoid ceramics (Kidder, Jennings, Shook 1946; Cheek 1977a, 1977b; Santley 1983; Sanders 1974, 1977). A recent direct examination of these ceramics (Foias n.d.) has shown that of all the ceramics found in the burials of Mounds A and B, only sixteen Thin

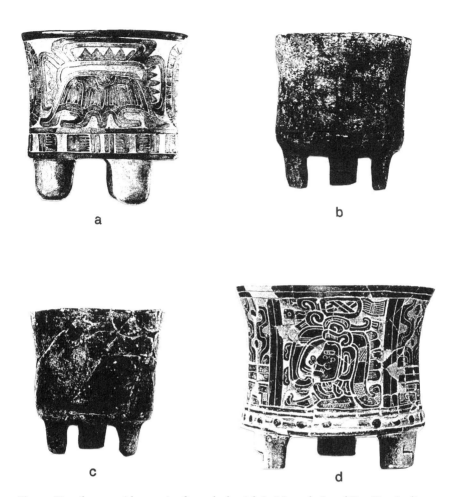

a

b

c

d

Fig. 3. Teotihuacanoid ceramics from the burials in Mounds A and B at Kaminaljuyu, Guatemala (after Kidder, Jennings, and Shook 1946: figs. 174c, 179e, 179g, 178c)

Orange vessels can be identified as Central Mexican imports, while the shape and decoration of only eight of the sixty-seven cylindrical tripods found suggests Central Mexican provenience (Fig. 3a). The other Teotihuacanoid ceramics were probably local copies given differences in shape and decoration (Fig. 3b–d). Furthermore, the Teotihuacanoid ceramics appear only in a very limited context: burials in Mounds A and B and the Palangana (Kidder, Jennings, and Shook 1946; Cheek 1977a). Very few Teotihuacanoid ceramics have been reported by the Pennsylvania State Project from other contexts (Wetherington 1978: 133; Sanders 1977: 401).

The present evidence suggests that these ceramics represent contact between the elites of Kaminaljuyu and Teotihuacan. Furthermore, it should be emphasized that these burials contain not only Teotihuacanoid ceramics, but also lowland Maya Tzakol vessels as well as Gulf Coast ceramics (Kidder, Jennings, and Shook 1946). Thus, Kaminaljuyu had contact with the lowland Maya and the Gulf Coast as well as with Teotihuacan. These ceramics appear to be in the burials of Kaminaljuyu lords who were drawing on exotic symbols of status reinforcement from foreign regions. It would be expected that Teotihuacan materials would be well-represented in such an assemblage. But the relative infrequency of true Central Mexican imports and the local mortuary style indicate that the buried elites were probably local lords involved in status-reinforcing contacts with both Teotihuacan and other regions. It does *not* necessarily follow from this that these contacts reflect any intense economic connection or control from Teotihuacan.

Meanwhile, in the lowlands, Juan Pedro Laporte has identified in the Mundo Perdido complex of Tikal an early presence of some ceramic features usually associated with Middle Classic highland contact. These include some types of slab tripod feet and cylinder vases (Laporte n.d.b; Laporte and Fialko 1987). Laporte's dating of these vessels predates the proposed late fourth-century Teotihuacan dynastic intrusion. He suggests that some Tikal slab tripods evolved locally, perhaps drawing on stylistic canons common not only at Teotihuacan but throughout the peripheral coastal lowlands (i.e., Veracruz, Tabasco, and the Pacific Coast; cf. Parsons 1978). Furthermore, Teotihuacanoid ceramics were found only in ritual contexts and special deposits (Laporte n.d.a, n.d.b; Laporte and Fialko 1987: 157). This evidence indicates a more complex and less chronologically focused Mexican "influence" at Tikal.

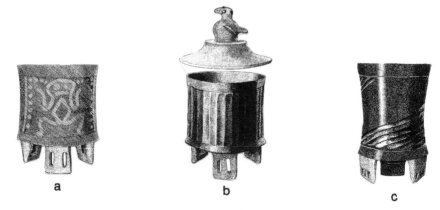

Fig. 4. Three examples of cylindrical tripods from Uaxactun, Guatemala (after R. E. Smith 1955: figs. 5f, 6l, 6p)

Teotihuacanoid ceramics appear with rarity at other Maya lowland sites. At Uaxactun, the Teotihuacanoid ceramics consist of forty-nine complete or partial cylindrical tripods, one *candelero* similar to one found at Monte Alban, ten copa-shaped vases, and seven Thin Orange fragments (R. Smith 1955). The design and form of cylindrical tripods suggest that they were all made in the Maya lowlands (Fig. 4). It is intriguing to note that certain Teotihuacanoid features in the Uaxactun ceramic data do not appear at Kaminaljuyu. Differences include the fairly common use on tripods of negative painting, fluting, and openwork slab feet at both Uaxactun and Teotihuacan, features that are rare at Kaminaljuyu (R. Smith 1955) (Fig. 4). Thus, if Mexican influence is indicated in Uaxactun's locally made, Maya-style slab-tripods, and other "Teotihuacanoid" vessels, it is probably derived from a source other than, or in addition to, Kaminaljuyu.

At Rio Azul, the discovery of two Early Classic tombs with Teotihuacanoid ceramics has led R. E. W. Adams (1986: 439) to suggest that "the men in Tombs 19 and 23 were important nobles from central Mexico attached to Ruler X and thus buried near him." But again, the cylindrical tripods in these tombs (Adams 1986) are in the Maya lowland style. Nineteen other cylindrical tripods were undecorated, and another has polychrome painting and Tajin-style scrolls. The murals of all the tombs are purely lowland Maya in style, and the burials beneath temples are in typical Maya fashion. It seems more probable, then, that the buried Rio Azul dignitaries were local Maya lowland elites.

There are a few ceramically documented cases of probable direct contact with Teotihuacan. The famous cache at Becan is one such example and is the

Fig. 5. An example of an Escuintla *incensario* showing the martial butterfly iconography (drawn after Berlo 1989: fig. 8.2)

only excavated and well-provenienced find of Teotihuacan figurines in the Maya area (Ball 1974). The cache was probably a commemorative one, placed in a structure "of crude talud-tablero form" (Ball 1974: 3). It consists of a large Teotihuacan-style hollow figurine within which were ten smaller solid ceramic figurines of deities and warriors, all of which were placed in a low cylindrical tripod decorated, though, with typical Maya iconography. This cache may represent an as yet still enigmatic case of direct Central Mexican contact.

Another set of materials often cited as evidence of direct Teotihuacan contact are the so-called "Escuintla Hoards" studied by Nicholas Hellmuth (1975, 1978) and Janet Berlo (1983, 1984, 1989). Berlo has hypothesized the existence of a Teotihuacano merchant-warrior presence on the South Coast of Guatemala in the Escuintla region. Her conclusions are based on detailed stylistic and iconographic studies of forty-two Escuintla *incensarios* (Fig. 5). The forty-two censers show a whole range of Teotihuacan influence, from *incensarios* closely resembling Teotihuacan examples, to some showing a combination of local constructs with Teotihuacan imagery, to others using local iconography with Veracruz-derived traits (Berlo 1984). Berlo believes that in Escuintla the censer cult became the focus for group ritual of a Teotihuacano "warrior/trader" community (Berlo 1983). Still, we should recall that these *incensarios* were locally made and have not yet been associated with any ceramic assemblage (intrusive or local).

A great number of cylindrical tripods were also part of the Escuintla hoards (Hellmuth 1975, 1978). In contrast to the Escuintla *incensarios,* these tripods do not show "pure" Teotihuacan characteristics. Rather, Berlo believes that the tripods are of poor workmanship, which may indicate that local potters had a lack of familiarity with the foreign iconography (Berlo 1989: 157). The Escuintla tripods differ from the Teotihuacan counterparts in many vessel form features (Hellmuth 1975: pls. 3, 6, 8, 9, 13, 16, 20c), as well as in their intermixture of Teotihuacan, Maya, and Gulf Coast iconography (Berlo 1984, 1989; Hellmuth 1978). Nevertheless, Berlo (1989) argues that, in spite of these differences, the Escuintla cylindrical tripods are more similar to Teotihuacan prototypes than are the "Teotihuacanoid" ceramics of Kaminaljuyu.

Critical evaluation of the Escuintla hoards is difficult because very few have been found in archaeological contexts. Edwin Shook's small excavations at Rio Seco and at Finca Toliman have produced the only sourced Teotihuacan material from the South Coast of Guatemala (Shook 1965). *Incensario* bases and cylindrical tripods were uncovered by Shook at these two sites. Their archaeological context in burials indicates the ritual significance of these Teotihuacan-related ceramics.

Another case of intensive contact between Teotihuacan and the Maya region is seen by Stephen Borhegyi (1965, 1972), Janet Berlo (1984), and Guillermo Mata Amado and Rolando R. Rubio C. (1987), in the *incensarios* found in Lake Amatitlan. More than 200 hourglass *incensario* bases were brought up from the lake bottom by Mata. All are near lakeshore Middle Classic sites. Berlo's stylistic study of the Amatitlan *incensarios* sees them as of local Maya style, Teotihuacanoid style, and in combinations of the two styles. An interesting Teotihuacanoid *incensario* from the Lavaderos offertory site in Lake Amatitlan consists of a standing human figure on top of a talud-tablero censer decorated with Teotihuacan symbols, such as shells, Reptile Eye glyphs, birds, and so forth (Mata and Rubio 1987; Berlo 1984: 149–150). But some features of this *incensario* type are more similar to Kaminaljuyu ones than to Teotihuacan ones: the talud-tablero featured on the censers has the 1:1 ratio found at Kaminaljuyu, and three moldings around each talud or tablero as found on Kaminaljuyu Structure D-III-1 (Mata and Rubio 1987: 200–201). Convincing interpretations of the lake ceramic offerings, like the Escuintla censers, is impeded by the lack of any clear association with complete non-ritual assemblages and settlement contexts. Berlo interprets the Amatitlan site as a pilgrimage center visited both by local Maya and Teotihuacanos from coastal enclaves. Yet these coastal enclaves, if they exist, have not yet been found.

The past ten years of settlement studies and excavations in Escuintla by Frederick Bove (1989, n.d.a) provide a more complete context in which to interpret this material. According to Bove, most of these hoards were locally made and indicate local, but Mexican-influenced, elite rituals rather than the existence of enclaves or Teotihuacanoid centers on the southern coast. He believes that the most probable explanation of this material is "that, similar to the situation at Tikal, the Teotihuacan-Mexican symbols were borrowed or introduced over a period of time and incorporated differently into societies" (1989: 10).

We would suggest that the Escuintla hoards and the Amatitlan censers may be explained by the introduction of rituals or cults during elite contacts, as suggested by iconographic studies by Berlo (1983), Schele (n.d.), and Taube (n.d.) (to be discussed below). Indeed, the present evidence of specialized isolated deposits tends to support the suggestion that it was primarily ideas, *not* populations, that were moving between Central Mexico, Veracruz, and these southeastern regions.

This brief review of some of the ceramic evidence for Teotihuacan contact with the Maya civilization indicates that Teotihuacanoid ceramics are found in small frequencies and in a very narrow range of contexts (ritual or mortuary). Joseph Ball's review of the ceramic interchange between the Maya and Teotihuacan arrives at the same conclusion: ceramic identities (such as Thin Orange pottery and the Becan cache) indicate the existence of exchanges, gift-presentations, or other practices in which ceramic vessels produced in, and symbolic of, one region were transported to another for purposes of establishing, affirming, or otherwise signifying real or fictive political, social, or kinship ties. (Ball 1983: 127)

Ceramic homologues, including all locally made Teotihuacanoid ceramics, were commissioned by the elites as status-reinforcing markers of their participation in a larger information sphere.

Ball's review also shows that there was a two-way relationship between the Maya civilization and Teotihuacan. Maya ceramics are found in abundance at Teotihuacan in the Merchant's Barrio together with a high concentration of Veracruz ceramics. Among the 500 Maya sherds from the Merchant's Barrio examined by Ball, most forms were typical of the southeastern through northwestern Maya lowland coastal zone, and most paste variants were similar to those of northwestern Campeche and northern Belize (Ball 1983: 137). It is interesting that this important ceramic connection is with neither Kaminaljuyu nor Tikal, underscoring the complexity of Middle Classic relations.

Overall, the ceramic evidence supports an interpretation of inter-elite exchange of status-reinforcing goods. The number of true Mexican imports is small and is consistently associated with elite rural contexts. These imports are always found in association with other Maya ceramics and artifacts and are usually in association with Maya architecture and burial patterns.

Additionally, many of the cylindrical tripods with slab feet and other locally made Teotihuacanoid vessels are just as likely to represent influence from Veracruz or the isthmian area (Laporte n.d.a, n.d.b; Laporte and Fialko 1987). The quantity, context, nature, and dating of the ceramics are all consistent with an interpretation of ongoing inter-elite exchanges of status-reinforcing ceramic gifts throughout the Early and "Middle" Classic periods. The elite interaction implied is one of an ongoing awareness, exchange, and mutual status reinforcement by the elites of both areas. Naturally, this interaction is more intense at the period of Teotihuacan's Middle Classic florescence as seen in fourth- to fifth-century Tikal and Kaminaljuyu. But at no site yet identified can we argue for the movement of Mexican populations or for Teotihuacan political or economic dominance.

Green Obsidian

Obsidian is one of the most traceable exchange materials. Robert Santley (1983) has suggested that Teotihuacan established an enclave at Kaminaljuyu so as to control obsidian distribution in the Maya area. Such trade is also considered to be indicative of exchange in other commodities (e.g., cacao) and so, of a more intense Teotihuacan economic or political interaction. Yet, even the degree to which the clearly Mexican green obsidian specifically indicates exchange or contact with Teotihuacan is debatable. Green obsidian was common at many centers in Mexico, Puebla, Tlaxcala, and Morelos during the Early and Middle Classic (Spence 1977). It is possible that the green obsidian seen at the Maya sites arrived through one or more intermediaries.

There are even greater problems with theories of a general Teotihuacan monopoly over obsidian (Santley 1983). The important obsidian source of Ixtepeque in the southern highlands, not included in Santley's study, has never been associated with Teotihuacan influence or control (Sharer 1983). Furthermore, Robert Zeitlin's (1982) obsidian study of the southern isthmus of Tehuantepec plots yet another Middle Classic obsidian interaction sphere unrelated to Teotihuacan or to the El Chayal sources. In the Classic period in this Tehuantepec region, most obsidian was from western and northern sources, probably controlled by Veracruz centers (Zeitlin 1982).

The most thorough critique of interpretations of the Middle Horizon as a Teotihuacan mercantile empire has been provided by John Clark's (1986) reanalysis of the obsidian workshops at Teotihuacan. Clark argues that many of the high concentrations of obsidian artifacts identified as workshops in Teotihuacan itself could be general refuse redeposited in middens by an organized "city trash service" (1986: 31). He also calculates that all of "the specialized obsidian tools used at Teotihuacan throughout its history could have easily been produced by fewer than 10 full-time specialists or 20 part-time specialists" (cf. Santley 1984: 41). Although these positions are still controversial, we would agree that there was far less obsidian trade with eastern Mesoamerica than generally imagined:

> All the Middle Horizon green Pachuca obsidian found outside the central Mexican plateau would only fill a couple of shoe boxes. . . . Apart from the prismatic blades, most items were of a symbolic-ceremonial character (i.e., bifaces, needles, sequins, figurines), as is apparent in the special contexts in which they are found and what they are found with. (Clark 1986: 64)

In the Maya area itself, we find that green obsidian appears in small quantities at many Maya sites: Altun Ha, Holmul, Becan, Dzibilchaltun, Palenque, Tikal, Uaxactun, and Yaxha. In the highland and coastal regions, it appears at Solano, Kaminaljuyu, and Balberta (Santley 1983; Bove n.d.a). Michael Spence (1977) examines the green obsidian found in the Maya area, concluding that, with the exception of Tikal, green obsidian has been found only in special caches and burials. At Kaminaljuyu, all green obsidian was found in burials from Mounds A and B of the Esperanza phase by Kidder, Jennings, and Shook (1946).

At Altun Ha and Holmul, Teotihuacan green obsidian caches have been dated to the beginning of the Early Classic period (A.D. 150–200) (Pring 1977; Merwin and Valliant 1932), nearly two centuries before the beginning of the Middle Classic, the period believed to represent contact with Teotihuacan (Parsons 1969). This chronological misalignment indicates that the concept of a chronologically focused "horizon" cannot be applied to the Maya interaction with Central Mexico.

Two cases merit special discussion: Tikal and Balberta. As remarked previously, at both of these sites, green obsidian is found in domestic refuse as well as in ritual burials and caches. Nevertheless, the size of the sample is still small: only 550 green fragments, representing 1% of the total obsidian, were reported from Tikal (Moholy-Nagy 1979; Moholy-Nagy, Asaro, and Stross 1984), while at Balberta, 123 examples were found, representing 2.7% of the total obsidian, and 65% were found with the cacao effigy offerings in the central platform, an elite context (Bove n.d.c).

It is clear that more careful attention should be given to depositional contexts at Teotihuacan, as well as its presumed "consumer" sites (Clark 1986). The diversity of alternative sources, the variability in dating, and the primarily ritual contexts, again indicate more varied and diffuse contacts in the exchange of Central Mexican obsidian. Rather than a Teotihuacan-dominated obsidian monopoly or cartel, the evidence is more reasonably interpreted as reflecting sporadic formal elite contacts, as well as indirect trade with Central Mexican sites. Green obsidian is even less focused in time than the ceramics, since green obsidian is found from the second century on. Trade monopoly models are inapplicable to this small green obsidian sample, and they seem equally inappropriate for modeling Maya-controlled southern highland obsidian sources.

Teotihuacan Architecture

The presence of talud-tablero construction at several Maya sites has been seen as evidence of strong Teotihuacan-Maya relations, or even of residence there by Teotihuacanos (Cheek 1977b; Sanders and Price 1968; Santley 1983, n.d.). Review of published evidence shows scattered and limited examples of talud-tablero architecture in the Maya area. The facade form is found at Kaminaljuyu, Solano, Tikal, Dzibilchaltun, and Tazumal (Brown 1977b; Coggins n.d.; Laporte n.d.a; Andrews 1981; Sharer 1978) (Fig. 6).

Robert Santley (n.d.) has reviewed the inter-site variability in the talud-tableros at several sites. He suggests that the ratio of talud to tablero height is a particularly sensitive and significant marker. Santley observes that the height of taluds relative to tableros is about 1.00 at Kaminaljuyu and Matacapan. Teotihuacan has a much higher ratio of 1.62 to 2.50 (n.d.). Dzibilchaltun and Solano have ratios closer to that of Teotihuacan (Sanders and Santley 1983). Santley interprets this data to indicate that Kaminaljuyu and Matacapan are indeed enclaves of Teotihuacan of a specific type. The

A

0   1 m.

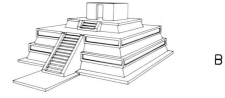

Fig. 6. Talud-tablero architecture from: (a) Teotihuacan and (b) Kaminaljuyu (drawn after Kidder, Jennings, and Shook 1946: figs. 11, 108)

B

variability in talud-tablero ratios is subject to another interpretation: the close tablero-talud ratio between Matacapan and Kaminaljuyu again suggests that the Teotihuacan influence at Kaminaljuyu and other Maya sites may have been transmitted through Gulf Coast centers (Laporte n.d.a; Santley 1983, n.d.).

Tikal has a number of talud-tablero structures such as Structure 5D-43, and several temples in the Mundo Perdido complex. But, Esther Pasztory (1978a: 109) has reinterpreted the architecture of Structure 5D-43 as of Gulf Coast derivation. In a more recent study, Laporte (n.d.a) examines the Early Classic sequence of talud-tablero facades on the Mundo Perdido pyramids 49 and 54, and on the Group 6-C palace. A variety of different forms of talud-tablero were found to date prior to the proposed Middle Classic dynastic intrusion. The talud-tablero and other features were found in the context of fully Maya Early Classic elite culture. They were elements in what Laporte believes was "a more continuous and more equivalent relationship between Teotihuacan and the Maya region" (n.d.a: 32–33). He contends that the talud-tablero seen in the Maya area may be characteristic of areas intermediate between the Valley of Mexico and Tikal, diffusing in an irregular manner across Mesoamerica in the Early Classic (n.d.a: 32–34). This interpretation would account for the early date and varied forms of talud-tablero at Tikal, as well as such variability at other sites.

Talud-tablero architecture at Kaminaljuyu has been found in Mounds A and B (Kidder, Jennings, and Shook 1946) (Fig. 6b), and in the Palangana (Cheek 1977a, 1977b). The similarities between the architectural style found at Teotihuacan and at this site are clear, and indicate close contact between the two cultures, but the Teotihuacan architectural style present at Kaminaljuyu involves several variations. Construction techniques used at Teotihuacan, such as the honeycomb pattern of the matrix and "the use of vertical tree trunks to redistribute the weight and transmit the stress forces directly to the ground," are not used at Kaminaljuyu (Cheek 1977a: 132). Kaminaljuyu's talud-tablero temples have a frontal platform or apron not found at Teotihuacan (Kidder, Jennings, and Shook 1946: 44; Cheek 1977a: 133–134). One Kaminaljuyu construction, Structure E-1, is similar to the *adoratorios* from the apartment compounds at Teotihuacan, but the building techniques are different. According to Charles Cheek, this "suggests again that the builders knew what the Teotihuacan building looked like, but did not know how it was built" (1977a: 134). Another structure, D-III-1, is characterized by tableros and taluds enclosed by moldings on only three sides instead of the four moldings typical of Teotihuacan (Rivera and Schávelzon 1984: 51–56). The temporal alignment of the appearance of talud-tablero architecture has also been overstated. In fact, it now appears that Tikal's stylistically distinctive talud-tableros may appear earlier than the more Teotihuacanoid examples at Kaminaljuyu (Laporte n.d.a, n.d.b).

In general, Central Mexican or Veracruz influences in architecture are more subtle and complex than previously believed. Probable processes include intermittent highland–lowland alliances, exchanges, pilgrimages, dynastic marriages, or other inter-elite contacts. The talud-tablero architectural style may have been integrated within local cultures as a result of interaction with Teotihuacan or with Veracruz, but apparently not within the context of a military takeover, military-merchant colony, or other movements of population (and architects). In some cases, talud-tablero facades may have been adopted for local political purposes from a corpus of elements widespread throughout Mesoamerica by the second century A.D.—a corpus not always traceable to Teotihuacan itself.

Teotihuacan Iconography

Recent interpretations of Maya iconography and epigraphy provide one of the most exciting new sources of information on Teotihuacan-Maya contact and the proposed Middle Horizon. Previous interpretations of Mexican motifs and representations in the Maya area were developed with only minimal information from epigraphy. A series of breakthroughs in phonetic hieroglyphic decipherment and historical interpretation have led to a great increase in the number of fully readable Maya texts. As a result, the iconography associated with these texts has been subject to recent reinterpretation, including those elements indicative of Mexican influence.

Several separate lines of iconographic evidence now seem to point to a very specific type of connection between these two Mesoamerican regions. Linda Schele (n.d.) has reinterpreted the iconography and inscriptions of Tikal's Stela 4 and Stela 31, Burials 10 and 40, Stela 5 at Uaxactun, and related materials. She identifies representations in many Maya stelae of Tlaloc, Mexican year signs, owl pectorals, spear-thrower darts, and Teotihuacan-style bags, as a specific complex of traits associated with ritualized warfare, often culminating in blood-letting and human sacrifice. Citing dozens of examples in the Early and Late Classic, Schele (n.d.) argues that the imagery, usually identified as Teotihuacan iconography, marks astrologically sanctioned Maya rituals of sacrifice often associated with Venus.

Among Schele's conclusions concerning the Early Classic iconography of Tikal is that the pose, texts, personal name, and presentation of Curl-Snout are consistent with lowland Maya stylistic canons, not only as seen in the Classic period, but as proposed by Freidel and Schele (1988) for the Late Preclassic period. Thus, she believes that the ruler, Curl-Snout, must have been a lowlander. Furthermore, most of the presumed Mexican or Kaminaljuyu elements seen in the inscriptions of Curl-Snout and his successor Stormy Sky can be explained in terms of the sacrificial rituals which those monuments celebrate, rather than by reference to outside influences. Schele does, however, argue for a Teotihuacan origin for the elements of the imagery of this sacrificial complex. These are seen in terms of a very Early Classic absorption of highland traits by the eclectic lowland Maya, rather than in terms of Middle Classic political or economic events (Schele n.d.).

Two other recent studies of the Teotihuacan iconography found on Maya ceramics and monuments have suggested that warrior cults originating at Teotihuacan may have spread to the Maya civilization (Berlo 1983, 1989; Taube n.d.). Berlo's studies discussed above also examined the iconographic content of the Teotihuacan *incensarios* found in the Escuintla region, at Lake Amatitlan, and in the Maya lowlands. She suggests that a great deal of the Teotihuacan imagery centers upon a martial butterfly deity—the iconography of which features the depiction of warriors carrying shields, spears, scapers, and other symbols associated with Teotihuacan warriors (see Fig. 5). According to Berlo, this great concern for martial iconography in Teotihuacan-related ceramics in Escuintla would have served the needs of a foreign military-merchant enclave on the southern coast of Guatemala (1984, 1989).

Although the iconography of the Lake Amatitlan *incensarios* includes this militaristic imagery, there is an even stronger component of rain god iconog-

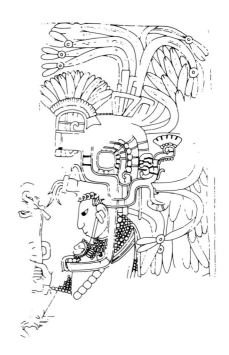

Fig. 7. An example of a Classic Maya figure with iconography associated with the War Serpent (drawn after Taube n.d.: fig. 6d)

raphy. This emphasis on rain gods is a new syncretism that draws from both Maya and Teotihuacan cultures (Berlo 1984: 202). Not surprisingly the *incensarios* found at Tikal show even less Teotihuacan influence; Berlo (1984: 210) calls them "a Maya interpretation of a foreign ceramics type." She suggests that in areas "where Teotihuacanos met sophisticated cultures on an equal footing, Teotihuacan artistic and cultural influence is absorbed into already living traditions" (Berlo 1984: 215).

The second study, by Karl Taube (n.d.), reinterprets some of this imagery as representing a War Serpent deity from Teotihuacan's Temple of Quetzal-coatl borrowed by the lowland Classic Maya. The rectangular Tlaloc image alternating with naturalistic depictions of Quetzalcoatl seen on the Temple of Quetzalcoatl has been identified by Taube as a solar fire-serpent deity complex ancestral to Xiuhcoatl of Aztec mythology and religion. This solar fire serpent deity, like its successor Xiuhcoatl, is associated with warfare (Taube n.d.: 38). Evidence for this cult of the War Serpent in the lowland Maya region comes from warrior costume features in many monuments, such as the platelet War Serpent headdress (Figs. 7 and 8), shell collars, protective goggles, trapeze-and-ray symbols, mirrors, as well as the so-called Jaguar Butterfly deity (Figs. 5 and 7). According to Taube, the War Serpent is directly identified with Maya rulership, especially "with one particular aspect of rulership, that of paramount war leader" (Taube n.d.: 39). He concludes

Fig. 8. Lintel 2 of Temple 1 at Tikal, Guatemala (drawing by William R. Coe [after Jones and Satterthwaite 1982: fig. 69])

that "the Teotihuacan sphere of influence may have included a solar war cult carried by proselytizing emissaries and warriors" (Taube n.d.: 40). Taube also identifies a representation on Lintel 2 of Temple 1 at Tikal of a specific Teotihuacan-Maya contact: Tikal's Ruler A sitting on the "Old Temple," alias Temple of Quetzalcoatl of Teotihuacan (n.d.: 18–26) (Fig. 8).

Taube's study has revised and refined Schele's (n.d.) and Berlo's earlier discussions of Maya cults of warfare. The Tlaloc imagery associated with ritual warfare now appears to be stylized references to the Teotihuacan Fire Serpent deity, although some conscious overlap or confounding of these deities is also probable. More importantly, Taube's interpretation of the Tikal Lintel 2 indicates that Maya lords were directly aware of the meaning of the Teotihuacan cult, and they attributed considerable importance to their Teotihuacan ties.

On the other hand, the nature of this Teotihuacan-Maya contact as described is still restricted and consistent with previous iconographic studies as well as other categories of evidence: the Tikal lintel and other Teotihuacanoid iconography is associated with rituals of warfare, specifically what Linda Schele and Mary Ellen Miller (1986) have referred to as "Venus wars." In fact, all of the iconographic studies have found that Teotihuacan iconography was related to cults of warfare. In each case, such imagery seems to be consistent with the new evidence of militaristic ritual and imagery at Teotihuacan itself (Sugiyama 1989; Cowgill n.d.).

In terms of the "horizon" concept, an additional problem is that the iconography dates from the beginning of the Classic period to its end—from at least the second to the ninth centuries (Schele n.d.; Schele and Miller 1986). The use of such iconography seems to depend on regional and historical factors within this 700-year period. For example, it is most common in the Usumacinta and Pasion regions at the very end of the Classic period when an accelerating pattern of warfare led to an emphasis in monumental art on this type of imagery (Schele and Miller 1986; Mathews and Willey n.d.; Houston n.d.; Demarest and Houston n.d.). Clearly, a "horizon" designation for this class of iconography would be misleading.

Teotihuacan Influence in the Maya Area: A General Assessment and Interpretation

The preceding review of the evidence in ceramics, lithics, architecture, and iconography confirms that Teotihuacan influence is present and scattered throughout the Maya area in the Classic period. Yet Maya materials in Teotihuacanoid or even Mexican style are very rare when reviewed systematically within the context of the full sample of lowland evidence. In any given site or period, such as the vaguely defined "Middle Classic," no component has yet been identified with a large quantity of Teotihuacan material or a large corpus of truly Mexican imagery. Furthermore, there is a broad chronological range to the Mexican elements in the Maya lowlands from the second to the ninth centuries.

It is this lack of chronological alignment that is most disturbing about our appraisal of the Teotihuacan evidence. Without such an alignment, what meaning does the "horizon" concept have? What is its utility in interpretation? Past specific historical scenarios for Middle Classic Teotihuacan-Maya contact were built upon the assumption of some degree of chronological contemporaneity for the many observed Mexican elements in the lowlands. Such an assumption seems to be only rarely justified.

Looking at all categories of evidence simultaneously, we see that even the three previously most convincing examples of Teotihuacan contact—"Middle Classic" Tikal, Kaminaljuyu, and Escuintla—were each different in nature and chronology. The proposed Teotihuacan enclave at Kaminaljuyu is subject to a variety of interpretations. Given the ceramic and architectural evidence it seems most probable that the Palangana and Mound A and B areas represent the use of Mexican symbology and exotics to reinforce the prestige of one segment of the ruling elite. Long-distance contacts were involved, but they are just as likely to have been with Matacapan or some other intermediary center as with Teotihuacan. The general nature of such contacts was probably that of long-distance trade, perhaps with elite intermarriage. The most recent evidence from Tikal also reveals that early contacts probably involved Gulf Coast centers and other Mexican regions as well as Teotihuacan. Again, it is likely that a Tikal elite lineage received these influences as an element in the enhancement of their local prestige.

On the Pacific Coast, new excavations in Escuintla have shown that much of the Mexican influence there begins even earlier in the third century and, in fact, more often represents contact with Veracruz than with Teotihuacan (Bove n.d.c). Still, it remains possible that a Mexican or a Veracruz enclave of some kind will be discovered on the South Coast.

How then are we to model Teotihuacan-Maya contact? What do we make of these disparate Mexican elements imported from Teotihuacan or imitated by local Maya elites?

The chronological evidence from all categories indicates that Maya-Teotihuacan contacts were continuous over a long period of time. The stylistic diversity in ceramic, obsidian, architectural, and iconographic evidence also precludes the possibility that Mexican-Maya relations were focused on a single process, series of historical events, or even a single time period. In all categories, over a long period, there is a mix of local imitations or variants with items of Veracruz, Central Mexican, or Teotihuacan style with a relatively small portion of true imports actually present. The implication is that there was a multiplicity of contacts of different types and intensity with various Mexican regions, Teotihuacan being only the most prominent and best known of these. Direct historical connections between elites are probable for Kaminaljuyu and Tikal, but even there local traditions predominate.

A consistent pattern seems to be that the western contacts are primarily limited to the elite subcomplex of ritual and mortuary practices, monumental art, and public architecture. The contact between Teotihuacan and the Maya polities was largely restricted to interaction between the elites of the two regions and interaction between the Maya elites themselves. The Teotihuacanoid features and the few actual trade goods were symbols of their association with the distant and powerful Central Mexican center. The warrior cults identified by the art historical work of Berlo, Schele, and Taube typify this kind of interaction. Elements of the Teotihuacan warrior cults were adopted at the beginning of the Classic period by admiring Maya elites in the lowland and were perhaps introduced more directly through

Mexican contacts on the Pacific Coast. In the lowlands this imagery was subsequently reworked, elaborated, and passed on to become a tradition that had its greatest florescence in the last two centuries of the Classic period. Thus, the Mexican military imagery in Late Classic Maya art resulted from a long tradition of inter-elite interaction. Again, the "horizon" concept and its proposed historical correlates seem singularly inappropriate to describe this process.

Cross-cultural studies have shown that status-reinforcing exotic goods, imagery, and cults tend to enhance power, wealth, and status, by implying contact or even (largely symbolic) political alliance with foreign realms. Political power is reinforced by the demonstration that the elites participate in a broader information sphere, most often one defined in geographical terms. By virtue of such a broader range of knowledge and activity, rulers' status and power could be increased—be they Panamanian chiefs (e.g., Helms 1976), Maya lords (e.g., Demarest 1988), or Thai kings (Tambiah 1977). This use of such status-reinforcing symbols pervades all pre-capitalist states (Blanton and Feinman 1984), but it is even stronger in weak states. The rulers of inchoate or archaic states need to reinforce their power through displays of participation in broader information spheres (Kurtz 1987; Claessen and Skalnik 1978; Claessen 1984). The Maya polities were certainly such inchoate states, the power of the elite being based heavily on the charisma of individual rulers (Demarest n.d., 1984: 138–150). Thus, fictitious or real associations of the Maya elite with the powerful Teotihuacan city-state through participation in exotic cults or through display of local copies of Teotihuacan ceramics, architecture, and painting, may have been helpful in maintaining their power over other centers and the population.

If such a broad and continuous lattice of status-reinforcing contacts between Mexican and Maya polities was in place, Mesoamerica was a more interactive and international community than many have envisioned (at least at the elite level). Yet, this elite awareness and exchange of ideas and information does not correspond in any way to the "horizon" model of a short period of close stylistic relationships, nor does it fit "world system" analogies of economic and political dominance by Central Mexican superpowers. Indeed, the murals at Cacaxtla (Quirarte 1983), and the Maya ceramics at Teotihuacan (Ball 1983), illustrate the multi-directional nature of Classic period interaction. The complex distribution of motifs and elements of related Puuc, Oaxacan, and Veracruz architecture and art styles also exemplify the close inter-elite communication network characteristic of the Mesoamerican world (Sharp 1978). The movement of Teotihuacan items, motifs, cults, or elements across Mesoamerica should be understood as only one of the many sets of symbols and ideas moving across this lattice of interaction.

THE HORIZON CONCEPT: THE VIEW FROM THE EAST

The horizon concept was originally intended as a chronological device. In retrospect, however, it tended to impose an interpretive structure of long periods of regional isolationism punctuated by brief epochs of international contact. In Mesoamerica, this interpretive framework led archaeologists to force Mexican elements artificially into the presumed "Middle Classic" horizon, just as it led them to force "Olmec" evidence into one or two "horizons." As demonstrated, neither horizon holds up under scrutiny even in chronological terms. The Preclassic period of interaction between the chiefdoms of Veracruz and those of other regions is now known to stretch from 1200 to 500 B.C. It is a continuous lattice of inter-elite relationships and exchanges of ideas, symbols, and perhaps goods—not a historically focused spread of a cultural complex, as once believed. Similarly, Maya-Mexican elite relationships were intense, complex, multi-directional, and unbroken throughout the Classic period.

In this sense, the horizon concept has only encouraged archaeologists to impose alignments of the evidence that have not survived rigorous dating and comparative studies. Ironically, the horizon concept—at least in the past decade—has come to encourage parochialism through the myth that interregional relations in Mesoamerica were important, but episodic. Lintel 2 at Tikal, the Cacaxtla murals, and many features of ceramics and architecture, all indicate that the elites of Mesoamerica were probably always very much aware of each other. The intensity of relationships may have varied, but there were apparently few breaks in exchanges of ideas and influences through a variety of mechanisms. Periods of localized style were more likely due to conscious definition of cultural boundaries than to a lack of interaction (cf. Barth 1969; Wobst 1977; Freidel 1981; Plog 1978; Schortman 1986; Ashmore, Schortman, and Urban 1987; Wright 1987; Demarest and Sharer 1986; Demarest 1986). We might conclude that the horizon concept, long a stimulus to research, has begun to obscure the interrelated nature of ancient Mesoamerica.

The search for more sophisticated approaches to modeling interregional interaction has now become a major area of study and discussion in archaeology. In the past, archaeologists have struggled with vague and shifting concepts of "diffusion" to guide interregional studies. Edward Schortman and Patricia Urban (1987: 45) have noted the basic problems of all diffusion models, which are also frequent problems in applications of the horizon concept:

(1) proving and not just assuming intercultural contact . . .; (2) failing to specify mechanisms through which diffusion occurred . . .; (3) understanding the internal cultural processes of evaluation and

modification a borrowed trait was subject to . . .; (4) specifying the local effects of an innovation on the recipient culture.

Subsequent models have sought a greater degree of specificity and, in some cases, have tried to avoid the assumption of a narrow chronological period or a single central source of shared elements. For example, J. Caldwell's (1964) interaction sphere model, first applied to the North American Hopewell, has also been used to model inter-elite contact in Mesoamerica and other regions (cf. Freidel 1979). Yet, in application, the model can lead toward a reliance on vaguely defined "influences." It has been useful in describing elite interaction, but the actual mechanisms (e.g., elite rituals, pilgrimages, gift exchange, intermarriage) are not always specified. Another related model that has been useful, if at times a bit vague, has been that of peer-polity interaction (e.g., Renfrew and Cherry 1986). Its applicability, however, is at the scale of interaction of small adjacent polities rather than long-distance contacts between regions (e.g., Sabloff 1986; Freidel 1986a).

It is now possible in many cases to reconstruct the precise nature of artifact-specific exchanges or contacts. For example, compositional studies (e.g., Bishop 1980; Bishop et al. 1986; Sidrys 1976; Rice et al. 1985) allow reconstruction of sources and trade routes in the movement of ceramics and lithics. Specific analogies and models for the exchange relations involved can then be compared with the evidence (e.g., Lamberg-Karlovsky 1975; Rathje 1977; Renfrew 1969; Wells 1980). Such trade models are a promising tool in terms of reconstructing specific economic exchanges, but they have generally failed to provide any understanding of the non-economic, cultural, or ideological impact of the exchange of ideas involved. In the case of Mesoamerica, this exchange of ideas was clearly far more important than its economic impact. Future studies on the nature of prehistoric trade will need to consider more completely the mechanisms of human contacts and their impact on the cultures involved.

In examining ideology and elite relations, epigraphic and iconographic studies have perhaps been most successful in replacing vague concepts like "horizon," "influence," and "interaction sphere" with a documentation of the specific nature of historical connections. Some initial successes in identification of contacts have been achieved. For example, the above-cited models from art history suggest conscious adoption of elements of Mexican cults and their ritual paraphernalia by the Maya elite (Berlo 1989; Schele n.d.; Taube n.d.). Other specific contacts identified from art historical studies include Ann Guillen's recent identification of a probable "Early Horizon" interregional marriage alliance (Guillen 1984; cf. Flannery 1968).

More disruptive contacts, at the level of small group or even mass migration also are now being modeled and debated in more specific terms. Population movements are presently proposed in terms of fairly rigorous criteria and tests (e.g., Kershaw 1978; Trigger 1968; du Toit and Safa 1975; Kemper 1975; Peterson 1968). Recent debates of possible migrations in Mesoamerica have begun to move to this more sophisticated level, and to test models with specific hypotheses regarding material correlates (e.g., Sheets 1983; Demarest 1988).

As our modeling achieves greater degrees of sophistication and specificity, we must be careful to avoid the previous pitfall of creating frameworks for interpretation that lead archaeologists to force the evidence into a preconceived form. One such fashionable, but somewhat leading, approach draws on I. Wallerstein's (1974) "World Systems Theory" and other modelings of modern international economies (e.g., Eckholm and Friedman 1979; Kohl 1979; Pailes and Whitecotton 1979; Blanton and Feinman 1984; Upham 1986). This new series of models allows us to consider the Mesoamerican horizon in more sophisticated terms, but it seems unlikely that these terms are appropriate to the Pre-Columbian world. Wallerstein's model posits a single, interconnected world economic system with closely dependent economies. This assumption of a single economic structure has been challenged for modern applications (e.g., Wolf 1982; Ragin and Chirot 1984; Nash 1981; Kohl 1979), and it seems particularly inappropriate for Pre-Columbian Mesoamerica. At the time of the proposed Early and Middle Horizons, Mesoamerica had a mixture of archaic market systems, redistributive chiefdoms, as well as simple reciprocal exchange systems. The degree of interrelatedness and interdependency of the polities and economies of Classic and Preclassic Mesoamerica was minimal compared to the modern World System. C. Ragin and D. Chirot (1984: 303–305) have criticized even the modern applicability of Wallerstein's model, citing its insensitivity to cultural differences, ethnicity, religion, language, and other non-economic factors. These flaws would be even more damaging in examining ancient Mesoamerican interaction, given the more limited nature and importance of long-distance exchange of goods, and the greater strength of regional ethnic traditions.

In essence, world-systems and other core-periphery or dependency theory models view the world as a network of *asymmetrical, economic* exchanges. These basic features make it inapplicable to Classic and Preclassic interaction. At those times, the Mesoamerican world does not appear to have been so centrally dominated, nor was there large-scale interregional economic exchange. The above review of the Early and Middle Horizons in eastern Mesoamerica finds no evidence that either the Olmec heartland or Central Mexico had any such intense, asymmetrical relationship with the Maya area or adjacent regions. Because of the lack of centralization of economic and political power in ancient Mesoamerica, attempts to apply core-periphery or world systems models have been forced to alter Wallerstein's model beyond recognition (e.g., Pailes and Whitecotton 1979; Upham 1986; Blanton and

Feinman 1984). For example, R. Blanton and G. Feinman (1984) focus on the exchange of status-reinforcing exotics and the ideological effect of their exchange. By so doing, they create a more accurate model of interregional interaction in Mesoamerica, but one that retains only the burden of Wallerstein's terminology.

In overview, we can characterize interactions between Mexico and the Maya area as having been continuous and important, but they were not of an economic nature and probably did not involve political or economic control. As described above, the most critical aspect of their continuous interregional contact was elite status-reinforcing trade and contacts, the exchange of ideas, and the spread of religious cults. Nonetheless these contacts may have been very important in their effects. For example, the spread of the Teotihuacan warrior cults gradually could have affected not only the rituals of warfare, but also the frequency of warfare, its intensity, and even the weapons used. These effects may have been felt later within Maya society as these cults subsequently evolved and were elaborated.

The horizon model may have outlived its utility. It has guided us to force periods of interaction into narrow chronological bands and interpret them in terms of Mexican dominance. As archaeologists continue to explore Mesoamerican interregional interaction, these errors can be avoided by adhering closely to the specific known dates and by reconstructing the precise nature of individual interactions, contacts, or exchanges. As documented above, recently scholars have had great success in such focused studies. Generalizations and overarching models for Mesoamerican interaction can then be built upon the documentation of such contacts, rather than by forcing evidence into preconceived molds. Such overarching frameworks can also serve as deductive structures and guides to research, but only if they are initially truly neutral in regard to the issues of the direction, intensity, and nature of the mechanisms involved (e.g., Schortman and Urban 1987). Only with an appreciation for the continuity, complexity, and diversity of the forms of interregional contact can we begin to reconstruct the rich tapestry of the ancient Mesoamerican world.

BIBLIOGRAPHY

ADAMS, RICHARD E. W.
  1986 Rio Azul. *National Geographic* 169 (4): 420–451.

ANDREWS V, E. WYLLYS
  1981 Dzibilchaltun. In *Supplement to the Handbook of Middle American Indians, vol. 1: Archaeology* (Jeremy A. Sabloff, ed.): 313–344. University of Texas Press, Austin.
  1986 Olmec Jades from Chacsinkin, Yucatan, and Maya Ceramics from La Venta, Tabasco. In *Research and Reflections in Archaeology and History: Essays in Honor of Doris Stone* (E. Wyllys Andrews V, ed.): 11–49. Middle American Research Institute, Pub. 57. Tulane University, New Orleans.
  1991 The Early Ceramic History of the Lowland Maya. In *Vision and Revision in Maya Studies* (Flora Clancy and Peter Harrison, eds.). University of New Mexico, Albuquerque.

ARROYO, BARBARA
  1990 *Patron funerario en Balberta, Escuintla: Algunas comparaciones con otros sitios e inferencias sobre su organización social.* BAR International Series 559. Oxford.

ASHMORE, WENDY, EDWARD SCHORTMAN, AND PATRICIA URBAN
  1987 The Classic Maya Fringe: Cultural Boundaries in the Southeast Mesoamerican Periphery. In *Polities and Partitions: Human Boundaries and the Growth of Complex Societies* (Kathryn M. Trinkaus, ed.): 157–178. Arizona State University, Tempe.

BALL, JOSEPH W.
  1974 A Teotihuacan-Style Cache from the Maya Lowlands. *Archaeology* 27 (1): 2–9.
  1983 Teotihuacan, the Maya, and Ceramic Interchange: A Contextual Perspective. In *Highland-Lowland Interaction in Mesoamerica: Interdisciplinary Approaches* (Arthur G. Miller, ed.): 125–143. Dumbarton Oaks, Washington, D.C.

BARTH, FREDERICK (ED.)
  1969 *Ethnic Groups and Boundaries.* Little, Brown, and Co., Boston.

BERLO, JANET
  1983 The Warrior and the Butterfly: Central Mexican Ideologies of Sacred Warfare and Teotihuacan Iconography. In *Text and Image in Pre-Columbian Art: Essays on the Interrelationship of the Verbal and Visual Arts* (Janet C. Berlo, ed.): 78–117. BAR International Series 180. Oxford.
  1984 *Teotihuacan Art Abroad: A Study of Metropolitan Style and Provincial Transformations in Incensario Workshops.* BAR International Series 199. Oxford.

1989   Art Historical Approaches to the Study of Teotihuacan-Related Ceramics from Escuintla, Guatemala. In *New Frontiers in the Archaeology of the Pacific Coast of Southern Mesoamerica* (Frederick Bove and Lynette Heller, eds.): 147–165. Anthropological Research Papers 39. Arizona State University, Tempe.

BISHOP, RON

1980   Aspects of Ceramic Compositional Modeling. In *Models and Methods in Regional Exchange* (R. Fry, ed.): 47–66. Society for American Archaeology Papers 1. Washington, D.C.

1984   Análisis por activación de neutrones de la cerámica de El Mirador. *Mesoamérica* 7. CIRMA, Woodstock, Vt.

BISHOP, RON, M. BEAUDRY, R. LEVENTHAL, AND ROBERT J. SHARER

1986   Compositional Analysis of Copador and Related Pottery in the Southeast Maya Area. In *The Southeast Maya Periphery* (P. Urban and E. Schortman, eds.): 143–167. University of Texas Press, Austin.

BLANTON, RICHARD, AND GARY FEINMAN

1984   The Mesoamerican World System. *American Anthropologist* 86: 673–682.

BORHEGYI, STEPHEN

1965   Archaeological Synthesis of the Guatemalan Highlands. In *Handbook of Middle American Indians, vol. 2: Archaeology of Southern Mesoamerica, part 1* (R. Wauchope, gen. ed., and G. R. Willey, vol. ed.): 3–58. University of Texas Press, Austin.

1972   Pre-Columbian Contacts—The Dryland Approach: The Impact and Influence of Teotihuacan Culture on the Pre-Columbian Civilizations of Mesoamerica. In *Man Across the Sea* (C. Reilly, ed.): 79–105. University of Texas Press, Austin.

BOVE, FREDERICK J.

1989   Dedicated to the Costeños. In *The Archaeology of the Pacific Coast and Highlands of Southern Mesoamerica* (Frederick Bove, ed.): 1–13. University of Arizona Press, Tucson.

n.d.a   The Evolution of Chiefdoms and States on the Pacific Coast of Guatemala: A Spatial Analysis. Ph.D. dissertation, University of California, Los Angeles, 1981.

n.d.b   Objectivos y resultados preliminares del Proyecto Balberta, Costa Sur. Paper presented at the Primer Simposio Sobre Investigaciones Arqueológicas de Guatemala, Museo Nacional de Arqueología y Etnología, Guatemala City, 1987.

n.d.c   Teotihuacan Impact on the Pacific Coast of Guatemala: Myth or Reality. Paper presented at 52nd Annual Meeting of the Society for American Archaeology, Toronto, 1987.

BROWN, KENNETH L.

1977a   Toward a Systematic Explanation of Culture Change Within the Middle Classic Period of the Valley of Guatemala. In *Teotihuacan and Kaminaljuyu: A Study in Prehistoric Cultural Contact* (William T. Sanders and Joseph W. Michels, eds.): 411–440. Pennsylvania State University Press, University Park.

1977b The Valley of Guatemala: A Highland Port of Trade. In *Teotihuacan and Kaminaljuyu: A Study in Prehistoric Culture Contact* (William T. Sanders and Joseph W. Michels, eds.): 205–396. Pennsylvania State University Press, University Park.

CALDWELL, J.
1964 Interaction Spheres in Prehistory. In *Hopewellian Studies* (J. Caldwell and R. Hall, eds.): 134–143. Illinois State Museum Papers, 12. Springfield, Ill.

CHASE, ARLEN F., AND PRUDENCE M. RICE (EDS.)
1985 *The Lowland Maya Postclassic.* University of Texas Press, Austin.

CHEEK, CHARLES D.
1977a Excavations at the Palangana and the Acropolis, Kaminaljuyu. In *Teotihuacan and Kaminaljuyu: A Study in Prehistoric Culture Contact* (W. Sanders and J. Michels, eds.): 1–204. Pennsylvania State University Press, University Park.
1977b Teotihuacan Influence at Kaminaljuyu. In *Teotihuacan and Kaminaljuyu: A Study in Prehistoric Culture Contact* (W. Sanders and J. Michels, eds.): 441–452. Pennsylvania State University Press, University Park.

CLARK, JOHN E.
1986 From Mountains to Molehill: A Critical Review of Teotihuacan's Obsidian Industry. In *Economic Aspects of Prehispanic Highland Mexico* (Barry L. Isaac, ed.): 23–74. Research in Economic Anthropology Supplement 2. JAI Press, Greenwich, Conn.

CLAESSEN, HENRI J.
1984 The Internal Dynamics of the Early State. *Current Anthropology* 25 (4): 365–379.

CLAESSEN, HENRI J., AND PETER SKALNIK (EDS.)
1978 *The Early State.* Studies in the Social Sciences 32. Mouton, The Hague, Netherlands.

COE, MICHAEL D.
1966 *An Early Stone Pectoral from Southeastern Mexico.* Studies in Pre-Columbian Art and Archaeology 1. Dumbarton Oaks, Washington, D.C.
1968 *America's First Civilization.* Smithsonian Institution Press, Washington, D.C.
1977 Olmec and Maya: A Study in Relationships. In *The Origins of Maya Civilization* (Richard E. W. Adams, ed.): 183–195. School of American Research Advanced Seminar Series. University of New Mexico Press, Albuquerque.
1982 *Mexico.* Thames and Hudson, New York.
1989 The Olmec Heartland: Evolution of Ideology. In *Regional Perspectives on the Olmec* (Robert Sharer and David Grove, eds.): 68–84. A School of

American Research Advanced Seminar. Cambridge University Press, Cambridge.

COE, WILLIAM

1965   Tikal: Ten years of Study of a Maya Ruin in the Lowlands of Guatemala. *Expedition* 8: 5–56.

1967   *Tikal: A Handbook of the Ancient Maya Ruins.* University of Pennsylvania Museum, Philadelphia.

COGGINS, CLEMENCY

1979   A New Order and the Role of the Calendar: Some Characteristics of the Middle Classic Period at Tikal. In *Maya Archaeology and Ethnohistory* (Norman Hammond and Gordon R. Willey, eds.): 38–50. University of Texas Press, Austin.

1980   The Shape of Time: Some Political Implications of a Four-part Figure. *American Antiquity* 45: 727–739.

n.d.   Painting and Drawing Styles at Tikal: An Historical and Iconographic Reconstruction. Ph.D. dissertation, Harvard University, Cambridge, Mass., 1975.

COWGILL, GEORGE

n.d.   Toward a Political History of Teotihuacan. In *Ideology and Cultural Evolution in the New World* (A. Demarest and G. Conrad, eds.). A School of Américan Research Press, Santa Fe.

DAHLIN, BRUCE

1984   A Colossus in Guatemala: The Preclassic City of El Mirador. *Archaeology* 37 (3): 18–25.

DEMAREST, ARTHUR A.

1984   Conclusions y especulaciones acerca de El Mirador. *Mesoamérica* 7: 138–150. CIRMA, Woodstock, Vt.

1986   *The Archaeology of Santa Leticia and the Rise of Maya Civilization.* Middle American Research Institute, Pub. 52. Tulane University, New Orleans.

1988   Political Evolution in the Maya Borderlands. In *The Southeast Classic Maya Zone* (Elizabeth Boone and Gordon Willey, eds.): 335–394. Dumbarton Oaks, Washington, D.C.

1989   The Olmec and the Rise of Civilization in Eastern Mesoamerica. In *Regional Perspectives on the Olmec* (R. Sharer and D. Grove, eds.): 303–344. School of American Research Advanced Seminar. Cambridge University Press, England.

n.d.   Ideology in Ancient Maya Cultural Evolution: The Dynamics of Galactic Polities. In *Ideology and Cultural Evolution in the New World* (A. Demarest and G. Conrad, eds.). A School of American Research Advanced Seminar. School of American Research Press, Santa Fe. (in press).

DEMAREST, ARTHUR A., AND STEVE HOUSTON

n.d.   The Dynamism and Heterogeneity of Ancient Maya States. Paper presented at the Society for American Archaeology Meetings, Atlanta, 1989.

DEMAREST, ARTHUR A., AND ROBERT J. SHARER

1986　The Late Preclassic Ceramic Spheres, Culture Areas, and Cultural Evolution in the Southeastern Highlands of Mesoamerica. In *The Southeast Maya Periphery* (Patrician Urban and Edward Schortman, eds.): 194–233. University of Texas Press, Austin.

DEMAREST, ARTHUR A., ROBERT J. SHARER, WILLIAM FOWLER, JR., ELEANOR KING, AND JOYCE FOWLER

1984　Las excavaciones. *Mesoamérica* 7: 14–52. CIRMA, Woodstock, Vt.

DUTOIT, B., AND H. SAFA (EDS.)

1975　*Migration and Urbanization.* Mouton, The Hague.

ECKHOLM, K., AND J. FRIEDMAN

1979　"Capital" Imperialism and Exploitation in Ancient World Systems. In *Power and Propaganda: A Symposium on Ancient Empires* (M. Larsen, ed.): 41–58. Academisk Forlag, Copenhagen.

FASH, JR., WILLIAM L.

1991　*Scribes, Warriors and Kings: The City of Copan and the Ancient Maya.* Thames and Hudson, London.

n.d.　A Middle Formative Cemetery from Copan, Honduras. Paper presented at the annual meeting of the American Anthropological Association, 1982. Washington, D.C.

FLANNERY, KENT V.

1968　The Olmec and the Valley of Oaxaca: A Model for Inter-regional Interaction in Formative Times. In *Dumbarton Oaks Conference on the Olmec* (E. Benson, ed.): 79–110. Dumbarton Oaks, Washington, D.C.

FOIAS, ANTONIA E.

n.d.　The Influence of Teotihuacan in the Maya Culture During the Middle Classic: A Reconsideration of the Ceramic Evidence from Kaminaljuyu, Uaxactun and Copan. B.A. honors thesis, Harvard University, Cambridge, Mass., 1987.

FOWLER, JR., WILLIAM R., ARTHUR A. DEMAREST, HELEN V. MICHEL, FRANK ASARO, AND FRED STROSS

1989　Sources of Obsidian from El Mirador, Guatemala: New Evidence on Preclassic Maya Interaction. *American Anthropologist* 91 (1): 159–168.

FREIDEL, DAVID A.

1979　Culture Areas and Interaction Spheres: Contrasting Approaches to the Emergence of Civilization in the Maya Lowlands. *American Antiquity* 44: 36–54.

1981　Civilizations as a State of Mind: The Cultural Evolutions of the Lowland Maya. In *The Transitions to Statehood in the New World* (Grant D. Jones and P. Kautz, eds.): 188–227. Cambridge University Press, England.

1986a　Maya Warfare: An Example of Peer Polity Interaction. In *Peer Polity Interaction and Socio-Political Change* (Colin Renfrew and John F. Cherry, eds.): 93–108. A School of American Research Advanced Seminar. Cambridge University Press, England.

1986b　The Monumental Architecture. In *Archaeology at Cerros, Belize, Central*

America: Volume 1, an Interim Report (Robin Robertson and David Freidel, eds.): 1–22. Southern Methodist University Press, Dallas.

FREIDEL, DAVID A., AND LINDA SCHELE

1988   Symbol and Power: A History of the Lowland Maya Cosmogram. In Maya Iconography (Elizabeth Benson and G. Griffin, eds.): 44–93. Princeton University Press.

GRAHAM, JOHN

1989   Olmec Diffusion: A Sculptural View from Pacific Guatemala. In Regional Perspectives on the Olmec (R. Sharer and D. Grove, eds.): 227–246. A School of American Research Advanced Seminar. Cambridge University Press, England.

GROVE, DAVID

1989   Olmec: What's in a Name?. In Regional Perspectives on the Olmec (R. Sharer and D. Grove, eds.): 8–16. A School of American Research Advanced Seminar. Cambridge University Press, Cambridge.

GUILLEN, ANN CYPHERS

1984   The Possible Role of a Woman in Formative Exchange. In Trade and Exchange in Early Mesoamerica (Kenneth Hirth, ed.): 125–146. University of New Mexico Press, Albuquerque.

HAMMOND, NORMAN

1985   Nohmul: A Prehistoric Maya Community in Belize. Excavations 1973–1983. BAR International Series 250. Oxford.

HAMMOND, NORMAN, S. DONAGHEY, C. GLEASON, J. C. STANEKO, D. VAN TUERENHOUT, AND L. J. KOSAKOWSKY

1987   Excavations at Nohmul, Belize, 1985. Journal of Field Archaeology 14 (3): 257–281.

HANSEN, RICHARD D.

n.d.   Excavations on Structure 34 and the Tigre Area, El Mirador, Peten, Guatemala: A New Look at the Preclassic Lowland Maya. M.A. thesis, Brigham Young University, Provo, 1984.

HATCH, MARION P.

1987a   "Proyecto Tiquisate": Recientes investigaciones arqueológicas en la Costa Sur de Guatemala. Cuadernos de Investigación no. 2–87. Universidad de San Carlos, Guatemala City.

1987b   La importancia de la cerámica utilitaria en arqueología, con observaciones sobre la prehistoria de Guatemala. Anales de la Academia de Geografía e Historia de Guatemala 61: 151–184.

HELMS, MARY W.

1976   Ancient Panama: Chiefs in Search of Power. University of Texas Press, Austin.

HELLMUTH, NICHOLAS M.

1975   The Escuintla Hoards: Teotihuacan Art in Guatemala. F.L.A.A.R. Progress Reports, 1 (2), Foundation for Latin American Anthropological Research.

1978   Teotihuacan Art in the Escuintla, Guatemala Region. In Middle Classic

Mesoamerica: A.D. 400–700 (Elizabeth Pasztory, ed.): 71–85. Columbia University Press, New York.

HOUSTON, STEPHEN
n.d.   The Inscriptions and Monumental Art of Dos Pilas, Guatemala: A Study of Classic Maya History and Politics. Ph.D. dissertation, Yale University, New Haven, 1987.

JOESINK-MANDEVILLE, LeROY V.
1977   Olmec-Maya Relationships: A Correlation of Linguistic Evidence with Archaeological Ceramics. *Journal of New World Archaeology* 2: 30–39.

JONES, CHRISTOPHER
1977   Inauguration Dates of Three Late Classic Rulers of Tikal, Guatemala. *American Antiquity* 42: 28–60.
n.d.   Tikal as a Trading Center: Why It Rose and Fell. Paper presented at the 43rd International Congress of Americanists. Vancouver, 1979.

JONES, CHRISTOPHER, AND LINTON SATTERTHWAITE
1982   *The Monuments and Inscriptions of Tikal: The Carved Monuments.* Tikal Report 33a. University Museum Publications, Philadelphia.

JOYCE, ROSEMARY, RICHARD EDGING, KARL LORENZ, AND SUSAN GILLESPIE
n.d.   Olmec Bloodletting: An Iconographic Study. Paper presented at the 6th Mesa Redonda de Palenque. 1986.

KEMPER, ROBERT
1975   Social Factors in Migration: The Case of Tzintzuntzenos in Mexico City. In *Migration and Urbanization* (B. DuToit and H. Safa, eds.): 225–244. Mouton, The Hague.

KERSHAW, A.
1978   Diffusion and Migration Studies in Geography. In *Diffusion and Migration: Their Roles in Cultural Development* (P. Duke, et al., eds.): 6–13. The University of Calgary Archaeological Association, Calgary.

KIDDER, ALFRED V., JESSE D. JENNINGS, AND EDWIN M. SHOOK
1946   *Excavations at Kaminaljuyu, Guatemala.* Carnegie Institution of Washington, Washington, D.C.

KOHL, PHILLP
1979   The "World Economy" in West Asia in the Third Millennium B.C. In *South Asian Archaeology 1977* (M. Taddei, ed.): 55–85. Instituto Universitario Orientale, Naples.

KURTZ, DONALD V.
1987   The Economics of Urbanization and State Formation at Teotihuacan. *Current Anthropology* 28 (3): 329–353.

LAMBERG-KARLOVSKY, C. C.
1975   Third Millennium Modes of Exchange and Modes of Production. In *Ancient Civilization and Trade* (Jeremy Sabloff and C. C. Lamberg-Karlovsky, eds.): 341–368. University of New Mexico, Albuquerque.

LAPORTE, JUAN PEDRO
n.d.a   Nuevas referencias para viejos problemas: Enfoques dinásticos sobre el

Clásico Temprano de Tikal. Paper presented at the seminar "Vision and Revision in Maya Studies." Albuquerque Museum and the University of New Mexico, 1987.

n.d.b   Alternativas del Clásico Temprano en la relación Tikal-Teotihuacan: Grupo 6C-XVI, Tikal, Peten, Guatemala. Ph.D. dissertation, Universidad Nacional Autónoma de Mexico, Ciudad de Mexico, 1989.

LAPORTE, JUAN PEDRO, AND VILMA FIALKO C.

1987   La cerámica del Clásico Temprano desde mundo perdido, Tikal: Una reevaluación. In *Maya Ceramics: Papers from the 1985 Maya Ceramics Conference* (P. Rice and R. Sharer, eds.): 123–182. BAR International Series 345 (i). Oxford.

LEE, JR., THOMAS A.

1989   Chiapas Olmec. In *Regional Perspectives on the Olmec* (Robert Sharer and David Grove, eds.): 198–226. A School of American Research Advanced Seminar. Cambridge University Press, England.

LOWE, GARETH W.

1977   The Mixe-Zoque as Competing Neighbors of the Early Lowland Maya. In *The Origins of Maya Civilization* (Richard E. W. Adams, ed.): 197–248. A School of American Research Advanced Seminar. University of New Mexico Press, Albuquerque.

1978   Eastern Mesoamerica. In *Chronologies in New World Archaeology* (R. E. Taylor and Clement W. Meighan, eds.): 331–393. Academic Press, New York.

1989   The Heartland Olmec: Evolution of Material Culture. In *Regional Perspectives on the Olmec* (Robert Sharer and David Grove, eds.): 33–67. A School of American Research Advanced Seminar. Cambridge University Press, Cambridge.

MARCUS, JOYCE

1989   Zapotec Chiefdoms and the Nature of Formative Religions. In *Regional Perspectives on the Olmec* (R. Sharer and D. Grove, eds.): 148–197. A School of American Research Advanced Seminar. Cambridge University Press, Cambridge.

MATA AMADO, GUILLERMO, AND R. R. RUBIO C.

1987   Incensarios talud-tablero del lago de Amatitlán, Guatemala. *Mesoamérica* 13: 185–203. CIRMA, Woodstock, Vt.

MATHENY, RAY T.

1980   (Ed.) *El Mirador, Peten, Guatemala: An Interim Report.* Papers of the New World Archaeological Foundation 45. Brigham Young University, Provo, Utah.

1986   Investigations at El Mirador, Petén, Guatemala. *National Geographic Research* 2: 332–353.

1987   Early States in the Maya Lowlands During the Late Preclassic Period: Edzna and El Mirador. In *City-States of the Maya: Art and Architecture* (Elizabeth P. Benson, ed.): 1–44. Rocky Mountain Institute for Pre-Columbian Studies, Denver.

MATHENY, RAY T., DEANNE L. GURR, DON W. FORSYTH, AND FOREST R. HAUCK
    1983   *Investigations at Edzna, Campeche, Mexico, vol. 1, part 1.: The Hydraulic System.* Papers of the New World Archaeological Foundation 46. Brigham Young University, Provo, Utah.

MATHEWS, PETER, AND GORDON R. WILLEY
    1991   Prehistoric Polities of the Pasion Region: Hieroglyphic Texts and Their Archaeological Settings. In *Classic Maya Political History: Hieroglyphic and Archaeological Evidence* (T. P. Culbert, ed.): 32–71. A School of American Research Advanced Seminar. Cambridge University Press, Cambridge.

MEDRANO, SONIA
    n.d.a   Arquitectura de Balberta. Paper presented at the Segundo Simposio Sobre Investigaciones Arqueológicas de Guatemala, Museo Nacional de Arqueología y Etnología, Guatemala City, 1988.
    n.d.b   Análisis preliminar de la cerámica Formativa y Clásica de Balberta, Escuintla (forthcoming).

MERWIN, R. E., AND G. C. VALLIANT
    1932   *The Ruins of Holmul, Guatemala.* Memoirs of the Peabody Museum 3(1). Harvard University Press, Cambridge, Mass.

MICHELS, JOSEPH W.
    1979   Some Sociological Observations on Obsidian Production at Kaminaljuyu, Guatemala. In *Maya Lithic Studies: Papers from the 1976 Belize Field Symposium, Special Report 4* (Thomas R. Hester and Norman Hammond, eds.): 109–118. 2nd printing. Center for Archaeological Research, University of Texas at San Antonio, San Antonio.

MILLER, ARTHUR G.
    1978   A Brief Outline of the Artistic Evidence for Classic Period Cultural Contact Between Maya Lowlands and Central Mexican Highlands. In *Middle Classic Mesoamerica: A.D. 400–700* (Esther Pasztory, ed.): 63–70. Columbia University Press, New York.

MOHOLY-NAGY, HATTULA
    1979   Spatial Distribution of Flint and Obsidian Artifacts at Tikal, Guatemala. In *Maya Lithic Studies: Papers from the 1976 Belize Field Symposium, Special Report 4* (T. Hester and N. Hammond, eds.): 91–108. 2nd printing. Center for Archaeological Research, University of Texas at San Antonio, San Antonio.

MOHOLY-NAGY, HATTULA, F. ASARO, AND F. H. STROSS
    1984   Tikal Obsidian: Sources and Typology. *American Antiquity* 49 (1): 104–117.

NASH, JUNE
    1981   Ethnographic Aspects of the World Capitalist System. *Annual Reviews of Anthropology,* 10: 393–423.

PAILES, R., AND J. WHITECOTTON
    1979   The Greater Southwest and the Mesoamerican "World System": An Exploratory Model of Frontier Relationships. In *The Frontier* 2 (W.

Savage, Jr. and S. Thompson, eds.): 105–121. University of Oklahoma Press, Norman.

PARSONS, LEE A.

1969   *Bilbao, Guatemala: An Archaeological Study of the Pacific Coast Cotzumal-huapa Region.* Publications in Anthropology 12. Milwaukee Public Museum, Milwaukee.

1978   The Peripheral Coastal Lowlands and the Middle Classic Period. In *Middle Classic Mesoamerica: A.D. 400–700* (Esther Pasztory, ed.): 25–34. Columbia University Press, New York.

PASZTORY, ESTHER

1978a   Artistic Traditions of the Middle Classic Period. In *Middle Classic Mesoamerica: A.D. 400–700* (Esther Pasztory, ed.): 108–142. Columbia University Press, New York.

1978b   Historical Synthesis of the Middle Classic Period. In *Middle Classic Mesoamerica: A.D. 400–700* (Esther Pasztory, ed.): 3–22. Columbia University Press, New York.

1978c   (Ed.) *Middle Classic Mesoamerica: A.D. 400–700.* Columbia University Press, New York.

PENDERGAST, DAVID M.

1981   Lamanai, Belize: Summary of Excavation Results, 1974–1980. *Journal of Field Archaeology* 8: 29–53.

PETERSON, W.

1968   Migration: Social Aspects. In *International Encyclopedia of the Social Sciences* 10: 286–292.

PLOG, STEPHEN

1978   Social Interaction and Stylistic Similarity: A Reanalysis. *Advances in Archaeological Method and Theory* 1: 143–182.

PRICE, BARBARA

1978   Secondary State Formation: An Explanatory Model. In *Origins of the State: The Anthropology of Political Evolution* (Ronald Cohen and Elman Service, eds.): 161–186. Ishi, Philadelphia.

PRING, D. C.

1977   The Dating of Teotihuacan Contact at Altun Ha: The New Evidence. *American Antiquity* 42 (4): 626–628.

PROSKOURIAKOFF, TATIANA

1962   The Artifacts of Mayapan. In *Mayapan, Yucatan, Mexico* (H. E. D. Pollock, Ralph L. Roys, Tatiana Proskouriakoff, and A. Ledyard Smith, eds.): 341–442. Carnegie Institution of Washington, Pub. 619. Washington, D.C.

QUIRARTE, JACINTO

1977   Early Art Styles of Mesoamerica and Early Classic Maya Art. In *Origins of Maya Civilization* (Richard E. W. Adams, ed.): 249–283. A School of American Research Advanced Seminar Series. University of New Mexico Press, Albuquerque.

1983   Outside Influence at Cacaxtla. In *Highland-Lowland Interaction in Meso-*

america: Interdisciplinary Approaches* (Arthur G. Miller, ed.): 201–222. Dumbarton Oaks, Washington, D.C.

RAGIN, C., AND D. CHIROT
  1984 The World System of Immanuel Wallerstein: Sociology and Politics as History. In *Vision and Method in Historical Sociology* (T. Skocpol, ed.): 276–312. Cambridge University Press, Cambridge.

RATHJE, WILLIAM
  1977 The Tikal Connection. In *The Origins of Maya Civilization* (R. Adams, ed.): 373–382. University of New Mexico Press, Albuquerque.

RATHJE, WILLIAM L., JEREMY A. SABLOFF, AND DAVID A. GREGORY
  1973 El descubrimiento de un jade olmeca en la Isla de Cozumel, Quintana Roo, Mexico. *Estudios de cultura Maya* 9: 85–91.

RATTRAY, EVELYN C.
  1977 Los contactos entre Teotihuacan y Veracruz. *Mesa Redonda* 15 (2): 301–311. Sociedad Mexicana de Antropología y Universidad de Guanajuato, Guanajuato, Mexico.

RENFREW, COLIN
  1969 Trade and Culture Process in European Prehistory. *Current Anthropology* 10: 151–169.

RENFREW, COLIN, AND JOHN CHERRY (EDS.)
  1986 *Peer Polity Interaction and Socio-Political Change.* Cambridge University Press, England.

RICE, PRUDENCE M., HELEN V. MICHEL, F. ASARO, AND F. STROSS
  1985 Provenience Analysis of Obsidians from the Central Peten Lakes Region, Guatemala. *American Antiquity* 50 (3): 591–604.

RIVERA, V., AND D. SCHÁVELZON
  1984 Los Tableros de Kaminaljuyu. *Cuadernos de Arquitectura Mesoamericana* 2: 51–56.

ROBERTSON, ROBIN, AND DAVID A. FREIDEL (EDS.)
  1986 *Archaeology at Cerros, Belize, Central America, vol. 1: An Interim Report.* Southern Methodist University Press, Dallas.

SABLOFF, JEREMY A.
  1986 Interaction Among Classic Maya Polities: A Preliminary Examination. In *Peer Polity Interaction and Socio-Political Change* (Colin Renfrew and John F. Cherry, eds.): 109–116. Cambridge University Press, Cambridge.

SANDERS, WILLIAM T.
  1974 Chiefdom to State: Political Evolution of Kaminaljuyu, Guatemala. In *Reconstructing Complex Societies: An Archaeological Colloquium* (Charlotte B. Moore, ed.) 20: 97–121. Supplement to the *Bulletin of the American Schools of Oriental Research.* Cambridge.
  1977 Ethnographic Analogy and the Teotihuacan Horizon Style. In *Teotihuacan and Kaminaljuyu: A Study in Prehistoric Culture Contact* (William T. Sanders and Joseph W. Michels, eds.): 397–410. Pennsylvania State University Press, University Park.

SANDERS, WILLIAM T., AND JOSEPH W. MICHELS (EDS.)
  1977   *Teotihuacan and Kaminaljuyu: A Study in Prehistoric Culture Contact.* Pennsylvania State University Press, University Park.

SANDERS, WILLIAM T., AND BARBARA J. PRICE
  1968   *Mesoamerica: The Evolution of a Civilization.* Random House, New York.

SANDERS, WILLIAM T., AND ROBERT SANTLEY
  1983   A Tale of Three Cities: Energetics and Urbanization in Prehispanic Central Mexico. In *Prehistoric Settlement Patterns: Essays in Honor of Gordon R. Willey* (Evon S. Vogt and Richard Leventhal, eds.): 243–291. University of New Mexico Press, Albuquerque.

SANTLEY, ROBERT S.
  1983   Obsidian Trade and Teotihuacan Influence in Mesoamerica. In *Highland-Lowland Interaction in Mesoamerica: Interdisciplinary Approaches* (Arthur G. Miller, ed.): 69–124. Dumbarton Oaks, Washington, D.C.
  1984   Obsidian Exchange, Economic Stratification, and the Evolution of Complex Society in the Basin of Mexico. In *Trade and Exchange in Early Mesoamerica* (Kenneth Hirth, ed.): 43–86. University of New Mexico Press, Albuquerque.
  n.d.   Teotihuacan Influence at Matacapan: Testing the Goodness of Fit of the Enclave Model. Paper presented at the 52nd annual meeting of the Society for American Archaeology. Toronto, 1987.

SCHELE, LINDA
  n.d.   The Tlaloc Complex in the Classic Period: War and the Interaction Between the Lowland Maya and Teotihuacan. Paper presented at the Symposium on The New Dynamics. Kimbell Art Museum, Fort Worth, 1986.

SCHELE, LINDA, AND MARY ALLEN MILLER
  1986   *The Blood of Kings: Dynasty and Ritual in Maya Art.* Kimbell Art Museum, Fort Worth.

SCHORTMAN, EDWARD
  1986   Maya/Non-Maya Interaction Along the Classic Southeast Maya Periphery: The View from the Lower Motagua Valley. In *The Southeast Maya Periphery* (Patricia Urban and Edward Schortman, eds.): 114–136. University of Texas Press, Austin.

SCHORTMAN, EDWARD M., AND PATRICIA A. URBAN
  1987   Modeling Interregional Interaction in Prehistory. In *Advances in Archaeological Method and Theory* 2: 37–95.

SHARER, ROBERT J.
  1978   (Ed.) *The Prehistory of Chalchuapa, El Salvador.* University of Pennsylvania Press, Philadelphia.
  1983   Interdisciplinary Approaches to the Study of Mesoamerican Highland-Lowland Interactions: A Summary View. In *Highland-Lowland Interactions in Mesoamerica: Interdisciplinary Approaches* (Arthur G. Miller, ed.): 241–260. Dumbarton Oaks, Washington, D.C.

1989   The Olmec and the Southeast Periphery of Mesoamerica. In *Regional Perspectives on the Olmec* (R. Sharer and D. Grove, eds.): 247–274. A School of American Research Advanced Seminar. Cambridge University Press, Cambridge.

SHARER, ROBERT J., AND DAVID GROVE (EDS.)
1989   *Regional Perspectives on the Olmec.* A School of American Research Advanced Seminar. Cambridge University Press, Cambridge.

SHARER, ROBERT J., AND DAVID W. SEDAT
1987   *Archaeological Investigations in the Northern Maya Highlands, Guatemala: Interaction and the Development of Maya Civilization.* The University Museum, University of Pennsylvania, Philadelphia.

SHARP, ROSEMARY
1978   Architecture as Interelite Communication in Preconquest Oaxaca, Veracruz, and Yucatan. In *Middle Classic Mesoamerica: A.D. 400–700* (Esther Pasztory, ed.): 158–171. Columbia University Press, New York.

SHEETS, PAYSON D.
1983   *Archaeology and Volcanism in Central America.* University of Texas Press, Austin.

SHOOK, EDWIN M.
1965   Archaeological Survey of the Pacific Coast of Guatemala. In *Handbook of Middle American Indians, vol. 2: Archaeology of Southern Mesoamerica, part 1* (R. Wauchope, gen. ed., and G. R. Willey, vol. ed.): 180–194. University of Texas Press, Austin.

SIDRYS, RAYMOND V.
1976   Classic Maya Obsidian Trade. *American Antiquity* 41 (4): 449–464.

SMITH, A. LEDYARD
1982   *Excavations at Seibal, Department of Peten, Guatemala: Major Architecture and Caches.* Memoirs of the Peabody Museum of Archaeology and Ethnology 15. Harvard University, Cambridge, Mass.

SMITH, R. E.
1955   *Ceramic Sequence at Uaxactun, Guatemala,* 2 vols. Middle American Research Institute Pub. 20. Tulane University, New Orleans.

SPENCE, MICHAEL W.
1977   Teotihuacan y el intercambio de obsidiana en Mesoamerica. *Mesa Redonda* 15 (2): 293–300. Sociedad Mexicana de Antropología y Universidad de Guanajuato, Guanajuato.
1981   Obsidian Production and the State in Teotihuacan. *American Antiquity* 46 (4): 769–788.

SUGIYAMA, SABURO
1989   Burials Dedicated to the Old Temple of Quetzalcoatl at Teotihuacan, Mexico. *American Antiquity* 54(1): 85–106.

TAMBIAH, STANLEY
1977   The Galactic Polity: The Structure of Traditional Kingdoms in Southeast Asia. *Annals of the New York Academy of Sciences* 293: 69–97.

Arthur A. Demarest and Antonia E. Foias

Arthur A. Demarest and Antonia E. Foias

TAUBE, KARL
    n.d.   The Temple of Quetzalcoatl and the Cult of Sacred War at Teoti-
           huacan. *RES* 21 (in press).

TOLSTOY, PAUL
    1989   Western Mesoamerican and the Olmec. In *Regional Perspectives on the
           Olmec* (Robert Sharer and David Grove, eds.): 275–302. A School of
           American Research Advanced Seminar. Cambridge University Press,
           Cambridge.

TRIGGER, B.
    1968   *Beyond History: The Methods of Prehistory*. Holt, Rinehart, and Winston,
           New York.

UPHAM, S.
    1986   Imperialists, Isolationists, World Systems and Political Realities: Per-
           spectives on Mesoamerican-Southwestern Interaction. In *Ripples in the
           Chichimec Sea* (R. McGuire and F. Mathien, eds.). Southern Illinois
           University Press, Carbondale, Ill.

VELÁSQUEZ, RICARDO
    1980   Recent Discoveries in the Caves of Loltun, Yucatan, Mexico. *Mexicon*
           2 (4): 53–54.

WALLERSTEIN, I.
    1974   *The Modern World System I*. Academic Press, New York.
    1980   *The Modern World System II*. Academic Press, New York

WELLS, P. S.
    1980   *Culture Contact and Culture Change: Early Iron Age Central Europe and the
           Mediterranean World*. Cambridge University Press, Cambridge.
    1987   Sociopolitical Exchange and Core-Periphery Interactions: An Example
           from Early Iron Age Europe. In *Polities and Partitions: Human Bound-
           aries and the Growth of Complex Societies* (Kathryn M. Trinkaus, ed.):
           141–156. Arizona State University, Tempe.

WETHERINGTON, RONALD K.
    1978   The Ceramic Chronology of Kaminaljuyu. In *The Ceramics of Kaminal-
           juyu, Guatemala* (R. K. Wetherington, ed.): 115–150. Pennsylvania
           State University Press, University Park.

WILLEY, GORDON R.
    1978   *Excavations at Seibal: Introduction to the Site and Its Setting*. Memoirs of
           the Peabody Museum 13 (1). Peabody Museum, Harvard University,
           Cambridge, Mass.

WILLEY, GORDON R., RICHARD LEVENTHAL, ARTHUR DEMAREST, AND WILLIAM FASH
    n.d.   *The Ceramics and Artifacts from the Domestic Settlement at Copan, Hondu-
           ras*. A Peabody Museum Memoir, Harvard University Press, Cam-
           bridge, Mass. (forthcoming).

WOBST, H.
    1977   Stylistic Behavior and Information Exchange. In *For the Director: Re-
           search Essays in Honor of James B. Griffin* (C. Cleland, ed.): 317–342.

Anthropological Papers, Museum of Anthropology. University of Michigan, Ann Arbor.

WOLF, ERIC

1982   *Europe and the People without History.* University of California Press, Berkeley.

WRIGHT, RITA

1987   The Frontier of Prehistoric Baluchistan and the Development of the Indus Civilization. In *Polities and Partitions: Human Boundaries and the Growth of Complex Societies* (Kathryn M. Trinkaus, ed.): 61–82. Arizona State University, Tempe.

ZEITLIN, ROBERT N.

1982   Toward a More Comprehensive Model of Interregional Commodity Distribution: Political Variables and Prehistoric Obsidian Procurement in Mesoamerica. *American Antiquity* 47 (2): 260–275.

Understanding Tiwanaku: Conquest, Colonization, and Clientage in the South Central Andes

ALAN L. KOLATA

UNIVERSITY OF CHICAGO

FROM THE PERSPECTIVE of the south central and southern Andes, a reconsideration of the horizon concept and its meaning could not, perhaps, have come at a better time. Only a few years ago there would have been precious little new data concerning the nature and impact of Tiwanaku in the cultural history of the Andes. Today that situation is changing dramatically.

Although the archaeology of Tiwanaku has been discussed and commented upon continuously since the days of Max Uhle, the number of substantive field projects designed to explore systematically the nature of the Tiwanaku polity is unfavorably disproportionate to the slew of speculation that currently passes for our understanding of that ancient state. It seems that Tiwanaku has been admired, remarked upon, and then subtly, if, at times, unwittingly, dismissed, simply because there was nothing new to say.

However, the past ten years have witnessed a renaissance of interest and of scholarly work on the complex phenomenon that was Tiwanaku. Recent field projects in southern Peru, northern Chile, and western Bolivia promise to alter radically current perceptions regarding Tiwanaku's role in the geopolitics of the ancient Andean world. Fresh, compelling interpretations of the political economy of Tiwanaku are forthcoming and, for the first time in a very long time, these interpretations will be embedded in conceptual frameworks supported by a newly generated corpus of primary field data.

Within the limited scope of this paper, I can only characterize in summary fashion the nature of these new data, and outline, in schematic form, the general contours of these emerging interpretive frameworks. Together this material speaks directly to the theme of this volume: what precisely do horizons and horizon styles signify, and, more specifically, how will our new understanding of Tiwanaku clarify the current puzzling historical processes that seem to underlie the phenomenon we refer to as the Andean Middle Horizon?

193

TIWANAKU AND THE HORIZON CONCEPT

Before proceeding to a discussion of the substantive new data on Tiwanaku that will, in my mind, force a thoroughgoing revision in our understanding of that culture and its transformations, it is appropriate to locate briefly the critical role of Tiwanaku in the intellectual history of the horizon concept and to define the fundamental identifying characteristics of Tiwanaku as a horizon style. In this way, we may gain an initial appreciation for the definition, utility, and limitations of the horizon concept within the context of the investigation of native Andean civilization.

Tiwanaku can rightfully take its place as one of the two principal cultural phenomena (the Inca, of course, being the other) that inspired the development of the horizon concept in Andean studies. Just prior to the turn of the last century, Max Uhle, working in Germany with photographs, drawings, and notes compiled primarily by Alfons Stübel, began his analysis of the monumental stone sculpture and architecture at the site of Tiwanaku. This work culminated in the impressive descriptive monograph, *Die Ruinenstaette von Tiahuanaco im Hochlande des alten Perú* (Stübel and Uhle 1892), which essentially defines Uhle's understanding of the form and content of the Tiwanaku sculptural style.

Perhaps more importantly for the genesis of the horizon concept, Uhle's investigations of selected aspects of Tiwanaku and Inca material culture in Europe inspired him to engage in primary field work with the apparently explicit intention of sorting out the broad temporal and spatial relationships of various archaeological cultures of the ancient Americas. As Uhle (1902: 754) himself described his objectives in an article written for *American Anthropologist* in 1902:

> Our ideas concerning the degree of civilization in Pre-Columbian times by the inhabitants of the older American countries are not yet entirely freed from the prejudiced notion of generally regarding the various types of ancient culture as merely local styles, each being ascribed in some ways to a different geographic area and to a different tribe;—we are still prone to see in them purely ethnical divisions and individual local types. In observing these types of culture we should pay attention particularly to their succession in time; for their importance as stylistic strata which succeeded and covered each other (and, for the greater part, covered a coextensive area) is far beyond that which they may possess as local types. We must introduce into the archaeology of the countries of America the leading points of view which enabled students to distinguish in European prehistory the successive Hallstadt, La Tene, German Conquest, and Merovingian periods.

Uhle first incorporated this scholarly objective of isolating "stylistic strata" and their "succession in time" into his field work during his excavations at the great Peruvian coastal site of Pachacamac in 1896. There, Uhle noted (1902: 754), he applied the successful method developed by Flinders Petrie in Egypt of establishing "the succession of styles by the gradually changing character of the contents of graves differing in age. . . ." Applying basic principles of stratification to grave lot material (principally ceramics), Uhle (1902: 756) recognized five temporally distinct stylistic units that he characterized from the oldest to more recent as: (1) "that of the classical style of Tiahuanaco," (2) "that of a local epigonal development of the same style," (3) "the period of the vessels painted white, red, and black," (4) "the period characterized by certain black vessels," and (5) "the period of the style of the Incas."

This sequence was elaborated in greater detail in Uhle's (1903) monograph on Pachacamac. During subsequent work in the Moche Valley and in other important Peruvian and Chilean coastal valleys, Uhle consistently encountered ceramics that, in his judgment, were related in form, motif, color scheme, and other such attributes to the "classical Tiahuanaco style" or to the variant of the "epigonal Tiahuanaco" style that he had isolated at Pachacamac (Uhle 1913, 1915, 1919).

Uhle's familiarity with the highland-coastal distribution of Inca material culture, and with the presumptive historical descriptions of the Inca as an expansive imperial state, led him ineluctably to the conclusions that the Bolivian site of Tiwanaku was the ultimate source of a distinctive and broadly distributed art style, and, by implication, that the city was the capital of an Andean empire similar in structure, if not in geographical scope, to the Inca. Although Uhle did not employ the language of cultural horizon, or horizon style, the basic concepts were implicit in his notation of "stylistic strata" and their "succession in time."

Even from its inception, however, the characterization of Tiwanaku as a historically unified stylistic and cultural stratum in the south central Andes was being eroded by the realization that many of the regional coastal variants of the Tiwanaku style were, in fact, substantially different from the "classic" Tiwanaku style, expressed most essentially in the corpus of stone sculptures from Tiwanaku and its proximal affiliated settlements around the southern shores of Lake Titicaca (Figs. 1–5). Uhle (1903: 24) himself recognized this stylistic divergence between *altiplano* and coastal materials, but seems not to have explored in any depth the potential social implications of this distinction. Somewhat later, Alfred Kroeber (1927) explicitly distilled Tiwanaku material culture into two readily distinguishable stylistic units: "Coast Tiahuanaco" and "Highland Tiahuanaco." Kroeber (1944, 1948, 1951) nevertheless continued to conceptualize the

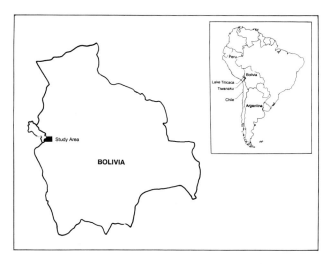

Fig. 1. Location map for Bolivia, Tiwanaku, and the study area of intensive agricultural production discussed in the text (after Kolata 1986: fig. 1)

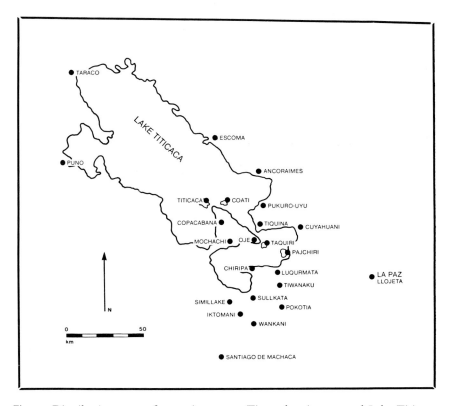

Fig. 2. Distribution map of some important Tiwanaku sites around Lake Titicaca

Fig. 3. Detail of the "Ponce Monolith" from the Kalasasaya temple at Tiwanaku

phenomenon of Tiwanaku as a cultural configuration within the frame work of a broad horizon style, an interpretation further elaborated by Gordon Willey (1945, 1948).

By the early 1940s, however, even the most vocal proponents of the horizon concept, who were engaged by its utility as a vehicle for organizing the space-time systematics of Andean culture history, began to appreciate that the actual historical situation in the south central Andes during the epoch of Tiwanaku emergence and florescence was dramatically more complex than might be accounted for by a single Inca-style regime of conquest

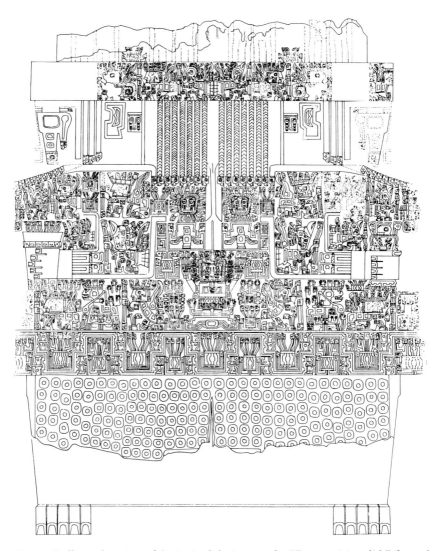

Fig. 4. Roll-out drawing of the incised designs on the "Bennett Monolith" from the Semi-subterranean Temple at Tiwanaku (redrawn from Posnansky 1945 I (2): fig. 117)

and territorial incorporation. Luis Valcarcel's (1932a, 1932b, 1935) publication of ceramic and stone sculptures from Pukara sites on the northern shore of Lake Titicaca brought into sharp relief the presence of a culture which possessed a vigorous art style that shared a substantial set of conventions and iconographic canons with Tiwanaku but was nevertheless clearly of autocthonous origin.

Fig. 5. Stone architectural element from Tiwanaku, possibly an architrave fragment, with a figure carved in high relief holding scepters, or staffs, and portrayed standing on a stepped-terrace temple mound. Traces of pigment still adhere to the sculpture, suggesting that this, and quite likely other Tiwanaku stone sculptures, were painted. The piece, 44 cm tall, is in the collections of the Museum für Völkerkunde, Dahlem, Berlin, catalogued as VA 10882, and was collected by Hettner, 1890 (photo: courtesy of Dieter Eisleb and the Museum für Völkerkunde, Dahlem, Berlin)

Alfred Kidder's (1943) subsequent excavations at Pukara in 1939, followed by archaeological survey in 1941, confirmed the essential independence of Pukara, and prompted him to remark (Kidder 1943: 40):

> It may be beating a dead horse, however, to raise the point here, but the demonstrated lack of Tiahuanaco extension in pure form to the northern Collao should lay the ghost of the "megalithic," or "Tiahuanaco" "empire" for good and all.

Farther to the north in the Ayacucho basin, Julio Tello's discovery of the extensive settlement at Wari (first published by Rowe, Collier, and Willey 1950), followed by the recovery in 1942 of elaborately painted ceremonial urns in a clearly Tiwanaku-related style from the Conchopata district of Ayacucho, altered archaeological perception of the source of Kroeber's old "Coast Tiahuanaco" material (Menzel 1968: 6; Wallace n.d.; see also Willey's 1948 article on horizon styles). A new orthodoxy began to emerge that identified Wari, and not Tiwanaku, as the true center of imperialistic expansion and the intellectual parent of the coastal Tiwanaku manifestations.

In this world view, Tiwanaku was no longer perceived as the sole, or, for that matter, even the principal distributive force behind the newly, if somewhat nebulously conceived "international style" now termed Wari-Tiwanaku. Most interpretations of the relationship between these two urban centers and their respective spheres of influence in the south central and southern Andes began to portray Tiwanaku as an essentially passive donor of a developed religious cult focused iconographically on the figure of the so-called Gateway, or "Staff God," together with its attendant symbols (Fig. 6; see Cook 1983 for other designations for this figure). These interpretations envisioned (unspecified) commercial interactions between Wari and Tiwanaku, brokered by merchant-missionaries who were instrumental in introducing the cult to Wari. There the cult of the "Staff God" became the catalyst for the formulation of a consciously fostered imperial ideology that was subsequently imposed by force of arms throughout the central Andes (Menzel 1964, 1968; Lumbreras 1974).

Subsequently, over the past decade, a number of other speculative reconstructions of the relationships, both between Tiwanaku and Wari specifically, and among Tiwanaku, Wari, and Pukara more generally, have been elaborated (Browman 1978, 1980, 1981; Isbell 1983; Cook 1983). Nevertheless, despite a growing data base for each of these three urban settlements (Pukara: Mujica 1978, 1985; Wari: Isbell 1977, 1980, 1986; Anders 1986; Spickard 1983; Brewster-Wray 1983; McEwan 1991; Tiwanaku: Ponce 1976, 1981a, 1981b; Kolata 1983, 1986, 1989), the precise nature of these relationships still remains a central problem in Andean culture history.

It is not my intention to contribute another leaf to the book of speculation concerning this admittedly important, but, to my mind, presently unresolv-

Fig. 6. Photograph (1908) of the "Gateway of the Sun" standing in its current location in the northwest corner of the Kalasasaya Temple (after Posnansky 1945: pl. XLV)

able problem. There remains a long row to hoe, particularly concerning the nature of the Tiwanaku polity, before any truly substantive and testable propositions are generated with respect to this now elusive problem of spatial, temporal, and cultural relationships. Therefore, my strategy here will be to reassess our current understanding of the structure of political economy in the Tiwanaku state. By focusing on the nature of Tiwanaku's endogenous and exogenous patterns of production, we will gain new insight into its perduring cultural influence in the ancient Andean world, and perhaps, a sharper and more complete perspective on the role of Tiwanaku in the evolution of the native Andean state.

As noted below, Tiwanaku cultural, political, and economic presence takes different forms in different geographic settings, both inside and outside of its heartland on the high plateau. In general, we may define three principal contexts for the expression of Tiwanaku cultural influence: (1) the

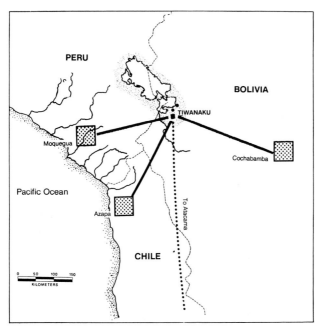

Fig. 7. Map of the Tiwanaku state's political geography. Shaded area in circum-Lake Titicaca basin illustrates distribution of the core, *altiplano* agricultural territory. Boxed areas represent agricultural colonies in lower altitude valleys. Dotted line indicates schematically llama caravan routes to the San Pedro de Atacama oasis discussed in the text

mountain slopes and *altiplano* of the Lake Titicaca basin; (2) the lower, warmer *yungas* zones that lie both to the east and west of the *altiplano* in the mesothermic valleys of Bolivia such as Cochabamba and in the coastal valleys of Peru and Chile such as Moquegua and Azapa; and (3) the vast, high plains to the south of the Titicaca basin in southern Bolivia and along the border of Chile such as in the San Pedro de Atacama region (Fig. 7). In each of these three sharply differentiated environmental zones, Tiwanaku material culture assumes varying forms and intensities of expression.

In the Lake Titicaca basin, we see the full panoply of Tiwanaku state action: an integrated network of densely populated, internally differentiated settlements distributed strategically across the landscape with the capacity of exploiting a variety of production zones. In the lower *yungas* region, Tiwanaku appears in many valleys in the form of large-scale colonizing populations, which, to judge by the scope and long-term persistence of occupation, were clearly established as permanent residences. Finally, in the more distant southerly reaches of the Tiwanaku sphere of influence, such as the high Atacama Oasis of Chile, its physical presence appears most prominently in elite mortuary and domestic contexts, suggesting a more specialized, fluid, and transactional quality to the relationship between the *altiplano* state and its local counterparts.

The fundamental identifying characteristics of Tiwanaku as a horizon style and its apparent spatial and chronological distribution will emerge in greater detail throughout the following discussion. However, those who wish to enhance their understanding of the essential elements of the Tiwanaku style should consult the remarkable two-volume graphic compendium of Tiwanaku material culture published by Arthur Posnansky (1945), along with Dwight Wallace's (n.d.) perceptive and still thought-provoking analysis of the relationship among the "Tiahuanaco horizon styles" (i.e., Tiwanaku, Wari, and Pukara).

POLITICAL ECONOMY AND HORIZON STYLES

Before embarking on my analysis of political economy in the Tiwanaku state, for the sake of clarity, I would like to characterize briefly some of my thoughts concerning the essential social, political, and cultural content of what we have called horizons, or horizon styles. The definition of a cultural horizon that I suggest here is, perhaps, unorthodox, and certainly differs from that employed by most contributors to this volume. If there is a fatal flaw in the concept of a cultural horizon, it resides precisely in a lack of specificity with respect to the kinds of social processes that generate and maintain identities, or at least non-random similarities, in material culture over space and time.

The first order assumption I make is that cultural horizons are intimately related to the political economy of states. From this perspective, a cultural horizon emerges as the direct result of shared participation in a single economic system. This does not imply, in some rigid fashion, a lack of ethnic differentiation or an absence of diversity in basic forms of production and exchange. Rather, the authentic cultural horizon reflects a systematic interaction of producers, consumers, managers, and economic intermediaries distributed over a relatively broad geographic area. The state, as the supraordinate form of political organization, provides the most efficient armature for this complex network of interaction, insuring through well-developed mechanisms of centralized control the survivability and long-term stability of the essential modes of economic and social production and reproduction.

However, within the ambit of the state's economic order, one can envision various degrees of participation. In the context of the preindustrial state, the essential wealth of nations was grounded in intensive agricultural production, most often centered in a core region under direct control of the central government. Frequently, although not invariably, this centralized control was expressed through a nested, hierarchical set of administrative and productive settlements. It is probably reasonably accurate to suggest that this core region of production consisted principally of an ethnically homogeneous base of peasant agriculturalists, who shared a common language, and participated in a mutually intelligible folk culture. This peasant base also shared a third characteristic: political and cultural domination by a ruling elite.

Again this is not to imply that core productive regions of preindustrial states entirely lacked ethnic diversity. The non-Aymara speaking, occupationally specialized Uru groups who lived along what Nathan Wachtel (1986) referred to as the "aquatic axis" within the heartland of the post-Tiwanaku Aymara kingdoms of the Lake Titicaca Basin are a trenchant case in point. Nevertheless, the principal productive force of these kingdoms resided in the Aymaraphone agriculturalists and pastoralists of the high *puna*.

The core region of production, then, reflects the most profound degree of participation in the state's economic order. In fact, its productive forces are so tightly bound to the economic order of the state that they may be considered isomorphic, or perhaps even constitutive of it.

At somewhat further remove, most agrarian states attempt to gain control of essential resources concentrated outside their primary core region. This is particularly true in the Andean region where the natural environment is characterized simultaneously by highly variable and remarkably compressed economic landscapes. The exploitation of peripheral zones takes two general forms: (1) direct colonization or expropriation of desired land or other resources, and (2) more indirect means of interregional exchange or trade, generally mediated by a professional class of merchants.

The first method of gaining access to these desired resources, of course, necessarily implies some form of coercive power exerted by the core region or its agents on the peripheries. The implicit threat of coercion may frequently be masked by the consciously fostered perception that the intrusive state and local populations are engaged in a mutually beneficial exchange of services and product or by the inculcation of a shared ideology that entails mass participation in public rituals, thereby embedding a notion of mutual interdependence and solidarity (Godelier 1977, 1978). In either case, or both taken together since in practice they are often conjoined, the end result will be to diffuse the social and economic tensions generated between the alien, intrusive state and the indigenous populations. The status quo of centralized control over labor, land, and production is thus affirmed at relatively low (from the perspective of the state) cost.

The second, more indirect method of gaining access to desired resources, although it may contain implicit elements of coercion, generally results from a relatively free and mutually beneficial exchange of information and goods. Here arrangements of status and power between state agents and authorities of local polities are more nearly equivalent, and the valuation of services and commodities in exchange transactions proceeds in a more flexible environment of negotiation rather than imposition.

THE POLITICAL ECONOMY OF THE TIWANAKU STATE

If we are to understand Tiwanaku, then, particularly from the analytical perspective of a cultural horizon, we must be able to reconstruct the nature and organization of both the endogenous and exogenous elements of that state's political economy. I begin my analysis of the political economy of the Tiwanaku state with the perhaps controversial proposition that Tiwanaku, like some of its contemporaneous counterparts in Peru, was a dynamic, expansive state, based squarely on an effective, surplus-producing system of intensive agriculture. This interpretation of Tiwanaku's political and economic system contradicts the perspective of Tiwanaku that, in the past two decades, has become a kind of orthodoxy in the archaeological literature in the United States and Peru. Here the settlement system of the Tiwanaku polity has been portrayed as a series of loosely linked ceremonial centers that lacked resident populations but that served as the focus of periodic pilgrimages from throughout the southern and central Andes (Lumbreras 1974).

From this perspective, Tiwanaku is distilled into a simple religious and artistic tradition that gradually diffused throughout the Andes through the activities of merchant-missionaries. Serious consideration that Tiwanaku might have played a forceful, independent, political role in the Andes during the Early Intermediate Period and the Middle Horizon was subsumed under the burden of the theory that the city of Wari was the only true political capital of empire in the Andes at this time (Menzel 1964, 1968). As Thomas Lynch (1983: 1) remarked, "the portrayal of Tiwanaku looks a bit like Central Andean chauvinism."

Even the most sophisticated reconstructions of Tiwanaku's political and economic impact on Andean culture history stress the primacy of long-distance exchange (of commodities and of ideologies) in integrating the Tiwanaku polity (Núñez and Dillehay 1979; Browman 1978, 1981). Because the appropriate data are only now beginning to emerge, none of these interpretations address the remarkable scale and complexity of Tiwanaku's indigenous agrarian system or the intensity of concern for massive agricultural reclamation evinced by the rulers of the Tiwanaku state in the Lake Titicaca basin and adjacent lands at lower elevations. How, then, can we reconcile the contradictions inherent in these apparently different models of Tiwanaku's political economy: one that emphasizes intensive agricultural production as a fundamental endogenous source of wealth for the nation, and the others that stress essentially exogenous sources of wealth such as long-distance exchange and religious pilgrimage?

By redefining our notion of the geopolitical boundaries of the old Tiwanaku state and by somewhat altering our perception of the nature of Tiwanaku exchange networks, the superficial tension between these different interpretations dissolves, and they may be seen to be essentially complementary. To this end, I believe that we can best conceptualize the essential contours of Tiwanaku political economy in terms of the long-term interaction among distinct production zones in core and periphery regions. First, I would argue that the essential geopolitical core of the Tiwanaku state consisted of a politically and economically integrated agricultural heartland reclaimed from the flat, marshy lands that ring Lake Titicaca. The fields in this core area provided the bulk of the state's considerable subsistence needs and accommodated the natural expansion of its demographic base (Kolata 1986, 1987, 1989). Large-scale herding of camelids in the adjacent high reaches of the *puna* complemented intensive tuber and grain agriculture in the lacustrine flatlands, creating a powerful core productive system capable of sustained yields (Yamamoto 1985; Tomoeda 1985). Although difficult to quantify precisely given the present lack of systematic research, it is evident from Tiwanaku middens tested to date that intensive exploitation of the lacustrine environment was a substantial, self-sustaining element of this pivotal productive system (Kolata 1986, 1989; Browman 1981). Lake Titicaca itself, and its smaller counterparts, provided fish, water fowl, edible aquatic plants, and abundant algae, which was used as a form of green manure to fertilize adjacent fields and, potentially, as fodder for camelids, as it is used today for cattle.

Secondly, the Tiwanaku state subsistence economy, although grounded in intensive *altiplano* agropastoralism, was not restricted to the food crops and camelid herds that can be produced and managed at high altitude. A key element of Tiwanaku state economic policy was colonization and subsequent control over regions ecologically distinct from that of the *altiplano*. The direct effect of this policy was the establishment of agricultural provinces in *yungas* zones through which the residents of Tiwanaku settlements on the high plateau enjoyed unmediated access to large quantities of important warm-land crops, such as maize and coca.

Finally, a third element played a critical role in the economic success and integration of the Tiwanaku polity: long-distance exchange through the medium of organized llama caravans. The most recent advances in the archaeology of Tiwanaku settlement and economy, however, have not concerned that state's presumptive long-distance exchange networks organized around caravan trade. Large-scale projects initiated within the past two years have begun to generate new, primary field data regarding the organization of agricultural production within the core of the Tiwanaku state in the high plateau of Bolivia, and in that state's agricultural provinces on the western slopes of the Andes in Peru and Chile. In short, the focus of current research has shifted from the exogenous to the endogenous elements of Tiwanaku political economy.

AGRICULTURAL PRODUCTION IN THE TIWANAKU STATE

For the past six years, my colleagues and I have been exploring the social and environmental dimensions of large-scale agricultural production in the sustaining hinterland of the city of Tiwanaku (Kolata 1989; Kolata and Ortloff 1989; Ortloff and Kolata 1989; Kolata 1991). In addition to fossil field systems and their associated features, we are currently excavating large areas of elite and commoner domestic residences at Tiwanaku and the poorly understood ritual and administrative centers of Lukurmata, Pajchiri, and Khonko Wankane. I believe that, even at this early juncture in the research, the results generated to date will require us to reassess the nature, structure, and organization of Tiwanaku, and its secondary centers in the *altiplano,* and thereby the impact of Tiwanaku in the geopolitical landscape of the Andean Middle Horizon.

For instance, we have demonstrated, through a systematic program of topographic mapping, intensive surface collection, and excavation that the site of Lukurmata was of a scale substantially larger than Wendell Bennett's sketch map from the 1930s would lead one to believe (Stanish 1989). The settlement extends far beyond the central acropolis of public architecture explored by Bennett to include extensive zones of domestic architecture, middens, agricultural fields, and storage structures (Fig. 8). We now estimate that the core settlement incorporates a minimum area of 2 km². Outlying habitation reflected in surface distributions of artifactual material extends to the east and west of the settlement.

The site itself is not an isolated temple complex, or a simple "vacant" ceremonial center. On the contrary, we may now state with confidence that this Tiwanaku regional secondary center was characterized by a dense population living in a variety of domestic settings distinguished by differences in status and occupation (Bermann 1989; Fig. 8 summarizes my current interpretation of internal community organization at Lukurmata). The presence of storage facilities within residences and the proximity of the massive raised field complexes of the adjacent Pampa Koani that I have previously associated with a Tiwanaku IV–V occupation (Kolata 1985, 1986, 1987, 1991) suggests an important administrative function for Lukurmata. The fact that Lukurmata is linked directly to the raised field complexes of the Pampa Koani by elevated roadbeds, or causeways, as well as to its companion secondary center of Pajchiri, and to Tiwanaku itself, enhances the viability of a reconstructed regional settlement system that emphasizes a structure characterized by hierarchy and centralized control (Fig. 9).

Even though our work at Pajchiri is still in its preliminary phases, survey operations have revealed that this settlement rivaled Lukurmata in size and complexity of architectural development, in both its public and domestic components. Our current estimate of maximum settlement size approaches 3.5 km² of public architecture, residences, and domestic terraces analogous

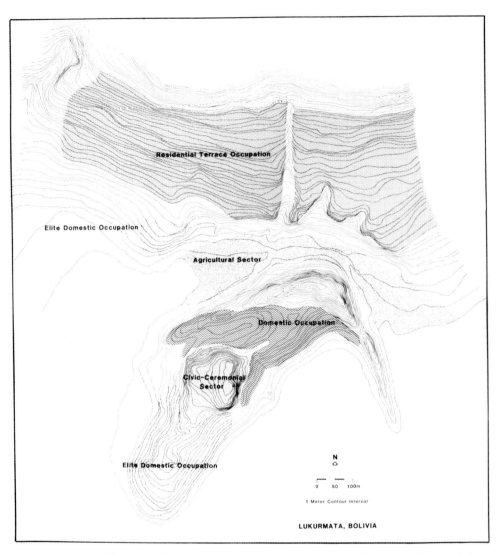

Fig. 8. Map of the Tiwanaku secondary urban center of Lukurmata (cf. Fig. 2). The map illustrates the distribution of general functional areas within the site. (See Kolata 1989, for a more detailed discussion of recent archaeological investigations at Lukurmata)

to those at Lukurmata. Moreover, Pajchiri, like Lukurmata, was supported by an elaborate, on-site sector of agricultural constructions (Ortloff and Kolata 1989). In the case of Pajchiri, these constructions are even more complex than those at Lukurmata, consisting of an interlinked set of aque-

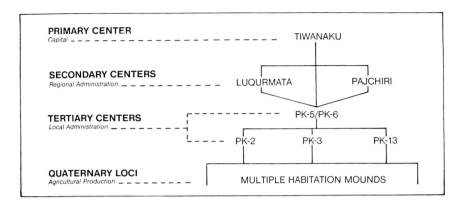

Fig. 9. Schematic representation of Tiwanaku's hierarchical settlement network (after Kolata 1986: fig. 8)

ducts, raised fields set on artificial, stepped terreplains, and a large, freshwater reservoir connected to the aqueduct uptakes by a canal (Ortloff and Kolata 1989). The entire system may have functioned to mitigate the problem of hypersalinization in lake-edge fields, and thereby maintain optimal production for the support of this pivotal administrative center, by permitting periodic fresh water flushing of the terreplains from small diversion structures set along stone-lined canals running on top of the aqueduct. We anticipate encountering sequential vertical construction of raised fields at Pajchiri similar to the three sets of superimposed, buried agricultural fields discovered in extensive excavations in the agricultural sector of Lukurmata (Kolata and Ortloff 1989).

In short, it is now very likely that Pajchiri, like Lukurmata, will be recharacterized as a densely populated, variegated settlement that performed important bureaucratic and administrative functions for the state, acting, in essence, as a local surrogate for the capital city of Tiwanaku. The principal political role of these secondary centers, located on either side of the Pampa Koani, was to manage the construction and maintenance of the impressive agricultural landscape that constituted the core productive zone for the capital.

I suspect that forthcoming excavations at the analogous regional Tiwanaku center of Khonko Wankane will reveal a similar demographic and functional profile as that of Lukurmata and Pajchiri. Given the size and functional complexity of these centers, I think it would not be inappropriate to speak of the Tiwanaku IV–V settlement pattern in the southern Titicaca basin as one articulated by a closely interacting network of cities centered in optimal lacustrine agricultural zones dominated by the apical center of Tiwanaku itself.

Yet Tiwanaku's interest in reclaiming agricultural land was not restricted to the immediate sustaining hinterland of the capital. A pattern of strategically located, state-built administrative centers near zones of potentially arable land, similar to that which has been documented for the Pampa Koani, may be perceived in the entire circum-Titicaca region during Tiwanaku phases III–V. Most of the known Tiwanaku satellite settlements of this type, such as Mocachi, Puente Yayes, Khonko Wankane, and the like, are situated along the southern and eastern rim of the lake. But there is clear evidence for intrusive Tiwanaku sites in the northern Titicaca basin as well, near Puno and on the island of Estevez (Núñez and Paredes 1978). In addition, Tiwanaku ceramics dating to phases III–V are documented for a wide area of Puno, which, certainly not coincidentally, encompasses a broad zone of fossil raised fields (Lennon n.d.; Erikson 1984, 1985; Charles Stanish, personal communication). This distinctive settlement pattern, when assessed against our new knowledge of the Pampa Koani rural zone, strongly implies that the state of Tiwanaku imposed a regional political unification of the Titicaca basin with an eye toward expanding its agricultural production, and thereby its fundamental sources of wealth, economic vitality, and political power.

Tiwanaku state expansion, intimately associated with the reclamation of agricultural land, proceeded well beyond the confines of the heartland in the high plateaus of the Titicaca basin. There is substantial and growing evidence that Tiwanaku directly colonized and subsequently controlled key economic resources of certain regions, such as the Cochabamba Valley of Bolivia, and the Azapa Valley of northern Chile, among others, which were ecologically distinct from the *altiplano*. One important region that we may identify as just such an economic province of the Tiwanaku state during its Tiwanaku IV–V florescence was the Moquegua Valley of southern Peru.

THE MOQUEGUA VALLEY: A TIWANAKU ECONOMIC PROVINCE

Recent research in the Moquegua Valley under the auspices of the *Programa Contisuyu* has begun to clarify the nature and extent of Tiwanaku state expansion from the *altiplano* to the western Andean slopes and coastal zones of southernmost Peru (Rice et al. 1989). Aridity and broken, difficult terrain severely constrain agriculture in the 140-km long drainage area of the Moquegua Valley. Although this drainage system rises above 5000 m, less than 20% of the catchment area lies within the zone of seasonal rainfall. Consequently, cultivation requires artificial, canal-based irrigation. Not surprisingly, the utilization of the scarce runoff is itself subject to topographic constraints that divide Moquegua agriculture into four ascending zones (Fig. 10). The second zone, which lies at the heart of the mid-valley, contains the largest expanse of arable land, composed of fertile flatlands formed around the confluence of the three major valley tributaries. This zone was the focus of heavy and long-term Tiwanaku occupation.

The Tiwanaku occupation of the Moquegua Valley was the subject of preliminary work in the 1960s (Disselhoff 1968; Ravines 1965). Current

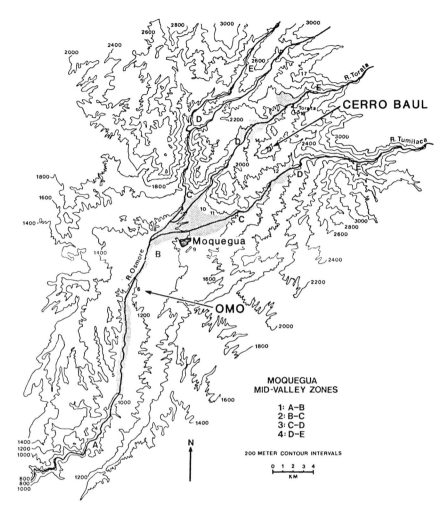

Fig. 10. Map of the middle Moquegua Valley, southern Peru, illustrating the distribution of arable land along the floodplains of the Osmore, Torata, and Tumilaca
rivers and the location of Tiwanaku sites at Omo and at the base of Cerro Baul
(redrawn from Moseley, Feldman, Goldstein, and Watanabe 1991: fig. 3; original
base map courtesy of Robert A. Feldman)

studies by Michael Moseley, Robert Feldman, Paul Goldstein, Garth
Bawden, and others have identified more than a dozen sites (Rice et al. 1989;
Moseley et al. 1991). Tiwanaku sites are concentrated in the lower agricultural zones where farming was supported by canal systems that reclaimed
relatively flat land (see Fig. 10). Associated settlements range from multi-
room farmsteads or hamlets to nucleated communities of several hundred

structures grouped around plazas. There are special-purpose sites such as the extensive settlement of Omo, where massive adobe architecture and formal, stepped terrace layout imply an administrative function (Goldstein n.d.). Other specialized sites include two mid-valley hills with large adjoining settlements that were heavily fortified with formidable masonry perimeter walls, and an exceptionally large cemetery that apparently served as the central burial ground for the mid-valley population (Chen Chen).

Three 50–150-room Tiwanaku settlements are situated at the base of Cerro Baul immediately adjacent to irrigated bottom lands of the Torata and Tumilaca rivers. However, there appears to be little or no Tiwanaku association with agricultural terraces at higher elevations. Additional Tiwanaku settlements and cemeteries cluster along the coast and in the lower reaches of the Rio Osmore, where Loreto Viejo has served as the type site defining the late Tiwanaku ceramic style of far southern Peru and northern Chile. Loreto Viejo, Chen Chen, and the other mid-valley sites have abundant decorated ceramics stylistically associated with Phase V of the Tiwanaku sequence. Local radiocarbon dates on this material range between ca. A.D. 900 and 1200. Tiwanaku IV material occurs less commonly than that of the later phase but is present in quantity at the large, but poorly understood site of Omo (Goldstein n.d.; Mosley et al. 1991). Unfortunately, at present, we have no local radiocarbon dates for the presumptive Tiwanaku IV material, but elsewhere this phase has been estimated to have begun after A.D. 400. (Ponce 1972; Kolata 1983, 1989).

In recent years, both ethnographic and archaeological research has demonstrated that ethnic groups of *altiplano* affiliation have periodically colonized or otherwise occupied key resource-bearing lands in the Osmore and other drainages to the south (Mujica 1985; Julien 1985). Preliminary evidence from work completed over the past two years strongly supports the interpretation that ethnic *altiplano* occupation in the Moquegua region was an ancient and profoundly influential geopolitical pattern (Mujica 1978). Both survey and tomb excavations have revealed substantial quantities of early *altiplano* ceramic materials including classic Pukara pottery from the northern Titicaca basin, and the fiber tempered wares characteristic of the Chiripa sites of the southern Titicaca basin.

If we combine this evidence with the history of Tiwanaku occupation outlined above, it is very difficult to escape the conclusion that, at various times, the Moquegua Valley was the object of resource-hungry *altiplano* ethnic groups wishing to expand their economic base. During the Tiwanaku regime, if not earlier, we can surely speak of Moquegua as an integrated economic province of an *altiplano* state.

I would not necessarily suggest, however, that the agriculturally oriented mid-valley region of the Osmore drainage was organized by the state administration of Tiwanaku in the same hierarchical fashion as in the Pampa Koani sustaining zone. Rather I would envision a more symbiotic relationship between state and provincial governments that encouraged a stronger measure of local autonomy in the organization of production. In contrast to the situation on the Pampa Koani where labor for reclaiming and maintaining productive agricultural lands was non-local (i.e., explicitly brought in by state government for that purpose) all evidence indicates that in the Moquegua Valley the land was worked by the local resident populations in part for their own benefit and secondarily for the benefit of the reigning political power from the *altiplano*. In return for a portion of the labor and product of the local Moquegua populations, the Tiwanaku state would have provided both a measure of political security and perhaps the technological and administrative expertise in developing massive reclamation projects that had been gained through centuries of creating analogous hydraulic works around the edges of the Lake Titicaca homeland.

In my historical reconstruction, then, the strategy of Tiwanaku state economic expansion entailed first developing a solid core of tightly controlled agricultural zones of which the Pampa Koani, as the immediate sustaining area of the capital city itself, was one of the most important. This agrarian core was engaged in the production of staple *altiplano* crops such as potato, oca, quinoa, and the like, and, in time, came to encompass the entire circum-Lake Titicaca region. This core of reclaimed land was the direct result of and dependent upon the actions of the Tiwanaku state government, or, more precisely, upon the actions of the elite classes that constituted supra-community government in the Tiwanaku polity.

The second critical element of Tiwanaku economic expansion entailed the movement into *yungas* regions of lower altitude, such as the Moquegua, Azapa, and Cochabamba Valleys, where important warm land crops such as maize, coca, and aji could be grown. Here state intervention was more indirect and local autonomy may not have been completely abrogated as in the case of the Pampa Koani. Nevertheless, despite its significant organizational differences from the core agricultural zones such as the Pampa Koani, the Moquegua region and its counterparts were in a real sense politically, economically, and to some degree, culturally embedded in an influential social matrix of *altiplano,* particularly Tiwanaku, origin. If he had been on the scene, Niccolo Machiavelli, author of the great Renaissance manual of statecraft, *The Prince,* would have admired the machinations of the state of Tiwanaku, for he has this to say about the most effective strategies of state expansion:

> plant colonies in one or two of those places which form as it were the keys of the land, for it is necessary either to do this or to maintain a large force of armed men. . . . but by maintaining a garrison instead of colonists, one will spend much more, and consume all of the revenues of the state in guarding it, so the acquisi-

tion will result in a loss. . . . In every way, therefore, a garrison is as useless as colonies are useful. (Machiavelli [1532], 1952: 37–38).

In this regard, the lords of Tiwanaku might have been the New World archetype for Machiavelli's prince. They were sensitive to the need to establish alliances with the local populations, perhaps even to inculcate a sense of loyalty and identification with the prestige and power of the state. Accordingly, they founded substantial colonies in the Moquegua region and elsewhere, creating in the process a pluralistic, multi-ethnic state.

CARAVANS AND CLIENTS: TIWANAKU EXCHANGE SYSTEMS

To complete this analysis of Tiwanaku state political economy, reference must be made to the third element of the economic system shaped by this *altiplano* polity: long distance exchange through the medium of organized llama caravans. This is the element of economic activity stressed so forcefully by David Browman (1978, 1981), who envisions Tiwanaku as a pilgrimage center of great ritual prestige that became the nexus of multiple, far-flung caravan routes operated by loosely confederated ethnic groups. Although I cannot agree with Browman's characterization of Tiwanaku as a weak confederation of ethnic groups bound solely by economic mutualism rather than by political imperative, I would agree that in the far reaches of Tiwanaku influence, in the area of San Pedro de Atacama, the central Chilean valleys, the Quebrada de Humahuaca in northwestern Argentina, the nature of the interaction between the *altiplano* polity and local populations was more attenuated than in the core regions of the Lake Titicaca basin and adjacent lands. This attenuation of direct state action, of course, is reflected in material culture: here Tiwanaku-related artifacts are concentrated disproportionately in elite domestic and mortuary contexts and consist principally of portable art associated with Tiwanaku state cult and belief systems.

I hypothesize that this long distance exchange was organized along the lines of a clientage relationship, in which the local elites of these distant lands maintained personal relationships with the lords of Tiwanaku, managing the production and exchange of desired commodities, and, simultaneously, appropriating emblems of status and authority from their *altiplano* patrons. Such a clientage relationship would account for the selective distribution of elite Tiwanaku material culture from tombs in these regions distant from the Tiwanaku homeland, particularly the heavy occurrences of textiles, elements of costume, and paraphernalia associated with the consumption of hallucinogenic drugs. More basic cultural patterns of settlement and local subsistence do not seem to have been altered directly by the interaction with the *altiplano* state.

I suspect that at least some of the far-ranging pack trains of llamas that articulated this mercantile element of Tiwanaku political economy were more highly organized and centrally administered than either Browman

(1980) or Núñez and Dillehay (1979) currently believe. Specifically, the main trunk route to the San Pedro de Atacama oasis may have been monopolized and forcefully administered by the state of Tiwanaku (see Fig. 7). The Atacama oasis probably served as an entrepôt, or transshipment point for other independent caravan traders who brought goods for exchange and distribution with established trading partners. Recent analyses of mortuary textiles in the San Pedro de Atacama oasis indicate the presence of substantial colonies of *altiplano* populations, most likely from the Tiwanaku core region around Lake Titicaca (A. Oakland-Rodman, personal communication). Such colonization, or enclaving of populations, emphasizes the geopolitical importance of the Atacama oasis to the lords of Tiwanaku.

From my perspective, the Tiwanaku state formalized key routes in the network of interregional communication maintained through llama caravans. In regions relatively close to the Titicaca basin (southern Peru, Cochabamba, northern Chile, Atacama), Tiwanaku founded substantial economic colonies that were linked directly to the capital and its satellite cities by state-managed caravans. In regions at further remove (Valliserrana, Quebrada de Humahuaca, western Puna of Argentina), the state operated more indirectly, through a clientage relationship, in which politically independent, and perhaps ethnically diverse caravan traders were funneled into the Atacama entrepôt.

ZONAL COMPLEMENTARITY AND POLITICAL ECONOMY IN THE TIWANAKU STATE

To what extent is the foregoing reconstruction of Tiwanaku political economy consonant with or reflective of the general model of "verticality," or, more broadly, economic complementarity in the Andes first explicitly formulated by John Murra (1964, 1968, 1972, 1985a, 1985b)? The model itself argues that highland Andean ethnic groups and polities persistently attempted to exert control over a maximum number of distinct, altitudinally stratified ecological zones in order to enhance and diversify agricultural production and to insure direct, unmediated access to other strategic resources (minerals [Shimada 1985], guano [Julien 1985], *cochayuyo* [Masuda 1985], etc.). Functionally equivalent analyses of "vertical control" have been applied to Andean societies across the continuum of sociopolitical complexity, from single villages in which reciprocal obligations among consanguinal and affinal kinsmen and their allies structured relations of production of relatively low energetic value, to large-scale colonizing states engaged in patterns of intensive production, labor allocation, and redistribution of surplus.

Over the past decade, driven by the stimulus of Murra's contribution, concepts of multi-ethnic exploitation of economic islands arrayed in "vertical archipelagos," large-scale colonization by highland societies of multiple, low-lying ecological "floors" or niches (Murra 1972), "compressed," "extended," (Brush 1976), and "micro" verticality (Salomon 1980), direct and indirect economic complementarity (Mujica 1978, 1985), "discontinuous territoriality" (Cock 1976) and even "horizontal archipelagos" (Shimada 1985) have all gained currency in the general explanatory frameworks that seek to link economy and polity in the Andes. It would not be an exaggeration to suggest, in fact, that models of verticality and zonal economic complementarity have become pervasive, influential, and, in the case of the south central Andes at least, dominant features of the intellectual landscape of Andean studies (see, for instance, the symposium papers compiled in Flores Ochoa 1978 and Masuda, Shimada, and Morris 1985).

However, even as the analytical perspective engendered by general models of zonal complementarity received increasingly broad, more inclusive, and perhaps at times, uncritical application, Murra (1985a) was cautioning that the notion of the "vertical archipelago" required careful, context-specific verification and that Andean scholars should not simply accept the verticality model as axiomatic. Murra (1985a) himself described some demographic and political conditions under which "vertical archipelagos" were not likely to emerge, or under which specific structural transformations of a given society's political economy would be anticipated (Murra 1985a: 18):

> [U]pon the expansion of the population which it controlled, the growth of the power of the authorities, the increasing difficulty of exercising effective control over rights maintained at the center by inhabitants settled in the "islands," the archipelago changes structurally. Contradictions appear between the interest of the lords and the *mitmaqkuna;* the relations of reciprocity and redistribution are weakened.

In situations of sustained demographic growth and increasing concentration of political power in the hands of elite interest groups such as hypothesized by Murra, we might anticipate that the previously symmetrical relationships between highland lords and outlying colonists through which the property and jural rights of the latter in their homeland were acknowledged and maintained would begin to change. I would suggest that the inevitable direction of this change could be toward increasing peripheralization of colonial enclaves. By this I do not mean that the political and economic relations between principal lords and their colonial subjects weakened. Quite the contrary: these social linkages, in fact, would have been strengthened. However, the intensification of these relations would not follow traditional lineaments characterized by reasonably balanced reciprocal rights and obligations between lord and subject. Rather, the essential character of these linkages, formerly embedded in the metaphor of kinship, would be "depersonalized," and reconstructed as asymmetrical relations of extraction in which the colonial enclaves and their inhabitants become little more than sources of surplus raw materials and labor for the state.

The transformation of discontinuously distributed, formerly kin-bonded colonial enclaves into true economic provinces of a centralized state characterizes the emergence of the Tiwanaku macro-polity between ca. A.D. 400 and 1000. If, after evaluating the data from regions such as the Moquegua, Azapa, and Cochabamba Valleys, we accept that this transformation occurred in the south central Andes during this time, it is clear that the vertical archipelago model developed by Murra (1968, 1972) in describing the Lupaqa polity's apparently non-coercive mechanisms of interzonal economic exchange is inappropriate when applied to the mature Tiwanaku state.

Rather I think we can more effectively frame the question of the nature of Tiwanaku's political economy in terms of interlocking sets of core-periphery relationships structured around multiple forms of complementary interactions: direct and indirect, centralized and decentralized, administered and autonomous (see Salomon 1985: 520, for a comprehensive diagram of institutions of Andean economic complementarity). The Tiwanaku state manipulated various institutional forms of both coercive and consensual economic complementarity (large-scale regional colonization, selective enclaving of populations, administered trade, clientage, barter) to intensify production, as well as to enhance its own political integration, following a principle of context-specific structuring of the relationships between the state and local populations.

Such a perspective on the nature of Tiwanaku political economy, as contrasted with a mechanical application of the vertical archipelago concept modeled along the lines of the Lupaqa colonizing state, affords a more convincing explanation of the high regional variability in Tiwanaku settlement patterns and material culture. Such a perspective also acknowledges that as states expand they incorporate a multiplicity of local populations possessing divergent demographic, political, and economic potentials. For instance, it is likely that some of the regions in the Lake Titicaca basin into which the Tiwanaku state expanded, such as the heartland of the old Pukara polity, contained nucleated settlements with high population density, large investment in labor-intensive systems of production, class stratification, and well-developed mechanisms for allocating and redistributing economic surplus. Other areas, however, such as the high *puna* of the Atacama, were characterized by relatively small-scale, widely distributed, kin-based communities that emphasized local community autonomy, with more inclusive economic relationships restricted to exchange based on principles of reciprocity. It is evident that an expansive state confronted with such social, economic, and behavioral heterogeneity would need to generate multiple, context-sensitive strategies to adjust the relationship between centrally imposed tributary modes of production and locally self-sustaining communal modes of production. In short, Tiwanaku as a state formation may be conceptualized as a dynamic, heterogeneous mosaic of populations linked (perhaps at times imperfectly) by a mosaic of policies focused on the economy of extraction which were devised by elite interest groups in the core polity of the Lake Titicaca basin.

TIWANAKU AS A CULTURAL HORIZON

Given the foregoing reflections on Tiwanaku political economy, what conclusions may we draw with respect to Tiwanaku as a cultural horizon, and more generally, to the utility of the horizon concept as an explanation of the archaeological distribution of Tiwanaku material culture? The answers to these questions essentially depend upon which spatial and temporal frames of reference one chooses to approach the problem.

That is, if we consider Tiwanaku from the frame of reference of its core region in the Lake Titicaca basin during the first millennium, there is little question that it constituted an authentic cultural horizon as an integrated, politically centralized state. If we analyze Tiwanaku from the frame of reference of its colonized agricultural provinces such as Moquegua, Cochabamba, and Azapa, we should consider it as a cultural horizon, but most likely only during the Tiwanaku IV and V phases and not earlier. Furthermore, as I have indicated, the essential content of this cultural horizon, even though in a contemporaneous context, may be very different in geographically separate regions: for instance, the precise forms of the sociology and organization of agricultural production in core and colonial regions was probably quite distinct.

Finally, if we consider Tiwanaku from the frame of reference of the distant regions of central Chile, and northwestern Argentina, we can legitimately use the horizon concept only in its incarnation as a strict chronological marker, methodologically binding style, time, and place. In these regions, the interaction with Tiwanaku cannot be conceptualized as pervasive, or something that dramatically alerted local patterns of subsistence and social organization. In short, a clientage relationship will not constitute a cultural horizon as I have defined it. Used in this flexible, context-specific manner, the concept of horizon retains vitality and describes, in essence, the political and economic actions of expansive state formations.

BIBLIOGRAPHY

ANDERS, MARTHA
1986 Wari Experiments in Statecraft: A View from Azangaro. In *Andean Archaeology: Papers in Memory of Clifford Evans* (Ramiro Matos M., Solveig A. Turpin, and Herbert Eling, Jr., eds.): 201–224. Monograph 27, Institute of Archaeology. University of California, Los Angeles.

BERMANN, MARC
1989 Una visión de las casas del período Tiwanaku en Lukurmata. In *Arqueología de Lukurmata,* 2 (Alan L. Kolata, ed.): 113–152. Instituto Nacional de Arqueología y Ediciones Puma Punku, La Paz, Bolivia.

BREWSTER-WRAY, CHRISTINE
1983 Spatial Patterning and the Function of a Huari Architectural Compound. In *Investigations of the Andean Past: Papers of the First Annual Northeast Conference on Andean Archaeology and Ethnology* (Daniel Sandweiss, ed.): 122–135. Latin American Studies Program. Cornell University, Ithaca, New York.

BROWMAN, DAVID
1978 Toward the Development of the Tiahuanaco (Tiwanaku) State. In *Advances in Andean Archaeology* (David Browman, ed.): 327–349. Mouton, The Hague, The Netherlands.
1980 Tiwanaku Expansion and Altiplano Economic Patterns. *Estudios Arqueológicos* 5: 107–120. Universidad de Chile, Antofagasta.
1981 New Light on Andean Tiwanaku. *American Scientist* 69 (4): 408–419.

BRUSH, STEPHEN
1976 *Mountain, Field and Family: The Economic and Human Ecology of an Andean Valley.* University of Pennsylvania Press, Philadelphia.

COCK, GUILLERMO
1976 La visita de los Conchucos por Cristobal Ponce de Leon, 1543. *Historia y Cultura* 10: 23–45.

COOK, ANITA
1983 Aspects of State Ideology in Huari and Tiwanaku Iconography: The Central Deity and Sacrificer. In *Investigations of the Andean Past: Papers of the First Annual Northeast Conference on Andean Archaeology and Ethnology* (Daniel Sandweiss, ed.): 161–185. Latin American Studies Program. Cornell University, Ithaca, New York.

DISSELHOFF, H.D.
1968 *Oasenstadte und Zaubersteine im Land der Inka.* Safari-Verlag, Berlin.

ERICKSON, CLARK
1984 Waru-waru: una tecnología agrícola del altiplano prehispánico. *Boletín del Instituto de estudios Aymaras,* ser. 2, 18: 4–37.
1985 Applications of Prehistoric Andean Technology: Experiments in Raised Field Agriculture, Huatta, Lake Titicaca 1981–1982. In *Prehistoric Inten-*

Alan L. Kolata

sive Agriculture in the Tropics (Ian Farrington, ed.): 209–232. BAR International Series, 232(i). Oxford.

FLORES OCHOA, JORGE (ED.)

1978   Organización social y complementariedad económica el los Andes Centrales. *Actes du 42e Congrès International des Américanistes* 4: 7–156. Paris.

GODELIER, MAURICE

1977   *Perspectives in Marxist Anthropology.* Cambridge University Press, Cambridge.

1978   Infrastructures, Societies and History. *Current Anthropology* 19: 763–771.

GOLDSTEIN, PAUL

n.d.   *Omo, A Tiwanaku Provincial Center in Moquegua, Peru.* Ph.D. dissertation, University of Chicago, Chicago, Illinois, 1989.

ISBELL, WILLIAM

1977   *The Rural Foundation for Urbanism.* University of Illinois Press, Urbana.

1980   La evolución del urbanismo y del estado en el Peru Tiwanakoide. *Estudíos Arqueológicos* 5: 121–132. Universidad de Chile, Antofagasta.

1983   Shared Ideology and Parallel Political Development: Huari and Tiwanaku. In *Investigations of the Andean Past: Papers of the First Annual Northeast Conference on Andean Archaeology and Ethnology* (Daniel Sandweiss, ed.): 186–208. Latin American Studies Program. Cornell University, Ithaca, New York.

1986   Emergence of City and State at Wari, Ayacucho, Peru during the Middle Horizon. In *Andean Archaeology: Papers in Memory of Clifford Evans.* (Ramiro Matos M., Solveig A. Turpin, and Herbert Eling, Jr., eds.): 189–200. Monograph 27, Institute of Archaeology, University of California, Los Angeles.

JULIEN, CATHERINE

1985   Guano and Resource Control in Sixteenth-Century Arequipa. In *Andean Ecology and Civilization* (Shozo Masuda, Izumi Shimada, and Craig Morris, eds.): 185–231. University of Tokyo Press, Tokyo.

KIDDER II, ALFRED

1943   *Some Early Sites in the Northern Titicaca Basin.* Papers of the Peabody Museum of Archaeology and Ethnology, Harvard University 27 (1). Cambridge, Mass.

KOLATA, ALAN L.

1983   The South Andes. In *Ancient South Americans* (Jesse Jennings, ed.): 241–284. W. H. Freeman & Co., San Francisco.

1985   El papel de la agricultura intensiva en la economía politíca del estado de Tiwanaku. *Diálogo Andino* 4: 11–38. Universidad de Tarapacá, Arica.

1986   The Agricultural Foundations of the Tiwanaku State: A View from the Heartland. *American Antiquity* 51: 748–762.

1987   Tiwanaku and its Hinterland. *Archaeology* 40 (1): 36–41.

1989   *Arqueología de Lukurmata, 2* (Alan L. Kolata, ed.). Instituto Nacional de Arqueología y Ediciones Puma Punku, La Paz, Bolivia.

1991   The Technology and Organization of Agricultural Production in the Tiwanaku State. *Latin American Antiquity* 2 (2): 99–125.

KOLATA, ALAN L., AND GRAY GRAFFAM
1989   Los campos elevados de Lukurmata, Bolivia. In *Arqueología de Lukurmata, 2* (Alan L. Kolata, ed.): 173–212. Instituto Nacional de Arqueología y Ediciones Puma Punku, La Paz, Bolivia.

KOLATA, ALAN L., AND CHARLES ORTLOFF
1989   Thermal Analysis of Tiwanaku Raised Field Systems in the Lake Titicaca Basin of Bolivia. *Journal of Archaeological Science* 16: 233–263.

KROEBER, ALFRED
1927   Coast and Highland in Prehistoric Peru. *American Anthropologist* 29: 625–653.
1944   *Archaeology in Peru in 1942.* Viking Fund Publications in Anthropology 4. New York.
1948   Summary and Interpretations. In *A Reappraisal of Peruvian Archaeology* (Wendell Bennett, ed.): 113–121. Memoirs of the Society for American Archaeology 4, Supplement to American Antiquity 13 (4), pt. 2.
1951   Great Art Styles of Ancient America. In *The Civilizations of Ancient America* (Sol Tax, ed.). Selected Papers of the 29th International Congress of Americanists, 1. University of Chicago Press, Chicago.

LENNON, THOMAS J.
n.d.   *Raised Fields of Lake Titicaca, Peru: A Prehispanic Water Management System.* Ph.D. dissertation, University of Colorado, Boulder, 1982.

LUMBRERAS, LUIS
1974   *Peoples and Cultures of Ancient Peru* (Betty Meggers, trans.). Smithsonian Institution, Washington, D.C.

LYNCH, THOMAS
1983   Camelid Pastoralism and the Emergence of Tiwanaku Civilization in the South-Central Andes. *World Archaeology* 15 (1): 1–14.

MACHIAVELLI, NICCOLO
1952   *The Prince* ([1532]; Luigi Ricci, trans.). New American Library of World Literature, Mentor, New York.

MASUDA, SHOZO
1985   Algae Collectors and Lomas. In *Andean Ecology and Civilization* (Shozo Masuda, Izumi Shimada, and Craig Morris, eds): 233–250. University of Tokyo Press, Tokyo.

MASUDA, SHOZO, IZUMI SHIMADA, AND CRAIG MORRIS (EDS.)
1985   *Andean Ecology and Civilization.* University of Tokyo Press, Tokyo.

McEWAN, GORDON
1991   Investigations at the Pikillacta Site: A Provincial Huari Center in the Valley of Cuzco. In *Huari Administrative Structure: Prehistoric Monumental Architecture and State Government* (William Isbell and Gordon McEwan, eds.): 93–119. Dumbarton Oaks, Washington, D.C.

Alan L. Kolata

MENZEL, DOROTHY
    1964   Style and Time in the Middle Horizon. *Ñawpa Pacha* 2: 1–105.
    1968   New Data on the Huari Empire in the Middle Horizon Epoch 2A. *Ñawpa Pacha* 6: 47–114.

MOSELEY, MICHAEL, ROBERT FELDMAN, PAUL GOLDSTEIN, AND LUIS WATANABE
    1991   Colonies and Conquest: Tiahuanaco and Huari in Moquegua. In *Huari Administrative Structure: Prehistoric Monumental Architecture and State Government* (William Isbell and Gordon McEwan, eds.): 121–140. Dumbarton Oaks Research Library and Collections, Washington, D.C.

MUJICA, ELIAS
    1978   Nueva hipótesis sobre el desarrollo temprano del altiplano del Titicaca y sus áreas de interacción. *Arte y Arqueología* 5–6: 285–308. Revista del Instituto de Estudios Bolivianos, La Paz.
    1985   Altiplano-Coast Relationships in the South-Central Andes: From Indirect to Direct Complementarity. In *Andean Ecology and Civilization* (Shozo Masuda, Izumi Shimada, and Craig Morris, eds.): 103–140. University of Tokyo Press, Tokyo.

MURRA, JOHN
    1964   Una apreciación etnológica de la visita. In *Visita hecha a la provincia de Chucuito por Garci Diez de San Miguel en el año 1567*. Documentos Regionales para la Etnología y Etnohistoria Andina 1: 421–444. Ediciones de la Casa de la Cultura del Perú, Lima.
    1968   An Aymara Kingdom in 1567. *Ethnohistory* 15 (2): 115–151.
    1972   El "control vertical" de un máximo de pisos ecológicos en la economía de las sociedades andinas. In *Visita de la Provincia de León de Huánuco en 1562* (John Murra, ed.): Documentos para la Historia y Etnología de Huánuco y la Selva Central 2: 427–476. Universidad Nacional Hermilio Valdizán, Huánuco.
1985a[1976] The Limits and Limitations of the "Vertical Archipelago" in the Andes. In *Andean Ecology and Civilization* (Shozo Masuda, Izumi Shimada, and Craig Morris, eds.): 15–20. University of Tokyo Press, Tokyo.
    1985b   "El Archipielago Vertical" Revisited. In *Andean Ecology and Civilization* (Shozo Masuda, Izumi Shimada, and Craig Morris, eds.): 3–13. University of Tokyo Press, Tokyo.

NÚÑEZ, LAUTARO, AND THOMAS DILLEHAY
    1979   *Movilidad giratoria, armonía social y desarollo en los Andes meridionales: Patrones de tráfico e interacción económica.* Universidad del Norte, Antofagasta.

NÚÑEZ, MARIO, AND ROLANDO PAREDES
    1978   Estevez: Un sitio de ocupación Tiwanaku. In *III Congreso Peruano del Hombre y Cultura Andina*, 2 (Ramiro Matos, ed.): 757–764. Lima.

ORTLOFF, CHARLES, AND ALAN L. KOLATA
    1989   Hydraulic Analysis of Tiwanaku Aqueduct Structures at Lukurmata and Pajchiri, Bolivia. *Journal of Archaeological Science* 16: 513–535.

PONCE SANGINES, CARLOS

    1972   *Tiwanaku: Espacio, tiempo y cultura; Ensayo de síntesis arqueológica.* Academia Nacional de Ciencias de Bolivia, publicación 30, La Paz.

    1976   *La cerámica de la Época I de Tiwanaku,* 2nd ed. Instituto Nacional de Arqueología, publicación 18, La Paz.

    1981a   *Descripción sumaria del templete semisubterraneo de Tiwanaku,* 5th rev. ed. Libreria y Editorial "Juventud," La Paz.

    1981b   *Tiwanaku: Espacio, tiempo y cultura; Ensayo de síntesis arqueológica,* 4th ed. Editorial "Los Amigos del Libro," La Paz and Cochabamba.

POSNANSKY, ARTHUR

    1945   *Tihuanacu, the Cradle of American Man,* 2 vols. J. J. Augustin, New York.

RAVINES, ROGGER

    1965   Investigaciones arqueológicas en el Perú. *Revista del Museo Nacional* 34: 247–254. Lima.

RICE, DON, CHARLES STANISH, AND PHILIP SCARR (EDS.)

    1989   *Ecology, Settlement and History in the Osmore Drainage, Peru.* BAR International Series 545 (i–ii). Oxford.

ROWE, JOHN, DONALD COLLIER, AND GORDON WILLEY

    1950   Reconnaisance Notes on the Site of Huari near Ayacucho, Peru. *American Antiquity* 16: 120–137.

SALOMON, FRANK

    1980   *Los señores étnicos de Quito en la época de los Incas.* Serie Pendorenos 10. Instituto Otavaleño de Antropología, Otavalo.

    1985   The Dynamic Potential of the Complementarity Concept. In *Andean Ecology and Civilization* (Shozo Masuda, Izumi Shimada, and Craig Morris, eds.): 511–531. University of Tokyo Press, Tokyo.

SHIMADA, IZUMI

    1985   Perception, Procurement, and Management of Resources: Archaeological Perspective. In *Andean Ecology and Civilization* (Shozo Masuda, Izumi Shimada, and Craig Morris, eds): 357–399. University of Tokyo Press, Tokyo.

SPICKARD, LYNDA

    1983   The Development of Huari Administrative Architecture. In *Investigations of the Andean Past: Papers of the First Annual Northeast Conference on Andean Archaeology and Ethnology* (Daniel Sandweiss, ed.): 136–160. Latin American Studies Program. Cornell University, Ithaca, New York.

STANISH, CHARLES

    1989   Tamaño y complejidad de los asentamientos nucleares de Tiwanaku. In *Arqueología de Lukurmata,* 2 (Alan L. Kolata, ed.): 41–58. Instituto Nacional de Arqueología y Ediciones Puma Punku, La Paz.

STÜBEL, ALFONS, AND MAX UHLE

    1892   *Die Ruinenstaette von Tiahuanaco im Hochlande des alten Perú.* Eine Kulturgeschichtliche Studie auf Grund selbstandiger Aufnahmen. Verlag von Karl W. Hiersmann, Leipzig.

TOMOEDA, HIROYASU

    1985   The Llama is My Chacra: Metaphor of Andean Pastoralists. In *Andean Ecology and Civilization* (Shozo Masuda, Izumi Shimada, and Craig Morris, eds.): 277–300. University of Tokyo Press, Tokyo.

UHLE, MAX

    1902   Types of Culture in Peru. *American Anthropologist* 4: 753–759.

    1903   *Pachacamac: Report of the William Pepper, M.D., LL.D. Peruvian Expedition of 1896.* Department of Archaeology, University of Pennsylvania, Philadelphia.

    1913   Los indios atacameños. *Revista Chilena de Historia y Geografía* 9: 105–111. Santiago.

    1915   Las tabletas y tubos de rape en Chile. *Revista Chilena de Historia y Geografía* 16: 114–136. Santiago.

    1919   La arqueología de Arica y Tacna. *Boletín de la Sociedad Ecuatoriana de Estudios Historicos Americanos* 8: 1–48. Quito.

VALCARCEL, LUIS

    1932a   El personaje mítico de Pukara. *Revista del Museo Nacional* 1 (1): 18–30. Lima.

    1932b   El gato de agua, sus representaciones en Pukara y Naska. *Revista del Museo Nacional* 1 (2): 3–27. Lima.

    1935   Litoesculturas y cerámica de Pukara. *Revista del Museo Nacional* 4 (1): 25–38. Lima.

WACHTEL, NATHAN

    1986   Men of the Water: The Uru Problem (Sixteenth and Seventeenth Centuries). In *Anthropological History of Andean Polities* (John Murra, Nathan Wachtel, and Jacques Revel, eds.): 283–310. Cambridge University Press, Cambridge.

WALLACE, DWIGHT

    n.d.   *The Tiahuanaco Horizon Styles in the Peruvian and Bolivian Highlands.* Ph.D. dissertation, University of California, Berkeley, 1957.

WILLEY, GORDON

    1945   Horizon Styles and Pottery Traditions in Peruvian Archaeology. *American Antiquity* 11: 49–56.

    1948   Functional Analysis of "Horizon Styles" in Peruvian Archaeology. In *A Reappraisal of Peruvian Archaeology* (Wendell Bennett, ed.): 8–15. Memoirs of the Society for American Archaeology 4, Supplement to *American Antiquity* 13 (4), part 2.

YAMAMOTO, NORIO

    1985   The Ecological Complementarity of Agro-Pastoralism: Some Comments. In *Andean Ecology and Civilization* (Shozo Masuda, Izumi Shimada, and Craig Morris, eds.): 85–100. University of Tokyo Press, Tokyo.

Congruence of Horizon with Polity: Huari and the Middle Horizon

RICHARD P. SCHAEDEL

UNIVERSITY OF TEXAS

THE APPLICATION OF HORIZONS to periodization schemes in the Andes goes back to Max Uhle (1913: 341) whence it was perpetuated by Kroeber (1944: O'Neale and Kroeber 1930: 24) and Willey (1945, 1948). It experienced a slight displacement (1946–56) headed by William Strong and later reinforced by Strong's (1948) and my joint efforts in Peru in 1953 (Schaedel 1953). Subsequently, John Rowe (1960) moved to reestablish the horizon cum early-middle-late concept in 1956 (see Lumbreras 1959: viii, and in Schaedel 1959: 33). This was, up to a certain point, debated in Peru in 1958 (Schaedel 1959), but thereafter most Andeanists in the U.S. and with some modifications in Peru, have adhered to the Rowe nomenclature. It is only fair to say that since 1958, I have tried to compromise with the conceptual implications of the horizon concept and attempted to use it, following my modified scheme at the Lima Mesa Redonda, where my proposed period of Great Fusion is equivalent to Rowe's Middle Horizon. In 1978, at the Society for American Archaeology meetings in Tucson, I attempted to utilize constructively the concept in a special symposium dedicated (one might say) to "making sense of" the horizon concept by establishing diagnostics of the Middle Horizon (Schaedel n.d.a.), which I shall shortly summarize. I bring to this colloquium mixed feelings regarding the utility of the concept, but since it has now been propagated among Mesoamericanists and may even be proposed for extension yet further afield in time and space, I want to present an objective view of how it conceivably could be used, based upon my experience with the concept and its use and misuse in the Andean context. In the least objectionable meaning (i.e., with the least sociocultural implications), horizons represent periods of high diffusion rates, opposed to periods of limited diffusion (called "periods" by Rowe) among prehistoric complex societies of the Andes. The preconditions of societies capable of producing great horizon styles are that they be both sedentary and surplus-producing. Prior to this situation, over a much broader time spectrum, and even after-

225

wards (insofar as the food-producing societies remain small-scale), the diffusionary process is encompassed within and described by the concept of interaction spheres. Good diagrammatic representations are illustrated in the
work of Richard MacNeish, Thomas Patterson, and David Browman (1975).

Has the concept proved a useful tool in helping us Andeanists reach
consensus and increasing control over an accurate periodization in the Andes
(as Rowe hoped, when he rejected the functional developmental scheme that
he called "stages" for what the Peruvians [Lumbreras 1959; Lumbreras in
Schaedel 1959: 32] call his time/space scheme)? Let us examine what connotations get associated with "horizons" and what can be done about using the
term with greater objectivity.

Even though Kubler (1984: 32) found the horizon concept already deeply
imbedded in the social science literature in the Americas (but particularly the
Andes) and hence not used in the art historian's way, it appears to be a
concept that Uhle brought to his periodization of the Andean prehistoric
sequence from art history theory, and hence subject to the metaphysics of
aesthetic process or style dynamics. Uhle (1913: 344) himself, in 1913, raises
objections to following the art historian's sequence "blindly," and maintains
that field work can and must be used to correct the expectation of art
historians working with museum specimens in reconstructing sequences (or
life spans of an art style).

Thus, it is necessary for us as social scientists to give meaning in social
science terms to the processes we see manifested in the spread of a great
horizon style, not to mention the internal dynamics of local or micro-
regional styles. John Rowe (1960: 628) anticipated my argument that horizons cannot be clearly defined by the great horizon style (Schaedel n.d.)
early on when he stated that the Early Horizon was marked not so much by
the diffusion of the Chavin style or Chavinoid styles, but by a pottery
technology of incomplete oxidation, dark color, and incised and pattern-
burnished surface finishing.

OPERATIONALIZATION OF THE HORIZON CONCEPT TO THE MIDDLE HORIZON

There is no need here to discuss further justification of the horizon concept in the Andes, other than to point out that its progenitor, Uhle, derived
it from validated ethnohistoric inferences (on the Late Horizon) relating to
supra-community aggregation in the Central Andes and assumptions (for
the Middle Horizon) that broad interregional hegemonies like the Inca state
were responsible for major socioeconomic changes. These changes were
ultimately reflected in material culture and iconography. This is implicit in
Uhle's use of the Inca empire as his last horizon (although it is clear that
Uhle never explicitly stated this or documented the tremendous amount of

archaeological evidence that he reviewed and subjectively relied upon in Chile, Ecuador, Peru, Bolivia, and perhaps Argentina).

The enunciation of the Tiahuanaco and epigonal horizons was developed gradually in Uhle's work, and they were systematized during his lifetime by A. L. Kroeber, William Strong, and Gordon Willey, the first two of whom recorded, described, and analyzed his excavations. Few authors until Willey seemed willing to make Uhle's implicit assumption about the Inca hegemony applicable to Tiahuanaco, and about this time (1946), Rafael Larco Hoyle and others introduced the bifurcation of the second horizon into a northern Huari sphere, radiating influences in all directions out of a center near Ayacucho, and a southern Tiahuanaco-centered sphere. Since then, the focus in dealing with this time period has been on whether or not (1) to accept the implicit assumption of political hegemony, (2) to make a second assumption (which might be labeled "religious hegemony" or "iconographic hegemony") to avoid premature inferences on processes of state formation, or (3) simply to abolish the term (a recent "heretic" trend that has yet to be formally pronounced).

The purpose of this paper is to review the utility of the concept (holding in abeyance, for the moment, whether one is committed to any of the three assumptions) as it has been applied to *ordering* various classes of archaeological data, including misapplications, in the hope of arriving at consensus regarding diagnostics. Finally, I hope to engender discussion on which of the three assumptions we may legitimately proceed to adopt or discard.

Since Uhle first established the Tiahuanaco phase as a pan-Peruvian phenomenon, the spread of what might best be called an "iconographic cluster" has been used as a diagnostic of a cultural manifestation that Uhle found separated early from late manifestations of what were generally labeled local cultures or local culture continua. These iconographic clusters (which could be on any scale and in any media) over time became identified with associated changes in technology and behavioral patterns (e.g., mortuary practices, head deformation), which in their turn have tended to be used to interpret the nature of the seemingly pan-Peruvian "phenomenon," but which could also be used independently of their associations as diagnostics. However, this process of the extension of diagnostics of the Middle Horizon has varied according to the region. This paper attempts to sum up most of the classes of diagnostics that have been identified, place them according to referent locations, and indicate whether the diagnostic is "intrusive" or transitory, or whether it is permanent, that is, resulted in a transformation of the affected culture continuum. A perception of the interrelationship of the several categories of criteria (not just the iconographic cluster) should produce a better understanding of the "phenomenon" and its future utility as a chronological yardstick, marking off local or regional cultural developments.

Richard P. Schaedel

Iconographic Clusters

The iconographic clusters to which I will now refer have been established first on the basis of shared iconographic elements of classic Tiahuanaco-style stonework (Stübel and Uhle 1892; Posnansky 1945) with Ancon textiles (Reiss and Stübel 1880–87) and Pachacamac pottery by Uhle (1903). A. Kroeber and W. Strong (1924) and W. Bennett (1934), using these same anchor points, continued to recognize the Middle Horizon presence in the restricted cluster base through the mid-1940s. With Larco's and Tello's pronouncements on Huari as the probable direct center of diffusion of these iconographic clusters in the Central Andes, mediating between Tiahuanaco and the coast, the base for this cluster was widened, though not substantially altered, and the iconographic cluster thought characteristic of Huari ceramics by A.D. 500–600 was taken as the new diagnostic, systematically applied by Dorothy Menzel (1964). Louis Stumer (1956) has presented the latest summary of the widened iconographic cluster in ceramics seen from the central coastal perspective. It is worth noting that both Menzel and Stumer include iconographic "influences" outside the cluster (Cajamarca-North Highland unidentified in the case of Menzel, and Recuay-Central Highland unidentified in the case of Stumer).

In addition to enlarging the iconographic cluster, which can vary depending upon whether the receiving or sending "culture" is the focus of analysis, the iconographic cluster technique has some periodizational modifications that may be slightly confusing and require comment. The Menzel approach is to include what was previously considered the last phase of the regional-classic (Early Intermediate, Mastercraftsmen, etc.) culture as Middle Horizon 1, thus augmenting to four the subdivisions into which the Middle Horizon was traditionally subdivided, whereas most authors begin the Middle Horizon with a Huari-Tiahuanaco influenced period (Rowe and Menzel 1967). Part of this problem of detecting the first intrusion of the Middle Horizon iconographic cluster arises from the lack of contexts where there is a stratigraphic sequence from the last phase of the Early Intermediate to the Middle Horizon (references to South Coast: Strong 1957; Central Coast: Strong and Corbett 1943; Stumer 1957; Bonavia 1963; North Coast: Ford 1949; Collier 1955).

There exists a certain consensus among authors as to the beginning of Middle Horizon, if we exclude the difference just referred to between Rowe and Menzel; but there is a trend to terminate the Middle Horizon early, according to the alleged demise of the Huari-Tiahuanacoid "influence" in the Ica Valley (Rowe and Menzel 1967; Menzel 1977). This presumably gives rise to the problem of reconstructing a regional coastal renascent culture, from about A.D. 900 to the time of Inca contact. On the North Coast, where the extant dynasty lists go back far enough to cover the Late Intermediate Period and impinge on Middle Horizon, we find that the regional dynasty responsible for the kingdom of Chimor, interpreting conservatively, begins around A.D. 1250 (Kosok 1964). We have no credible basis, either archaeologically or ethnohistorically, for assuming an earlier date for what can be legitimately called Chimu, that is, the political label for the ethnic group responsible for the kingdom of Chimor and by all odds the largest of Late Intermediate Period polities. Therefore, it seems hypothetically useless to propose a series of earlier regional cultures (as yet totally unidentified in the ethnohistoric records, except for the Lambayeque region) which we should call Chimu. What evidence we have from the southern North Coast valleys (Nepeña, Santa, Casma, and apparently Huarmey) suggests that the late Middle Horizon style (Black-White-Red) marks the last pre-Chimu phase. If Chimu is to be a meaningful term, as an adjective referring to a late pre-Incaic kingdom, Chimor, that spread north and south out of the Moche north bank after A.D. 1300, it would little serve our purpose to refer to the local and regional cultural developments by this term. We have, furthermore, enough documentation on the Lambayeque Valley to define one of these regional styles, occupying a time placement somewhere between A.D. 800 and 1100 known as Lambayeque (Zevallos 1971) and later well documented and rebaptized as Sican by Shimada (1982). Although it doubtlessly did influence the formation of what became Classic Chimu pottery, it clearly has an independent trajectory, both as a pottery style and as a presumed polity.

For these reasons, I propose a 1200 date for the beginning of the Late Intermediate Period. It makes for a closer approximation of the archaeological date to which the ethnohistoric data can refer, which is relevant to the immediate pre-Inca societies and is more likely to represent the material state of aggregation or disaggregation of these broad ethnic entities, which we may decode from the ethnohistorical references, than would a longer time frame. I invoke Christopher Hawkes' (1954: 159–160) argument here regarding the distinction between telehistoric and parahistoric.

If we postpone for the moment consideration of the evidence for the iconographic cluster on pottery, we may address ourselves to other media on which the cluster appears, insofar as it relates to broader technological diagnostics. Dorothy Menzel (1977), in her later work, uses textiles and wood, and Christopher Donnan (1976), although confining his study to Mochica, brings in metal, shell, bone, and inlay, to broaden significantly the media field upon which the iconographic cluster may be played. I used monumental stone sculpture (Schaedel n.d.a.), and Duccio Bonavia (1974), Christopher Donnan (1976), and I (Schaedel 1951b, 1978) have used mural painting. Nonetheless, despite the fact that the universe tends to diminish numerically as the artifact increases in size, there may be a compensating factor in that the larger the specimen, the greater significance attached to it. In this connection, then, I refer to the seminal study of the Middle Horizon tapestry textile design by Alan Sawyer (1963), which broadly encompasses specimens from Menzel's Middle Horizon epochs 1 and 2 over a wide coastal area.

Unfortunately, similar concentration on the later epochs of Middle Horizon in textile iconography and technique has not been attempted, although Menzel's (1977: 32–36) effort on Chimucapac painted and woven textiles breaks important new ground. The long-recognized relationship between Pachacamac (Gretzner and Gaffron collection, Ubbelohde-Doering 1967: 84) and Pacatnamu textiles (Keatinge 1978), remains to be explicated. In a similar fashion, extending the iconographic cluster on textile analysis to northern Chile where specimens of Tiahuanaco originals have been found (Munizaga 1957: 119, fig. 4), and comparing them with Sawyer's (1963) presumed Huari-derived textiles would clarify the nature of the spread of the Tiahuanaco cluster to Huari, which has not been elucidated from either stonework (Schaedel 1953) or pottery (see Cook 1983, 1984–85, 1987, for more recent attempts to reformulate the iconographic problem).

Dorothy Menzel (1977) has added to her summary of the Middle Horizon diagnostics on pottery (1964, 1968) throughout the coastal area, and Carol Mackey (1982) seeks a non-Huari derivation of one North Coast Middle Horizon style, while John Smith (1978) attempts to relate the Recuay stylistic input to Middle Horizon styles. Later on we shall attempt to analyze some of these by vectorial breakdown. I only want to add to Menzel's placement and derivation of Middle Horizon styles the positioning of the cursive styles, for example, Kroeber's (1926) Cursive tripod and the non-Tiahuanacoid ware that Uhle first found in association with Huari wares on the Huaca del Sol (Kroeber 1925). On the basis of the survey of the North Coast valleys by Smith (n.d.b) and Herbert Eling's and my research at Cerro Cañocillo and Ventanillas (Schaedel n.d.b.) in the Jequetepeque Valley, the placement of the "floral cursive" and other Cajamarca-derived Middle Horizon variants (which Thatcher [1978] was able to seriate in Huamachuco, and Ravines [1968] recorded in the Central Highlands) can be anchored to those coastal sequences in which Moche V precedes and classic Chimu follows, for the Jequetepeque and Zaña Valleys. The Cajamarca wares are widespread in these two valleys (with only sporadic Huari polychrome pieces), relatively sparse in the Chicama and Moche valleys to the south, and virtually absent south of Moche. In the Lambayeque and Leche areas to the north they are also sparse. Izumi Shimada (1982) places Middle Sican culture in this time frame in the Leche Valley.

This distribution of Cajamarca (and occasionally Huari-associated) wares along the North Coast lends strength to a proposed "corridor" of Huari diffusion from Cajamarca-Huamachuco-Callejón de Huaylas-Huarihuillca-Huari, dropping east-west to the coast via Jequetepeque and Zaña. One or more similar corridors presumably existed, with a Huari-Callejón node between the south bank of the Santa and Huarmey Rivers. A final northern-most east-west link to the Huari-Cajamarca corridor is suggested by Ramiro Matos' (1965–66) finds in the upper Piura region, an omission in the otherwise rather complete survey of Middle Horizon ceramics in the Menzel trilogy (1964, 1968, 1977). Rather than quote from Matos, we reproduce his first chart (Fig. 1).

	Vicús	Yécala	Callingará 2 y 3?	Santa Rosa	El Bronce	Mostrante	Monte de los Padres	Talanqueras	Malamatanzas	Pabur	Zapotal	TOTALES
Chavinod/Cupisnique	40	33	—	—	—	15	—	13	12	11	1	125
Cupisnique Transit.	15	26	—	—	—	15	5	7	18	9	—	95
Garbanzal	16	21	—	—	—	—	1	—	—	—	—	38
Vicús Blanco/Rojo	84	25	30	20	22	23	7	13	20	10	8	263
Vicús Negativo	126	70	22	18	15	18	3	11	39	15	14	355
Vicús Monocromo	138	82	36	25	29	48	6	10	34	15	17	440
Mochica I	16	13	—	—	—	—	8	7	10	1	—	55
Mochica II	1	5	—	—	—	—	—	6	5	—	—	17
Mochica III	—	2	—	—	—	—	2	5	3	—	—	12
Mochica IV	—	—	—	—	—	—	—	2	—	—	—	2
Mochica V	6	10	—	—	—	—	7	12	12	5	—	52
Mochica/Huari	—	—	—	—	—	—	—	4	2	—	—	6
Huari Norteño	—	2	2	—	—	—	6	12	20	5	1	47
Cajamarca	23	11	10	—	10	23	12	17	30	9	3	148
Estilos Tardíos	10	5	21	27	27	87	—	—	2	5	10	194
No identificados	10	—	4	5	12	16	4	—	—	—	6	57
	485	305	125	95	115	245	65	117	205	85	60	1902

NOTA: Los fragmentos fueron recogidos indistintamente, sin ningún control estadístico definido.

Fig. 1. Distribution of ceramic styles by sites in the upper Piura region (after Matos 1965–66: fig. 1)

I pass briefly over the iconographic cluster applied to stone sculpture, for few new pieces have been reported to clarify the pattern or nature of diffusion since my summary of the art in 1952 (Schaedel n.d.a.). The most significant finding here probably relates to the small stone puma that Larco published (n.d.) and indicated as coming from Pallasca (Fig. 2). It fulfills a "missing link" in my earlier attempt (Schaedel n.d.a.) to find an iconographic connection between the early Middle Horizon stone sculpture styles

Richard P. Schaedel

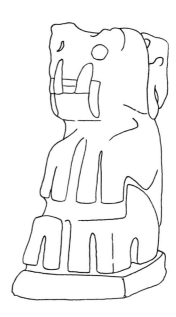

Fig. 2. Puma from Pallasca (re-drawn after Larco n.d.)

of the Pallasca central area, the Pomebamba peripheral area, Huari, the Tiahuanaco and Pukara central areas, and the Titicaca peripheral areas.

In defining the universe of stone sculpture styles in 1952, I established a grouping of statues for the Pallasca central area called the Bold Salient style, contrasting it with the two styles with which it guarded the closest similarity: the Tiahuanaco planimetric and the Huari planimetric. The small puma reproduced by Larco (n.d.: pl. 1) would conform to this Bold Salient style. It is unique in that the feline is presented completely in the round, in a threatening position, as in Tiahuanaco chacha-pumas and in the one example from Huari (Fig. 3a). This similarity in large monumental stone sculpture is related both to the technology of sculpting by planes and to the gross representational form. (See Posnansky's [1945: 221, fig. 136] illustration of an incomplete statue and his observation on the technical specificity of pieces produced in this technique.)

Nevertheless, the fact that the bold relief felines occur individually in Pallasca (and here they seem to come mostly from Pashash) and in Tiahuanaco (where, as Posnansky observed, the chacha-pumas are usually paired) gives this iconographic feature particular compositional importance. It is rather likely that the Bold Salient pumas in both Tiahuanaco and Pallasca formed flanking pairs to a central figure (Fig. 4). In the Tiahuanaco repertoire of motifs, the central figures of the planimetric style which would correspond are the caryatid-like figures of the Gateway of the Sun. There are some eleven of these, two of which are double (Posnansky dubs them appropriately "antice-

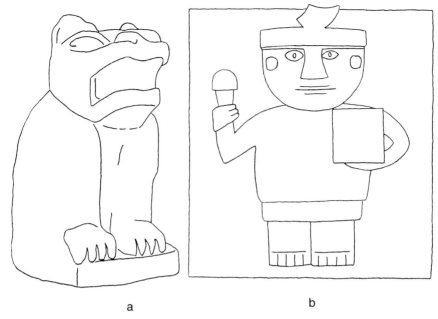

a   b

Fig. 3. (a) Puma from Huari; (b) Urcon caryatid-like figure

Fig. 4. Pumas flanking a central figure

phalic"). There are fourteen chacha-pumas from Tiahuanaco, and at least one from Copacabana. The only other free-standing figure that would be centrally placed is the standing black statue with hands at side (Posnansky 1945: fig. 134). The Urcon (in the Pomebamba peripheral area) caryatid-like figure could represent the center piece for the free-standing Pallasca puma (Fig. 3b).

Although the shield-and-club motifs of the Urcon bold relief are not seen on Huari or Tiahuanaco stone sculpture, the analogy with Huari pottery can be seen by comparing Menzel's illustration of a standing figure of the Atarco A style (1977: pl. XXXIX, 46).

The likelihood of syncretism between Tiahuanaco, Huari, and Recuay has been suggested (Schaedel 1952; Smith n.d.a), and a much more compelling argument can be made than Menzel makes for Huari-Mochica. Here it would be appropriate only to indicate that there seems to be strong evidence for a monumental sculpture diagnostic of central-figure-and-flanking-felines in a technique of salient and recessed planes, which links the Pallasca, Huari, and Tiahuanaco areas. I presume this linkage dates from the earliest phases of the Middle Horizon.

Though there is additional stone sculpture evidence to link the North Highland with Huari, particularly with head tenons and puma lintels (see McCown 1945; Bennett 1944), the arguments for doing so are more involved and could well relate to a later phase of the Middle Horizon. My purpose here is to verify the existence of a Middle Horizon highland corridor from Huari to Cajamarca (implicit since Bennett's work at Huari, and since emphasized by Lumbreras and Menzel) *prior to the extension of Huari to the North Coast* (i.e., north of the Santa). This would be particularly significant in explicating the diferent routes and timing of the Huari (Middle Horizon) 2 and 3 currents into the Chicama and Moche, via the Jequetepeque, from a nodal point in Cajamarca, at about the same time or somewhat later than currents with a nodal point in Pachacamac were diffusing up the North Coast to Casma, Nepeña, and Santa.

Another technology that has relevance both as technology and as a field for the iconographic cluster as a diagnostic of the Middle Horizon is woodcarving. Menzel reports on the Huaca del Sol wooden *kero* (Fig. 5; Menzel 1977: Fig. 90) excavated by Uhle, and closely related (Middle Horizon 1B) iconographically is the *kero* from Cahuachi in A. Lapiner's (1976) work, illustrated in Fig. 6. Guano Island wood sculpture, examples of which were exhaustively assembled by George Kubler (1948), affords a broad geographic, if not a quantitative, range of examples from the Early Intermediate to the Late Intermediate Periods. The wooden staff at Pachacamac (Kosok 1965), the epoch 3 or 4 statuary (Huaca Dragon [Schaedel 1951a]; Moche [Menzel 1977: fig. 96]), and numerous pieces for the South Coast (e.g., snuff tubes with and without provenience [Schmidt 1929]), provide an excellent basis for the kind of iconographic cluster that Menzel and Stumer compiled for Middle Horizon pottery. Indeed, as in the case of painted textiles, wood sculpture seems to have had its florescence in the Andes during the Middle Horizon. Much of it seems to have to do with processional ritual.

The range of decorated examples of bone and shell from Middle Horizon

Fig. 5. Carving on the wooden *kero* from the Huaca del Sol (redrawn after Menzel 1977: fig. 90)

Fig. 6. Carved figure on the wooden *kero* from Cahuachi (redrawn after Lapiner 1976: figs. 568–569)

is not, to my knowledge, as yet adequate to provide still another field for extending iconographic cluster analysis. The objects in metal of which there are enough specimens for this type of analysis can best be studied at the technological level, thanks particularly to the advances in this approach by Heather Lechtman (1979).

The universe of mural painting, while small, is significant in the areas in which it is found. The Huaca Dragon, for example, provides an excellent repertory for the Middle Horizon 3 iconography, not unlike that of the Sun Gate of Tiahuanaco for Middle Horizon 1, in that the murals show a gamut of two-dimensional motifs that are distinct from the wooden sculpture in the round found inside the shrine; Duccio Bonavia (1974) has shown the intrusive mural sequence for Middle Horizon 1 and 2 in Moche.

We also have unusual documentation for the preceding Early Intermediate Period on the North Coast, covering a span of four valleys and two time periods (Bonavia 1974). Fragments to reconstruct the Central Coast developments from Middle Horizon through Late Intermediate have been assembled by Bonavia (1974: figs. 59–72), although his caution in stylistic interpretation will doubtless leave this documentation largely unnoticed. For this reason, let me remark on the similarity between principal figures on the painted walls of Huadca (in the Rimac; Fig. 7b) and Chankillo (in the Casma; Fig. 7a), also obscurely published by Rosa Fung (1971). If one assumes that the mural painting of El Purgatorio and the low reliefs of Chotuna, on the North Coast (Christopher Donnan, personal communication; Schaedel 1966a), are roughly contemporaneous with the Huadca-Pachacamac painting on the Central Coast (Middle Horizon 3), then the iconographic heterogenization in Middle Horizon 3–4 by region, between adjacent valleys, comes more clearly into focus. Conversely, for the North Highlands, a widespread iconographic similarity is shown by the squatting central figure on stone at Tinyash and Pajaten. This observation anticipates concluding observations regarding the Janus-type character of the Middle Horizon phenomenon.

Technology

A second class of diagnostics that has been associated with Middle Horizon, although less explicitly and consistently, is technologic. This refers to commonalities in changed behavior patterns, rather than presumptive belief systems, which we were referring to in the iconographic cluster. Although the two may be closely linked, this is not necessarily so. Hence, the convenience in making the distinction in the technological diagnostic. I will refer briefly to three characteristics only: material, forms, and technique.

Pottery, despite providing our best quantitative universe of the several technologies, at this stage of analysis does not yet provide us the basis for much in the way of commonalities. This is probably because the raw material category depends on local conditions, and we have not yet enough analysis of clay provenience to identify the widely travelled pieces from the locally produced varieties. In terms of material (i.e., paste and firing technique), about the best generalization that has held up for Middle Horizon is that of oxidized firing, providing a neutral field for polychrome decoration, and this technique marks all but the last phase. Obviously, in areas where polychrome was previously predominant (i.e., Nazca, Recuay, Nievería [Lima], and Cajamarca) the innovation is more difficult to determine (Lumbreras 1974: 111–149).

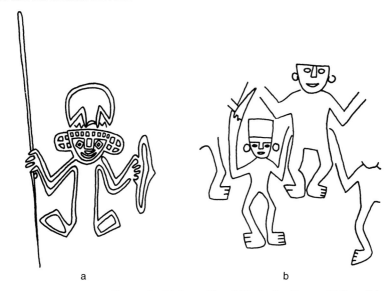

Fig. 7. Figures on wall murals: (a) from Chankillo in the Casma Valley; (b) from Huadca in the Rimac (redrawn after Fung 1971: op. 45 and cover)

Fortunately, in all these styles, significant differences in thickness and paste make discrimination, even at this stage, probable. Also, the persistence of a reduced firing minority tradition in late Early Intermediate in Central and North Coast pottery is almost as significant (Stumer 1957).

The technique characteristics have definite regional variations, and however important and valid they may be as diagnostics, we cannot discuss them here because of the complexity of the data (see Schaedel's [1979] and Menzel's [1964] dilemma regarding the spread of mold-made pottery).

Form is the category that over wide areas has shown us the most commonalities in pottery technology. Obvious to all is the *kero* (cylindrical goblet or tumbler with flaring base and rim), the hallmark of the Tiahuanaco-to-Huari-to-North Andes movement. The next most frequent form (implicitly but not explicitly recognized by Kroeber [1944] and many others) would be the rotund-face collar jar. It would appear that there are other forms that can be traced to one or another node of Huari or Tiahuanaco expansion (e.g., tripods, divergent and usually conical spouts), but the comprehensive survey and analysis of specimens has yet to be done. What can be stated on the basis of the form distribution so far reported is that the *kero,* the tripod, and the divergent conical spouts are evanescent forms on *pottery,* while the rotund-face collar jar persists, at least on the Central and North Coasts, until the Spanish Conquest or later.

Textile Technology

A few summary observations are relevant, since much of the vast bibliography on textile techniques has yet to distinguish Late Intermediate from Middle Horizon procedures. Alan Sawyer's generalization on Highland Tiahuanaco shirts represents the best statement on commonalities in the weaving technology:

> The unusual weaving tradition manifested in the structure of these shirts is not one found on the coast of Peru prior to the Tiahuanaco occupation. It contrasts markedly with the regional techniques used in weaving "Coastal Tiahuanaco" textiles found in the same cemeteries and often in the same graves. It appears logical to conclude that the Tiahuanaco tapestry shirt reflects a distinctive and long established Highland weaving tradition. It is quite possible that it was a garment worn only by the officials of the Tiahuanaco Empire and made only in those areas. It is interesting to note that the official garments of the later Inca Empire, which borrowed much from the Tiahuanaco culture, were woven on similar wide looms. . . . (Sawyer 1963: 35).

This is a clear-cut example of the evanescent (temporary or intrusive) diagnostic. Analyses of other wide-loom coastal Tiahuanaco textiles have been made, implying that they represent introduction of techniques, design structure, material (dyes), and use of the dark field, but these analyses have yet to be systematized.

Similar to the problem of origin and path of diffusion of mold-pressed ware in pottery is the appearance and diffusion of the painted and stamped technique on textiles, as a Middle Horizon diagnostic for the North Central Coast. In other words, the appearance (or reappearance after Chavin times, of painted textiles on the South Coast) seems to be diagnostic of Middle Horizon 2 along the coast. There seems reason to believe that one can establish a periodization through Middle Horizon 3 or 4 (by Menzel's classification), but the point and time of origin and latest manifestation are shrouded in mystery.

In terms of form in textiles, one can add to the tunic-shirt (Sawyer 1963) the peaked, four-cornered hat (Wardle 1949) and its representation in wood and pottery as more of a "stove-pipe" headdress (Vreeland 1977).

Metallurgical and Wood Technologies

Metallurgical studies are advancing to the point where we may possibly come to some technique and material innovations corresponding to the Middle Horizon. The old diagnostic of silver and bronze technique needs either to be refined or dropped, as both metals seem to antedate Middle Horizon on the North Coast (Kroeber 1944). Heather Lechtman (1979) distinguishes Middle Horizon from Mochica technology. In terms of metallurgical forms, the principle of angularity seems to be applicable to Middle Horizon masks and to painting on a metallic surface.

In wood technology, there is some likelihood that light balsa wood represents a material diagnostic. Free-standing idols may prove to be a form (see Bennett 1946: 128, pl. 56), and certainly the wooden *kero* already alluded to from Cahuachi and Huaca del Sol would indicate that the form is probably introduced in this medium in the Middle Horizon 1. In this case, we have a clear illustration of the permanent diagnostic, carried on in later periods in wood and metal, with straight-sided tending to supercede the Middle Horizon's predominantly, but not exclusively, curved sides. I can report that fragments of a wooden *kero* were recovered from University of Trujillo frieze-clearing tests at Pañamarca in 1952–53; these were at the base of a wall similar to Uhle's find (Menzel 1977: 40).

Non-Monumental Lithic Technology

I can report on the presence in Batan Grande of an incised stone *kero* in a grave lot or cache, shown by the *huaqueros* in Chiclayo to Dr. Rodríguez Suy Suy and myself, which was later decommissioned by the Inspección de Monumentos in Chiclayo. The scattered reporting on small lithic artifacts is, to date, insufficient to warrant speculation on how this medium might have been diagnostic.

Other Technologies Reflecting Behavior Patterns

Mortuary practices. Dorothy Menzel (1964: 70, 148) has summed up the evidence for the South and Central Coasts. My rapid review of the North Coast indicates that flexed burial tends to be generally diagnostic of Middle Horizon, but there is conflicting evidence on whether Classic Chimu burials revert to extended position. Menzel reminds us that Uhle found Mochica burials in flexed position at Moche. It is still premature to characterize this complex as a temporary or permanent diagnostic.

Rearing practices, manifested by cranial deformation, appear to provide a fruitful area for investigation. The normal Central and North Coast patterns are summed up by Marshall Newman (1948), but refinement of typology by Pedo Weiss (1962) would seem to show more emphasis on occipital flattening as coastal. The tabular recta type seems more common before and after the Middle Horizon, and the annular type (*llautu*) seems to be Highland-derived when it is found on the South Coast. Good associations of cranial material from single component sites might provide evidence that seems to be reflected in the Middle Horizon pottery, that the annular and bilobial deformations were introduced into the Central and North Coasts at this time (Weiss 1962).

Richard P. Schaedel

Rites of passage. Menzel (1977: 107) shows one of the Middle Horizon pots with lip-plug, and I found a face sherd in a Middle Horizon cemetery at the foot of Chancayillo (Chankillo) with a similar trait, not unlike the blackware pot reproduced by Weiss (1962: fig. 8). The lip-plug is a south Andean trait, pre-Middle Horizon, along with the snuff-tube tablet complex. Its presence in the Central Andes is probably diagnostic of the Middle Horizon, and it would be an evanescent trait, reflecting presumed life-cycle markings of some Highland peoples.

Architecture and engineering. Gordon Willey has summed up the changes for the Viru valley (1953: 344–422), and I have referred to them in the other valleys of the North Coast (Schaedel 1966a), as Donald Proulx (1973) has done for the Nepeña. Because most of the individual structures have their antecedent forms in the region, Middle Horizon architecture seldom can prove diagnostic for form alone, and much more research on plans of structural types is required before we have a representative universe. Much the same can be said of construction materials. One form, which I have tentatively proposed as diagnostic of Middle Horizon 1B, is the concentric *castillo,* and it would be an evanescent form (Schaedel 1966b). Willey's freestanding walled enclosure would be a permanent diagnostic; he draws out the implications of this form for urban systems (1971: 164). Subsequently, Gordon McEwan (1990) summed up this proposed connection.

Extremely important and likely to emerge as diagnostics of the Middle Horizon are engineering techniques, but little study has been devoted to eliciting these principles. One area of study where Middle Horizon principles might be discovered is the foundation engineering of the *quebrada* settlements, whereby in earth moving, leveling is calibrated with embankment building, a technique that seems to replace buttressing on the North Coast. (Examples of late Moche buttressing techniques carried on into Sican monumental structures are explained by Shimada [1982] and were observed by Kroeber [1930] from the Jequetepeque Valley north to Purgatorio.)

Systemic Features

Examples of systems as diagnostics are at once less tangible but more revealing in terms of intepreting the nature of our phenomenon and deciding which of the three assumptions about Middle Horizon "hegemony" one should adopt. Gordon Willey tentatively postulates the existence of such systemic features when he states of the Middle Horizon:

> It was a social, political and religious turning point rather than a technological one. . . . economic effects were probably the major ones. . . . at this time state control of the distribution of foodstuffs on a wide territorial scale came into being. This system with its storehouses, highways, garrisons and control stations is well known from Inca archaeology and ethnohistory. (1971: 164)

Its pattern was laid down in the Middle Horizon.

Just as in the case of our research on architecture (Schaedel 1966a), the identification of features relating to systems has been attempted only sporadically. Much argument rages over what might be termed a garrison, an administrative building, a palace, and so forth. Storehouse units and clusters are only now being explicated (Morris n.d.; Dillehay 1977). Still, certain broad diagnostics of systems, such as water supply features including drainage and canal intakes, boundary walls, zoning segments, intra- and extra-community roads, can be detected, and seem to parallel what I called in my 1966 paper "Tiahuanacoid occupation" (Schaedel 1966b). Basically, these systemic features were identified in order to analyze and understand the urbanization process. Other systemic features more directly related to state formation, which are likely to be reflected in Middle Horizon settlement patterns, are the ones alluded to by Willey for bulking and storage centralization/transportation and patterns in the development of field as opposed to plot agriculture. Some inkling of the development of this last transformation is to be found in the work of Herbert Eling (1978) and Antonio Rodríguez Suy Suy (1971).

The applicability of systemic evidence as diagnostic of the Middle Horizon would involve us in an overall interpretative review of regional late-period developments throughout the Central Andes. Much of this is not well documented and is controversial; for example, the alleged deurbanization on the South Coast (Rowe 1963) or the time of Jauja-Mantaro urban florescence (Parsons and Hastings n.d.). Our purpose here is simply to emphasize a class of systemic diagnostics as most decisive in establishing one assumption as more acceptable than another.

Discussion

In presenting the various classes of diagnostics, I have intentionally moved from the more specific (upon which there would be more likely consensus) to those where less agreement exists (usually the more general). Assessing these three classes in terms of utility, the iconographic cluster has fared best. As manipulated by Menzel (1964, 1968, 1977) for north, central, and south highlands and as far as Moche on the north Andean coast, particularly in 1977 (Menzel 1977), the composite and multinucleated panorama of the Middle Horizon iconography seems to show a pattern of (1) first Tiahuanaco-Huari interface and (2) fertilization with a Huari-inspired dissemination of patterns (i.e., Huari admixture to basic Tiahuanaco icons) to secondary centers, or nodes (e.g., Pachacamac and perhaps a highland node between Huari and Cajamarca) for (3) subsequent redissemination to more distant areas. The distribution of the iconographic cluster in the North Coast tends to confirm my proposition in 1966 about the nature of the Tiahuanacoid occupation to encompass the Viru valley and possibly the south bank of the Moche, while also confirming what Willey (1953: 380–381) hypothesized in his paper on diffusion-acculturation, that is, that the area to the north (possibly beginning with the north bank of the Moche, the Chicama, Jequetepeque-Lambayeque) constituted a "hinterland" or refuge zone for the Mochica (a case history of which the research findings at Pampa Grande as capital of a retreating Moche hegemony document [Shimada 1982]). This refuge area would correspond in my alternate paradigm to the tripartite Middle Horizon expansion-penetration-persistence or degeneration, in which phase 2 and 3 (degeneration) are constituted by interactions of rival contemporaneous cultures and no occupation, properly speaking, takes place. A similar testing of the Middle Horizon penetration-occupation hypothesis could be made in juxtaposing the Central Coast area of heavy Huari presence in the Lurin, with only sporadic early Middle Horizon 1 occupation of the neighboring Rimac and Chillon.

The intricacies of stylistic change and recombination between Huari Middle Horizon styles and rival contemporary styles have only been examined in detail for Ica (Menzel et al. 1964) and more generally by Stumer (1956) for the near North Central Coast, wherein he summarizes the combined findings of Uhle, Kroeber, Strong, and collaborators who worked on Uhle's collection from Ancon, Supe, and Chancay, establishing a three-phase breakdown, on stylistic grounds, for the "Middle Period." Menzel's later review of Kroeber for the South Coast division indicates that the Huari occupation lasted less than in the north, since she closes her four "Middle Horizon" phases with a period (prior to A.D. 1000!) with the designation "great cultural revival at Ica." If this be the case, the North Central Coast, and indeed Pachacamac itself, which Menzel credits with being the main stylistic crater on the coast (however it was linked to Huari during the Middle Horizon) lasted and evolved in the Pachacamac "great horizon style tradition" well into the eleventh century (see Menzel's chronological table [1977: 85]).

To summarize the state of the art on the Central Coast Middle Horizon iconographic cluster diagnosis, Menzel's phases 2–4 at Ica are represented at all Central Coast valleys (perhaps with the exception of one), but that there are later phases (largely characterized by either a version of what Kroeber (1926: 271) called Black-White-Red Geometric or Epigonal (Bennett's Coastal Tiahuanaco), which last far longer in all of the Central Coast valleys, except in the Rimac and Chillon (Stumer 1956; Dillehay 1977), where the later phases are absent. It is doubly surprising that Menzel's (1977: 88–89) chart shows no presence of these two widespread Middle Horizon styles in Chancay (as represented by the Uhle grave lots), since they are defined in Kroeber's 1926 study.

In the North Coast area, unfortunately, we can make no state-of-the-art conclusion. This is because of utter confusion over the years in using the term *Chimu* with variant modifiers and designata. Even if we leave the terminological nightmare to one side (e.g., Early Chimu = former Middle Chimu or Proto-Chimu = Moche phases 1–5, etc.), the real problem lies in distinguishing the Classic Chimu (i.e., Kingdom of Chimor) pottery style from the several styles with which it has been confused (which are regionally and temporally distinct, but which also overlap in short areas of time and space). A case in point is Willey's mislabeling of the Huaca Dragon iconography (and it is the single largest icon-bearing monument in the Andes, second only to Tiahuanaco's sun door) as being very "typically Chimú," whereas I had spent a monograph demonstrating by many arguments that it anteceded, however closely, the classic Chimu style (Schaedel 1966a). The application of the iconographic cluster to the Middle Horizon on the North Coast becomes particularly weak when we have no careful breakdown of the icons by period or area after Moche. In such a case as the friezes of the Dragon, they can be compared in technique and motives with the friezes in the compounds at Chan Chan, which can be taken as representative of classical Chimu. There is hardly a single icon to compare, nor are there similarities in composition (vertical and horizontal panels) nor in the color of the friezes. As Ann Marie Helsley (n.d.) has shown, the closest parallels to the Huaca Dragon style are in the Huari-influenced Santa-style pottery, illustrated by Rebeca Carrión Cachot (1959), and alluded to in Julio Tello's (1956) work for Casma, and originally "discovered" as one of the intermediate styles between Proto-Chimu and Late Chimu by Uhle and labeled simply "post-Tiahuanaco" at Moche Site A (Kroeber 1925: 209) and another piece of which is reproduced in Menzel (1977: fig. 94), where she assigns it as Middle Horizon 2B in time. Subsequently, some excessively large panels of painted cloth have come to light, some from Viru and some with an assumed Central Coast provenience, that relate to the Dragon vertical panel iconography.

Izumi Shimada's (1982) recent work on the stratigraphy of Leche valley (particularly the area around Batan Grande) has enabled him to isolate the characteristics of the so-called Lambayeque style and to specify two phases, which he now labels Middle and Late Sican. This style, like the Casma and Huaylas styles, has a strong blackware strain, modeled in high and low relief and has frequently been confused with classic Chimu.

It is necessary to emphasize the fact that, however inadequately, the styles of Santa, Huaylas, and Lambayeque on the North Coast have been described and illustrated. The Classic Chimu with which the blackware or reduced-fired component of these styles is so often confused has been neither adequately described nor illustrated. Since Kroeber's 1925 and 1926 publications where he treats Late Chimu as a presumably well-recognized style (see 1925: 209), everyone has assumed Late Chimu (or what we should prefer to call Classic Chimu) is a well-known and easily defined style. We have just reviewed the evidence to show that it is confused in the southern

North Coast valleys with the Casma and Santa styles (their blackware components) because it shares with them commonalities of gross surface treatment and paste, although it would appear that the Classic Chimu does not carry the particular ritualistic iconographic load and the "busy" composition of southern North Coast styles.

Disentangling the Middle Sican blackware from Classic Chimu is somewhat easier, but there are blackware strains in Late Sican, and presumably other local blackwares of the Middle Period in the valleys from Lambayeque south to the Moche (similar to San Juan molded in the Viru valley) that are often confused with Classic Chimu. Although these blackwares, like those on the southern North Coast, share similarities in gross surface treatment and paste, they tend to be iconographically more parsimonious than even Classic Chimu in use of pressed ware for ritualistic panels and resort more to appliqué additions than to full three-dimensional modeling.

The clues for the determination of the end of the Middle Horizon and the onset of Classic Chimu in the iconographic cluster on the pottery still require a large representative collection of Classic Chimu. That, it is hoped, will be forthcoming when the Martínez Compañón collection (which is 90% Chimu and presumably of Chan Chan provenience and which exists in the Museo Americano in Madrid) is adequately documented.

The other classes of diagnostics (technology and systemic features) would seem to lend further weight to the hypothesis of a political hegemony for the Middle Horizon; there has been little negative evidence to indicate that, in zones where Huari Middle Horizon 2 presence is *not* detected, we are dealing with phenomena of the type Willey (1953) and I (1966b) mentioned long ago.

Summing up, then, in the area of technological and systemic diagnostics, there is a need to test them rigorously in the later phases of Middle Horizon, where such diagnostics would provide a surer interpretation than does the badly garbled iconographic clustering, of the interplay of late Huari-influenced groups with non-Huari rival contemporaneous groups, some of which crystallize in Late Intermediate periods as ethnohistorically identifiable ethnic groups (Rostworowski 1977; Netherly n.d.).

This points up the Janus-type character of the Middle Horizon concept. Looked at from the point of view of emerging Late Intermediate states and later disaggregated *señoríos* (chiefdoms), one tends to de-emphasize the intrusive Huari and Huari-associated features that show up in cluster analysis. Looked at from the spread and depth of penetration of Huari traits, one tends to overemphasize these same elements. In this sense, the overview of iconographic cluster analysis shows that this contradictory tendency of the Middle Horizon does not help to *order* the data in late phases of Middle Horizon. It can only be usefully applied with confirmation from changes in technology and systems, especially as their reality is given for the first time some feeble support from ethnohistory.

OPERATIONALIZATION OF HORIZON CONCEPT BY VECTORS

I have tried to introduce three classes of phenomena that could be diffused in any horizon: iconographic clusters, technologies, and systems. A pragmatic definition, then, of *horizon* for the archaeologist is a configuration that reflects a diffusionary process in which the diffused material consists of a patchwork quilt of artifacts, techniques, and systems (inferred from the artifacts) within a broad area, anchor points of which we may refer to as *nodes,* from whose contexts one may attempt to reconstruct the agency of diffusion.

As corollaries of this definition: (1) The scale must be markedly large in space. Thus a horizon can only be differentiated from the dynamics of a period in a relative sense. In the regional styles such as Gallinazo, Recuay, and Moche, we have diffusion within a broad region, yet no one has used the term *horizon* to describe their expansion. (Or is it legitimate to speak of a Moche IV horizon or a Nazca 5 horizon?) (2) In the case of Willey's (1948) proposition that if only a technique got diffused, however broad the area, it probably did not constitute a horizon, he applied his horizon concept to White-Red and Negative painting. This implies that, although the other sets of phenomena can be present in the diffusion, the *sine qua non* is the iconographic cluster, which we have isolated as the best objective representation of "the great style." This also resolves the problem posed by Rowe in talking of the several styles that a horizon can have. What relates the styles is the iconographic cluster. (3) The significance of the horizon should be fully weighted by the three sets of evidence in order to conceptualize the true nature of *what* was being diffused before addressing the hypothetical question of the agency or agencies of diffusion, which ultimately have to be analyzed to solve for the meaning of the horizon-producing configuration. In conceptualizing the *what* of diffusion one weighs the distinct sets of phenomena, checking those that were selected out for diffusion against those that were not. This exercise enables one to establish, in the case of the Chavin or the "Early Horizon" for example, just how much of the alleged "cultist" content can be disaggregated from things that might imply economically or politically significant content (e.g., domesticated plants or a construction device).

After one specifies that the horizon is constituted by a widely diffused bundle of phenomena (which we will call the content of the horizon or *what* was diffused), one must specify or at least tentatively formulate the agency or agencies of diffusion. All that this means, in a relative sense, is to show that the nodes between which the currents of diffusion flow are in some patterned relationship, in the sense of a donor-recipient situation that may or may not support some implied site hierarchy. We, as social scientists, are fishing for a mode sufficiently broad to encompass all the social processes that might underlie the explication of these currents of diffusion, and we need to use one that does not predispose us to one or another preconceived process, such as state formation, a Kula ring, Hanseatic league, or a great religious movement.

I suggest, therefore, that we apply a model of aggregation along the lines of Richard Adams' coordinating and centralizing groups (Adams 1975: 173ff). Although Adams uses his model with a heavy emphasis on the evolution of political forms in human society, we need not concern ourselves with what precise percentage of the force that brings and holds the coordinated or centralized group together is sacred or secular in nature to use his model. It is clear from his discussion that the pre-state societies rely more upon dogma or religious power than do the states; and in looking at the models of early aggregation of either the coordinated or the centralized type that might explicate a given horizon, weighting of the religious (sacred, ceremonial, etc.) should be manifest both in content and in the circumstantial evidence at the nodes (presumably architectural).

The usefulness of Adams' model is that it allows for very loosely joined formats in the case of coordination, which may mask an early or anticipatory stage of a centralization process in which the non-political motivation for the aggregation might predominate over the political. Unfortunately, Adams makes no explicit allusion to the special kind of coordination process that characterized the spread of a great religion, which insofar as we know about it in recorded history (e.g., spread of Islam; Carolingian hegemony in Western Europe; Buddhistic penetration of China) could provide the basis for a horizon-like spread rather unlike the expansion of an even more complex political hegemony. The other aspect of the spread of a great religion is that (at least in pre-industrial societies) it is a process totally divorced from necessary and sufficient preconditions and that one can postulate for *economically* and *politically* motivated aggregations that give rise to the universe of coordination and centralization processes that Adams was explicating.

It is useful to have this model of the total range of possibilities for aggregation in societies so that we make the horizon concept into an operational tool for analysis, rather than an impressionistic will-o'-the-wisp chimaera-type creature—a floating balloon containing within it the great horizon style (or complex of related styles) ready to shatter at the slightest prick.

What we have concluded up to now, then, is that the horizon is the product of a special kind of exaggerated diffusion that is reflecting one of two classes of aggregating processes that Adams defined as coordination and centralization. None has been operationalized on archaeological data so far, but I believe it would be a worthwhile exercise to apply this model in an area of successive horizon configurations to see if it would be possible to delimit coordination-type aggregation from centralization.

At the present state of the art, it is perhaps more appropriate to delineate two models of aggregation. For the sake of argument we can call both sets

246

illustrative of Adams' centralization processes. One is enforced diffusion, and the other is spontaneous diffusion. In the case of the Incaic Andes (and certainly also for Aztec Mesoamerica) we know from ethnohistory and history how the "enforced diffusion" took place and what universe of phenomena were affected. In both areas we would like to address the question: was the Middle Horizon a case of spontaneous or forced diffusion? Obviously, in the Andean situation, we are referring to two diffusion spheres, and it might well be that the solving for the X (enforced diffusion) would give us "enforced" in one sphere (e.g., Huari) and Y in the other (e.g., Tiahuanaco). It would be my methodological suggestion that separate patterns for enforced diffusion be extrapolated from the Inca and Aztec models. One should then superimpose some compromise template over the Andean area in Middle Horizon to see how the two spheres differ significantly or not for the model. In operationalizing this model, one should define the Middle Horizon with special attention to what I refer to as the content and nodes so that there is: (1) a specified minimum of clustering of diffused elements; (2) careful attention to fine-line time correlations, avoiding (where possible) subjective decisions based upon stylistic analysis that allow for shifting alignments of center and subcenters; and (3) careful contextual placement of the nodes so as to be able to measure (however crudely) the diffusionary impact of the agency of diffusion.

Concluding this part of the applicability of the horizon concept or its operationalization in the abstract, I just want to note the obvious. I propose the extension back in time of a model of statehood, which in material culture terms can be characterized by a pattern of enforced diffusion. I am proposing this simply to substitute for the lamentable a priori modeling of states in early post-sedentaristic societies based upon ad hoc criteria such as site stratification or implied corvée labor systems (extrapolated from monumental architecture). When we can work from parahistorical to telehistorical models of state formation we may move through the Late to the Middle Horizons, and only after affirming the existence of an enforced diffusionary pattern in the Middle Horizon should we attempt the assessment of such a model for the Early Horizon.

In this symposium, we have three papers besides my own dealing with Andean horizons. Before showing you how I practice what I preach in terms of the alleged Huari Horizon, I will comment briefly on how I find the three papers in accord or disaccord with my theoretical position. Because of the apparent fit in the archaeological evidence between the diffusion of the Tiahuanaco iconography through the agency of a Huari-based polity (be that diffusion politically, economically, or religiously—or any combination thereof—motivated) with the old Tiahuanaco and the newer Middle Horizon (second wave of pan-Peruvian diffusion), it has been implicitly assumed and just as implicitly disavowed that there must be congruence between horizon and polity. For the extreme case of the application of this "built-in" assumption, we have the proponents of statehood for Chavin de Huantar. Richard Burger's paper on Chavin indicates an awareness of the built-in assumptions, and it avoids the pitfalls of using horizon as an interpretational crutch.

Alan Kolata's paper on the Tiahuanaco sphere of the Middle Horizon accepts and proceeds on the assumption that horizon is congruent with polity and not only polity, but the most developed polity of them all—the state. This illustrates how we should not operationalize horizon, because, as he himself states, he uses horizon to justify an a priori position.

In John Hyslop's paper on the Late Horizon, themes and variations of an obviously enforced diffusionary pattern are expounded in which the thrust is in emphasizing the variation. My own research on the Inca state and the enforced diffusion it represented has led me to emphasize the commonalities (the forest as opposed to Hyslop's trees of variation). Lest we lose sight of the magnificent vectorial patterns of Tahuantinsuyu by analyzing some of the patchwork quilt of eighty-odd component provinces with their intraregional vectorial diffusionary swirls and eddies, I want to cite Baron von Humboldt, who was perhaps the first scientific observer to encompass Tahuantinsuyu physically. A free translation goes as follows:

> All the remains of Peruvian architecture scattered along the Cordillera from Cuzco to Cayambe, from the southern latitude to the Equator, present an identical character, both in the dressing of the stone as in the form of the doors, symmetric distribution of the niches and complete lack of external adornment. And so great is this uniformity of construction that all the tambos, guesthouses situated along the principal roads, called in Peru houses or palaces of the Inca, appear to be copies, one of the other (Humboldt 1878[1821]: 54–55).

TRIVECTORIAL ANALYSIS: OPERATIONALIZATION OF HORIZON CONCEPT TO THE HUARI SPHERE

Except perhaps in its presumptive homeland on the Bolivian plateau, the Tiahuanaco style nowhere appears alone but is regularly associated with the supposedly derivative Epigonal *or with local styles* or both. On the other hand, it is the one style other than the Inca that is found over almost all of Peru (Kroeber 1925: 212).

What degree (if any) of congruence between Middle Horizon and Huari polity would be expected? To what extent is this borne out in the case of the spread (diffusionary process associated) with Huari within the commonly accepted meaning of Middle Horizon? It should be obvious that neither is there any "fit" in the diffusion of Tiahuanaco iconography through the agency of a Huari-based polity with the Middle Horizon, nor is it to be expected. But it is worth summing up, in a manner of synthesizing what we consider to be the social science parameters of the horizon concept, how the diffusionary process of Huari interdigitates with the other diffusionary processes detectable in the archaeological evidence that characterize the Middle Horizon, as well as how it can be characterized as differing from them. To do this I propose a trivector analysis: (1) the Tiahuanaco vector (the elements diffused through the diffusion agency), however we now characterize it; (2) the Huari vector; and (3) the various vectors that, because of their iconographic heterogeneity, we can at this time only lump as marginal vectors. By this term we mean agencies spatially located within, between, or on the peripheries of the other two diffusionary agencies, which interact with one of the other vectors in major diffusionary processes but in more limited spheres.

The emphasis here is on the Huari diffusionary process, because that was my assignment, but I could not disaggregate the Huari processual data without referring to the other diffusionary processes. The ways in which the tertiary or marginal vectors are spatially delimited is illustrated in the case of Moche V pottery, which seems to be totally coastal and is restricted to the northern North Coast, with its southern limit in the Chicama and possibly north bank of the Moche Valley. A spatially delimited Central Coast vector (not yet precisely defined, but the center of which may well be Chimucapac and is associated with the diffusion of pressed-ware) is bounded on the south by the Chillon, with predominantly coastal dimensions except for possible pockets in the Callejon del Huaylas. A far northern vector (which may conceivably reach into Ecuador), associated with the diffusion of paddle ware, can be illustrative of a peripheral vector; and a southern peripheral vector (in which pottery is only one of the media) in the Chilean-Atacameño area can represent the southern periphery (Núñez and Dillehay 1979).

The integration of these tertiary vectors as "cultures" capable of emitting their own waves as well as transforming or passing on other cultural currents cannot be even summarily done here, as they have not been recognized as such. All we have so far on the Central Coast, for example, are accounts where a Huari node was hypothesized and a number of sites where contemporaneously apparent autonomous cultures subsisted (Menzel 1977), characterized by certain material culture elements that were diffused north along with Huari iconography but with little Huari iconographic content. The clearest candidate for an intermediate highland vector is the "Recuay Culture" between A.D. 800 and 1100 (Smith n.d.a), which builds upon the Wilkawain-Tiahuanaco phase originally postulated by Wendell Bennett (1944).

In order to illustrate the change in normal vector analysis of cultural diffusion through regular exchange—as opposed to the exacerbation of concentrated diffusionary currents that should characterize a horizon—let me recall the amazing contemporary grave lots Louis Stumer (1958) found at Huaquerones, where the autogenous Central Coast Early Intermediate Period culture (Proto-Lima or Nieveria) was interacting with Nazca, Huari (via Nazca?), Callejon de Huaylas (Recuay), and Moche V cultures, seemingly, prior to large diffusionary centralization (before the eruption of the Middle Horizon). Here we would alter Menzel's (1977) yardstick for the beginning of the Middle Horizon (which seems to begin ca. A.D. 600 in her chronological table) to place Stumer's Nieveria phase at Huaquerones as terminal Early Intermediate Period because it is clearly *before* the prevailing waves of diffusion of the Middle Horizon break out. Ruth Shady Solis' (1982) study of Nieveria follows Menzel's placement and also shows the rapid disappearance of the Nieveria style in the Huari iconographic cluster in Middle Horizon 2. If we then superimpose the univector situation reconstructed from Uhle's (1903) Pachacamac findings over the tentatively reconstructed pattern in Stumer's Huaquerones find, the predominance of the Huari (which Uhle, not knowing of Huari's existence, labeled the Tiahuanaco) iconographic cluster is overwhelming.

My triple macro-vector analysis was actually developed in crude form to handle the ceramic distribution in my multiple-valley study (Casma to Motupe Valleys) in which I was essentially seriating the architecture and settlement types while working out refinements of the ceramic sequence inherited from the Viru valley group (applicable to valleys from Chicama to the south) and Bennett's (1939) sequence for the Lambayeque region (for the valleys from Chicama to Motupe). To handle the variation within the Middle Horizon wares and other media like textiles on which motifs were diffused, I subdivided the hypothesized time frame (A.D. 700–1200) into three flexible phases. "A" constituted the first appearance of the Huari iconographic cluster (including Huari-associated) that could be identified in intervening nodes between Huari and the North Coast. Hence, San Nicolas molded ware (by Viru Valley terminology), which can be related to the Central Coast pressed-molded ware (Menzel 1977: 45–47) and which carries Huari iconography without colors, could be used to validate a site with an "A" placement just as well as the familiar polychrome with Huari motifs (see Menzel 1977: figs. 109a and 110, where both wares are in the same grave). Whatever the mechanism, this pressed-ware with heavy symbolic load appears as a south-north vector that I would call intermediate, because it is not present in artifacts bearing the Huari iconographic cluster in the long Huari-Pachacamac polychrome trajectory (manifest in pottery and textiles) south of Ancon (the nodal center of which would be Pachacamac); but the ware appears in prototypical form in late Early Intermediate Period at Ancon and Chancay (e.g., Teatino [Bonavia 1963; Schaedel 1979]), acquiring momentum in the Supe and continuing north to the Lambayeque Valley (Schaedel 1979). Shady and Ruiz (1979) write about this vector as though it were reflecting some Central Coast local culture, but do not identify it with any domain.

In a similar vein, during the "A" phase, we could consider the association of Uhle's finds on the south platform of the Huaca del Sol (Site A), wherein artifacts of the Huari iconographic cluster and Cajamarca influence are in association. As I pointed out earlier, the likelihood is that this "Coastal Cajamarca" vector is coming from north to south via the Cajamarca basin-Jequetepeque Valley and down further south via the Chicama to the Moche. In this case, Cajamarca ware is like coastal pressed-ware, reflecting an inter-mediate vector (and flowing in what would be a contradictory direction from the principal Middle Horizon early coastal wave from the Central and to the near North Coast).

By the time of my second phase ("B"), the majority of the North Coast valleys fall in line with this overall south to north macro-vector, although the iconographic content is a mixture of mostly intermediate vectorial and little original Huari (though much Huari-derived) content. In the northern valleys (Motupe–Zaña), this trend produced localized trends that begin to replace the large horizon vector during phase "B," for example, the emer-gence of the Sican style. Compare this with what look like local trends reflected in the Chornancap friezes in Lambayeque (Donnan 1984) and those reflected in the Mocupe friezes in the Zaña Valley (Alva and Alva 1984), and several ill-defined "eclectic" styles (usually with one strain of cursive polychrome–presumably Cajamarca-derived) from the Jequetepeque to Viru Valleys (Kroeber 1926; Collier 1955: esp. fig. 1). In the valleys from Santa to Casma, the Black-White-Red and reduced and oxidized fired pressed-wares reported by Julio Tello (1956) for the Casma and Rebeca Carrión Cachot (1959) for the Santa, was recently illustrated from Uhle's excavations in Chimucapac (Menzel 1977). Dorothy Menzel tries to sepa-rate what would be the equivalent of my "A" phase (Menzel's MH 2) from "B" (Menzel's MH 3; cf. Menzel 1977: figs. 60, 61, 64, 65, 68 with Carrión 1959: passim).

In my phase "C" (more or less a combination of part of Menzel's MH 3 [in Moche] and 4 [south of Moche]), in the North Coast valleys, the Middle Horizon content (in the way of "derived iconographic cluster") diminishes further, and the local developments of phase 2 give rise to a north to south vector, which is marked by the spread of the paddle-ware technique, as well as fine wares with exceptionally low iconographic loads. This period proba-bly characterizes the florescence of Purgatorio, the building of Apurle, and the building of Huacas Tacaynamo and Dragon in the Moche.

Summing up the North Coast findings of what we may impressionistically describe as a vector analysis of Middle Horizon diffusionary trends, we have the first current, originating around the northern Rimac-Chillon, which con-stituted a basically south to north sweep, with a curious eddying around the

Richard P. Schaedel

Santa, followed shortly thereafter by a loop-shaped vectorial movement emanating either through the highlands directly from Huari or from Rimac-Chillon up to the Callejon de Huaylas via Cajamarca–Jequetepeque to the Chicama–Moche. At the northern end of the Middle Horizon parameters, the vectors stabilize in a predominantly south to north direction for the south-central area in phase 2 (by A.D. 1000) and begin to produce intermediate-type localized shifts, with prevailing north to south vectors dominating the third phase (A.D. 1000–1200) in the Motupe–Moche region, and finally erupting over the stabilized pattern of the south central area in the next 200 years.

I sketch out this plan for analyzing horizons in the area I know best. I have had enough experience to know that it can be equally well applied in the southern periphery. Such vector analysis can be conveniently diagrammed according to the motif and technology used; and the points where such units tend to concentrate can be designated "nodes" to avoid any predetermined judgment as the agency of diffusion. It is felt that by plotting the diffusionary processes in this form, one can arrive at the most adequate definition of the agency of diffusion. This analysis preferably should be done in combination with excavation at the nodal points to find the architectural correspondence to the presumed function of the diffusionary agent.

CONCLUSION

At the outset of my presentation, I indicated my ambivalence about the utility of the horizon concept and my reluctant efforts at coming to terms with it for periodizational purposes. In the main body of the paper I suggested how it might best be operationalized so as to be a helpful tool of analysis instead of the misleading balloon of homogeneity masking a plethora of built-in assumptions that it has come to be. I have reviewed some problems with the concept as expounded by my colleagues in the Andes and finally proposed a way of making the concept meaningful, specifically for the Middle Horizon with regard to the Huari sphere. My exercise in operationalization leads me to the conclusion that it requires too much self-discipline to expect many Andeanists to follow suit; and it is much easier to *abuse* than *use* the concept analytically. I am forced to the conclusion that the horizon concept has outlived its usefulness, certainly for the Andes, because it leads to confusing the establishment of chronology with the interpretation of cultural history. We do not need it for the Late Horizon; it becomes extremely difficult to define its spatial and temporal parameters for the Middle Horizon; and its longevity, as far as I can understand the much-debated significance of radiocarbon dates for the Early Horizon, makes it more inappropriate as a term than a simple epoch designation would be.

The curious coast/highland counterpoint of Andean history and prehistory accounts for the utility of "horizon" to describe impressionistically the dynamics of the highlands periodically erupting over the coastal civiliza-

252

tions. The Mesoamerican situation did not seem to provide pan-Mesoamerican counterpoint. The Mesoamerican chronology, however, was not perceived early on as one dominated by "pan-Mesoamerican" movement, but rather one in which regional strengths were the characteristic hallmark, with shifting regional polarities marking the intensity peaks of Mesoamerican culture through time. It has been only in the past two or three decades that Olmec and Teotihuacan "influence" began to assume the configuration of horizon spreads. It seems to this Andeanist, who has a reasonable familiarity with Mesoamerican prehistory, that affixing to them an ex post facto label of horizons—implying, however innocuously, similar diffusionary processes—will obfuscate rather than accelerate our understanding of the processes identifying their growth and decline.

Richard P. Schaedel

BIBLIOGRAPHY

ADAMS, RICHARD N.
 1975 *Energy and Structure.* The University of Texas Press, Austin.
ALVA, WALTER A., AND SUSANA MENESES DE ALVA
 1984 Los murales de Ucupe en el valle de Zaña, norte del Perú. *Beiträge zur Allgemeinen und Vergleichenden Archäologie* 5 (1983): 336–360. Deutsches Archäologisches Institut, Bonn.
BENNETT, WENDELL C.
 1934 *Excavations at Tiahuanaco.* Anthropological Papers of the American Museum of Natural History 34 (1). New York.
 1939 *Archaeology of the North Coast of Peru: An Account of Exploration and Excavation in the Virú and Lambayeque Valleys.* Anthropological Papers of the American Museum of Natural History 37 (1). New York.
 1944 *The North Highlands of Peru. Excavations in the Callejón de Huaylas and at Chavín de Huantar.* Anthropological Papers of the American Museum of Natural History 39 (1). New York.
 1946 The Archaeology of the Central Andes. In *Handbook of South American Indians* 12: 122–135.
 1953 *Excavations at Wari, Ayacucho, Peru.* Yale University Papers in Anthropology 49. New Haven.
BONAVIA, DUCCIO
 1963 Sobre el estilo teatino. *Revista del Museo Nacional* 31: 43–94. Lima.
 1974 *Ricchata Quellccani: Pinturas Murales Prehispánicas.* Fondo del Libro del Banco Industrial del Perú. Lima.
CARRIÓN CACHOT, REBECA
 1959 *La religión en el antiguo Perú: Norte y centro de la costa, Período Post-Clásico.* Tipografía Peruana, S.A., Lima.
COLLIER, DONALD
 1955 *Cultural Chronology and Change as Reflected in the Ceramics of the Viru Valley, Peru.* Fieldiana: Anthropology 43. Chicago Natural History Museum, Chicago.
COOK, ANITA
 1983 Aspects of State Ideology in Huari and Tiwanaku Iconography: The Central Deity and Sacrificer. In *Investigations of the Andean Past* (D. Sandweiss, (ed.): 161–185. Latin American Studies Program. Cornell University, Ithaca, New York.
 1984–85 The Middle Horizon Ceramic Offerings from Chonchopata. *Ñawpa Pacha* 22–23: 49–90.
 1987 Ideological Origins of an Andean Conquest State. *Archaeology,* July/Aug.: 27–33.
DILLEHAY, TOM D.
 1977 Un estudio de almacenamiento. *Cuadernos* 24–25: 25–37. Lima.

DISSELHOFF, HANS D.

1941   Acerca del problema de un estilo "Chimu Medio." *Revista del Museo Nacional* 10: 51–62. Lima.

1958   Tumbas de San José de Moro (Provincia de Pacasmayo, Peru). *Proceedings:* 364–367. 32nd International Congress of Americanists, Copenhagen.

DONNAN, CHRISTOPHER

1972   Moche-Huari Murals from Northern Peru. *Archaeology* 25 (2): 85–95.

1973   A Pre-Columbian Smelter from Northern Peru. *Archaeology* 26 (4): 289–297.

1976   *Moche Art and Iconography.* UCLA Latin American Studies 33. UCLA Center Publications, Los Angeles.

1984   Ancient Murals from Chornancap, Peru. *Archaeology* 37 (3): 32–37.

ELING, HERBERT H., JR.

1978   Interpretaciones preliminares del sistema de riego antiguo de Talambo en el valle de Jequetepeque, Perú. In *El Hombre y la Cultura Andina* 2: 401–419. Lima.

FORD, JAMES A.

1949   *Cultural Dating of Prehistoric Sites in the Viru Valley, Peru.* Anthropological Papers of the American Museum of Natural History 43 (1): 29–89. New York.

1954   The History of a Peruvian Valley. In *Readings from Scientific American: New World Archaeology:* 164–170. W. H. Newman, San Francisco.

FUNG, ROSA

1971   *Apuntes Arqueológicos* 1. Universidad Nacional Mayor de San Marcos. Lima.

GONZALEZ, LETICIA, AND RICHARD P. SCHAEDEL

1977   Enrique (Hans Heinrich) Bruening, un hamburgés en el Perú. *Humboldt* 64: 76–80.

HAWKES, CHRISTOPHER

1954   Archaeological Theory and Method: Some Suggestions from the Old World. *American Anthropologist* 56: 155–168.

HELSLEY, ANN MARIE

n.d.   The Friezes of Huaca El Dragón: An Interpretation. M.A. thesis, Department of Anthropology, University of Texas at Austin, 1985.

HUMBOLDT, ALEJANDRO DE

1878   Sitios de las cordilleras y monumentos de los pueblos indígenas de América. Traducido por Bernardo Giner, Madrid. Imprenta y Librería de Gaspar.

KEATINGE, RICHARD W.

1978   The Pacatnamu Textiles. *Archaeology* 31 (2): 30–41.

KOSOK, PAUL

1965   *Life, Land and Water in Ancient Peru.* Long Island University Press, New York.

KROEBER, A. L.

1925   The Uhle Pottery Collections from Moche. *University of California Publications in American Archaeology and Ethnology* 21: 191–234. Berkeley.

1926   *Archaeological Explorations in Peru, Part I: Ancient Pottery from Trujillo.* Field Museum of Natural History, Anthropology Memoirs 2 (1). Chicago.

1930   *Archaeological Explorations in Peru, Part II: The Northern Coast.* First Marshall Field Archaeological Expedition in Peru. Field Museum of Natural History, Anthropology Memoirs 2 (2). Chicago.

1944   *Peruvian Archaeology in 1942.* Viking Fund Publications in Anthropology 4. New York.

1948   Summary and Interpretations. In *A Reappraisal of Peruvian Archaeology* (Wendell C. Bennett, ed.). Memoirs of the Society for American Archaeology 13 (4), pt. 2: 113–122.

KROEBER, A. L., AND WILLIAM DUNCAN STRONG

1924   The Uhle Collections from Chincha. *University of California Publications in American Archaeology and Ethnology* 21 (5). Berkeley.

KUBLER, GEORGE

1948   Towards Absolute Time: Guano Archaeology. In *A Reappraisal of Peruvian Archaeology* (Wendell C. Bennett, ed.). Memoirs of the Society for American Archaeology 13 (4), pt. 2: 29–50.

1984   *The Art and Architecture of Ancient America: The Mexican, Mayan and Andean Peoples.* Penguin Books, Baltimore.

LAPINER, A.

1976   *Precolumbian Art of South America.* Harry N. Abrams, New York.

LARCO HOYLE, RAFAEL

1948   *Cronología arqueológica del norte del Perú.* Hacienda Chiclín, Trujillo, Perú.

n.d.   Escultura lítica del Perú pre-colombino. Serie: Orígenes del Arte Peruano, 2. Escultura Lítica. Instituto de Arte Contemporaneo, Lima.

LECHTMAN, HEATHER

1979   Issues in Andean Metallurgy. In *Pre-Columbian Metallurgy of South America* (Elizabeth P. Benson, ed.): 1–40. Dumbarton Oaks, Washington, D.C.

LOTHROP, SAMUEL K.

1951   Peruvian Metallurgy. *Proceedings of the 29th International Congress of Americanists* 1: 219–223. New York.

LUMBRERAS, LUIS

1959   Panorama histórico de la arqueología Peruana. *Actos y Trabajos del II Congreso Nacional de la Historia del Perú* 1: 3–16. Lima.

1974   *The Peoples and Cultures of Ancient Peru* (Betty Meggers, trans.). Smithsonian Institution, Washington, D.C.

MACKEY, CAROL J.

1982   The Middle Horizon as Viewed from the Moche Valley. In *Chan Chan: Andean Desert City* (Michael E. Moseley and Kent C. Day, eds.): 321–331. University of New Mexico Press, Albuquerque.

MacNeish, Richard S., Thomas C. Patterson, and David Browman
  1975 *The Central Peruvian Prehistoric Interaction Sphere.* Papers of the Robert S. Peabody Foundation for Archaeology 7. Phillips Academy, Andover.

Matos, Ramiro
  1965–66 Algunos consideraciones sobre el estilo de Vicús. *Revista del Museo Nacional* 34: 89–130. Lima.

McCown, Theodore
  1945 Pre-Incaic Huamachuco: Survey and Excavations in the Region of Huamachuco and Cajabamba. *University of California Publications in American Archaeology and Ethnology* 34: 223–399. Berkeley.

McEwan, Gordon
  1990 Some Formal Correspondences between the Imperial Architecture of Wari and Chimu Cultures of Ancient Peru. *Latin American Antiquity* 1 (2): 97–116.

Menzel, Dorothy
  1964 Style and Time in the Middle Horizon. *Ñawpa Pacha* 2: 1–106.
  1968 New Data on the Huari Empire in Middle Horizon Epoch 2A. *Ñawpa Pacha* 6: 47–114.
  1977 *The Archaeology of Ancient Peru and the Work of Max Uhle.* R. H. Lowie Museum of Anthropology, Berkeley.

Menzel, Dorothy, John Howland Rowe, and Laurence Emmett
  1964 The Paracas Pottery of Ica: A Study in Style and Time. University of California Publications in American Archaeology and Ethnology 50. University of California Press, Berkeley and Los Angeles.

Morris, Craig
  n.d. Storage in Tahuantinsuyu. Ph.D. dissertation, University of Chicago, 1967.

Muelle, Jorge C.
  1954 Acerca del estilo Chimu Medio. *Revista del Museo Nacional* 23: 182–197. Lima.

Munizaga, Carlos
  1957 Secuencias culturales de la zona de Arica. *Arqueología Chilena* (Richard P. Schaedel, ed.). Centro de Estudios Arqueológicos, Universidad de Chile, Santiago.

Netherly, Patricia
  n.d. Local Level Lords on the North Coast of Peru. Ph.D. dissertation. Cornell University, Ithaca, N.Y., 1977.

Newman, Marshall T.
  1948 A Summary of the Racial History of the Peruvian Area. In *A Reappraisal of Peruvian Archaeology* (Wendell C. Bennett, ed.). Memoirs of the Society for American Archaeology 13 (4), pt. 2: 16–19.

Nuñez, Lautaro, and Tom D. Dillehay
  1979 Movilidad giratoria, armonía social y desarrollo en los Andes meridio-

nales. Patrones de tráfico e interacción económica. Universidad del Norte, Antofagasta, Chile.

O'NEALE, LILA M., AND ALFRED LOUIS KROEBER
1930 *Textile Periods in Ancient Peru.* University Publications in American Archaeology and Ethnology 28 (2): 23–56. University of California Press, Berkeley.

PARSONS, JEFFREY R., AND CHARLES M. HASTINGS
n.d. Prehistoric Settlement Patterns in the Upper Mantaro, Peru. A progress report for the 1975 field season. Submitted to the Instituto Nacional de Cultura, 1977. Mimeographed.

PATTERSON, CLAIR
1971 Native Copper, Silver and Gold Accessible to Early Metallurgists. *American Antiquity* 36 (3): 286–321.

POSNANSKY, ARTHUR
1945 *Tihuanacu, the Cradle of American Man,* 2 vols. J. J. Augustin, New York.

PROULX, DONALD A.
1973 *Archaeological Investigations in the Nepeña Valley, Peru.* Research Report 13. University of Massachusetts, Amherst.

RAVINES SÁNCHEZ, ROGGER
1986 Un depósito de ofrendas del Horizonte Medio en la Sierra Central del Perú. *Ñawpa Pacha* 6: 19–45.

REISS, WILHELM, AND ALPHONSE STÜBEL
1880–87 *The Necropolis of Ancon in Peru,* 3 vols. Berlin.

RODRÍGUEZ SUY SUY, ANTONIO
1971 Irrigación prehistorica en el valle de Moche. *Transcripción de investigaciones de particulares,* 1. Centro Nacional de Capacitación e Investigación para la Reforma Agraria. Trujillo.

ROSTWOROWSKI DE DIEZ CANSECO, MARÍA
1977 *Etnía y sociedad.* Instituto de Estudios Peruanos, Lima.

ROWE, JOHN HOWLAND
1960 Cultural Unity and Diversification in Peruvian Archaeology. In *Man and Cultures: Selected Papers of the Fifth International Congress of Anthropological and Ethnological Science:* 627–631. Philadelphia.
1962 Stages and Periods in Archaeological Interpretation. *Southwest Journal of Anthropology* 18 (1): 40–54.
1963 Urban Settlements in Ancient Peru. *Ñawpa Pacha* 1: 1–27.
1978 Introduction. In *Peruvian Archaeology: Selected Readings* (J. H. Rowe and D. Menzel, eds.), Peek Publications, Palo Alto, Calif.

ROWE, JOHN HOWLAND, AND DOROTHY MENZEL (EDS.)
1967 *Peruvian Archaeology: Selected Readings.* Peek Publications, Palo Alto, Calif.

SAWYER, ALAN
1963 Tiahuanaco Tapestry Design. *Textile Museum Journal* 1 (2): 27–38.

SCHAEDEL, RICHARD P.
   1951a   Wooden Idols from Peru. *Archaeology* 4 (1): 16–22.
   1951b   Mochica Murals from Pañamarca, Peru. *Archaeology* 4 (3): 145–154.
   1953   Mesa redonda para regularizar la terminología arqueológica peruana. *Boletín de la Sociedad para la Antropología Peruana* 1: 3–18. Lima.
   1957   Highlights of Andean Archaeology, 1954–1956. *Archaeology* 10 (2): 93–99.
   1959   Terminología para la arqueología peruana. *Actos y Trabajos del II Congreso Nacional de la Historia del Perú, Época Prehispánica* 1: 30–46. Lima.
   1966a   The Huaca el Dragón. *Journal de la Société des Américanistes* 15 (2): 383–495. Paris.
   1966b   Incipient Urbanization and Secularization in Tiahuanacoid Peru. *American Antiquity* 31 (3): 338–344.
   1966c   Urban Growth and Ekistics on the Peruvian Coast. *Actas y Memorias del 36 Congreso Internacional de Americanistas* 1: 536–539. Seville.
   1978   The Huaca Pintada of Illimo. *Archaeology* 31 (1): 27–39.
   1979   The Confluence of the Pressed Ware and Paddle Ware Traditions in Coastal Peru. *Estudios Americanistas, 2, Homenaje a H. Trimborn*. Haus Völker und Kulturen, Anthropos-Institut, Bonn.
   n.d.a.   An Analysis of Central Andean Stone Sculpture. Ph.D. dissertation, Department of Anthropology, Yale University, 1952. University Microfilms, Ann Arbor.
   n.d.b.   Informe de los trabajos de Cañoncillo, valle de Jequetepeque. Patronato Nacional de Arqueología, Instituto Nacional de Cultura, Lima, 1976.

SCHMIDT, M.
   1929   *Kunst und Kultur von Peru.* Propyläen-Verlag, Berlin.

SHADY SOLÍS, RUTH
   1982   La cultura Nievería y la interacción social en el mundo andino en la época Huari. *Arqueológicas* 19: 8–108. Lima.

SHADY SOLÍS, RUTH, AND ARTURO RUIZ
   1979   Evidence for Interregional Relationships during the Middle Horizon on the North Central Coast of Peru. *American Antiquity* 44 (4): 676–684.

SHIMADA, IZUMI
   1982   Horizontal Archipelago and Coast-Highland Interaction in North Peru. In *El Hombre y su ambiente en los Andes Centrales* (Luis Millones and Hiroyasu Tomoeda, ed.): 137–210. Senri Ethnological Series 10. National Museum of Ethnology. Senri, Osaka, Japan.

SMITH, JR., JOHN W.
   n.d.a   The Recuay Culture: A Reconstruction Based on Artistic Motifs. University Microfilms International, Ann Arbor, 1978.
   n.d.b   Report on Mid and Upper Valley Reconnaissance of North Coast Valleys between Zaña and Santa. Unpublished ms.

STRONG, WILLIAM DUNCAN
   1948   Cultural Epochs and Refuse Stratigraphy in Peruvian Archaeology. In

Richard P. Schaedel

A Reappraisal of Peruvian Archaeology (Wendell C. Bennett, ed.). Memoirs of the Society for American Archaeology 13 (4), pt. 2: 93–102.

1957   Paracas, Nazca, and Tiahuanacoid Relationships in South Coastal Peru. Society for American Archaeology Memoir 13. Menasha, Wisconsin.

STRONG, WILLIAM DUNCAN, AND J. M. CORBETT

1943   A Ceramic Sequence at Pachacamac. In Archaeological Studies in Peru, 1941–1942 (W. D. Strong, G. R. Willey, and J. M. Corbett, eds.). Columbia University Studies in Archaeology and Ethnology 1 (2). New York.

STRONG, WILLIAM DUNCAN, AND CLIFFORD EVANS

1943   Cultural Stratigraphy in the Virú Valley, Northern Peru. Columbia University Studies in Archaeology and Ethnology 4. New York.

STÜBEL, ALPHONSE, AND MAX UHLE

1892   Die Ruinenstaette von Tiahuanaco. Leipzig.

STUMER, LOUIS M.

1956   Development of Peruvian Coastal Tiahuanaco Styles. American Antiquity 22 (1): 59–68.

1957   Cerámica negra de estilo Maranga. Revista del Museo Nacional 26: 272–289. Lima.

1958   Contactos foráneos en la arquitectura (sic) de la Costa Central. Revista del Museo Nacional 27 (2): 11–30. Lima.

TELLO, JULIO C.

1942   Origen y desarrollo de las civilizaciones prehistóricas andinas. 37 Congreso Internacional de Americanistas, Actas y Memorias 1: 589–720. Lima.

1956   Arqueología del Valle de Casma. San Marcos. Lima.

THATCHER, JR., JOHN P.

1978   Early Intermediate Period and Middle Horizon 1B Ceramic Assemblages of Huamachuco, North Highlands, Peru. Ñawpa Pacha 10–12 (1972–1974): 109–127.

UBBELOHDE-DOERING, HEINRICH

1967   On the Royal Highways of the Inca. Praeger, New York.

UHLE, MAX

1902   Types of Culture in Peru. American Anthropologist 4: 753–759.

1903   Pachacamac: Report of the William Pepper, M.D., LL.D., Peruvian Expedition of 1896 (C. Grosse, trans.). University of Pennsylvania, Department of Archaeology. Philadelphia.

1913   Zur Chronologie der alten Culturen von Ica. Journal de la Société des Américanistes de Paris n.s. 10: 341–367. Paris.

VREELAND, JAMES

1977   Ancient Andean Textiles: Clothes for the Dead. Archaeology 30 (3): 166–178.

WARDLE, H. NEWELL

1949   A Rare Peruvian Tapestry Bonnet. Proceedings of the International Congress of Americanists: 216–218. New York.

WASSÉN, S. HENRY

  1965   The Use of Some Specific Kinds of South American Indian Snuff-Related Paraphernalia. *Ethnologiska Studier* 28: 1–116. Goteborg.

WEISS, PEDRO H.

  1962   Tipología de las deformaciones cefálicas de los antiguos peruanos según la osteología cultural. *Revista del Museo Nacional* 31: 15–42. Lima.

WILLEY, GORDON R.

  1945   Horizon Styles and Pottery Traditions in Peruvian Archaeology. *American Antiquity* 11 (1): 49–56.

  1948   Functional Analysis of "Horizon Styles" in Peruvian Archaeology. In *A Reappraisal of Peruvian Archaeology* (Wendell C. Bennett, ed.). Memoirs of the Society for American Archaeology 13 (4), pt. 2: 113–122.

  1953   A Pattern of Diffusion-Acculturation. *Southwest Journal of Anthropology* 9 (4): 369–383.

  1971   *An Introduction to American Archaeology. Volume II: South America.* Prentice-Hall Inc., Englewood Cliffs, N.J.

ZEVALLOS QUIÑONES, JORGE

  1971   Cerámica de la cultura "Lambayeque." *Lambayeque* 1. Trujillo.

The Toltec Horizon in Mesoamerica: New Perspectives on an Old Issue

RICHARD A. DIEHL

UNIVERSITY OF ALABAMA

P RIOR TO THE 1986 DUMBARTON OAKS CONFERENCE on Latin American Horizons, archaeologists and art historians generally accepted the existence of three Pre-Columbian horizons in Mesoamerica: Olmec, Teotihuacan, and Aztec or Mexica. In the past some scholars have proposed a fourth, or Toltec, horizon, named for the inhabitants of ancient Tollan or Tula. Although the reality of a Toltec horizon has not been widely accepted, most scholars agree that the issue deserves closer examination than it has received (cf. Price 1976: 20).

In this paper I examine the evidence, both old and new, for a Toltec horizon. I conclude that there is considerable evidence for a horizon between A.D. 950 and 1150 and that its spread can be attributed to the Toltecs of Tula, Hidalgo. I hasten to emphasize that the existence of the horizon and its attribution to the Toltecs are two separate issues, and the former can be true even if the latter is not. Thus my position is contrary to that of Esther Pasztory, Cecelia Klein and Emily Umberger, and other contributors to this volume who reject the value of the horizon concept or deny the reality of particular horizons. Despite the faults that my colleagues find with it, I believe that the concept is valid in a general sense and, for reasons that should become apparent, useful in reconstructing Mesoamerican prehistory during the Early Postclassic period.

BACKGROUND

Rebecca Stone-Miller (this volume) has reviewed the horizon concept, and her discussion need not be repeated here. However, I must briefly discuss one class of frequently neglected evidence that is important in my formulation of the Toltec horizon; that which G. R. Willey and P. Phillips (1958: 33) called "highly specialized artifact types" and "peculiar ritual assemblages." First, however, a little background is in order.

Most scholars employ some version of Willey and Phillips' (1958) definition of horizon. Drawing upon the work of Max Uhle (1913) and A. L. Kroeber (1944) in the central Andes, Willey and Phillips defined horizons as a "primarily spatial continuity represented by cultural traits and assemblages whose nature and mode of occurrence permit the assumption of a broad and rapid spread" (Willey and Phillips 1958: 33). For Willey and Phillips, horizons serve the archaeologist primarily as a means of investigating external relations over large areas within a reasonably restricted span of time. They recognize that the traits (horizon markers) that occur in the archaeological record achieved their spread through diffusion and suggest that the agents behind the spread were "individuals or organized groups, such as trading companies, religious bodies, armies, and migrating populations" (Willey and Phillips 1958: 51).

According to Willey and Phillips, horizons are usually characterized by the presence of a horizon style, "a specialized cultural continuum represented by the wide distribution of a recognizable art style" (Willey and Phillips 1958: 32). However, they recognize that other kinds of cultural data may also be used to define horizons, including "highly specialized artifact types, widely traded objects, new technologies, unusual modes of burial, or peculiar ritual assemblages—*in other words any kind of archaeological evidence that indicates a rapid spread of new ideas over a wide geographic space*" (Willey and Phillips 1958: 32, emphasis added).

Even though Willey and Phillips took care to propose multiple lines of evidence, most discussions of Pre-Columbian horizons concentrate on styles and stylistic analyses while ignoring other kinds of information. However, archaeologists frequently document widespread occurrences of well-defined artifact types that do not exhibit stylistic unity but whose mere acceptance by other societies must indicate cultural contacts of the intensity implied by the horizon concept. These artifacts are often ritual objects, which certainly qualify as "highly specialized artifact types" whether or not they formed a functional complex or "peculiar ritual assemblage." Several such artifact classes that existed in Mesoamerica in the two centuries after A.D. 950 helps us to identify the Toltec horizon.

THE TOLTEC HORIZON

In the past archaeologists have considered three lines of evidence for a Toltec horizon: (1) the Mixteca-Puebla horizon style, (2) the spatial distribution of Tohil plumbate and Silho or X-Fine Orange ceramic wares; and (3) the central Mexican or "Toltec" presence at Chichen Itza. Each of these is a controversial topic about which a broad spectrum of opinions exists, so it is not surprising that some authorities accept them as evidence for a Toltec horizon while others do not. However, in each instance there is new information not previously considered in the context of a Toltec horizon. Therefore, I will briefly discuss each of them in turn.

The Mixteca-Puebla Horizon Style

The Mixteca-Puebla Horizon Style is a highly distinctive art style believed to originate in southern Puebla and northern Oaxaca at about A.D. 800, after which it spread to the rest of Mesoamerica (Nicholson 1960). The defining hallmarks of the style include geometric delineation, standardized symbols that are not so highly stylized as to obscure their natural models, and vivid polychrome designs. According to Nicholson:

> These generalities are much less important in distinguishing the style from others in Mesoamerica than certain specific ways of representing various symbols. The presence of even one of these symbols or a characteristic grouping is often enough in itself to define the presence of the style. Among the most highly individual symbols are: solar and lunar disks, celestial and terrestrial bands, the Venus or bright star symbol, skulls and skeletons (with double outlined bones), jade or *chalchihuitl,* water, fire and flame, heart, war (*atl-tlachinolli,* shield, arrows, and banner), mountain or place, "downy feather ball," flower (many variants), stylized eyes as stars, stepped fret (*xicalcoliuqui*), sliced spiral shell (*ehecacozcatl*), and the twenty *tonalpohualli* signs. One of the most frequent and diagnostic symbol groups is the row of alternating skulls and crossed bones (often combined with hearts, severed hands, etc.). Zoomorphic forms are quite distinctive and easily recognizable, particularly serpents (frequently feathered, *quetzalcoatl,* or sectioned, *xiuhcoatl*), jaguars, deer, rabbits, and spiders. The many deities depicted are highly individualized and usually accompanied by special, clearly distinguishable insignia. (Nicholson 1960: 614)

Nicholson identified several possible regional variants, including Mixtec, Tula-based Toltec, Valley of Mexico, and Veracruz substyles, and suggested that future investigators would be able to define at least two major sequential substages, which he labeled "Toltec" and "Post-Toltec" or "Cholulteca." He defined the geographical range of the style beyond its homeland to include northwest Mexico, the Veracruz coastal lowlands, and Chichen Itza. Later variants occur at Tulum, Quintana Roo, and Santa Rita, Belize, and somewhat weaker expressions are seen in Chiapas, Guatemala, and the Mesoamerican southeastern frontier region.

Despite Nicholson's caveats about the preliminary nature of his formulation (Nicholson 1960: 616; see also Nicholson 1982), the Mixteca-Puebla concept achieved great popularity and continues to play an important role in most reconstructions of Mesoamerican prehistory. Although various authors examined specific aspects of the concept (e.g., Paddock 1982; Brockington 1982; Ramsey 1982; Stone 1982; Lind n.d.; Schávelzon 1980), it never received the systematic evaluation Nicholson called for in his original paper until Michael E. Smith and Cynthia M. Heath-Smith published an indepth critique in 1980.

Smith and Heath-Smith argue that Nicholson and his followers have created "inappropriate models and faulty interpretations of Postclassic Mesoamerican cultural dynamics" (Smith and Heath-Smith 1980: 15) by failing to distinguish three distinct phenomena. They call these three phenomena (1) the Postclassic Religious Style, (2) the Mixtec Codex Style, and (3) the Mixteca-Puebla Regional Ceramic Sphere. Smith and Heath-Smith define the Postclassic Religious Style as "a collection of standardized religious symbols that were popular throughout Mesoamerica, beginning in the Early Postclassic period"; the Mixtec Codex style as "a highly distinctive Late Postclassic polychrome narrative style most commonly associated with codices, murals, and ceramics of the Mixteca-Puebla region"; and the Mixteca-Puebla Regional Ceramic Sphere as "the local ceramic complexes of the Mixteca-Puebla region which share several stylistic features" (Smith and Heath-Smith 1980: 15).

Smith and Heath-Smith maintain that Nicholson's version of the Mixteca-Puebla concept has fostered a flawed historical reconstruction of the spread of the Mixteca-Puebla style, which they call the "Waves of Influence" diffusion model. According to them, the model tries to account for the spread of all the components of the Mixteca-Puebla style as a unitary phenomenon emanating from a single source area in the central Mexican highlands. They criticize this model as an overly simplistic recontruction that does not fit the data, and instead propose a "non-nuclear spatial model" in which the Postclassic Religious Style, the Mixtec Codex Style, and the Mixteca-Puebla Ceramic Sphere arose at different times and in different places.

I find these propositions convincing and tentatively accept them. Since the Mixtec Codex Style and the Mixteca-Puebla Ceramic Sphere postdate A.D. 1200, they are not relevant to an examination of the Toltec horizon. However, the Postclassic Religious Style is directly germane to the issue and thus deserves closer examination.

At the beginning of their article Smith and Heath-Smith (1980: 18) restrict the Postclassic Religious Style to the Early Postclassic, but later they say that it appears "in widely separated areas of Mesoamerica at various times during the Postclassic period." The motifs include stepped frets, feathered serpents, and other widespread symbols commonly found as painted designs on ceramics (Fig. 1). They relate the style to a long-lived elite religious system that spread along newly established commercial networks after A.D. 800 and continued to function until the Spanish Conquest and argue that the style

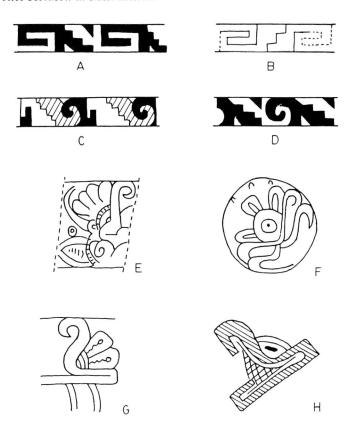

Fig. 1. Elements and motifs of the Postclassic Religious Style. Original sources: (A) Tizatlan, Tlaxcala; (B) Tizapan el Alto, Jalisco; (C) Nicoya, Costa Rica; (D) Valley of Oaxaca, Oaxaca; (E) Tizapan el Alto, Jalisco; (F) Culhuacan, Valley of Mexico; (G) Tizapan el Alto, Jalisco; (H) Nicoya, Costa Rica (after Smith and Heath-Smith 1980: fig. 1)

and the belief system it expresses fail to qualify as a horizon because seven centuries is far too long for a horizon.

I believe that they have been too quick to reject the Postclassic Religious Style as a horizon. The crucial determinant of a style's value as a horizon marker is not its longevity but rather the speed of its spread. If the Postclassic Religious Style achieved a wide geographical spread in a century or less, its initial stages surely represent a true horizon, which only later evolved into a generalized elite religious system. Unfortunately, the Meso-american regional and site chronologies for the tenth century are not pre-cise enough to support the idea of a horizon style composed of Postclassic

Religious Style "Mixteca-Puebla" elements. Although future investigations will undoubtedly refine these chronologies and provide detailed, temporarily sensitive stylistic analyses of Mixteca-Puebla-related materials, at the present we cannot define the relationship between the Postclassic Religious Style and a Toltec horizon.

Plumbate and Silho Fine Orange Ceramics

Tohil Plumbate and Silho Fine Orange (formerly called X-Fine Orange) pottery are two highly distinctive and well-studied Mesoamerican ceramic tradewares. Their unusual forms, surfaces, and pastes led to their recognition as horizon markers long before Willey and Phillips formalized the horizon concept (Shepard 1948; Smith 1958), and they are still recognized as such today (cf. Fahmel-Beyer 1988). The extensive literature dealing with them includes several recent studies that employed neutron activation and other chemical characterization techniques to help define the locales where they were produced (Neff and Bishop 1988; Rands, Bishop, and Sabloff 1982). In addition, a recent monograph by Bernd Fahmel-Beyer (1988) examines their distribution and the role they played in Toltec Mesoamerica.

Plumbate is a lustrous ware produced for at least 600 years (ca. A.D. 600–1200) on the south Pacific Coast near the Mexico-Guatemala border (Lee 1978; Neff and Bishop 1988). Tohil is the most recent variant of the Plumbate tradition, and it differs from earlier Plumbate pottery in temper and characteristic vessel forms. Tohil's very distinctive glassy-rock temper suggests a highly localized homeland, which Hector Neff and Ronald Bishop place within a few kilometers of the international border. Until recently archaeologists believed that Tohil Plumbate forms were restricted to effigy jars, goblets, and a few other unusual shapes, but new studies of clay chemical composition indicate that simple Tohil forms were produced for local consumption simultaneously with the more elaborate "export wares" (Figs. 2, 3) (Lee 1978: 293; Neff and Bishop 1988: 519).

Tohil Plumbate was transported over greater distances than any known Mesoamerican pottery; examples are reported from Panama and Nicaragua on the southeast to Nayarit and the Huasteca on Mesoamerica's northeast frontier (Fig. 4). It is especially abundant at Tula where it greatly outnumbers all other foreign trade ceramics (Cobean n.d.; Diehl 1983: 115). The

Fig. 3. (opposite, below) Tohil Plumbate pottery vessels found at Tula, Hidalgo. (A) bird effigy; (B) tripod jar; (C) flat-bottomed jar; (D) eagle-warrior effigy head from Tohil Plumbate vessel. The three vessels were part of a cache located in a subfloor storage pit in a house near the north edge of the city. (See Diehl, Lomas, and Wynn 1974, for complete information on the find.)

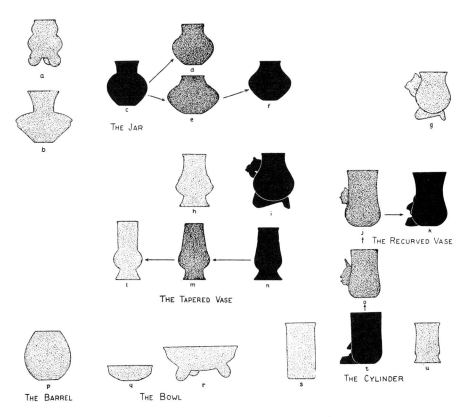

Fig. 2. Tohil Plumbate vessel forms (after Shepard 1948: fig. 1). Scale approximately ⅟₇

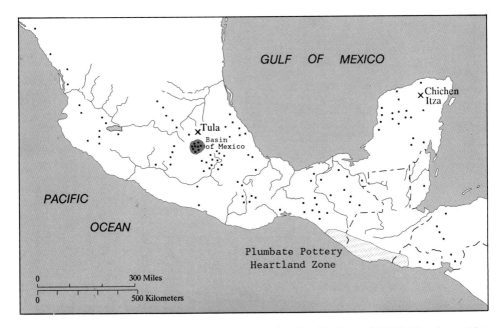

Fig. 4. Map of Mesoamerica showing the distribution of Tohil Plumbate. This impressionistic map shows a sample of reported finds of Tohil Plumbate (drawn from more accurate and detailed maps in Fahmel-Beyer 1988: 69–85)

stylistic and iconographic similarities Tohil vessels share with the Tula-Toltec art style have prompted much speculation about connections between Tula and the Plumbate potters because the eagle warriors, Tlalocs, Xipes, bearded old men, dogs, and turkeys commonly depicted on fancy Tohil vessels are much more at home iconographically in the central Mexican highlands than in the Plumbate homeland (cf. Coe 1984: 132). Thomas Lee (1978) suggests that Xoconusco potters produced vessels with central Mexican-influenced iconography in response to tribute demands by Toltec conquerors or merchants, while Hector Neff interprets the new styles as a voluntary response to growing external markets (Neff n.d., cited in Neff and Bishop 1988).

Silho Fine Orange pottery was manufactured in the Gulf Coast lowlands between southern Veracruz and Campeche, perhaps in the lower Usumacinta drainage in the centuries A.D. 900–1200 (Rands et al. 1982: 332). Like Tohil Plumbate, it is but one type in a long sequence of Fine Orange ceramics manufactured between A.D. 650 and 1500. The name refers to the characteristic homogeneous fine orange paste that lacks visible temper.

According to Robert Smith (1958: 154) the principal vessel forms include the pyriform vase with three hollow bulbous feet or bell-shaped pedestals;

cylindrical vases with pedestals; globular jars; flat-bottomed, basal-break tripod plates with hollow, bell-shaped feet; round-sided bowls; and convex-bottomed, basal-break tripods (Figs. 5, 6). Decoration includes painting, incision, gouging, and modeling. Black-painted decorative motifs include step frets, bands of bird, floral designs, and scrolls, while modeled effigy vessels depict humans and animals. Many of these forms and motifs are similar and even identical to characteristic Tohil Plumbate shapes and designs manufactured at essentially the same time a few hundred kilometers away.

Although not as widely distributed as Tohil Plumbate, Silho Fine Orange appears to occur in much greater quantities at the sites where it is found. Known occurrences outside its homeland include Yucatan, the Pasion drainage, Chiapas, highland Guatemala, Belize, and central Mexico (Fig. 7) (Rands et al. 1982; R. Smith 1958; R. Smith and Gifford 1965). Interestingly enough, none has been identified at Tula, although Jorge R. Acosta (cited in Davies 1977: 283) reports a sherd from near the city. This apparent absence may simply reflect the lack of excavations in urban elite residences, and its sporadic occurrence in central and north-central Mexico suggests it will eventually appear at Tula as well.

Chichen Itza and Its Toltec Connections

Chichen Itza's place in Mesoamerican prehistory and especially its relationship with Tula have perplexed scholars for over a century. As a result of his pioneering research at both centers, Désiré Charnay (1887) was the first to note striking similarities between their sculptures. Since his time, research at both sites has enormously expanded the inventory of architectural, artistic, and other traits shared by these two centers. According to C. Kristan-Graham (n.d.: 66), this impressive list includes "feathered serpent columns, atlantids, chacmools, *cipactli* glyphs, banquettes decorated with processional reliefs, colonnaded halls, similarly attired armed profile figures, and low relief images of feathered serpents, composite man-bird-serpent creatures posed frontally, profile raptors, canines and felines" (Figs. 8, 9). She goes on to observe, "What is so striking about the Tula-Chichen relationship is that the shared traits are not marginal but rather so numerous and central to the art style of each site that they actually typify the imagery of both cities" (Kristan-Graham n.d.: 66). In fact, the evidence indicates that despite the 1,100 kms that separate them, these two communities were more alike than any other two archaeological sites in Pre-Columbian America.

Although most scholars agree that Tula and Chichen Itza were partners in a very special relationship, the nature of that relationship is a matter of heated dispute. Recently published reconstructions include propositions that: (1) Tula-based Toltecs established a colony at Chichen or conquered an existing community; (2) a similar campaign of colonization or conquest was

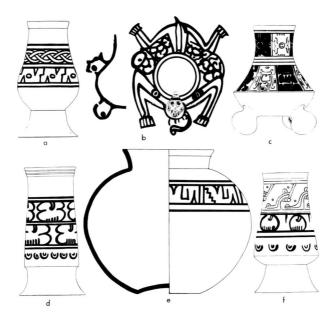

Fig. 5. Silho Fine Orange forms and decorations from the Már-quez collection. Height of (F) 19.9 cm (after Smith 1958: fig. 3)

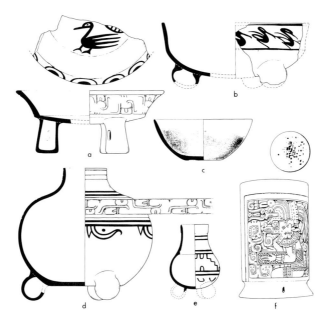

Fig. 6. Silho Fine Orange forms and decorations from Chichen Itza (A–E) and Moxviquil (F). Height of (D) 21.5 cm (after Smith 1958: fig. 4)

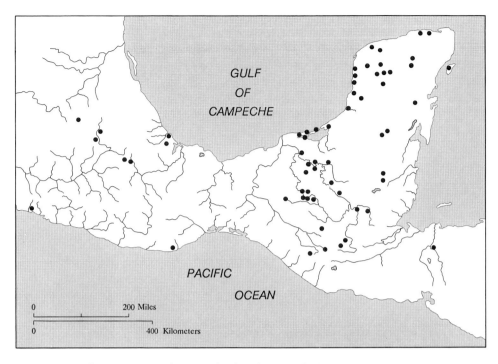

Fig. 7. Map of Mesoamerica showing the distribution of Silho Fine Orange pottery (after Fahmel-Beyer 1988: 62–63)

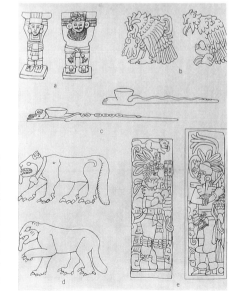

Fig. 8. Comparison of motifs and designs from Chichen Itza and Tula; (a) Atlantean figures (left, Tula; right, Chichen Itza); (b) eagles with human hearts from sculptured panels (left, Tula; right, Chichen Itza); (c) pottery pipes (upper, Tula; lower, Chichen Itza); (d) jaguars in relief (top, Tula; bottom, Chichen Itza); (e) figures from sculptured columns (left, Tula; right, Chichen Itza) (after Weaver 1981: 366)

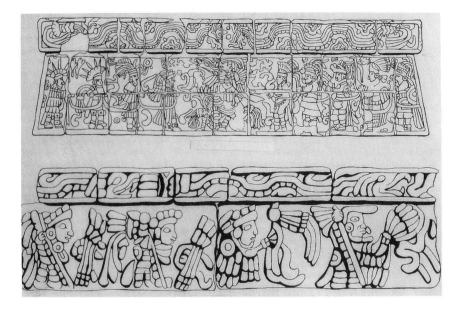

Fig. 9. Comparison of designs from Chichen Itza and Tula. Banquette facades showing processions of lavishly dressed figures with feathered serpent cornices (after Weaver 1981: 367)

carried out by the Putun or Chontal, Toltec-influenced merchants based in the Campeche-Tabasco lowlands; (3) Chichen was a basically Maya community that maintained contacts with Teotihuacan, Tula, and other central Mexican and Gulf Coast centers for at least five centuries (ca. A.D. 600–1200); and (4) Maya from Chichen exerted stylistic and perhaps social, political, and economic influence on the Gulf Coast and central Mexico, including even Tula itself. The existence of such diversity indicates the dimensions of the problem, but even more amazing is the fact that they are all based upon the same archaeological, ethnohistorical, artistic, and epigraphic data sets!

Charnay (1887) was the first to propose that Toltecs from Tula conquered the local Maya population. According to this interpretation, central Mexican Toltecs, led by an individual named Quetzalcoatl (Feathered Serpent, known as Kukulkan in Yucatan), conquered Yucatan during the tenth century and established their capital at Chichen. From this vantage point they could control overland trade, the coastal maritime trade route that skirted the peninsula, and the large salt beds on the North Coast. Except for an early disclaimer by Daniel Brinton (1887), scholars generally accepted this reconstruction until quite recently.

Alfred M. Tozzer's monumental *Chichen Itza and Its Cenote of Sacrifice*

(1957), an exhaustive two-volume synthesis of everything known about Chichen and its role in Yucatecan prehistory, is the benchmark work on the topic of Toltec-Maya relationships. Tozzer proposed a five-period site chronology (Chichen I through V, with appropriate subdivisions) in which he attempted to organize the various data sets into a coherent historical reconstruction. Chichen I (Late/Terminal Classic [A.D. 600–948, based upon the Goodman-Martinez-Thompson correlation]) was a regional variant of Classic Maya culture with hieroglyphic inscriptions, Puuc-style architecture, and other Late Classic diagnostics. Period II (A.D. 948–1145) marked the initial central Mexican incursion into Yucatan during which the invaders subjugated the peninsula, established their capital at Chichen Itza, introduced the feathered serpent cult, and created a hybrid Toltec-Maya culture. The foreigners consolidated their position in period III, a time of florescence (A.D. 1145–1260), but civil war led to Chichen's abandonment at its end. Mayapan emerged as the dominant community on the peninsula during Chichen IV (A.D. 1260–1450), and period V marked the years of political breakup between the abandonment of Mayapan and the Spanish Conquest.

As Charles Lincoln (1986: 144) has observed, many archaeologists who accepted Tozzer's reconstruction were uncomfortable with its many inconsistencies. Thus many new interpretations have appeared in recent years (cf. Andrews and Robles 1985; Ball 1986; Ball and Taschek 1989; Chase 1986; Chase and Chase 1985; Cohodas, 1978, 1989; Kelley 1968, 1983, 1984; and Lincoln 1986). C. Kristan-Graham's doctoral dissertation (Kristan-Graham n.d.: 64–98) contains a particularly useful synthesis of the issues, as does Lincoln (1986), even though I reject many of the latter's interpretations.

Many of the disagreements over the relationships between Chichen and Tula result from gaps and inconsistencies in the archaeological data base for Yucatan. The primary source of archaeological information on Chichen is the Carnegie Institution of Washington project conducted by Sylvanus G. Morley, Karl Ruppert, Earl Morris, George Vaillant, and others during the 1920s. These investigations were high-quality efforts for their time and some (e.g., the work of Earl Morris and his collaborators at the Temple of the Warriors [Morris, Charlot, and Morris 1931]), remain unsurpassed in their technical achievements and careful attention to detail. However, the investigators were not asking the questions we ask today, they lacked the sophisticated techniques we now take for granted, and their data cannot serve purposes they did not foresee. Furthermore, they failed to achieve one of their basic goals, a well-grounded archaeological site chronology. More recent investigations have made significant contributions in this direction, but Chichen Itza remains one of the most poorly dated major Pre-Columbian centers in Mesoamerica.

Recent attempts to define Chichen's role in Mesoamerican prehistory focus on three interrelated themes:

Richard A. Diehl

1. Chronology
2. The sources and nature of foreign influences at Chichen Itza
3. The direction in which contacts moved between Chichen and the rest of Mesoamerica

Chronology

Archaeologists do not agree upon Chichen Itza's internal chronology, placement in absolute time, and relationships to other Yucatecan sites. The issues are so complex that I cannot begin to do them justice in this paper; therefore I will restrict my discussion to those aspects of the problem that are relevant to my specific topic. From this perspective, the issue can be stated very simply. If central Mexican influence occurred at Chichen in the centuries from A.D. 850 to 1200, it could have come from Tula. If it arrived earlier than 850 or later than 1200, it cannot be the result of contacts with Tula because Tula was only a minor center prior to 850 and lay in ruins by 1200.

Tozzer's chronology and others like it do not present any problems in this regard. His Chichen periods II and III (A.D. 948–1260) fit nicely with Tula's florescence. However, this chronology has been challenged by several scholars in recent years. Lee Parsons (1969) argues that many of Chichen's central Mexican architectural traits actually belong to a seventh-century Teotihuacanoid horizon, and Marvin Cohodas (1978) has proposed that Chichen Itza's ballcourts were constructed at approximately the same time. David Kelley's (1983) correlation of the Maya and Christian calendars provides some support for this early placement of Chichen but the ideas of all three scholars have been greeted with skepticism by many.

Charles Lincoln (1986) occupies the other chronological extreme with his assertion that Chichen Itza postdates 1200, claiming that "Chichen Itza *by any criteria* must be more closely related to Tenochitilan than to Tula or Teotihuacan" (1986: 189, emphasis in original). The reasoning behind this is not clear but may be contained in an earlier statement on the same page that "only the Aztec imperial capital of Tenochtitlan is fully comparable in scope and urban character to Chichen Itza." I cannot help but wonder whether Lincoln and I are talking about the same archaeological site; the Chichen Itza I know is impressive but hardly comparable to the Aztec capital in size or complexity. In any case, Lincoln fails to provide any supporting evidence of his desire to move the chronology forward.

Eight radiocarbon determinations provide the only independent archaeological information relevant to the dating of Chichen Itza. Four of the samples were associated with Toltec-style materials, while the others came from Puuc-style structures and contexts. Two of these associated with Toltec-style remains were found in Balankanche cave; the other two came from a *zapote* lintel in the Castillo (Andrews 1970: 63–64).

The Balankanche dates are particularly important because the charcoal meets so many of the requirements for a suitable sample. The wood is from small plant stems and branches used as torches, assuring that the wood death-date is contemporaneous with the burning. Furthermore, the possibility of mixed samples of different ages is minimized because the cave served as a shrine for only a short time and then was sealed. Finally, the samples were found inside braziers that are virtually identical stylistically to braziers commonly found at Tula. Both determinations yielded identical dates, A.D. 860 ± 100 (LJ-272, LJ-273). Although two determinations are not enough to inspire complete confidence, their one-sigma range certainly suggests strong Toltec influence on Chichen Itza ritual activities during the time when Tula was approaching its height as a Mesoamerican imperial center.

The two lintel samples provided dates of A.D. 790 ± 70 (Y-262) and 810 ± 100 (Y-626b), dates whose midpoints are too early to fit comfortably with Tula's florescence. However, two factors may account for this anomaly. An old beam taken from an existing building, perhaps the Castillo substructure, may have been reused; or the radiocarbon determinations may reflect the death date of the heart wood within the tree many years before it was felled rather than the date of the construction of the Castillo. Similar cases to both suggestions have been reported at Teotihuacan (Kovar 1966; Millon 1973: 60–61).

Thus, despite their obvious similarities, the contemporaneity of Tula and Chichen Itza remains an unresolved issue and will continue to plague scholars until archaeologists create a sound chronology. Such a chronology must include detailed, stratigraphically based, ceramic and architectural sequences and an absolute chronology anchored in time with radiocarbon, obsidian hydration, or other chronometric evidence. Only then can we begin to correlate the ethnohistoric documentary accounts with the archaeology.

The Source and Nature of Central Mexican Influence at Chichen Itza

According to Tozzer and his followers, the central Mexican religion and artistic canons that the Toltecs imposed upon the Maya of Chichen Itza resulted in the emergence of a hybridized Toltec-Maya style rather than a slavish imitation of central Mexican Toltec art. Tozzer hypothesized that, since the small contingent of conquerors did not include artisans and craftsmen, they conscripted local laborers and sculptors trained in local Maya ideas and techniques. This, coupled with the rapid assimilation of many Maya attitudes and culture traits by the conquerors, resulted in the new and vigorous Toltec-Maya style.

In recent times J. Eric S. Thompson's "Putun Hypothesis" (1970) has largely replaced Tozzer's historical reconstruction. Thompson proposed that Toltecized Maya-speaking merchants from Campeche and eastern Tabasco, called the Putun, played a major role in Yucatecan affairs after A.D. 700. According to Thompson's interpretation of the archaeology and ethnohistorical documents, the Putun established control over a circumpeninsular maritime commercial route, conquered Chichen Itza, and founded their capital on the site in two sequential stages. Central Mexican influence was already evident during the first stage but did not become so visibly dominant until the second stage of the process.

Following Thompson's lead, most recent interpretations have emphasized the Putun instead of the Toltecs as the agents who introduced Mexican elements to Yucatan. However, several questions remain unanswered. If the Putun or a Putun-Toltec alliance introduced central Mexican cults, iconography, and styles into Yucatan, why is there no evidence of these things in their Campeche-Tabasco homeland? Using negative evidence is always treacherous business in archaeology, and only a few Early Postclassic sites are known in the western Maya lowlands, but even the antiquities market seems to lack Toltec or Maya-Toltec materials from the Putun area. We might not expect to find stone monuments and architectural sculpture in the swampy, alluvial Putun homeland, but this does not account for the apparent lack of Toltec or Toltec-inspired art in other media.

Several explanations can be offered for this curious state of affairs. The Toltecs may have had a less visible impact on the Putun homeland centers than at Chichen Itza. Perhaps the Putun were nothing more than a minor element in Chichen Itza's new elite. Perhaps the Putun role in the entire business has been misinterpreted or greatly exaggerated. We need to learn much more about the archaeology of the Putun homeland before we can choose between these alternatives, but until we do, the marked similarities between Chichen Itza and Tula cannot be explained by invoking these shadowy coastal peoples.

The Direction of Cultural Contacts

Most scholars are convinced that contacts and influences went from central Mexico to Yucatan, but George Kubler (1961, 1962, 1984: 288) has argued the reverse. According to him, Maya from Chichen Itza introduced "Toltec" influence into Tula and that highland city was a stylistic outpost of the Yucatecan center. He maintains that what we call the Toltec style crystallized at Chichen Itza out of earlier Maya ideas and was taken to central Mexico where it was adopted by Tula's elite. Thus, argues Kubler, the first stage of the style is visible in Yucatan but not at Tula. Alberto Ruz Lhuillier (1962) countered Kubler's assertions in a well-reasoned rejoinder that convinced most scholars (but see Lincoln 1986: 188).

Kubler and Ruz both neglected a crucial point which needs to be emphasized. Kubler used structures erected near the end of Tula's history as his standards of comparison. However, the Toltec capital was occupied for several centuries, and it is the earliest remains, not the latest, that are relevant in such a comparison. If Tula's early art and architecture were radically different from the later "Toltec" corpus, Kubler's assertion that the new elements were introduced from outside might have some validity.

Unfortunately, Tula's earliest public architecture and art remains unstudied. Tula Chico, the major civic precinct during the Corral phase, has never been excavated, and nothing is known about the associated art (Matos 1974; Cobean 1982; Diehl 1983). In addition, we know that the Tula Grande structures on which Kubler based his comparisons contain older substructures. Acosta identified seven sequential construction phases in the Palacio de Quetzalcoatl, three in Pyramid B, and several earlier buildings beneath the floors of the Palacio Quemado (cf. Diehl 1989). None of these early structures has been exposed, and it is premature to argue that the Toltec style was imported in toto from afar until we know more about them and Tula's other early buildings.

Summary

The information we have on the Postclassic Religious Style, Tohil Plumbate and Silho Fine Orange pottery, and Tula-Chichen connections is strongly indicative of a horizon even though there is no "horizon style" in the usual sense of the term. The preceding discussion presents a variety of evidence for serious, highly developed contacts among many widely separated societies during the Early Postclassic period. Most of the evidence is not new, although recent investigations have clarified many important issues, particularly regarding the ceramic tradewares and the Mixteca-Puebla concept.

NEW EVIDENCE FOR AN EARLY POSTCLASSIC HORIZON

An unusual assemblage of ceramic ritual objects constitutes another line of evidence for an Early Postclassic horizon. The assemblage includes at least three items commonly found at Tula and many other Mesoamerican centers during the ninth and tenth centuries: (1) large ceramic braziers decorated with conical appliqué nubbins and Tlaloc faces; (2) wheeled animal effigy figurines; and (3) hand-held censers with tubular handles, open-work carving on the bowl, and two supports. Although in the past archaeologists have noted the widespread distribution of these items, they have not considered them as evidence for a horizon.

There is no evidence that the three formed a functional set employed together in specific ceremonies, and I use the term *assemblage* to refer to a group of objects utilized at one point in time for a specific class of human behavior, in this case, ritual. Other artifact classes may be included in the assemblage when we know more about their history and distribution; ceramic flutes, smoking pipes, and Mazapan-style "gingerbread" figurines are possible candidates for future inclusion.

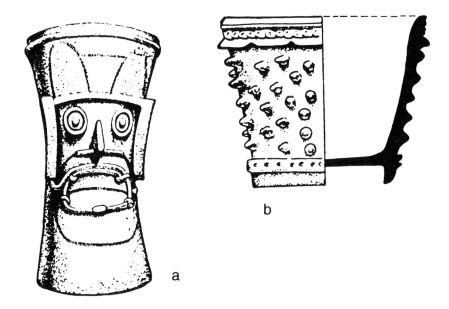

Fig. 10. Early Postclassic braziers from Tula, Abra Coarse Brown type. The hourglass-shaped vessel on the left has a Tlaloc face, the flared-wall vessel on the right is decorated with conical nubbins and finger-impressed clay strips (from Diehl 1983: fig. 25)

All three classes of objects included in the assemblage were frequently encountered in excavations carried out by the University of Missouri-Columbia Tula Archaeological Project. These excavations uncovered eleven Tollan phase (A.D. 950–1150/1200) houses and a small temple in the Canal Locality and portions of another house at the Corral Locality, both near the northern boundary of the ancient Toltec capital. Much of the following discussion is based upon the results of those excavations, which are reported in detail in Diehl (1983) and Healan (1989).

Braziers

Ceramic vessels used as containers for fires or smoldering embers first appeared in Mesoamerica during the Late Formative period. Two quite distinctive forms became popular after the eighth century: large bowls with flat bottoms and outflaring walls and biconical, hourglass-shaped vessels (Fig. 10). Although similar vessels occur in Late Postclassic ceramic assemblages in the Basin of Mexico and elsewhere, they are readily distinguishable from Early Postclassic types. In fact, they are so distinctive that they may ultimately prove to be just as useful horizon markers as Tohil Plumbate and Silho Fine Orange.

Complete vessels of both shapes tend to be quite large, with heights of 100 cm and rim diameters of 70 cm not uncommon. They almost invariably have a coarse paste fabric, smoothed but unpolished surfaces, and exterior decorations constructed of appliqué clay elements. These elements include solid conical spikes; horizontal fillets or flanges, often with finger impressions, placed near the rim; and clay strips forming readily identifiable Tlaloc faces. Most braziers retain remnants of post-fired red, white, blue, or orange paint.

Both classes of braziers have a wide geographical distribution, and strikingly similar vessels are reported from central Mexico, the northern Mesoamerican periphery, the Gulf Coast lowlands, northern Yucatan, highland Guatemala, El Salvador, and Honduras. Specific designs and combinations of elements vary from one site to another and even within single phases at a given site. For example, the Tollan phase Abra Coarse Brown brazier type manufactured at Tula includes six distinct varieties (Cobean n.d.: 516–550) (Fig. 11). Most Tula varieties have analogues elsewhere in Mesoamerica, but no other site has more than two of the six Tula varieties. We do not know where the Early Postclassic brazier form originated, but regardless of where that happened, the diversity of Tula's brazier complex suggests that the idea reached its highest development at at the Toltec capital.

Braziers have been recovered from various depositional and use contexts, including domestic debris, temple refuse, and offertory caches at Balankanche cave, Chichen Itza (Cobean n.d.: 516–550; Andrews 1970). Most of the Tula pieces in Robert Cobean's sample were either associated with domestic refuse or the neighborhood temple and appear to have been used in domestic ritual rather than routine daily activities (Cobean n.d.: 516–550; Stocker and Healan 1989).

Wheeled Animal Effigy Figurines

Animal figurines mounted on wheels (see Fig. 12) are much more common than most Mesoamericanists realize, and at least 150 complete or fragmentary examples are recorded in the literature (Diehl and Mandeville 1987). Unfortunately, almost none of the complete examples comes from controlled documented excavations. Those for which we have reasonably secure and datable archaeological contexts were made and used between A.D. 950 and 1200, despite suggestions that the tradition began during the Late Classic period (Medellin Zenil 1960).

Wheeled figurines exhibit considerable stylistic and technological variability (Boggs 1973) and although we do not understand the spatial distribution of this variability, its existence suggests that individual pieces were manufactured locally at each site. They have been found in central Mexico, Michoacan, Guerrero, northern and central Veracruz, and El Salvador. The University of Missouri excavations at Tula recovered seventy-seven wheels,

a

b   c

Fig. 11. Abra Coarse Brown type brazier fragments from Tula; (a) Tlaloc eye fragment found associated with a small temple in the Canal Locality excavations; (b–c) are rims from cylindrical vessels (from Diehl 1983: monochrome pl. 40)

body fragments, and heads, the largest sample known from any site (Diehl and Mandeville 1987). Large-scale excavations in other Early Postclassic sites should recover many more wheeled figurines in the future.

The most common forms have handmade bodies with moldmade heads. Solid bodies are common in central Mexico and central Veracruz, while hollow bodies seem to predominate in northern Veracruz, Michoacan, Guer-

Fig. 12. Wheeled animal effigy figurine (drawing based on a complete example from Panuco, Veracruz, reported by Ekholm 1946)

rero, and El Salvador. Dogs and coyotes predominate but deer, jaguars, crocodilians, and iguanas have been identified as well. Many pieces have remnants of post-fired paint.

The functions of wheeled figurines are not known. Although often called toys, they probably had ritual uses similar to the equally puzzling functions of most Mesoamerican figurines that lack wheels. At Tula they appear only in domestic refuse, suggesting that they served in household rituals, not public or temple celebrations. The same may not have been true everywhere.

Openwork censers

Handled censers first appeared in Mesoamerica during the eighth century. Two basic varieties are known: "frying pan" censers with outflaring walled bowls and tubular handles, and smaller "openwork censers" that feature globular bodies with openings carved into the sides, two small supports at the front, and tubular handles that also served as third supports (Fig. 13). Openwork censers are much more widespread than the frying pan variety; they have been reported from Tula, the Basin of Mexico, Puebla, Oaxaca, Yucatan, and the highlands of Guatemala. They are called Mixtec censers by some but there is no evidence that Mixtec speakers invented the form, fostered its diffusion, or used them more than anyone else.

At Tula the Alicia openwork type is the Tollan phase variant of this censer form (Cobean n.d.: 564–571). Their distinguishing characteristics include jar-like bodies with rectangular or triangular openings, cylindrical necks, and outflaring rims with polished red upper surfaces. Vessel exteriors are frequently decorated with incised human faces, skulls, punctate designs, and horizontal rows of small clay appliqué flanges. At times appliqué strips on the upper surface of handles suggest the tail of a lizard or cayman. Those found by Acosta in his excavations at Tula Grande probably functioned in

283

Fig. 13. Openwork handled censers. Top: Alicia Openwork type from Tula; bottom: from the Sacred Cenote at Chichen Itza (Top, after Diehl: 1983; fig. 25; bottom photo, Coggins and Share [1984: 109])

temple or public rituals, but the examples Cobean reported were recovered in domestic refuse.

Discussion

Several significant points can be made about the ritual assemblage just described:

1. The three classes of objects served ritual functions. There is no evidence to suggest that they functioned in daily utilitarian contexts nor any reason to assume such a function. Braziers are the only possible exception. It is conceivable that they were used for cooking, but their elaborate decoration, the Tlaloc symbolism depicted on some of them,

the common occurrence of burnt areas and other evidence for hearths on house floors, and the fact that Abra Coarse vessels are never associated with kitchens all argue against this supposition.

2. Although some of these objects served in temple rituals at Tula and perhaps elsewhere, they all functioned in household settings as well. This implies that they permeated every social and organizational level of Toltec society down to the family. We do not know if the same held true elsewhere in Mesoamerica because we lack the essential provenance data from other sites.

3. The objects in the assemblage were not reserved for the exclusive use of the elite, at least not at Tula. Although the Canal Locality residents did not belong to the lowest status groups in Tula Toltec society, they were certainly not members of the elite (Diehl 1981, 1983; 68–96; Healan 1977,1989). The situation elsewhere is unclear for the reasons given above, but the Tula data suggest that these horizon markers functioned on every level of Mesoamerican society. The obvious implication is that scholars must be careful not to restrict their search for horizon markers too narrowly on elite cultural manifestations.

4. The three components of the complex appear to have originated in different regions of Mesoamerica. This may surprise some but should not. An implicit assumption underlying most uses of the horizon concept holds that all of its components originated at a single place and spread outward from there. This is what Smith and Heath-Smith basically, and I believe correctly, criticize in their attack on the Mixteca-Puebla "Waves of Influence" scenario. Conventional wisdom among Mesoamericanists suggests that urban centers are the only sources of creativity and hearths of invention in complex societies—what Don Rice (this volume) calls the "set of center-margin or core-periphery relations implicit in the construction of horizons." He goes on to say that "centers of origins for particular styles are assumed, and styles 'move' from those centers to more peripheral regions." However, both general world history and Mesoamerican studies provide abundant instances in which the reality of what happened was not that neat or simple.

Teotihuacan sheds some interesting light on this proposition. Until recently archaeologists assumed that because talud and tablero architecture, tripod cylindrical vases, and Thin Orange pottery were common in the city and excellent horizon markers elsewhere, they must have originated at Teotihuacan itself. However, recent investigations indicate that "typical Teotihuacan" talud and tablero architectural profiles may be older in Puebla and Tlaxcala than at Teotihuacan, "typical Teotihuacan" tripod vases grew out of an older ceramic tradition in central and southern Veracruz, and "typical Teotihuacan" Thin Orange pottery was manufactured in Puebla (Garcia Cook 1981: 256–262;

Rattray 1978, 1979, 1990). For whatever reasons, Teotihuacanos enthusiastically accepted these foreign ideas and integrated them so completely into their culture that they came to symbolize Teotihuacan. Later these ideas and, in some cases, the actual objects embodying them were exported to foreign regions under the aegis of Teotihuacan commercial, colonial, or military agents. Even though Teotihuacanos had borrowed them rather than invent them, the city was responsible for their dissemination. In that sense they are indeed excellent Teotihuacan horizon markers.

A similar process probably accounts for the dissemination of braziers, wheeled animal figurines, and openwork censers. There is no evidence that the inhabitants of Tula invented any of them. Ancestral forms of the braziers seem to be indigenous to the Guatemala highlands, although the home of the specific Early Postlassic forms is unknown. Wheeled animal figurines are thought to originate in central Veracruz, and central Mexico may be the homeland of openwork censers. Despite their widely separated origins, all three objects were thoroughly integrated into Toltec household ritual by A.D. 950, early enough for Tula to have served as the donor in the diffusion process to other areas.

5. The formal similarities shared by the three classes of objects at different sites indicate that similar ideas and beliefs were widely disseminated in Early Postclassic Mesoamerica, but their stylistic and, at times, technological variability suggests that the actual objects were manufactured locally. Thus, their distribution does not indicate trade in the way that Tohil Plumbate, Silho Fine Orange, and sourced obsidian indicate the movement of actual goods. The hypothesis of local manufacture remains to be tested by neutron activation analysis or other archaeometric techniques but the available evidence suggests that ideas rather than objects were transmitted from group to group. It is precisely the movement of ideas that is the central concern of the horizon concept.

SUMMARY AND CONCLUSIONS

During the course of the tenth century, Tula emerged as central Mexico's dominant polity and possibly the largest city in Mesoamerica. In the decades which followed, the Toltecs established an "empire" of unknown dimensions, complexity, and duration. One aspect of this imperial expansion centered on Chichen Itza, with which the Toltecs established close ties or even political domination.

Toltec commercial networks extended far beyond the apparent boundaries of the empire. Altough Toltec merchants were not the only traders who traveled Mesoamerica in search of markets, exotic raw materials, and fine luxury products (Diehl 1983: 140–157), Tula's size, complexity, and status as Mesoamerica's most powerful state suggests that Tula traders were perhaps more active and covered more territory than their contemporaries. These Toltec merchants moved ideas as well as tangible goods. The ideas were not commodities traded in the marketplace, as some have suggested for the lowland Maya in earlier times, but rather cultural beliefs and practices. Some may have been propogated deliberately, others surely passed from donor to recipient without any conscious intent. Many originated at or near Tula but others must have been learned from the peoples whom they encountered while away from home. The specific mechanisms of diffusion are not known. New cults and rituals may have been introduced along with the appropriate paraphernalia, or local traditional religious practices may have incorporated the new ideas and associated technology. The inhabitants of Tula were recipients as well as donors and some of the ideas seem to have been integrated into the basic fabric of Tula-Toltec life.

The diffusion of the·ideas and beliefs represented by the three classes of ritual objects may have followed very complex routes of transmission. They could have moved from Tula to new areas; from their original homelands to Tula first and only later to other places; or may even have by-passed Tula initially. Perhaps wheeled figurines and the ideology they embodied arrived in El Salvador before reaching Tula. Regardless of the specific historical sequence of events, new and unique exotic goods and ideas spread throughout Mesoamerica. Tohil Plumbate, Silho Fine Orange, and green Pachuca obsidian are the only objects for which there is evidence for actual trade (e.g., Andrews et al. 1988). Ceramics with Postclassic Religious Style motifs, braziers, wheeled animal effigies, and openwork censers were locally made material manifestations of the ideas.

These goods and ideas circulated far enough and fast enough to qualify as a horizon even if Tula was not the original source of the concepts. Mass migrations or missionary activities need not be invoked; ordinary commerce of the type major central Mexican states normally engaged in easily accounts for what we see in the archaeological record. I believe that Toltec merchants were the agents of that diffusion, introducing foreign goods and concepts wherever they went and that they played such a critical role in the spread of the horizon that it should be named for them. Calling the horizon Toltec does not gloss over the historical complexities or the contributions of other societies, nor does it necessarily imply Tula's military or economic control of the regions that participated in the horizon. Such a claim reads more into the situation than the evidence warrants.

In a similar vein, although the discovery of this or any horizon is a significant step, we must be careful not to assign too much weight to the presence of a horizon. I believe that many of my colleagues in this symposium have done precisely that by expecting too much payoff from the recognition of a horizon and then discarding the entire concept when it fails to live up to their expectations. In the case of the Toltec horizon, it is true that it can function as a chronological tool to help us date archaeological occupations, just as Tohil Plumbate and Silho Fine Orange have been used for decades. However, modern chronometric techniques such as radiocarbon and obsidian hydration dating have reduced the value, or at least the need for, horizons as chronological tools, and if chronology were the primary benefit resulting from recognition of a Toltec horizon, writing this paper would not have been worth my effort.

The truth is that horizons have more important functions than chronology. They alert us to certain kinds of contacts among ancient societies, contacts of an unusually strong and visible nature (at least as preserved in the archaeological record). Mere recognition of a horizon does not explain the processes and events that initiated the contacts or the dynamics that grew out of the contact situation, but it does provide insights about when and where to focus our investigations. For example, recognition of the Toltec horizon suggests the need for renewed field research of specific kinds at particular sites and regions. These might include Tula, Chichen Itza, Cihuatan in El Salvador, or the villages that produced Tohil Plumbate. Such research should be designed to answer questions about the nature, duration, and impact of contacts with other groups. The study of these particular cultural dynamics is greatly facilitated by the horizon concept; without it we could not formulate the kinds of questions and research strategies needed to understand what happened in prehistory and why.

BIBLIOGRAPHY

Andrews, Anthony P., Tomás Gallareta Negrón, Fernando Robles
Castellanos, Rafael Cobos Palma, and Pura Cervera Rivero
    1988   Isla Cerritos: An Itzá Trading Port on the North Coast of Yucatán,
            Mexico. *National Geographic Research* 4 (2): 196–207.

Andrews, Anthony P., and Fernando Robles Castellanos
    1985   Chichen Itza and Coba: An Itza-Maya Standoff in Early Postclassic
            Yucatan. In *The Lowland Maya Postclassic* (Arlen F. Chase and Prudence
            M. Rice, eds.): 62–72. University of Texas Press, Austin.

Andrews IV, E. Wyllys
    1970   *Balankanche, Throne of the Tiger Priest.* Middle American Research Insti-
            tute Pub. 32. Tulane University, New Orleans.

Ball, Joseph W.
    1986   Campeche, the Itza, and the Postclassic: A Study in Ethnohistorical
            Archaeology. In *Late Lowland Maya Civilization* (Jeremy A. Sabloff
            and E. Wyllys Andrews V, eds.): 379–408. University of New Mexico
            Press, Albuquerque.

Ball, Joseph W., and Jennifer T. Taschek
    1989   Teotihuacan's Fall and the Rise of the Itza: Realignments and Role
            Changes in the Terminal Classic Maya Lowlands. In *Mesoamerica af-
            ter the Decline of Teotihuacan: A. D. 700–900* (Richard A. Diehl and
            Janet Catherine Berlo, eds.): 187–200. Dumbarton Oaks, Washing-
            ton, D.C.

Boggs, Stanley
    1973   *Salvadoran Varieties of Wheeled Figurines.* Contributions to Mesoamer-
            ican Archaeology 1. Institute of Maya Studies of the Museum of Sci-
            ence, Miami.

Brinton, Daniel
    1887   Were the Toltecs a Historic Nationality? *American Philosophical Society
            Proceedings* 24: 229–241, Philadelphia.

Brockington, Donald L.
    1982   Spatial and Temporal Variations in Mixtec-Style Ceramics in Southern
            Oaxaca. In *Aspects of the Mixteca-Puebla Style and Mixtec and Central
            Mexican Culture in Southern Mesoamerica* (Doris Stone, ed.). Middle
            American Research Institute Occasional Paper 4: 7–14. Tulane Univer-
            sity, New Orleans.

Charnay, Désiré
    1887   *The Ancient Cities of the New World.* Harper, New York.

Chase, Arlen F.
    1986   Time Depth or Vacuum: The 11.3.0.0.0 Correlation and the Lowland
            Maya Postclassic. In *Late Lowland Maya Civilization* (Jeremy A. Sabloff

and E. Wyllys Andrews V, eds.): 99–140. University of New Mexico Press, Albuquerque.

CHASE, ARLEN F., AND DIANE CHASE

1985   Postclassic Spatial and Temporal Frames for the Lowland Maya: A Background. In *The Lowland Maya Postclassic* (Arlen F. Chase and Prudence M. Rice, eds.): 9–22. University of Texas Press, Austin.

COBEAN, ROBERT

1982   Investigaciones recientes en Tula Chico, Hidalgo. In *Estudios sobre la antigua ciudad de Tula.* Instituto Nacional de Antropología e Historia, Colección Científica 121. Mexico.

n.d.   The Pre-Aztec Ceramics of Tula, Hidalgo, Mexico. Ph.D. dissertation, Harvard University, 1978.

COE, MICHAEL D.

1984   *Mexico,* 4th ed. Thames and Hudson, New York.

COGGINS, CLEMENCY, AND ORRIN C. SHANE III (EDS.)

1984   *Cenote of Sacrifice: Maya Treasures from the Sacred Well at Chichén Itzá.* University of Texas Press, Austin.

COHODAS, MARVIN

1978   Diverse Architectural Styles and the Ball Game Cult: The Late Middle Classic Period in Yucatan. In *Middle Classic Mesoamerica, A. D. 400–700* (Esther Pasztory, ed.): 86–107. Columbia University Press, New York.

1989   The Epiclassic Problem: A Review and Alternative Model. In *Mesoamerica after the Decline of Teotihuacan: A. D. 700–900* (Richard A. Diehl and Janet C. Berlo, eds.): 219–240. Dumbarton Oaks, Washington, D.C.

DAVIES, C. B. NIGEL

1977   *The Toltecs until the Fall of Tula.* University of Oklahoma Press, Norman.

DIEHL, RICHARD A.

1981   Tula. In *Supplement to the Handbook of Middle American Indians: Volume One, Archaeology* (Jeremy A. Sabloff and Victoria Reifler Bricker, eds.): 277–295. University of Texas Press, Austin.

1983   *Tula: The Toltec Capital of Ancient Mexico.* Thames and Hudson, London.

1989   Previous Investigations at Tula. In *Tula of the Toltecs: Excavations and Survey* (Dan M. Healan, ed.): 13–29. University of Iowa Press, Iowa City.

DIEHL, RICHARD A., AND MARGARET MANDEVILLE

1987   Tula and Wheeled Animal Effigies in Mesoamerica. *Antiquity* 61 (232): 239–246.

DIEHL, RICHARD A., ROGER LOMAS, AND JACK T. WYNN

1974   Toltec Trade with Central America: New Light and Evidence. *Archaeology* 27: 182–187.

EKHOLM, GORDON F.

1946   Wheeled Toys in Mexico. *American Antiquity* 11 (4): 222–228.

FAHMEL-BEYER, BERND
 1981 Continuidad y cambio en dos tradiciones cerámicas postclásicas de Mesoamérica. *Anales de Antropología* 18 (1): 85–97. Mexico City.
 1988 *Mesoamérica Tolteca: Sus cerámicas de comercio principales*. Instituto de Investigaciones Antropológicas. Universidad Nacional Autónoma de México, Mexico.

GARCÍA COOK, ANGEL
 1981 The Historical Importance of Tlaxcala in the Cultural Development of the Central Highlands. In *Supplement to the Handbook of Middle American Indians: Volume One, Archaeology* (Jeremy A. Sabloff and Victoria Reifler Bricker, eds.): 244–276. University of Texas Press, Austin.

HEALAN, DAN M.
 1977 Archaeological Implications of Daily Life in Tollan, Mexico. *World Archaeology* 9: 140–165.

HEALAN, DAN M. (ED.)
 1989 *Tula of the Toltecs: Excavations and Survey*. University of Iowa Press, Iowa City.

KELLEY, DAVID
 1968 Kakupacal and the Itzas. *Estudios de Cultura Maya* 7: 255–268.
 1983 The Maya Calendar Correlation Problem. In *Civilization in the Ancient Americas: Essays in Honor of Gordon R. Willey* (Robert M. Leventhal and Alan L. Kolata, eds.): 157–208. University of New Mexico Press, Albuquerque, and Peabody Museum, Harvard University, Cambridge, Mass.
 1984 The Toltec Empire in Yucatan. *Quarterly Review in Archaeology* 5 (1): 12–13.

KOVAR, ANTON
 1966 Problems in Radiocarbon Dating at Teotihuacan. *American Antiquity* 31: 427–430.

KRISTAN-GRAHAM, CYNTHIA
 n.d. Art, Rulership and the Mesoamerican Body Politic at Tula and Chichén Itzá. Ph.D. dissertation, University of California at Los Angeles, 1989.

KROEBER, ALFRED L.
 1944 *Peruvian Archaeology in 1942*. Viking Fund Publications in Anthropology 4. New York.

KUBLER, GEORGE
 1961 Chichen Itza y Tula. *Estudios de Cultura Maya* 1: 47–79.
 1962 *The Art and Architecture of Ancient America: The Mexican, Maya, and Andean Peoples*. Penguin, Harmondsworth, England.
 1984 *The Art and Architecture of Ancient America: The Mexican, Maya, and Andean Peoples,* 3rd ed. Penguin, Harmondsworth, England.

LEE JR., THOMAS A.
 1978 The Origin and Development of Plumbate Pottery. *Revista Mexicana de Antropología* 24 (3): 287–300.

Richard A. Diehl

LINCOLN, CHARLES E.
    1986   The Chronology of Chichen Itza: A Review of the Literature. In *Late Lowland Maya Civilization* (Jeremy A. Sabloff and E. Wyllys Andrews V, eds.): 141–196. University of New Mexico Press, Albuquerque.

LIND, MICHAEL
    n.d.   Mixtec Polychrome Pottery: A Comparison of Late Preconquest Polychrome Pottery from Cholula, Oaxaca, and the Chinantla. M.A. thesis, Department of Anthropology, University of the Americas, Mexico City, 1967.

MATOS M., EDUARDO
    1974   Exploraciones en la Microarea: Tula Chico y la Plaza Charnay. In *Projecto Tula: 1a Parte*. Colección Científica 15. Instituto Nacional de Antropología e Historia, Mexico.

MEDELLIN ZENIL, ALFONSO
    1960   Nopiloa, un stitio clásico del Veracruz central. *La Palabra y el Hombre* 4 (13): 37–48.

MILLON, RENÉ
    1973   *Urbanization at Teotihuacán, Mexico. Volume One, The Teotihuacán Map. Part One: The Text*. University of Texas Press, Austin.

MORLEY, SYLVANUS G.
    1946   *The Ancient Maya*. Stanford University Press, Palo Alto, Calif.

MORRIS, EARL, JEAN CHARLOT, AND ANN MORRIS
    1931   *The Temple of the Warriors*, 2 vols. Carnegie Institution of Washington Pub. 406. Washington, D.C.

NEFF, HECTOR
    n.d.   Developmental History of the Plumbate Pottery Industry in the Eastern Soconusco Region, A.D. 600 through A.D. 1250. Ph.D. dissertation, University of California, Santa Barbara, 1984.

NEFF, HECTOR, AND RONALD L. BISHOP
    1988   Plumbate Origins and Development. *American Antiquity* 53: 505–522.

NICHOLSON, H. B.
    1960   The Mixteca-Puebla Concept in Mesoamerican Archaeology: A Reexamination. In *Men and Cultures: Selected Papers of the Fifth International Congress of Anthropological and Ethnological Sciences* (Anthony F. C. Wallace, ed.): 612–617. University of Pennsylvania Press, Philadelphia.
    1982   The Mixteca-Puebla Concept Revisited. In *The Art and Iconography of Late Post-Classic Central Mexico* (Elizabeth H. Boone, ed.): 227–254. Dumbarton Oaks, Washington, D.C.

PADDOCK, JOHN
    1982   Mixteca-Puebla Style in the Valley of Oaxaca. In *Aspects of the Mixteca-Puebla Style and Mixtec and Central Mexican Culture in Southern Mesoamerica* (Doris Stone, ed.). Middle American Research Institute Occasional Paper 4: 3–6. Tulane University, New Orleans.

Parsons, Lee
    1969   *Bilbao, Guatemala: An Archaeological Study of the Pacific Coast Cotzumalhuapa Region,* 2. Milwaukee Public Museum Publication in Anthropology 42. Milwaukee.

Price, Barbara J.
    1976   A Chronological Framework for Cultural Development in Mesoamerica. In *The Valley of Mexico: Studies in Pre-Hispanic Ecology and Society* (Eric R. Wolf, ed.): 13–21. University of New Mexico Press, Albuquerque.

Ramsey, James R.
    1982   An Examination of Mixtec Iconography. In *Aspects of the Mixteca-Puebla Style and Mixtec and Central Mexican Culture in Southern Mesoamerica* (Doris Stone, ed.). Middle American Research Institute Occasional Paper 4: 33–42. Tulane University, New Orleans.

Rands, Robert, Ronald L. Bishop, and Jeremy A. Sabloff
    1982   Maya Fine Paste Ceramics: An Archaeological Perspective. In *Analysis of Fine Paste Ceramics* (Jeremy A. Sabloff, ed.): Memoirs of the Peabody Museum of Archaeology and Ethnology 15 (2). Harvard University, Cambridge, Mass.

Rattray, Evelyn C.
    1978   Los contactos entre Teotihuacan y Veracruz. In *XV Mesa Redonda* 2: 301–312. Sociedad Mexicana de Antropología, Mexico.
    1979   La cerámica de Teotihuacan: Relaciones exteriores y cronología. *Anales de Antropología* 16: 51–70.
    1990   New Findings on the Origins of Thin Orange Ceramics. *Ancient Mesoamerica* 1 (2): 181–195.

Ruz Lhuillier, Alberto
    1962   Chichén Itzá y Tula: Comentarios a un ensayo. *Estudios de Cultura Maya* 2: 205–220.

Schávelzon, Daniel
    1980   *El complejo arqueológico Mixteca-Puebla: Notas para una redefinición cultural.* Universidad Nacional Autónoma de México, Mexico, D.F.

Shepard, Anna O.
    1948   *Plumbate–A Mesoamerican Trade Ware.* Carnegie Institution of Washington Pub. 573. Washington, D.C.

Smith, Michael E., and Cynthia M. Heath-Smith
    1980   Waves of Influence in Postclassic Mesoamerica? A Critique of the Mixteca-Puebla Concept. *Anthropology* 4 (2): 15–49. State Univeristy of New York, Stony Brook.

Smith, Robert E.
    1958   The Place of Fine Orange Pottery in Mesoamerican Archaeology. *American Antiquity* 24: 151–160.

Smith, Robert E., and James C. Gifford
    1965   Pottery of the Maya Lowlands. In *Handbook of Middle American Indians:*

Volume Two, Archaeology of Southern Mesoamerica, Part One (Gordon R. Willey and Robert Wauchope, eds.): 498–534. University of Texas Press, Austin.

STOCKER, TERRY, AND DAN M. HEALAN

1989   The East Group and Nearby Remains. In *Tula of the Toltecs; Excavations and Surveys* (Dan M. Healan, ed.): 149–162. University of Iowa Press, Iowa City.

STONE, DORIS

1982   Cultural Radiations from the Central and Southern Highlands of Mexico into Costa Rica. In *Aspects of the Mixteca-Puebla Style and Mixtec and Central Mexican Culture in Southern Mesoamerica* (Doris Stone, ed.). Middle American Research Institute Occasional Paper 4: 61–70. Tulane University, New Orleans.

THOMPSON, J. ERIC S.

1956   *The Rise and Fall of the Ancient Maya.* University of Oklahoma Press, Norman.

1970   *Maya History and Religion.* University of Oklahoma Press, Norman.

TOZZER, ALFRED M.

1957   *Chichen Itza and Its Cenote of Sacrifice: A Comparative Study of Contemporaneous Maya and Toltec.* Memoirs of the Peabody Museum 11–12. Harvard University, Cambridge, Mass.

UHLE, MAX

1913   Die Ruinen von Moche. *Journal de la Société des Américanistes de Paris* 10: 95–117.

WEAVER, MURIEL PORTER

1981   *The Aztecs, Maya, and Their Predecessors.* 2nd ed. Academic Press, New York.

WILLEY, GORDON R., AND PHILIP PHILLPS

1958   *Method and Theory in American Archaeology.* University of Chicago Press, Chicago.

Aztec Art and Imperial Expansion

EMILY UMBERGER

ARIZONA STATE UNIVERSITY

CECELIA F. KLEIN

UNIVERSITY OF CALIFORNIA, LOS ANGELES

IN 1972, WHEN A GROUP of archaeologists meeting in Santa Fe adapted a system of alternating horizons and intermediate periods to Mesoamerican chronology, they divided the traditional Postclassic (A.D. 900–1521) into three parts and named the last part the Late Horizon. Because this period was linked principally with the hegemony of the Mexica-Aztecs of Tenochtitlan, Barbara Price (1976: 20), in presenting the new nomenclature, chose as the beginning date 1325, the recorded year of foundation of that city. Subsequently, William T. Sanders, Jeffrey R. Parsons, and Robert S. Santley (1979: 467, 471, 162) chose 1350, the beginning of an extended period of political unification of the Basin of Mexico under first Texcoco, then Azcapotzalco, and finally Tenochtitlan. They saw this political unity as reflected archaeologically in the standardization of ceramics (the Aztec III ceramic complex) throughout the area, a great increase in size and number of settlements, and changes in production patterns and usage of particular ecological zones.

Price and Sanders, Parsons, and Santley considered their Late Horizon to be a pan-Mesoamerican horizon as well, linked with the expansion of the empire of the Aztec Triple Alliance,[1] which was formed in 1431 at the end of the war of independence from the Tepanecs (Price 1976: 20; Sanders et al. 1979: 94). The chief diagnostic of the horizon was Aztec III Black-on-Orange (B/O) ceramics. Price (1976: 20) also listed Cholulteca polychrome

---

[1] It is the people of this confederation, dominated by the Mexica of Tenochtitlan, that we will refer to as the Aztecs. Many of the problems to be discussed below in relation to ideas about the Aztec horizon are due to wide variations in the use of the term *Aztec*. Sometimes it is meant narrowly, as here, to refer to the culture of the Mexica and their neighbors in the Valley of Mexico especially during imperial times. But sometimes it is used to designate all cultural manifestations in Central Mexico (the states of Mexico, Morelos, Hidalgo, and Puebla) during the period from 1200 to 1521. This is an unacceptable definition.

ceramics, other Mixteca-Puebla style ceramics, and "the double-stairway, twin-temple pyramid encountered at least as far south as Guatemala," acknowledging that some of these components were "technically non-Aztec" and even pre-dating Aztec times.

The concept of an Aztec-influenced horizon was actually not new in 1972. One can find the term *Aztec horizon* and assumptions about widespread Aztec influence scattered through earlier literature. In addition to sculptures of obvious Aztec derivation and a few buildings at recognizable Aztec sites, other forms sometimes credited to Aztec imperialism are buildings with round platforms, the two-slope *alfarda*, so-called Mixteca-Puebla design conventions and motifs in media besides ceramics, and "Mexican" deity images. Thus, the possible markers of the late Aztec horizon include distributed artifacts of Aztec and non-Aztec manufacture (notably ceramics) and local manifestations of widespread forms, motifs, and style traits in several media.

Notwithstanding these sporadic allusions to Aztec influence, the concept of a Mesoamerican, Aztec-related horizon has not been embraced by scholars. Even those who accept the new terminology in general and include it in their time charts may speak of Olmec and Teotihuacan horizons in their texts, but rarely mention an Aztec horizon. For instance, Blanton et al. (1981: 50, 151) have a Late Horizon in the Central Mexican column of their chronological chart of Mesoamerica, but in the text speak of a Late Aztec period.[2] Yet, although there has been some criticism of the terminology in general (e.g., Flannery 1977), only one scholar, Michael Smith (1987: 39), has verbalized his objections to the Late Horizon specifically. He rejects its use, moreover, even within Central Mexico.

The problem is that the diagnostic ceramic of the horizon, Aztec B/O, predates the political rise of the Aztecs by eighty years and has so far resisted division into stylistic phases. Sanders, Parsons, and Santley (1979: 467) had originally expected that with time the Late Horizon would be divided into pre-imperial and imperial phases, but Smith points out that the term *horizon*, by definition, inhibits such chronological refinement. Likewise, he (1987: 38) notes that Aztec III B/O is not an accurate marker of Triple Alliance activities outside the Basin, although it has been assumed to be so by a number of scholars.

Other Aztec archaeologists and historians seem to be in agreement in not accepting the new terminology, although without stating their reasons. The only aspect of the new chronology that has been adopted generally is the division of the traditional Postclassic into three rather than two parts—a division that takes into account the special nature and importance of the time

---

[2] They also chose to use different dating systems for different areas in preference to applying a single chronological schema to Mesoamerica as a whole.

between the fall of Toltec Tula around 1200 and the mid-fourteenth-century florescence of the communities around Lake Texcoco. Yet, as indicated above, the new terminology is avoided. Scholars speak rather of the Early (950–1150), Middle (1150–1350), and Late (1350–1521) Postclassic phases or use ceramic phase names or other designations.

The fact is, however, that no one, whatever his or her position on the magnitude of Aztec influence in late Mesoamerica, has attempted to determine systematically which forms, style traits, and motifs actually can be linked to the activities of the Aztec state, and to map their distribution. Only "Mixteca-Puebla" polychrome ceramics have been examined previously, and these have been rejected (convincingly) as horizon markers because they pertain to several different traditions spanning 700 years (M. Smith and Heath-Smith 1980). This paper, then, is a first attempt to give an overall picture by critically examining a variety of media. In the process, we will reject many of the other proposed horizon markers as invalid on the basis of their having spread, like "Mixteca-Puebla" ceramics, before the rise of the Aztec empire. In the end we will come closer to a definition of an imperial Aztec archaeological horizon, but it is a reduced horizon whose markers include buildings at a handful of sites, sculptures mostly in Central Mexico and northern Veracruz, and B/O ceramics (with qualifications). Even allowing for future archaeological discoveries and more refined studies, one cannot help but note, therefore, the obvious contrast between the effect of Aztec imperialism on the material record and that of the contemporary Inca state, whose distinctive forms are easily recognized and distributed across the expanse of its empire. In part this difference can be attributed to the limited nature of Aztec hegemony, and in part, as we will suggest, to the way in which material objects and visual forms were used by the Aztec state.

EXPANSE OF THE AZTEC EMPIRE[3]

On the basis of tribute lists and historical sources, Robert Barlow (1949) reconstructed the provinces of the Aztec empire as having covered the Central Mexican states of Mexico, Hidalgo, Morelos, and Puebla and large parts of Guerrero, Veracruz, and Oaxaca, as well as the Soconusco (Xoconochco) area on the Chiapas-Guatemala border. Although Barlow acknowledged the presence of independent regions like Tlaxcala within the empire, his map implies a solidarity, extent, and degree of control that have been challenged in recent years by several scholars. Ross Hassig (1984) has argued that the Aztec empire was a "hegemonic" empire, relying on psychological coercion and non-Aztec people for maintenance, and that the number of Aztecs abroad was relatively small. Michael Smith (n.d.b) and Frances Berdan

---

[3] For the chronology and expanse of the empire, see Ross Hassig (1988) and Robert Barlow (1949), respectively.

(n.d.) have emphasized that the Aztecs controlled certain towns on the map, not solid areas of land. They have also pointed out that some provinces were strategic in nature and less under the control of the empire than were the tributary provinces. This new view of the empire accords better with the material record to be described below.

CERAMICS

All Aztec-period ceramics are problematic when considered as markers of an Aztec imperial horizon. Aztec III B/O is found in different parts of the empire, but it appears outside the Basin before Aztec imperial expansion, examples having been found in quantities in Morelos in the chronological phase dated before conquest by the Triple Alliance (M. Smith 1987). Aztec IV B/O, which may date from the early sixteenth century on (Charlton 1979: 205; Sanders et al. 1979: 467), appears outside Central Mexico, but only in very small amounts where numbers are reported (Guerrero may turn out to be an exception). Burnished red ware, or Guinda, was manufactured in the Basin and other parts of Central Mexico (M. Smith 1990) and occurs in quantity with Aztec III B/O in the empire. However, it is also found in earlier, Middle Postclassic contexts as far away as central Veracruz (Stark 1990). Cholulteca polychromes from various, more distant non-Basin sources are sometimes mentioned as contemporary with and accompanying Aztec wares in the empire (e.g., Adams 1977: 286), but they too have been found in earlier contexts in Oaxaca and Veracruz (Bernal 1948–49: 40–41; Stark 1990). Finally, Chalco Polychrome, a Middle Postclassic Basin of Mexico ware with possible extensions into Late Postclassic times (Parsons et al. 1982: 446), has not been reported in the empire. Thus, despite the problem of its pre-imperial appearance outside the Basin, Aztec III B/O is the only ware with a time span approximating that of the empire and with a significant distribution in areas under Aztec control. The following is a survey of this distribution. It includes references to local imitations, although one must bear in mind that some of these could have been made after the Spanish Conquest and subsequent breakdown of long-distance trade (Charlton 1979: 206).[4]

Outside the Basin, few areas in Central Mexico have been surveyed, but ceramics are reported from a number of excavated sites. At Tula in the north, large quantities of both Aztec III and IV B/O were found in surface survey and in excavations (Acosta 1956; Mastache and Crespo 1974: 76–77). In the Toluca area to the west Aztec III B/O has also been reported at Tlacotepec, Tecaxic-Calixtlahuaca, Teotenango, and further south at Malinalco. In Morelos it is reported at Cuernavaca, Coatlan, Coatetelco, Yautepec, and at other sites studied by M. Smith and Kenneth Hirth, respectively.

[4] See M. Smith (1990) for analysis of quantities in places where numbers are reported. See Charlton (1979) on the continued production of Aztec ceramics in the Colonial period.

To the east it has been found at Tulancingo (Hidalgo), Rio Zahuapan (Tlaxcala), Cholula, Cuauhtinchan, and Tepexi El Viejo (all in Puebla).⁵ Given the spotty archaeological record and lack of detailed analysis at most sites studied, one cannot generalize about distribution of Aztec III B/O even in Central Mexico. Nor is it known where, besides Morelos, it appeared before Aztec imperial incursion.

In Guerrero Aztec sherds are found frequently in the north, where written sources document the presence of large Aztec colonies and high officials at the fortresses of Oztoma (Oztuma), Teloloapan, and Alahuiztlan (Durán 1967, 2: 351–355; Codex Mendoza 1925: 18r). In surveys of the Teloloapan-Oztuma and nearby Cocula areas, Aztec III and IV B/O sherds were reported as common (Lister 1971: 628; Cabrera 1986: 193–194). Likewise, surveys around Tepecoacuilco, the former provincial capital, and in the Balsas River Valley between Tetela and Mezcala further south revealed Aztec ceramics and imitations throughout (Greengo 1967; Rodríguez 1986: 168). However, the pattern changes in the Xochipala area, where Aztec III B/O was apparent at only one site (Schmidt 1986: 112). Farther south only small scatterings of Aztec III and IV B/O are reported (Lister 1971: 628–629).

In contrast to Guerrero, the area covered by the modern state of Oaxaca, reportedly numerous times under Aztec attack from the 1450s on, has so far yielded very few Aztec ceramics, even at those sites believed to have been settled by the invader or to have had high imperial officials. The most interesting representation, although a small quantity, was found at Coixtlahuaca (Coayxtlahuacan) in the Mixteca Alta, which had an imperial governor (Durán 1967, 2: 195). Ignacio Bernal (1948–49: 40) found, in excavated pits, tombs, burials, and offerings, Aztec III B/O and Guinda as well as a local ceramic with orange slip and black paint emulating Aztec wares. Further east and south Aztec sherds occasionally appear in the Nochixtlan and Tamazulapan valleys (Spores 1984: 229, note 40), but little else is reported. One would expect to find Aztec ceramics in the Valley of Oaxaca, a well-surveyed area, given that it was the locus of two high officials and an imperial colony (Codex Mendoza 1925: 17v; Durán 1967, 2: 225–239). Richard Blanton (1983: 318), however, discovered only ten Aztec III B/O sherds on a spur of Monte Alban near modern-day Oaxaca City. The explanation seems to be provided in Motecuhzoma's own statement that he would command "the nearby nations to . . . provide [the colonists] with pots, plates, bowls, vases, and grinding stones" (Durán 1967, 2: 238).

With rare exceptions, late-period sites on the Gulf Coast have been poorly explored (and only one survey area on the central coast has been published), but significant remains are reported, and in all probability more will be found. Historical sources help explain these greater evidences of Aztec pres-

⁵ See M. Smith (1990) for references.

Emily Umberger and Cecelia F. Klein

ence on the Gulf Coast. The important routes to the south passed through Veracruz and, in addition, thousands migrated there from Central Mexico in different periods at times of famine in the highlands and after epidemics on the coast (Durán 1967, 2: 244; Herrera 1952, 9: Déc. 4, bk. 7, chap. 8: 211–212).

In northern Veracruz, Aztec III B/O is present at Castillo de Teayo (Felipe Solís, personal communication), an unexcavated site with an Aztec-style pyramid and sculptural remains, which must have had an Aztec enclave or colony, probably Aztec Tezapotitlan (Breton 1920). Gordon Ekholm (1953: 417; 1944: 432–433) found Aztec III B/O at various sites in the nearby Valley of Tuxpan and noted Aztec III stylistic influence in the decorations on Tancol Brown-on-Buff, a Huastec ware. Central Mexican ceramics have likewise been reported from coastal Totonac sites in central Veracruz, some of which have been explored but are not well published. Aztec III B/O and "Aztecoid" ceramics as well as Central Mexican style censers, stamps, and temple models seem to have been found at Cempoala (García Payón 1971: 540, 542; Medellín 1960: 160). Aztec ceramics are mentioned for several other sites, among them Quiahuiztlan (Medellín 1960: 160, 200–201).

The greatest quantity of Central Mexican ceramics reported at a single site in the outer empire was excavated at Huatusco (M. Smith 1990), a town in the Olmeca/Popoloca area farther south, which seems to have been the site of another Aztec enclave (Medellín 1952). Found there were a strong representation of Aztec III B/O (5.22 %), imitations of Aztec III B/O (9.92 %), *tlemaitls* or long-handled ladle braziers (15.51 %), and biconical braziers (Medellín 1952: 44, 53–66, 81; 1960: 138, 143). Late Aztec and Aztecoid wares likewise occur at Cuetlaxtlan (Medellín 1952: 57 and elsewhere; 1960: 138, 143), an unpublished site that had an Aztec governor (Durán 1967, 2: 182). Eroded, probably late Aztec orange ware ceramics are also reported from the Orizaba obsidian mine site (Stocker and Cobean 1984: 85–86). Finally, in the recently surveyed Mixtequilla area to the southeast, Aztec III B/O (probably local imitations) and Texcoco Molded, another Late Postclassic ware, were collected (Stark 1990; see also Medellín 1960: 147; Torres Guzmán 1962). Given the lack of documentary evidence of Aztec presence, Barbara Stark suggests indirect influence through Cuetlaxtlan or another town in the Aztec network.

Another area with reported Aztec ceramics is the Tehuacan Valley on the border between Puebla and Oaxaca, an area on an important trade route and apparently allied with the imperial network (Hassig 1988: 329–330). Aztec III B/O was noted on the surface around the modern city of Tehuacan, at the archaeological site of Tehuacan Viejo, and at Cozcatlan (Nicholson 1955: 119; M. Smith 1990: tables 1–2).

It is well known from both Central Mexican and local sources that Aztec merchants, officials, and warriors were operating well beyond the core of provinces controlled by the empire, especially at Xicalanco, an important trading center bordering the northern Maya lowlands, and that the Aztecs were forging some kind of link with the Yucatec Maya (Scholes and Roys 1968: 29–30, 34–35, 77; Chase 1986: 137–138; Robles and Andrews 1986: 97). Nevertheless, except for distant resemblances between some local ceramics and Aztec wares (e.g., Berlin 1960: 140; Rice and Rice 1985: 172), there is a dearth of Aztec finds in the Maya Lowlands.

Further south, the Aztecs controlled the coastal province of Xoconochco adjacent to the Maya Highlands and some places in the Isthmus of Tehuantepec and Chiapas en route there (e.g., Navarrete 1966: 7–8; Codex Mendoza 1925: 13r–13v, 18r, 47r; Durán 1967, 2: 383–389). But the only Aztec sherds known are small amounts collected in the Xoconochco province (Navarrete 1976: 361). Carlos Navarrete (1966: 68–72, 97) also suggests relationships of local orange and red wares in Chiapa de Corzo to Aztec III B/O and Guinda; again these are tentative. The situation in the adjacent Maya highlands matches that in the northern lowlands. Significant Aztec contacts from 1500 onward are documented (Carmack 1981: 141–145), but no Aztec ceramics have been reported.

Several written sources mention an Aztec invasion of Nicaragua under Motecuhzoma II, and it is possible that the Aztecs penetrated as far south as Panama, given a claim that two years before the Spaniards arrived a large army of flesh-eating men came from the north (Lothrop 1926, 1: 10–11). Still, no Aztec-related remains have been found in lower Central America, with the exception of a B/O vase from San Miguel, El Salvador (Navarrete 1965). In certain parts of Nicaragua and Costa Rica relatively late ceramics, like Vallejo Polychrome from the Guanacaste-Nicoya region, are decorated with figurative motifs that some scholars have argued are of Central Mexican origin. Most of the motifs mentioned, however, appear elsewhere in Mesoamerica on ceramics decorated in the "Mixteca-Puebla" style. Samuel Lothrop (1926, 2: 399) concluded that the Aztec contribution in the area was "not great," but cited the "earth monster" (Fig. 1) as one example of Aztec influence (cf. Lothrop 1926: pls. 83–84 with fig. 90). Although the creature does resemble the Aztec earth monster, a relatively rare form in Mesoamerica, the two rayed objects that flank the body make it resemble as well the creature on an Early Postclassic vessel from Amapa, Nayarit (Meighan 1976: pl. 148a). Thus, it is questionable whether this Central American form is the result of Aztec influence.

In summary then, outside Central Mexico there seem to be moderate amounts of Aztec ceramics in northern Guerrero and central Veracruz; possibly similar amounts in the Tehuacan Valley and northern Veracruz (an unsurveyed area); an unusually high proportion at Huatusco; very small numbers in both the Mixteca Alta and Valley of Oaxaca; and little beyond these areas. Examples of close imitations and local hybrids are recorded in

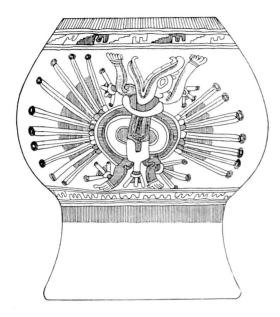

Fig. 1. "Earth Monster" on Vallejo Polychrome pedestal bowl, Late Period VI (A.D. 1200–1550), Guanacaste-Nicoya zone (after Lothrop 1926: pl. 85b).

places that also have imported Aztec wares—northern Guerrero, different places in Veracruz, and Coixtlahuaca. Connections with more distant styles in Chiapas and the northern Maya area are tentative. The problem noted by M. Smith of the pre-imperial distribution of Aztec III B/O is especially pertinent to the central provinces and probably Guerrero. In further distant areas, the chances are greater that Aztec III ceramics were distributed in imperial times—for instance, in central Veracruz. However, Central Mexican wares, notably Guinda, are also found in Middle Postclassic contexts there (Stark 1990), indicating earlier long-distance contacts.

ARCHITECTURE

Several structures outside the Basin of Mexico are commonly accepted as Aztec productions, and we agree that those at the following six sites appear to have been built/rebuilt or commissioned by Aztecs: Tecaxic-Calixtlahuaca and Malinalco in the State of Mexico, Tepoztlan in Morelos, Oztuma in Guerrero, and Huatusco and Castillo de Teayo in Veracruz. Notwithstanding the identification of these structures as in some sense Aztec, we have been unable to identify any widespread architectural traits per se as definitive signs of Aztec influence. The problem is, in part, that there are too few structures for generalization and, in part, that so little Aztec architecture has been excavated even in the Basin of Mexico. For all but one example (Huatusco), the identification is based less on overall form than on small details, associated sculptures, and/or written documentation of a significant Aztec presence.

From examination of the evidence, we have thus concluded that the Aztecs were not responsible for the spread of forms like the two-slope *alfarda,* the double temple, and the round, "wind god" temple, either in Central Mexico or further afield. In fact, the few surviving architectural traits that appear to be unique to the late Aztec period in the Basin are rarely found abroad. The pyramid at Teopanzolco in Cuernavaca and structures at the site of Cempoala in Veracruz are also rejected as having been influenced in any demonstrable way by the imperial Aztecs.

Written evidence indicates that colonies from Basin of Mexico towns were settled at various places in the Toluca Basin soon after conquest of that area in the 1470s, and that the settlements at Tecaxic and Calix-tlahuacan were held by the Aztec ruler Axayacatl (García Payón 1936: 198–199; Hernández 1950: 237, 247). At the archaeological site now called Tecaxic-Calixtlahuaca, between the modern towns of those names, the last of the four building phases is characterized by a change from gray stone to black and red basalt. Seven buildings were rebuilt or expanded during this final period, which José García Payón called the Aztec-Matlatzinca phase (García Payón 1956–57; Marquina 1964: 223–233). However, the only recognizable Aztec traits are the tenoned skulls and quoining with alternating horizontal and vertical stones on one small platform (Marquina 1964: 231, photo 94).

Archaeology at the site on the hill above Malinalco likewise indicates its use as a local center long before Aztec arrival (Galván 1984: 167ff). Conquered by the Aztecs in the 1470s (Galván 1984: 157, 159), it was the locus of a ceremony of allegiance by local lords to Ahuitzotl in the 1480s. However, Aztec building activities there commenced only after 1501. These activities were directed from Tenochtitlan (Townsend 1982: 121, 131). The well-known rock-cut temple and Structure III were obvious results, to judge by the attached sculptures and a mural, respectively, and are representative of the imperial style of Motecuhzoma II's time. Parts, if not all, of the presently visible complex, then, were built for imperial ceremonies on an earlier site, which also had mythical/political associations for the Aztecs as the settling place of an enemy sister of the Aztec war god (Townsend 1982: 119).

The Tepozteco temple on a ridge above Tepoztlan is another site associated with imperial ceremonies, and established on an older shrine, this one being for an important *pulque* god (Paso y Troncoso 1905–06, 6: 238, 244). The temple has been identified in the past as Aztec principally because of a pair of imperial-style reliefs bearing the name of the Aztec ruler Ahuitzotl (Fig. 2) and the date of his death, which were once set into the side of the pyramid platform (Seler 1960–61, 2: 200–214; 3: 487–513, fig. 10). However, to judge by the ceramics in the fill of the base and on the surface, the lower pyramid platform may predate the presence of the Triple Alliance in the area (Michael Smith, personal communication). The inscriptions on

Fig. 2. Plaque with hieroglyphic name of Ahuitzotl, once set into side of Tepozteco pyramid. Museo Nacional de Antropología, Mexico

sculptures indicate Aztec use at the time of Ahuitzotl's death in 1502 and the New Fire Ceremony of 1507 (Umberger n.d.a: 139–141).

At Oztuma in Guerrero, a place with a documented Aztec colony, fortifications, and two high officials, the ruins so far investigated are located on two adjoining ridges (Lister 1941, and others). Atop Cerro Malinche is a unique triangular fortification, and on Cerro Oztuma are a series of terraces, platforms, and rectangular rooms that probably correspond to the sixteenth-century description of a temple, "captain's house," and soldiers' houses (Paso y Troncoso 1905–06, 6: 113; Lister 1941: 212, 215). The Aztec structures were apparently built at the site of an earlier fort (M. Smith n.d.b). However, Aztec and earlier phases have not been distinguished from each other, and there is nothing, in fact, that can be identified as specifically Aztec.

The outermost pyramid at Huatusco (Fig. 3), the site of an Aztec enclave in Veracruz, is the last of four phases and is unusual in still having part of its upper roof (Medellín 1952: 24–28 and drawings; 1960: 143–144, pl. 87). It is the temple especially—its height, proportions, mansard form, and panels with tenoned bosses—that makes the structure recognizable as Aztec (Medellín 1952; cf. Codex Ixtlilxochitl 1976: 112v). The final building identified as Aztec is also in Veracruz—the Castillo de Teayo pyramid (Fig. 4). Covering at least one earlier structure, this temple has several traits found in late Aztec architecture: a distinctive molding on the upper *alfardas* and exterior shrine wall, buttresses flanking the stairs, and projecting stones on the *taludes* (Solís 1986: 76). According to Felipe Solís Olguin, the structure was in the process of

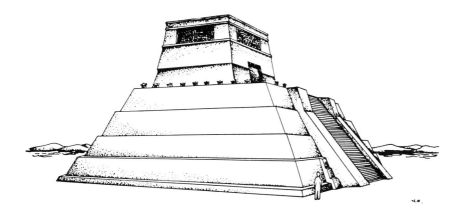

Fig. 3. Reconstruction drawing of pyramid at Huatusco, Veracruz (after Medellín 1960: pl. 87)

Fig. 4. Pyramid at Castillo de Teayo, Veracruz

being rebuilt, and perhaps the temple on top, which is strangely small for the platform, would have eventually more closely resembled an Aztec temple.

Having identified those structures that seem to have been built by Aztecs, we will now examine the evidence of more general Aztec influence on Mesoamerican architecture, which we find negligible. A case in point is the two-slope *alfarda,* or sloping panel framing a stairway, characterized by a vertical upper part (e.g., Figs. 3, 4) that has been suggested as indicating

Aztec influence abroad (Kubler 1973: 36). This general type is common in Late Postclassic Mesoamerica, with some variations consistent with regional architectural styles. It is found in Central Mexico (e.g., at Tenayuca), Veracruz (Cempoala), the Yucatan Peninsula (Tulum and Mayapan), and as far away as Tazumal, El Salvador. One distinctive variant is typical of the highland Maya area (see Fig. 7) and is found also at some sites in Veracruz (e.g., Cempoala). In this variant the vertical section projects slightly like a cornice.

However, the dates and locations of its appearance in various areas of Mesoamerica negate the two-slope *alfarda*'s use as a diagnostic of Aztec influence abroad. At the site of Teopanzolco in Cuernavaca the two-slope *alfarda* appears on the earlier of the two phases of the double temple, a phase that was built before the arrival of the Triple Alliance (Michael Smith n.d.a). It also appears at Early Postclassic Tula (Stocker 1986: fig. 1) and at Chichen Itza, where sculptures project horizontally from the vertical upper part. The earliest known example of the distinctive highland Maya version

Fig. 5. Binder-molding (here with double outline) on two-slope *alfarda,* Phase V stairway, Templo Mayor, Tenochtitlan

appears in Guatemala at Zacaleu during the Late Classic (Woodbury and Trik 1953, 1: 24, 28–29; 2: fig. 174c).

Although the presence of two-slope *alfardas* at Late Mesoamerican sites cannot be seen as the result of Aztec influence, it is possible that particular treatments can. There is, in fact, a late Aztec version with a distinctive binder-molding, which appears on late phases in the Basin of Mexico (Fig. 5). Interestingly, with one exception (that we know of), the binder-molding is not found outside the Basin, not even on imperial structures at Malinalco and Tepoztlan. The one example is the Castillo de Teayo pyramid (Solís 1986: 74–77).

It can also be demonstrated that the occurrence of double pyramids at late Mesoamerican sites outside the Basin was not a matter of Aztec influence, either in Central Mexico or in distant places. The most important Aztec example of a double pyramid was the Templo Mayor of Tenochtitlan, a four- or five-tiered, west-facing pyramid of rectangular plan with two broad stairways leading to two shrines (see Marquina 1960). Within the Basin double temples are or were known to be located at Tenayuca (Fig. 6), Tlatelolco, Santa Cecilia Acatitlan, Texcoco, and Tlacopan (the latter two known only in illustrations [Codex Ixtlilxochitl 1976: 112v; Codex Telleriano-Remensis 1899: 40r]). The earliest of these temples was built at Tenayuca (Tenayucan), a prominent settlement during the Middle Postclassic period, apparently in about 1150 or before (see ceramic data in Acosta [1965]). The first phase of the

Fig. 6. Reconstruction drawing of double-temple pyramid, Tenayuca, Mexico (after Departmento de Monumentos Artísticos 1935: pl. 23)

Fig. 7. Close-up of reconstruction drawing by Tatiana Proskouriakoff of Group A, Cahyup, Department of Baja Verapaz, Guatemala (after A. Smith 1955: fig. 26)

Tenochtitlan temple was probably built 200 years later in the early fourteenth century, as indicated by written histories and confirmed by archaeological remains (Matos 1981: 50).

Outside the Basin, the double pyramid at the Teopanzolco site in Cuernavaca is usually identified as an Aztec structure, the implication being that influence came from Tenochtitlan after conquest of the area in the 1430s. However, on the basis of associated ceramics, Michael Smith (n.d.a) asserts that both building phases of the pyramid predate the Triple Alliance conquest of Cuauhnahuac and suggests that its builders were emulating Tenayuca rather than Tenochtitlan.

Double temples are also found at much greater distances from Tenochtitlan, in both the highland and lowland Maya areas. The better-known highland examples of double and twin pyramids occur at sites like Cahyup (Fig. 7) and Mixco Viejo, respectively (A. Smith 1955; Fox 1987: 202–203, 211, 219, 228–243 passim). That Tatiana Proskouriakoff thought a direct connection with Aztec architecture likely is apparent in drawings, like the one reproduced here (Fig. 7), in which she topped double temples with Aztec-style roofs derived from Central Mexican manuscript illustrations. However, although written evidence indicates that the Aztecs had significant contacts with the highland Maya after 1500, recent archaeological work points to another scenario. At Cawinal the change from a single to double-temple pyramid has been radiocarbon dated to around 1350, 150 years prior to Aztec arrival in the area (Alain Ichon, cited in Fox 1987: 228ff., fig. 7.14). Such a radiocarbon date is inconclusive evidence, given the short time span, but it is not the only argument against Aztec influence. John Fox, following Florence Sloane (n.d.), interprets the appearance of double temples as a local innovation in response to the political expansion of the Quiche state, and as only one aspect of a complex of changes that are best explained on the regional level. In addition, from our perspective, the location of twin and double temples only in the zone between the Quiche and Cakchiquel states and not at the capitals (Fox 1987: 230) makes it most unlikely that their building was the result of alliance with or emulation of the Aztecs.

Interestingly, there are less well known double temples in the Maya lowlands, at Mayapan and Dzibilichaltun in the north and at El Chile on the Usumacinta River (Shook 1952: 248–249; E. Andrews 1965: fig. 5; Maler 1903: 96–97, fig. 35). The first may date from the Late Postclassic period, but the other two are probably earlier, given the dates of florescence of these sites. In any event, none of these Maya temples resembles Central Mexican examples. Some highland examples, like the one at Cawinal, have multiple stairways around all four sides of their platforms, in contrast to the Central Mexican stairways, which are on the front only. Others, like the twin temples at Mixco Viejo, are set on separate platforms (A. Smith 1955: fig. 40). Thus, although double temples appeared in Central Mexico centuries earlier than in highland Guatemala, the evidence does not point to Aztec influence as a viable explanation.

Also sometimes suggested as resulting from Aztec influence are round temples of late date appearing at sites thought to have been under Aztec domination.[6] Late Aztec round temples take different forms, some with rectangular sections added, and most are on earlier structures of unknown age. Written sources tell of important round structures in Tenochtitlan, notably one near the Templo Mayor dedicated to the wind god (Marquina 1960: 67–72). The only round temple of any size discovered in that area, Structure B (now under the Cathedral), consists of joined round and rectangular parts, with the stairway on the east-facing rectangular side. It seems to have only one tier, which stands on a large rectangular platform (Cabrera 1979: 60, plan 4, drawing following p. 50). A similar east-facing structure found to the southwest of the Templo Mayor of Tlatelolco had an Ehecatl (wind god) sculpture buried with other remains in front (Román 1991). The

---

[6] Marquina's (1960: photo 21) assumption of a direct historical connection between round temples in Central Mexico and Veracruz is evident in his use of the temple at Cempoala as the model for the wind god's temple in his reconstruction of the ceremonial precinct of Tenochtitlan (before recent archaeology in the area).

round pyramid at Huexotla east of the lake, the penultimate pyramid at the spot (L. Batres removed the outer structure), has a round plan with staircase on the east side and, perhaps, three tiers without cornices (Batres 1904: 14–15, illus.). Another round temple at Ixtapaluca Viejo in the southern lake area (Contreras 1976: 24–25), the last of three phases, has two tiers and combines round and rectangular parts with the stairway rising in three stages on the rectangular side. At Malinalco, the famous Aztec rock-cut temple, although set into the hill and lacking the back of the platform, is related in having a round chamber and a rectangular forechamber and stair-case in front (Marquina 1964: 206–212). It recalls the description of the Tenochtitlan Ehecatl temple in its monster maw entrance, but apparently it was not dedicated to the wind god, to judge by its sculptures.

Outside the Basin, the last of four phases of Structure 3 at Tecaxic-Calixtlahuaca (Fig. 8) is a round pyramid in general form like the Huejotla inner pyramid, but with cornices. Dated to the time of Aztec occupancy of the site, it is usually given as the prime example of an Aztec wind god temple, an idea supported by the imperial-style Ehecatl sculpture that was discovered under the platform. However, the earliest of the four phases is also a round temple, dated by ceramics in the fill to Teotihuacan times (García Payón 1956–57), and its basic form is repeated in the later versions with changes in slope and cornice treatment. Whether the slope and cornices of the final phase are particularly Aztec in style is not known. Nor was the first temple at this site the only round pyramid in Central Mexico before the Late Postclassic period. The El Corral temple at Tula, which dates to Early Postclassic times, affirms that the building type with rectangular extensions (here on front and back) was developed by the Toltecs (Acosta 1974: 48–49, figs. 1–4, plan 1).

Two other important round pyramids appear in Veracruz, one at Cempoala and the other at Calera or Oceloapan (Marquina 1964: 469–475; Pollock 1936: 70–74, figs. 23–24; Medellín 1960: pl. 102). Both phases of the Cempoala pyramid combine round and rectangular parts. The Oceloa-pan pyramid, which has not been excavated, is of the same type but with an additional small rectangular section on the rear. In attempting to counter the idea of Aztec influence on these two structures, H.E.D. Pollock (1936: 82–83, 169) pointed out that they have not been dated by ceramic evidence, that they resemble a buried structure at Cholula, and that there were earlier Central Mexican infusions in the area. That the Aztecs were responsible for these forms, then, is doubtful.

In summary, although more archaeological work is badly needed in all areas, it is obvious that the imperial leadership did not initiate extensive building projects in the empire. Four of the sites identified had a documented Aztec population and two were sites of sacred/mythical importance deco-rated with imperially commissioned works. Given the reports of conquest

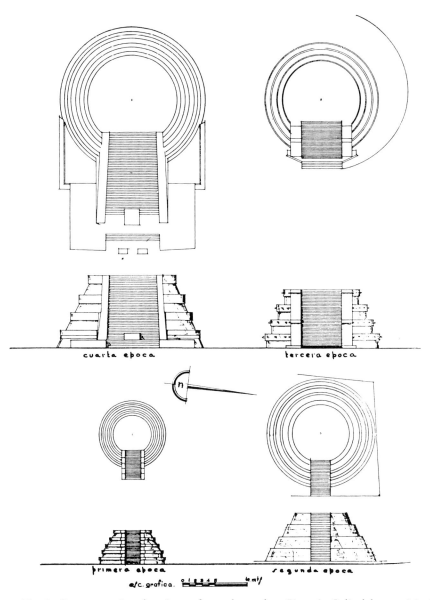

Fig. 8. Reconstruction drawings of round temple at Tecaxic-Calixtlahuaca, Mexico
(after Marquina 1964: pl. 65)

and colonization of parts of Guerrero and Oaxaca, it is surprising that little architecture has so far been discovered in either place that bears recognizable signs of Aztec influence. The fort at Oztuma is unique in the archaeological record and the residences and civic-ceremonial architecture have not been examined from this point of view.

There are recognizable Aztec architectural traits at two places in Vera cruz, Castillo and Huatusco, and one would expect more in this relatively unexplored area, given the presence of Aztec-related ceramics and sculptures and the mentions of migrations in written sources. However, we should investigate places known to have been controlled by the Aztecs, like Xico Viejo (Fewkes 1907: 246–248), before seeing artistic similarities in places with looser affiliations, such as Cempoala, which was conquered just before the Spanish Conquest and was probably a strategic province (Frances Berdan, personal communication). Because of its historical importance in chronicles of the Conquest and because it is one of the few late sites to have been reconstructed, forms at Cempoala are often compared to Aztec architecture, sometimes with the implication that they were the result of Aztec imposition. However, as seen in the discussions of the local *alfarda* treatment and the round temple, this cannot be demonstrated with present evidence.

The Aztec mark on Mesoamerican architecture may eventually be found in subtler changes that vary according to local circumstances and the nature of Central Mexican presence. But most likely these traits will be limited to places where Central Mexicans were residing or places of mythico-religious importance. In the meantime, Aztec imperial expansion cannot be made responsible for the spread of such major forms as the two-slope *alfarda* and the double-temple pyramid.

PAINTING

The influence of the Aztec painting style in other areas of Mesoamerica is likewise difficult to analyze because of the small number of extant examples in the Basin. Although written sources make it clear that the Aztecs produced a large number of murals and painted manuscripts, only a few murals and paintings on objects have survived,[7] and there are no pre-Hispanic

---

[7] The corpus of Aztec paintings from the Basin of Mexico includes: the paintings of skulls and crossed bones on the sides of altars at Tlatelolco and Tenayuca (Villagra 1971: figs. 33, 29); a recently discovered mural of Cipactonal and Oxomoco on a Tlatelolco temple (Guil'liem Arroyo 1991); a stylized Tlaloc image on an archaizing Teotihuacan-type temple platform in Tenochtitlan (Matos 1964); paintings on two other Teotihuacan-style platforms flanking the Templo Mayor (López Portillo et al. 1981: pls. on 262–263, 276–277); fragments of figural murals inside the Phase II Tlaloc temple of the Templo Mayor (López Portillo et al. 1981: pl. on 159; Matos 1985: 91); a badly abraded cave painting from San Cristobal Ecatepec (Villagra 1971: fig. 32); and two painted boxes found in Tizapan (Villagra 1971: fig. 31). Murals are also rumored to have decorated the interior wall of the Temple of the Eagles at Tenochtitlan, but

Aztec manuscripts. The earliest attempts to define an Aztec painting style were based on apparent Pre-Conquest traits in colonial painted manuscripts, as determined by comparison with Aztec relief carvings and Pre-Conquest Mixtec and Borgia Group manuscripts (e.g., Robertson 1959). The conclusions drawn, however, were so general as to be applicable to all Mesoamerican painting executed in the "Mixteca-Puebla" style.

H. B. Nicholson (1966: 261; 1971: 119, 123) clarified the situation somewhat by defining Aztec pictorialism as "marked throughout by greater realism, plus certain iconographic differences." More recently, Elizabeth Boone (1982) has identified a number of specific characteristics of the late Aztecs' more naturalistic interpretation of wide-spread motifs. Traits include more extensive use of curved lines, occasional distinction between left and right feet, and figural proportions in which heads are generally smaller and bodies taller (at least in comparison to Mixtec figures). Aztec relief carvings provide other modes of rendering and iconographic motifs that can be cited as particular to Aztec two-dimensional art. On the basis of these criteria, at present only one mural painting outside the Basin of Mexico can be called Aztec or Aztec-influenced with any certainty: the now-lost warrior procession mural inside Structure III at Malinalco (Fig. 9). The figural proportions are comparable to Aztec figures, as are the differentiation of left and right feet (Boone 1982: 155, 158), costume parts, body decorations, and more natural contours.

The other Late Postclassic murals west of the Isthmus of Tehuantepec are at Tizatlan in Tlaxcala, Mitla in Oaxaca, and Cempoala in Veracruz. Among examples in the Maya area east of the Isthmus are those at Tulum and Santa Rita in the northern lowlands and Iximche and Utatlan in the southern highlands. Most of these exhibit "Mixteca-Puebla" or "Mexican" traits in different degrees, leading Donald Robertson (1970) to refer to an International Style. The murals on the altars at Tizatlan are stylistically close to the Codex Borgia (Marquina 1964: 236–238), attributed variously to Puebla, Tlaxcala, Veracruz, the Tehuacan Valley, and even the Mixteca area. The murals at the Zapotec site of Mitla are in Mixtec style (Kubler 1984: 176–177), and the figures are stylized like those in Mixtec and Borgia Group codices. The Temple of the Faces at Cempoala is decorated with painted symbols of celestial bodies, which are also usually compared with Borgia Group and Mixtec codices (Marquina 1964: 469, pl. 137). The murals in the northern Maya lowlands exhibit Mixtec/Mexican sky bands, solar rays, and other motifs. Arthur Miller (1982: 74–75) hypothesized that those at Tulum, the latest at the site, were the work of an intrusive group,

---

they are not readily visible and have not been published. Only the paintings at the Templo Mayor can be dated (those on Phase II being pre-imperial, and the others being from the imperial period). Remains of painted details on sculptures also give more information on the painter's art.

Fig. 9. Mural with procession of costumed warriors, Structure III, Malinalco, Mexico (after Villagra 1971: fig. 30)

either Aztec merchants or Putun-Nahua laying the way for an Aztec invasion of the Yucatan from Xicalanco. However, nothing there is specifically Aztec. The now lost murals on Mound 1 at Santa Rita actually have more Mixtec/Mexican characteristics than those at Tulum, but again nothing unique to Aztec art (see Quirarte 1982: 54). George Kubler (1984: 319), in fact, suggests that a dating in the Late Classic or Early Postclassic is not precluded by present evidence.

In the southern highlands, the Temple 2 murals at Iximche (Fig. 10) represent a single person repeated in different attitudes (Guillemin 1965: 17, 28–29). Other fragments, one a similar warrior figure, were found in the main palace at Utatlan, where written sources say paintings commemorating past rulers were located. This warrior is probably performing a ritual dance of a type recorded in Quiche sources, and his accouterments can also be identified as local (Carmack 1981: 295–299, figs. 9.12–9.13). Unlike the Tulum and Santa Rita murals, no lowland Maya traits are apparent. Elizabeth Boone (personal communication) sees closer parallels in the Iximche murals with Borgia Group than Mixtec codices. Alternating skulls and crossed bones in basic format similar to those painted on Structure 24 at Iximche (Guillemin 1965: illus. p. 16) are common on altars in the Basin of Mexico, where they have an early Postclassic precedent at Tula (Acosta 1974: fig. 7). A Maya precedent in a Late Classic relief on an altar at Uxmal

Fig. 10. Painting of figure on interior of Temple 2, Iximché, Guatemala (after Navarrete 1976: fig. 18)

in the northern lowlands (G. Andrews 1975: fig. 226), in fact, is not as close to the Iximche mural as the Central Mexican examples. However, this Mexican type is also found on "Mixteca-Puebla" ceramics in highland Guatemala (Navarrete 1976: fig. 29). In summary, it is possible that the painting and some of the pieces of minor art in highland Guatemala (e.g., Navarrete 1976: fig. 36c) resulted from Aztec contact, but the evidence is inconclusive and other possibilities must be entertained.

The only painting outside Central Mexico that might qualify as near-Aztec in style is the pictograph of a striding warrior on Cerro Naranjo in Chiapas (Navarrete 1976: fig. 20). Interestingly, although this site is fairly far outside the territory controlled by the Quiche, the serrated neckpiece on the figure recalls the solar rays on the warriors at Utatlan and Iximche—perhaps indicating a connection with that area rather than Central Mexico.

Certainly the mechanisms for spreading the Aztec pictorial style existed, particularly in the form of painted manuscripts in which imperial records were kept and in the person of artists who accompanied officials abroad. When Cortés was in Veracruz, the Aztec governor of a nearby province (possibly Cuetlaxtlan or Tochtepec) brought with him "great painters, of which there were many in Mexico [Tenochtitlan]," whose depictions of Cortés, his companions, horses, and equipment were sent to Motecuhzoma (Díaz 1984, 1: 161 ff). Although it is difficult to generalize from the few existing examples, Boone (n.d.) has found strong Aztec influences in colonial painted manuscripts from Tula and Huichapan in Hidalgo, Azoyu in Guerrero, and Tuxpan in northern Veracruz, probably indicating the diffusion of the Aztec style to places dominated by the empire through traveling scribes and imperial documents. In contrast, she has distinguished a variant

Central Mexican style in nearby Tlaxcala, an area that remained independent of the empire. She also notes that Mixtec manuscripts, despite Aztec conquests in that area, form a stylistically distinct group, seemingly uninfluenced by Central Mexico.

At present, then, the only Pre-Conquest painting outside the Basin of Mexico that has specifically Aztec characteristics is the Malinalco mural. Colonial manuscript examples are found in a few other places of the eastern and western empire, perhaps the result of the presence of Aztec painters in imperial times, but there is no Pre-Conquest archaeological evidence of this influence.

SCULPTURE

The Aztecs' most distinctive art form remaining to us is stone sculpture. Important state monuments are large, relief-covered forms, most of which served as sacrificial stones, platforms, seats, and altars. In addition to the major deity images, which are only known in written accounts, many human and animal figures once performed subsidiary roles in architectural settings, for example, serpents and standard bearers decorating the Templo Mayor. Another important class consists of carvings on rock faces and boulders. Tenochca artists emulated Toltec and other ancient styles and included "Mixteca-Puebla" motifs in reliefs. Stylistically, late Aztec sculpture is notable for careful modeling of forms and detailing. Easily recognized is a prevalent figure type with ears in the full round and a low hairline with "sideburns."

That this style did not begin to resemble its final form until after 1450 has become increasingly apparent in recent years. Associated with the pre-1450 phases of the Templo Mayor are roughly carved figural sculptures, like the *chacmool* on Phase II, with details painted on a stuccoed surface (Fig. 11). More finely carved and naturalistic figures (Fig. 12) appear in offering chambers in Phases IV and IVb, dated 1454 and 1469, respectively (Matos 1981). The sacrificial stone found in Mexico City in 1988 was probably carved in the 1460s (Pérez-Castro et al. 1989), but it is obvious from comparison with the later Tizoc Stone, which it closely resembles in form, that the imperial style was still in formation. The first datable Tenochca monument in the mature imperial style is the Coyolxauhqui Stone, set at the foot of the Phase IVb temple stairway, which dates from 1469 (Matos 1981); the stone itself may date from then or a few years later. Thus, the development of a complex, professionally executed official carving style followed the Aztecs' political rise by decades.

Despite the innovations and importance of this new style, its spread outside the Basin of Mexico is not as great as sometimes implied; the corpus of sculptures called Aztec (in the narrower sense used in this paper) has to be reduced. In Central Mexico problematic pieces are the many roughly

Fig. 11. *Chacmool* in situ on Phase II, Templo Mayor, Tenochtitlan

Fig. 12. *Pulque* deity sculpture from Offering 6 on Phase IVb, Templo Mayor of Tenochtitlan

carved, anthropomorphic images made either before or independent of influence from the distinctive late style. In the Basin of Mexico, there are several recognizable pre-1450 types of figural sculptures. In addition to *chacmools* there are roughly carved, life-size standard bearers, like the eight buried on Templo Mayor Phase III before 1454 (Matos 1981). Other examples have been found at Tenayuca, Azcapotzalco, and Coatlinchan (Solís 1976: nos. 8–10; Field Museum, cat. no. 96530). A group of smaller figures found in the interior of the pyramid at Tenayuca and elsewhere in the Basin must be earlier in date, because of this location (Departamento de Monumentos Artísticos 1935: 276–277, figs. 19–21, 29, 31). It is unknown whether roughly carved figural sculptures further afield in Morelos (Solís 1976: nos. 13–14), Tlaxcala, and Puebla (Fig. 13) were made in pre-imperial or imperial times, but, whatever their dates, they should not be considered as influenced by Aztec art unless they have traits specific to the late, imperial style.

Sculptures that reveal such Aztec traits outside the Basin fall into three categories: rock and boulder carvings, architectural sculptures, and freestanding sculptures (the majority figural). Most are found in the Central Mexican states of Mexico, Morelos, and Puebla (to the west and south of the Basin) and in northern Veracruz, with only infrequent examples in other parts. In Central Mexico, freestanding and architectural sculptures are found at the sites with architecture discussed above—Tecaxic-Calixtlahuaca, Malinalco, and Tepoztlan—as well as the sacred site of Tula (Tollan). With the exception of three examples near the Gulf Coast,[8] most rock and boulder reliefs are in Central Mexico too (at Tula, Acacingo, Coatlan, Huaxtepec, Cuernavaca, and Huacachula).[9] And like the complexes at Malinalco and Tepoztlan, these display imperial imagery or are related to Tenochca concerns by written passages. For example, the relief near Tula representing Quetzalcoatl and Chalchiuhtlicue was carved at the time of ceremonies held in Tenochtitlan in 1500 to stop a devastating flood (Umberger n.d.a: 157–164).

At Tula, in addition to the rock reliefs, imperial-style sculptures said to be from the site include a colossal toad and a serpent with human face emerging from its jaws (Mayer 1844: fig. on 275; Peñafiel 1890: pls. 163–167). At Tecaxic-Calixtlahuaca imperial-style sculptures include a life-size wind god (Fig. 14) buried in the platform of the round temple and a kneeling death goddess (INAH 1960: 28, 30). Other human, deity, and animal sculptures

---

[8] At Tusapan, Castillo, and Texolo (Nebel 1963: pl. 35; Solís 1981: pl. 42b; Fewkes 1907: 247–248, pl. 108).

[9] Krickeberg 1969: 30–47, 52–75, 95–109, 124–130, 147–157, figs. 17–18, 34, 79–80, 102–104, pls. 15–20, 24–26, 30, 32, 34–37, 39–40, 42–43, 58–60, 62, 69–74. The carvings on the Cerro de la Campana, Acatlan, Puebla, may also be Aztec or Aztec-influenced (Krickeberg 1969: 109–123, figs. 64, 77).

Fig. 13. Large Tlaloc figure, collected in Hecilango,
Atlixco, Puebla (photo:
courtesy of the Museum für
Völkerkunde, Vienna)

Fig. 14. Ehecatl, excavated from platform of round temple at Tecaxic-Calixtlahuaca, Mexico (after Marquina 1964: photo 91). (Museo Nacional de Antropología,
Mexico)

found in the Matlatzinca-Toluca area—at Tecaxic-Calixtlahuaca, Tlacotepec, Teotenango, and Tenancingo—are less refined but are Aztec types
and show characteristics of the late style (e.g., Field Museum, cat. nos.
94902–94903; Alvarez 1983: pl. 7a–b; Nicholson 1977: 154, 164, fig. 9).
Fine, carved wooden drums with imperial Aztec imagery came from
Teotenango and Malinalco (Saville 1925: pls. 36a, 42–45). In this area, in
addition to the mostly architectural sculptures at the imperial shrine at
Malinalco, is the rock carving at Acacingo, probably commemorative of the
1507 New Fire Ceremony in Tenochtitlan (Umberger 1987: 94–95).

Aztec sculptures from the Tepozteco *pulque* god temple in Morelos include
the imperial name and date plaques that were once set into the platform (see
Fig. 2), reliefs on the benches and piers, a ballcourt ring commemorating the
foundation of Tenochtitlan, and a 2 Reed date (Seler 1960–61, 3: 487–513,
figs. 13–21; 2: 213, fig. 21; Umberger n.d.a: 139–141, figs. 106, 108). The
rock reliefs at Huaxtepec may represent previous Aztec rulers; and the boulder carving called the Chimalli Stone in Cuernavaca may commemorate the
death of Motecuhzoma I (Umberger n.d.a: 167–168). A few Aztec-style

sculptures, mostly small deity figures, have been found at Cuernavaca, Xochicalco, Coatetelco, and elsewhere in Morelos (e.g., Peñafiel 1910: 25–26, pl. 113; Solís 1982: figs. 23, 38; Noriega 1953: 268–269; INAH 1978: figs. 6–7, 10, 16–17).

In southern Puebla, Aztec-style sculptures have been reported principally at Huacachula and Tepeaca (Tepeacac). The latter was the provincial capital and had an Aztec "garrison," a major market, and a governor (Díaz 1984, 2: 486; Durán 1967, 2: 162). Guillermo Dupaix (1969, voyage 1: figs. 1–4) illustrates Aztec-looking sculptures from Tepeaca but their present whereabouts are unknown. The Huacachula reliefs, including boulder sculptures, have motifs of imperial iconography, one bearing a solar disk; another a composite eagle-serpent-jaguar and a shield; and another featuring the date 1 Flint, usually associated with the Aztec god Huitzilopochtli.[10] Some figural and animal sculptures in the regional museum in Puebla also display late Aztec traits,[11] as do sculptures in Mexican, American, and European museums said to have been collected in that state.[12] To the north of the Tepeacac province was the territory controlled by three enemy polities, Tlaxcalla, Huexotzinco, and Chololaan, which remained independent of the Triple Alliance for most of their Pre-Conquest history (Tlaxcalla until the Spanish Conquest). A few Aztec pieces were reportedly collected from these places (e.g., a fine human mask in Basel from Tizatlan, Tlaxcala [Bankmann 1983]), but generally there is a gap. Among the late-period, local style sculptures found in Tlaxcala (in the State Museum), some show derivation from Toltec forms but no influence from Aztec art.

The sculptures just mentioned from the central provinces include imperial monuments and scattered local productions, but no regional styles can be defined. In contrast, a recognizable regional style did flourish in the Castillo area of northern Veracruz, where fifty-one Aztec-style sculptures were found (Solís 1981). About twenty others in this and unrelated Aztec styles have been attributed to the general area.[13] In the Castillo style corpus, differences in artists, degree of provinciality in relation to the imperial Aztec style, and local attributes are evident. The subjects are mostly anthropomorphic figures and include the gods Tlaloc, Xipe, Chalchiuhtlicue, *amacalli*

---

[10] For sculpture from Huacachula, see Dupaix (1969, voyage 1: figs. 21–24), Krickeberg (1969: 57–68, pls. 30, 34–37), Noriega (1953: 258–259), and Horcasitas (1979: 163, illus., mislabeled Huaxtepec).

[11] E.g., a standing Chalchiuhtlicue and a dog (for the last, see Nicholson with Keber 1983: 120–121).

[12] An important greenstone fire serpent, now at Dumbarton Oaks, is labeled Puebla in an early illustration (Departamento de Monumentos Artísticos 1935: figs. 15–16 following p. 263). Other figural sculptures include an *amacalli* goddess and a Chalchiuhtlicue in the Museo Nacional (Solís 1985: fig. 13; 1982: 100, fig. 35) and a Xochipilli and Chalchiuhtlicue in Mannheim, the latter two from San Agustín del Palmar (Krickeberg 1960).

[13] E.g., Fuente and Gutiérrez 1980: pls. 178, 297.

Fig. 15. *Pulque* god Ometochtli from Poza Larga, Papantla, Veracruz. Museo Nacional de Antropología e Historia, Mexico

Fig. 16. Columnar stela, Castillo de Teayo, at site (after Seler 1960–61, 2: 417, fig. 8)

(fertility) deities, Quetzalcoatl, Mixcoatl, and the Pulque God. Aztec motifs and carving characteristics tend to indicate a date of inception after 1450; that is, during the period of Aztec imperial incursion. Among several sculptures that were apparently carved by sculptors well versed in the Aztec style are a seated standard bearer, a *pulque* god (Fig. 15), and a relief of a female deity from the nearby hill of La Chinola (Solís 1981: pls. 43, 47, 56). Another monument has imperial motifs (Fig. 16). Although provincial in carving style, this columnar stela bears the dates 13 Reed and 1 Flint, the dates of the birth of the sun and the beginning of the empire (Umberger n.d.a: 134–135). Local characteristics are also evident, some pointing to Huastec affiliations. The geometric treatment of human forms and costume parts, for instance, indicates the participation of Huastec carvers (Umberger n.d.b; cf. Solís 1981: pl. 11, right, with Fuente and Gutiérrez 1980: pl. 108b). Thus, the Castillo sculptures form a hybrid corpus reflecting a complex historical situation, the general outlines of which can be only vaguely understood at this point.[14]

Aztec-looking sculptures have been found further south on the Gulf Coast, but these scattered examples do not constitute a regional style or styles. Two interesting pieces, one found at Xico Viejo and the other said to be from there, show affinities with the Castillo corpus (Fewkes 1907: 246–247, 250–251, figs. 45–46, pl. 106; Fuente and Gutiérrez 1980: 176–178, pl. 175). Alfonso Medellín Zenil (1952: 83, illus. p. 85) mentions remains of several sculptures at Huatusco (most very damaged) but illustrates only one Aztec-style *amacalli* goddess (see also Dupaix 1969: voyage 1, figs. 12–15). A *chacmool* with Aztec dates and a large cylindrical stone with sun disk are from Cotaxtla, and three Aztec figural sculptures are from the Tlacotalpan region (Cuellar 1981: fig. C.T.2.0; Galindo y Villa 1912: 146–147, pl. 46; Stirling 1965: 722, figs. 10–11). A handful of others from the general area are published (Fewkes 1907: 266–268, figs. 62–64), and several possibly Aztec sculptures are in the state museum in Xalapa. Among pieces in non-local collections is the famous head of a dead man in the Museo Nacional, which is attributed to Veracruz (Bernal 1969: no. 41).

Another important group of Aztec-style sculptures, although few in number, was found in the Tehuacan Valley, at the cities of Tehuacan, Cozcatlan, and Teotitlan. These include two well-known figures from Cozcatlan (Fig. 17), the head of a death god from Teotitlan (Seler 1960–61, 2: 321, fig. 47b), and a gladiatorial stone from Tehuacan (Nicholson 1955), which were evidently carved by artists very familiar with the imperial style. That there may have been other examples indicated by the mention of two famous deity figures at Teotitlan (Paso y Troncoso 1905–06, 4: 216).[15] Although the Cozcatlan figure sculptures represent deity types similar to those of the Mexica, the dates on their heads, presumably their calendric names, are not inscriptions found in Central Mexico and do not pertain to the Aztec deities that the figures resemble (Coatlicue and the fire god Xiuhtecuhtli). Given that there were no resident Aztecs in the area and that the indigenous people were Nahuatl-speakers culturally related to the Aztecs, it is likely that the images

[14] The artistic relationship between the eastern empire and Tenochtitlan is difficult to reconstruct because of the pre-existing monumental sculptural traditions on the Gulf Coast. Scholars have suggested possible precedents for Aztec sculpture types in Olmec and Huastec figural sculptures, Classic Veracruz ceramic figures and stone skeuomorphs of ballgame equipment, and animal sculptures at Los Idolos (e.g., Kubler 1984: 97–98; Klein n.d.; Scott 1982). Cecelia Klein (n.d.) suggests both inspiration from Veracruz and also the possibility that Huastec sculptors participated in the formation of the more naturalistic figure style that appeared in Tenochtitlan in the 1450s, at the time that the Aztecs were making incursions into their territory.

[15] Another death deity sculpture found at Loma Bonita near Tuxtepec, Aztec Tochtepec (Müller 1980), and similar to the Cozcatlan female may indicate a wider range for the artist/artists who produced them.

Fig. 17. Drawing of two figures, probably representing local deities Cihuacoatl and her son Xelhua, found at Cozcatlan, Puebla (after Seler 1960–61, 2: 789, figs. 4a–4b, 5a) (Museo Nacional de Antropología e Historia, Mexico)

represent the comparable local deities mentioned in written sources— Cihuacoatl and her son Xelhua (Paso y Troncoso 1905–06, 5: 47; Umberger n.d.b).

In conclusion, state-commissioned monuments are generally lacking in the outer empire; only one sculpture at Castillo has an official inscription relating to Tenochtitlan, and it is provincial in style. Other sculptures bearing definable Aztec-style features likewise seldom appear outside Central Mexico. Exceptions are in areas of the eastern empire, where a provincial style is found at Castillo in northern Veracruz, and individual pieces are scattered further south and in the Tehuacan Valley. The high number of sculptures in northern Veracruz appears to be the result of immigrants from Central Mexico, while the sculptures from the Tehuacan Valley are the only examples that presently seem to indicate emulation of Aztec art among non-Aztecs. A few other Aztec sculptures have been attributed to Guerrero and Oaxaca[16] and to fur-

[16] Of the four Aztec-style sculptures found in Guerrero, the only one of monumental size is a

ther distant places outside the empire.[17] Other, distant "Mexican" styles, for instance in highland Guatemala, are not considered by us to have a direct historical relationship to Aztec productions (e.g., Navarrete 1976: figs. 21–23, 25–26).

CONCLUSION

Considering the ultimate expanse of the Triple Alliance empire, diplomatic contacts, and economic networks, Aztec-inspired forms are surprisingly scarce in most areas outside Central Mexico. As Ronald Spores (1984: 63; 229, note 40) notes in the case of the Mixteca, in many parts there is "virtually nothing in the archaeological record to suggest political domination . . . by an external power." This situation parallels what is known of the structure and ambitions of the Aztec state. The Aztecs altered political hierarchies and economic networks in the Basin (Hodge n.d.) and consolidated control of elites in nearby provinces through a combination of coercion and cooptation, emphasizing the dire consequences of rebellion and the benefits of alliance (e.g., M. Smith 1986). These nearby groups were also more easily suppressed by Mexica forces if the need arose. Outside the core area although the Aztecs practiced some of the same tactics (e.g., political marriages as far away as highland Guatemala), they were dealing with a vast area and groups that, in many cases were culturally different. As Ross Hassig (1984) has emphasized, in the outer empire they exerted relatively little direct territorial control. There were high officials at key locations and colonies of Central Mexicans in several places, but local rulers and officials of conquered polities were usually retained, and frontier garrisons were often manned and border wars waged by local soldiers.

There is one category of objects disseminated by the Aztecs—that of prestige and ritual paraphernalia and precious gifts. Clothing, jewelry, and other personal adornments were distributed to foreigners by the ruler at state ceremonies in Tenochtitlan (e.g., Durán 1967, 2: 279). Although these probably included redistributed tribute, at least some were Tenochtitlan productions (Sahagún 1950–82, bk. 9: 91). Masks, weapons, ritual paraphernalia, and other items were also sent abroad on the occasion of the initiation of aggression or negotiations with foreigners (e.g., Durán 1967, 2: 78–79; Klein 1986: 145–146). However, there is almost nothing in the archaeological record that reflects these practices. Presumably, some examples of late style goldwork found in the empire (e.g., Nicholson with Keber 1983: nos. 73–75) could be

---

stela from Huitzuco (Seler 1960–1961, 2: 753–760, figs. 37–44). The evidence is even more meager in Oaxaca: one Xipe sculpture was found in Oaxaca City (Paddock 1975) and others are attributed to Oaxaca in museum records (e.g., a fine squash said to be from Mitla [Nicholson with Keber 1983: no. 41]).

[17] E.g., an obsidian mask supposedly from Chiapas (Mayer 1844: 274, illus. on 273).

(and have been) considered Aztec gifts to foreign rulers, but, as in the case of other media, there is a problem with distinguishing Aztec from Mixtec metal-work (Bray 1989). There are very few examples from Tenochtitlan.

The Aztecs actually seem to have been more involved in absorbing luxury goods, artworks, and even "styles" than in distributing them. In addition to great amounts of tribute in textiles, precious stones, metalwork, and other items, patron deities of conquered polities were "captured" and taken back to Tenochtitlan to be imprisoned in the main precinct (Sahagún 1950–82, bk. 2: 182). The Templo Mayor excavations reveal a similar pattern of acquisitiveness in the numerous examples of imported or looted *sacra,* especially greenstone objects from Guerrero and the Mixteca Alta, which were placed in offerings. This centripetal tendency was also manifested in the Aztecs' collection of antiques and emulation of and "quotes" from the art of other cultures (Umberger 1987). The Aztecs emphasized the importance of their capital as a center, drawing outsiders and goods toward it and disseminating only a limited number of forms, most of which have not survived in the archaeological record. There were state shrines and monuments in some important places in Central Mexico but otherwise no great building projects. Thus, the spread of archaeologically recognizable architectural and artistic characteristics was limited and resulted from processes mostly outside direct state control—among these, the movement of Central Mexican peoples, trade, and, demonstrable to a lesser extent, foreign emulation.

It is possible, then, to speak of a horizon based on Aztec III B/O in Central Mexico, northern Guerrero, and parts of the eastern empire, but only with the understanding that it is not synonymous with imperial activities, especially in areas near the Basin. One can also speak of a sculptural horizon style corresponding to imperial times in Central Mexico and areas in the east. Except for the regional style in northern Veracruz and the few other sculptures with certain provenience, however, this is a horizon reconstructed from often uncertain collection records, without internal material or stylistic confirmation of origin. Otherwise, in many respects, the effect of the Aztec empire on the material record is still to be defined. It is probable that in the future scholars in various regions will be able to isolate local configurations of evidence of changes corresponding to imperial times, as Michael Smith (1987) has done in Morelos. It is also probable that future excavation of Aztec-period sites will reveal more recognizable Aztec remains in places where Aztecs were residing and lead to a clearer perception of Aztec architectural forms and to a refinement of ceramic phases. But the effect of the empire on its provinces may be more often apparent in indications of increased local production (Smith 1987 and elsewhere), for instance in textile production as evidenced by spindle whorls, than in obvious intrusions of foreign ideas. Whatever the outcome, we expect that our basic perception that the Aztecs were not responsible for the spread of a number of important Postclassic forms will still hold true.

Acknowledgments Emily Umberger wishes to thank Dumbarton Oaks and her colleagues in the 1986 Aztec empire summer seminar, Frances Berdan, Richard Blanton, Elizabeth Boone, Mary Hodge, and Michael Smith. She is grateful to the Graduate College at Arizona State University for a release-time and research grant in the fall of 1987. She has also benefited from discussions with and comments by George Cowgill, Tom Cummins, Stephen Houston, Thomas Reese, Wendy Schonfeld, Felipe Solís, and Barbara Stark.

Cecelia F. Klein is grateful for a 1985–86 U.C.L.A. Art Council Faculty Grant in support of this project and for the special assistance of Barbara Voorhies, Thomas Michael Blake, John Paddock, Elizabeth Boone, Ana Luisa Izquierdo, and Holly Barnet-Sanchez.

Modern geographical and place names are used when referring to archaeological sites, and sixteenth-century Nahuatl spellings when referring to the Aztec-period places. Further results of the summer seminar will appear in a book, *Aztec Imperial Strategies,* co-authored by Berdan, Blanton, Boone, Hodge, Smith, and Umberger.

BIBLIOGRAPHY

ACOSTA, JORGE R.

1956   Resumen de los informes de las exploraciones arqueológicas cn Tula, Hgo. Durante las VI, VII y VIII temporadas, 1946–1950. *Anales del Instituto Nacional de Antropología e Historia (1954)* 8 (37): 37–115. Mexico.

1965   Tenayuca, exploraciones de 1963. *Anales del Instituto Nacional de Antropología e Historia* 17: 117–125. Mexico.

1974   La pirámide de El Corral de Tula, Hgo. In *Proyecto Tula (primera parte)* (Eduardo Matos Moctezuma, ed.): 27–49. Instituto Nacional de Antropología e Historia, Mexico.

ADAMS, RICHARD E. W.

1977   *Prehistoric Mesoamerica.* Little, Brown, Boston.

ALVAREZ, CARLOS A.

1983   Las esculturas de Teotenango. *Estudios de Cultura Náhuatl* 16: 233–264. Mexico.

ANDREWS, E. WYLLYS

1965   Archaeology and Prehistory in the Northern Maya Lowlands: An Introduction. In *Handbook of Middle American Indians* 2 (Robert Wauchope and Gordon R. Willey, eds.): 288–330. University of Texas Press, Austin.

ANDREWS, GEORGE F.

1975   *Maya Cities: Placemaking and Urbanization.* University of Oklahoma Press, Norman.

BANKMANN, ULF

1983   Eine Jadeitmaske aus Tizatlan, Tlaxcala. *Mexicon* 5 (5): 80–84.

BARLOW, ROBERT H.

1949   *The Extent of the Empire of the Culhua Mexica.* Ibero-Americana 28. University of California Press, Berkeley.

BATRES, LEOPOLDO

1904   *Exploraciones en Huexotla, Texcoco y "El Gavilan."* J. I. Guerrero, Mexico.

BERDAN, FRANCES F.

n.d.   Political and Economic Geography of the Eastern Aztec Realm. Paper presented at the 86th Annual Meeting of the American Anthropological Association, Chicago, 1987.

BERLIN, HEINRICH

1960   *Late Pottery Horizons of Tabasco, Mexico.* Carnegie Institution of Washington, Pub. 606. Washington, D.C.

BERNAL, IGNACIO

1948–49   Exploraciones en Coixtlahuaca, Oaxaca. *Revista Mexicana de Estudios Antropológicos* 10: 5–76. Mexico.

1969   *Museo Nacional de Antropología de México: Arqueología.* Aguilar, Mexico.

Emily Umberger and Cecelia F. Klein

BLANTON, RICHARD E.
  1983 The Aztec Garrison of "Acatepec." In *The Cloud People* (Kent V. Flannery and Joyce Marcus, eds.): 318. Academic Press, New York.

BLANTON, RICHARD E., STEPHEN A. KOWALEWSKI, GARY FEINMAN, AND JILL APPEL
  1981 *Ancient Mesoamerica, a Comparison of Three Regions.* Cambridge University Press, Cambridge.

BOONE, ELIZABETH HILL
  1982 Towards a More Precise Definition of the Aztec Painting Style. In *Pre-Columbian Art History: Selected Readings* (Alana Cordy-Collins, ed.): 153–168. Peek Publications, Palo Alto, Calif.
  n.d. Regional Variation in the Painted Manuscripts of the Aztec Empire. Paper presented at the 86th Annual Meeting of the American Anthropological Association, Chicago, 1987.

BRAY, WARWICK
  1989 Fine Metal Jewelry from Southern Mexico. In *Homenaje a José Luis Lorenzo* (Lorena Mirambell, coordinator): 243–275. Colección Científica 188, serie Prehistoria, Instituto Nacional de Antropología e Historia, Mexico.

BRETON, A. C.
  1920 An Ancient Mexican Picture-Map. *Man* 10: 17–20.

CABRERA CASTRO, RUBÉN
  1979 Restos arquitectónicos del recinto sagrado en excavaciones del Metro y de la recimentación de la Catedral y Sagrario. In *El recinto sagrado de México-Tenochtitlán, excavaciones 1968–69 y 1975–76* (Constanza Vega Sosa, ed.): 55–66. Instituto Nacional de Antropología e Historia, Mexico.
  1986 El Proyecto arqueológico "Cocula." Resultados generales. In *Arqueología y Etnohistoria del Estado de Guerrero*: 173–200. Instituto Nacional de Antropología e Historia, Mexico.

CARMACK, ROBERT M.
  1981 *The Quiché Mayas of Utatlán: The Evolution of a Highland Guatemala Kingdom.* University of Oklahoma Press, Norman.

CHARLTON, THOMAS H.
  1979 The Aztec-Early Colonial Transition in the Teotihuacan Valley. *Acts of the XLII International Congress of Americanists, Paris, 1976* 9-B: 199–208.

CHASE, ARLEN F.
  1986 Time Depth or Vacuum: The 11.3.0.0.0 Correlation and the Lowland Maya Postclassic. In *Late Lowland Maya Civilization: Classic to Postclassic* (Jeremy A. Sabloff and E. Wyllys Andrews V, eds.): 99–140. University of New Mexico Press, Albuquerque.

CODEX IXTLILXOCHITL
  1976 *Codex Ixtlilxochitl, Bibliothèque Nationale, Paris (Ms. Mexicain 65–71)* (Jacqueline de Durand-Forest, commentator). Akademische Druck- und Verlagsanstalt, Graz.

CODEX MENDOZA
    1925   *Colección de Mendoza o Códice Mendocino.* Talleres Gráficos del Museo Nacional de Antropología, Historia, y Etnografía, Mexico.

CODEX TELLERIANO-REMENSIS
    1899   *Codex Telleriano-Remensis* (E. T. Hamy, intro.). Duc de Loubat, Paris.

CONTRERAS SÁNCHEZ, EDUARDO
    1976   La zona arqueológica de Acozac, México (Temporada 1973–1974). *Boletín del Instituto Nacional de Antropología e Historia* (época 2) 16: 19–26. Mexico.

CUELLAR, ALFREDO
    1981   *Tezcatzoncatl escultórico: El "Chac-Mool" (El dios mesoamericano del vino).* Avangráfica, Mexico.

DEPARTMENTO DE MONUMENTOS ARTÍSTICOS
    1935   *Tenayuca.* Talleres Gráficos del Museo Nacional de Arqueología, Historia y Etnografía, Mexico.

DÍAZ DEL CASTILLO, BERNAL
    1984   *Historia verdadera de la conquista de la Nueva España,* 2 vols. (Miguel León-Portilla, ed.). Hermanos García Noblejas, Madrid.

DUPAIX, GUILLERMO
    1969   *Expediciones acerca de los antiguos monumentos de la Nueva España, 1805–1807* (José Alcina Franch, intro. and notes). José Porrúa Turanzas, Madrid.

DURÁN, FRAY DIEGO
    1967   *Historia de las indias de Nueva España e islas de la tierra firme,* 2 vols. (Angel Ma. Garibay K., ed.). Porrúa, Mexico.

EKHOLM, GORDON F.
    1944   *Excavations at Tampico and Panuco in the Huasteca, Mexico.* Anthropological Papers of the American Museum of Natural History 38 (5). New York.
    1953   Notas arqueológicas sobre el Valle de Tuxpan y áreas circunvecinas. *Revista Mexicana de Estudios Antropológicos* 13 (2/3): 413–421. Mexico.

FEWKES, JESSE WALTER
    1907   Certain Antiquities of Eastern Mexico. *25th Annual Report of the Bureau of American Ethnology, 1903–04:* 221–284. Washington, D.C.

FLANNERY, KENT V.
    1977   A Setting for Cultural Evolution. *Science* 196: 759–761.

FOX, JOHN W.
    1987   *Maya Postclassic State Formation: Segmentary Lineage Migration in Advancing Frontiers.* Cambridge University Press, Cambridge.

FUENTE, BEATRIZ DE LA, AND NELLY GUTIÉRREZ SOLANA
    1980   *Escultura huasteca en piedra: Catálogo.* Instituto de Investigaciones Estéticas, Universidad Nacional Autónoma de México, Mexico.

GALINDO Y VILLA, JESÚS
    1912   *Las ruinas de Cempoala y del templo del Tajín.* Mexico.

GALVÁN VILLEGAS, LUÍS JAVIER
1984   *Aspectos generales de la arqueología de Malinalco, Estado de México.* Instituto Nacional de Antropología e Historia, Mexico.

GARCÍA PAYÓN, JOSÉ
1936   *La zona arqueológica de Tecaxic-Calixtlahuaca y los Matlatzincas.* Part 1. Secretaría de Educación Pública, Mexico.
1956–57   Síntesis de las investigaciones en Tecaxic-Calixtlahuaca. *Revista Mexicana de Estudios Antropológicos* 14: 157–159. Mexico.
1971   Archaeology of Central Veracruz. In *Handbook of Middle American Indians* 11 (Robert Wauchope, Gordon F. Ekholm, and Ignacio Bernal, eds.): 505–542. University of Texas Press, Austin.

GREENGO, ROBERT
1967   Reconocimiento arqueológico en el noroeste de Guerrero. *Boletín del Instituto Nacional de Antropología e Historia* 29: 6–10. Mexico.

GUILLEMIN, JORGE F.
1965   *Iximché, capital del antiguo reino cakchiquel.* Instituto de Antropología e Historia de Guatemala, Guatemala.

GUIL'LIAM ARROYO, SALVADOR
1991   Discovery of a Painted Mural at Tlatelolco. In *To Change Place: Aztec Ceremonial Landscapes* (Davíd Carrasco, ed.): 20–30. University Press of Colorado, Niwot.

HASSIG, ROSS
1984   The Aztec Empire: A Reappraisal. In *Five Centuries of Law and Politics in Central Mexico* (Ronald Spores and Ross Hassig, eds.): 15–24. Publications in Anthropology 30. Vanderbilt University, Nashville.
1988   *Aztec Warfare: Imperial Expansion and Political Control.* University of Oklahoma Press, Norman.

HERNÁNDEZ RODRÍGUEZ, ROSAURA
1950   Documentos relacionados con San Bartolomé Tlatelolco. *Memorias de la Academia Mexicana de la Historia* 9 (1): 233–250. Mexico.

HERRERA, ANTONIO DE
1952   *Historia General de los Hechos de los Castellanos en las Islas y Tierrafirme del Mar Océano,* Vol. 9. La Real Academia de la Historia, Madrid.

HODGE, MARY G.
n.d.   Formation of an Empire: The Development of Regional Hierarchies in the Aztec Empire's Center. Paper presented at the 86th Annual Meeting of the American Anthropological Association, Chicago, 1987.

HORCASITAS, FERNANDO
1979   *The Aztecs Then and Now.* Minutiae Mexicana, Mexico.

INAH (INSTITUTO NACIONAL DE ANTROPOLOGÍA E HISTORIA)
1960   *Calixtlahuaca, Official Guide.* INAH, Mexico.
1978   *El Museo de Cuahtetelco, Guía Official.* INAH, Mexico.

KLEIN, CECELIA F.

1986   Masking Empire: The Material Effects of Masks in Aztec Mexico. *Art History* 9 (2): 135–166.

n.d.   On the Sources of Aztec Art. Paper presented at the Annual Meeting of the College Art Association, Los Angeles, 1977.

KRICKEBERG, WALTER

1960   Xochipilli und Chalchiuhtlicue: Zwei Aztekische Steinfiguren in der Völkerkundliche Sammlung der Stadt Mannheim. *Baessler-Archiv* n.s. 8: 1–30.

1969   *Felsbilder Mexicos, als Historische, Religiöse und Kunstdenkmäler.* Verlag von Dietrich Reimer, Berlin.

KUBLER, GEORGE

1973   Iconographic Aspects of Architectural Profiles at Teotihuacan and in Mesoamerica. In *The Iconography of Middle American Sculpture:* 24–39. Metropolitan Museum of Art, New York.

1984   *Art and Architecture of Ancient America: The Mexican, Maya, and Andean Peoples,* 3rd ed. Penguin Books, Harmondsworth.

LISTER, ROBERT H.

1941   Cerro Oztuma, Guerrero. *El México Antiguo* 5 (7–10): 209–220. Mexico.

1971   Archaeological Synthesis of Guerrero. In *Handbook of Middle American Indians* 11 (Robert Wauchope, Gordon F. Ekholm, and Ignacio Bernal, eds.): 619–631. University of Texas Press, Austin.

LÓPEZ PORTILLO, JOSÉ, MIGUEL LEÓN-PORTILLA, AND EDUARDO MATOS

1981   *El Templo Mayor.* Bancomer and Beatrice Trueblood, Mexico.

LOTHROP, SAMUEL K.

1926   *Pottery of Costa Rica and Nicaragua,* 2 vols. Contributions 8. Museum of the American Indian, Heye Foundation, New York.

MALER, TEOBERT

1903   Researches in the Central Portion of the Usumasintla Valley. *Memoirs of the Peabody Museum of American Archaeology and Ethnology* 2 (2): 96–98.

MARQUINA, IGNACIO

1960   *El Templo Mayor de México.* Instituto Nacional de Antropología e Historia, Mexico.

1964   *Arquitectura prehispánica.* Instituto Nacional de Antropología e Historia, Mexico.

MASTACHE, ALBA GUADALUPE, AND ANA MARÍA CRESPO

1974   La ocupación prehispánica en el área de Tula, Hgo. In *Proyecto Tula (1a Parte)* (Eduardo Matos Moctezuma, coord.): 71–103. Colección Científica 15. Instituto Nacional de Antropología e Historia, Mexico.

MATOS MOCTEZUMA, EDUARDO

1964   El adoratorio decorado de las Calles de Argentina. *Anales del Instituto Nacional de Antropología e Historia* 17: 127–138. Mexico.

1981   *Una visita al Templo Mayor de Tenochtitlán.* Instituto Nacional de Antropología e Historia, Mexico.

1985   *Official Guide: The Great Temple.* Instituto Nacional de Antropología e Historia/SALVAT, Mexico.

MAYER, BRANZ

1844   *Mexico As It Was and As It Is.* New World Press, New York.

MEDELLÍN ZENIL, ALFONSO

1952   *Exploraciones en Quauhtochco, Temporada I.* Gobierno del Estado de Veracruz, Departamento de Antropología, y Instituto Nacional de Antropología e Historia, Jalapa.

1960   *Cerámicas del Totonacapan: Exploraciones arqueológicas en el centro de Veracruz.* Instituto de Antropología, Universidad Veracruzana, Jalapa.

MEIGHAN, CLEMENT W.

1976   *The Archaeology of Amapa, Nayarit.* The Institute of Archaeology, University of California, Los Angeles.

MILLER, ARTHUR G.

1982   *On the Edge of the Sea: Mural Painting at Tancah-Tulum, Quintana Roo, Mexico.* Dumbarton Oaks, Washington, D.C.

MÜLLER, FLORENCIA

1980   Una escultura en piedra de Loma Bonita, Tuxtepec, Oaxaca. *Antropología e Historia, Boletín del Instituto Nacional de Antropología e Historia* (época 3) 30: 45–48. Mexico.

NAVARRETE, CARLOS

1965   Una vasija azteca en la República de El Salvador. *Boletín del Instituto Nacional de Antropología e Historia* 29: 7–8. Mexico.

1966   *The Chiapanec, History and Cuture.* Papers of the New World Archaeological Foundation 16. Brigham Young University, Provo, Utah.

1976   Algunas influencias mexicanas en el área maya meridional durante el Postclásico Tardío. *Estudios de Cultura Náhuatl* 12: 345–382. Mexico.

NEBEL, CARLOS

1963   *Viaje pintoresco y arqueológico sobre la parte mas interesante de la Republica Mexicana, en los años transcurridos desde 1829 hasta 1834.* Librería de Manuel Porrúa, Mexico.

NICHOLSON, H. B.

1955   The Temalacatl of Tehuacan. *El México Antiguo* 8: 95–134. Mexico.

1966   The Mixteca-Puebla Concept in Mesoamerican Archaeology: A Reexamination. In *Ancient Mesoamerica. Selected Readings* (John A. Graham, ed.): 258–263. Peek Publications, Palo Alto, Calif.

1971   Major Sculpture in Pre-Hispanic Central Mexico. In *Handbook of Middle American Indians* 10 (Robert Wauchope, ed.): 395–446. University of Texas Press, Austin.

1977   An Aztec Stone Image of a Fertility Goddess (and Addendum). In *Pre-Columbian Art History: Selected Readings* (Alana Cordy-Collins and Jean Stern, eds.): 145–165. Peek Publications, Palo Alto, Calif.

NICHOLSON, H. B., WITH ELOISE QUIÑONES KEBER

1983   *Art of Aztec Mexico, Treasures of Tenochtitlan.* National Gallery of Art, Washington, D.C.

NORIEGA, RAÚL
 1953   *La Piedra del Sol y 16 monumentos del México antiguo; Símbolos y claves.* Editorial Superación, Mexico.

PADDOCK, JOHN
 1975   Trás el centro de Huaxyacac azteca. *Boletín* 4: 5–10. Centro Regional de Oaxaca, Instituto Nacional de Antropología e Historia, Oaxaca.

PARSONS, JEFFREY R., ELIZABETH BRUMFIEL, MARY H. PARSONS, AND DAVID J. WILSON
 1982   *Prehispanic Settlement Patterns in the Southern Valley of Mexico: The Chalco-Xochimilco Region.* Memoirs of the Museum of Anthropology 14. University of Michigan, Ann Arbor.

PASO Y TRONCOSO, FRANCISCO DEL (ED.)
 1905–06   *Papeles de Nueva España,* 6 vols. Sucesores de Rivandeneyra, Madrid.

PEÑAFIEL, ANTONIO
 1890   *Monumentos de arte mexicano antiguo: Ornamentación, mitología, tributos y monumentos,* 3 vols. in 5. A. Asher and Co., Berlin.
 1910   *Destrucción del Templo Mayor de México antiguo y los monumentos encontrados en la ciudad, en las excavaciones de 1897 y 1902.* Secretaria de Fomento, Mexico.

PÉREZ-CASTRO, GUILLERMO, ET AL.
 1989   El Cuauhxicalli de Moctezuma I. *Arqueología* 5: 132–151. Instituto Nacional de Antropología e Historia, Mexico.

POLLOCK, H. E. D.
 1936   *Round Structures of Aboriginal Middle America.* Carnegie Institution of Washington Pub. 471. Washington, D.C.

PRICE, BARBARA J.
 1976   A Chronological Framework for Cultural Development in Mesoamerica. In *The Valley of Mexico, Studies in Prehispanic Ecology and Society* (Eric R. Wolf, ed.): 13–21. University of New Mexico Press, Albuquerque.

QUIRARTE, JACINTO
 1982   The Santa Rita Murals: A Review. In *Aspects of the Mixteca-Puebla Style and Mixtec and Central Mexican Culture in Southern Mesoamerica:* 43–59. Middle American Research Institute, Occasional Paper 4. Tulane University, New Orleans.

RICE, PRUDENCE M., AND DON S. RICE
 1985   Topoxte, Macanche, and the Central Peten Postclassic. In *The Lowland Maya Postclassic* (Arlen F. Chase and Prudence M. Rice, eds.): 166–183. University of Texas Press, Austin.

ROBERTSON, DONALD
 1959   *Mexican Manuscript Painting of the Early Colonial Period: The Metropolitan Schools.* Yale University Press, New Haven.
 1970   The Tulum Murals: The International Style of the Late Post-Classic. *Proceedings of the 38th International Congress of Americanists, 1968* 2: 77–88. Stuttgart-Munich.

ROBLES CASTELLANOS, FERNANDO, AND ANTHONY P. ANDREWS

    1986   A Review and Synthesis of Recent Postclassic Archaeology in Northern Yucatan. In *Late Lowland Maya Civilization: Classic to Postclassic* (Jeremy A. Sabloff and E. Wyllys Andrews V, eds.): 53–98. University of New Mexico Press, Albuquerque.

RODRÍGUEZ BETANCOURT, FELIPE

    1986   Desarrollo cultural en la región de Mezcala-Tetela del Río. In *Arqueología y Etnohistoria del Estado de Guerrero:* 155–170. Instituto Nacional de Antropología e Historia, Mexico.

ROMÁN BERRELLEZA, JUAN ALBERTO

    1991   A Study of Skeletal Materials at Tlatelolco. In *To Change Place: Aztec Ceremonial Landscapes* (Davíd Carrasco, ed.): 9–19. University Press of Colorado, Niwot.

SAHAGÚN, FRAY BERNARDINO DE

    1950–82   *Florentine Codex, General History of the Things of New Spain* (Arthur J. O. Anderson and Charles E. Dibble, trans. and eds.). 12 books in 13 vols. School of American Research and the University of Utah Press, Santa Fe.

SANDERS, WILLIAM T., JEFFREY R. PARSONS, AND ROBERT S. SANTLEY

    1979   *The Basin of Mexico: Ecological Processes in the Evolution of a Civilization.* Academic Press, New York.

SAVILLE, MARSHALL

    1896   The Temple of Tepoztlan, Mexico. *American Museum of Natural History Bulletin* 8: 221–226.

    1925   The Wood-Carver's Art in Ancient Mexico. *Contributions from the Museum of the American Indian, Heye Foundation* 6. New York.

SCHMIDT, PAUL

    1986   Secuencia arqueológica de Xochipala. In *Arqueología y Etnohistoria del Estado de Guerrero:* 107–116. Instituto Nacional de Antropología e Historia, Mexico.

SCHOLES, FRANCE V., AND RALPH L. ROYS

    1968   *The Maya Chontal Indians of Acalan-Tixchel: A Contribution to the History and Ethnography of the Yucatan Peninsula,* 2nd ed. University of Oklahoma Press, Norman.

SCOTT, JOHN F.

    1982   The Monuments of Los Idolos, Veracruz. *Journal of New World Archaeology* 5 (1): 10–23.

SELER, EDUARD

    1960–61   *Gesammelte Abhandlungen zur Amerikanischen Sprach- und Altertumskunde,* 5 vols. Akademische Druck- und Verlagsanstalt, Graz.

SHOOK, EDWIN

    1952   The Great Wall and Other Features of Mayapan. *Carnegie Institution of Washington, Yearbook* 51: 247–251.

SLOANE, FLORENCE
    n.d.   Ideology and the Frontier: A Hypothesis of a Quiché Innovation in Religion. Paper presented at the 39th Annual Meeting of the Society for American Archaeology, Washington, 1974.

SMITH, A. LEDYARD
    1955   *Archaeological Reconnaissance in Central Guatemala.* Carnegie Institution of Washington Pub. 608. Washington, D.C.

SMITH, MICHAEL E.
    1986   The Role of Social Stratification in the Aztec Empire: A View from the Provinces. *American Anthropologist* 88 (1): 70–91.
    1987   The Expansion of the Aztec Empire: A Case Study in the Correlation of Diachronic Archaeological and Ethnohistorical Data. *American Antiquity* 52 (1): 37–54.
    1990   Long-Distance Trade under the Aztec Empire: The Archaeological Evidence. *Ancient Mesoamerica* I: 153–169.
    n.d.a   Economic Regions in Postclassic Central Mexico: A Trial Formulation. Paper presented at the 48th Annual Meeting of the Society for American Archaeology, Pittsburgh, 1983.
    n.d.b   Imperial Strategies in the Western Portion of the Aztec Empire. Paper presented at the 86th Annual Meeting of the American Anthropological Association, Chicago, 1987.

SMITH, MICHAEL E., AND CYNTHIA M. HEATH-SMITH
    1980   Waves of Influence in Postclassic Mesoamerica? A Critique of the Mixteca-Puebla Concept. *Anthropology* 4 (2): 15–50.

SOLÍS OLGUIN, FELIPE R.
    1976   *La escultura mexica del Museo de Santa Cecilia Acatitlán, Estado de México.* Instituto Nacional de Antropología e Historia, Mexico.
    1981   *Escultura del Castillo de Teayo, Veracruz, Mexico, Catálogo.* Instituto de Investigaciones Estéticas, Universidad Nacional Autónoma de México, Mexico.
    1982   The Formal Pattern of Anthropomorphic Sculpture and the Ideology of the Aztec State. *The Art and Iconography of Late Post-Classic Central Mexico* (Elizabeth P. Benson, organizer; Elizabeth Hill Boone, ed.): 73–110. Dumbarton Oaks, Washington, D.C.
    1985   Arte, estado y sociedad: La escultura antropomorfa de México-Tenochtitlán. In *Mesoamérica y el Centro de México* (Jesús Monjarás-Ruiz, Rosa Brambila, and Emma Pérez-Rocha, eds): 393–429. Instituto Nacional de Antropología, Mexico.
    1986   La estructura piramidal de Castillo de Teayo: Un edificio en proceso constructivo o un peculiar estilo arquitectónico. In *Cuadernos de Arquitectura Mesoamerica* 8: 73–79. División de Estudios de Posgrado, Facultad de Arquitectura, Universidad Nacional Autónoma de México, Mexico.

SPORES, RONALD
    1984   *The Mixtecs in Ancient and Colonial Times.* University of Oklahoma Press, Norman.

STARK, BARBARA

1990   The Gulf Coast and the Central Highlands of Mexico: Alternative Models for Interaction. *Research in Economic Anthropology* 12: 243–285.

STIRLING, MATTHEW W.

1965   Monumental Sculpture of Southern Veracruz and Tabasco. In *Handbook of Middle American Indians* 3 (Robert Wauchope and Gordon R. Willey, eds.): 716–738. University of Texas Press, Austin.

STOCKER, TERRY

1986   Wild Growing Plant Utilization by the Otomi Indians. *Mexicon* 8 (4): 81–84. Berlin.

STOCKER, T. L., AND R. H. COBEAN

1984   Preliminary Report on the Obsidian Mines at Pico de Orizaba, Veracruz. In *Prehistoric Quarries and Lithic Production* (Jonathon E. Ericson and Barbara A. Purdy, eds.): 83–95. Cambridge University Press, Cambridge.

TORRES GUZMÁN, MANUEL

1962   Exploraciones realizadas por el Instituto de Antropología de la Universidad Veracruzana. *Boletín del Instituto Nacional de Antropología e Historia* 10: 5. Mexico.

TOWNSEND, RICHARD F.

1982   Malinalco and the Lords of Tenochtitlan. In *The Art and Iconography of Late Post-Classic Central Mexico* (Elizabeth Hill Boone, ed.): 111–140. Dumbarton Oaks, Washington, D.C.

UMBERGER, EMILY

1987   Antiques, Revivals, and References to the Past in Aztec Art. *Res* 13: 62–105.

n.d.a   Aztec Sculptures, Hieroglyphs, and History. Ph.D. dissertation, Department of Art History and Archaeology, Columbia University, 1981. University Microfilms, Ann Arbor.

n.d.b   Aztec-Style Sculptures in Eastern Mesoamerica: Two Cases. Paper presented at the Annual Meeting of the American Anthropological Association, Phoenix, 1988.

VILLAGRA CALETI, AGUSTÍN

1971   Mural Painting in Central Mexico. In *Handbook of Middle American Indians* 10 (Robert Wauchope, Gordon F. Ekholm, and Ignacio Bernal, eds.): 135–156. University of Texas Press, Austin.

WOODBURY, RICHARD B., AND AUBREY S. TRIK

1953   *The Ruins of Zaculeu, Guatemala,* 2 vols. United Fruit Company and William Byrd Press, Richmond.

Factors Influencing the Transmission and Distribution of Inka Cultural Materials Throughout Tawantinsuyu

JOHN HYSLOP

INSTITUTE OF ANDEAN RESEARCH

THERE CAN BE LITTLE DOUBT that the Inka state created the most widespread archaeological horizon of all native American civilizations. Inka artifacts and public works span 5,500 km from the Colombian-Ecuadoran border to a point somewhat south of Santiago, Chile (Fig. 1). If there ever was a horizon in American prehistory, the Inka most thoroughly fits the traditional definitions of the concept.[1] This horizon was created in somewhat less than a century. It is expressed somewhat differently from region to region. We probably know more about the cultural factors causing variations in it than is the case with any other American horizon.

The variations in the material remains are crucial, because, if we understand what has caused them, we learn a great deal more not only about Inkas, but about the people they ruled. The factors discussed below appear to have been important in creating the variations in the horizon. None of these factors is an isolated determinant but rather an influence that might be modified or inoperative when other conditions are present. Nevertheless, the following factors are useful tools for evaluating the cultural materials of

---

[1] For the history and definitions of the term *horizon* see G. R. Willey and P. Phillips (1958: 29–33) and J. Rowe (1962). The concept was first introduced into Andean archaeology by Max Uhle. Willey and Phillips (1958: 33) define *horizon* as "a primarily spatial continuity represented by cultural traits and assemblages whose nature and mode of occurrence permit the assumption of a broad and rapid spread." Rowe (1962: 48) notes that the precision of chronology has improved to the point that "horizon styles" could not be taken "as sufficient indication of contemporaneity." Using the master chronological sequence from the Ica Valley, he defined the Andean Horizons (Early, Middle, and Late) according to their appearances in Ica. His Late Horizon coincides with the entrance of Inka (Phase A of the Tacaroca style) at Ica, about A.D. 1476. The term *Late Horizon* has been used by some scholars to refer to the Inka style throughout the Andes, although in some areas it occurred before the Inka occupation of Ica. This would appear to be an inaccurate usage of the term as proposed by Rowe.

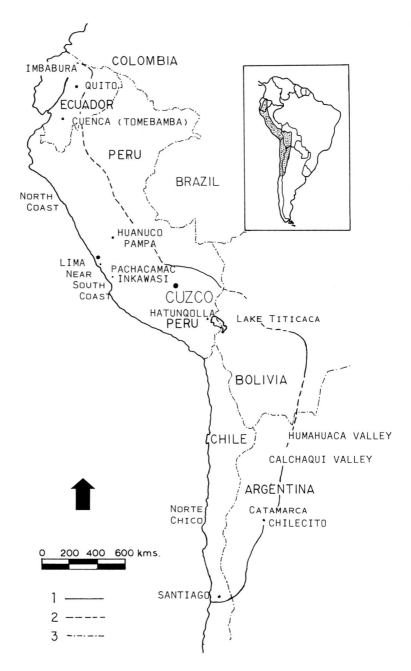

Fig. 1. Map of Tawantinsuyu, the Inka Empire. (1) Relatively well-defined boundary; (2) poorly defined boundary; (3) boundary of modern republics

the Inka horizon. In this discussion I shall limit myself primarily to two aspects of Inka materials: pottery and architecture.[2]

THE STRENGTH AND COMPLEXITY OF LOCAL (NON-INKA) CRAFT AND BUILDING TRADITIONS

Local pottery traditions in the Andes doubtlessly affected the nature of Inka pottery in most areas of the state outside of the Cuzco area. Speaking in the most general terms, throughout much of Tawantinsuyu one finds Inka pottery that looks the same and different at the same time. These variations are due in part to local ceramic traditions that leave their imprint on Inka pottery. Thus, while there are standard Inka pottery shapes and designs, it frequently is not difficult to distinguish local traits in an Inka vessel and tell from which zone it has come, although its provenance has not been recorded.

I have observed that Inka ceramic shapes and forms were replicated more successfully in many parts of the state than were the traditional Cuzco designs used on them (Fig. 2). Nevertheless, in almost no part of the Inka state (with possible exception of unique burial or ceremonial contexts) does one find nearly the complete assembly of shapes that occurs in the Cuzco area. The reasons for this are not altogether clear, but in some cases it is apparent that local forms of bowls, jars, and pots replace their Inka equivalent (Hyslop n.d.: 144–148). Other special Inka forms such as the *florero* (a long-necked bottle; Fig. 2, no. 12) are found rarely, if ever, outside of the Cuzco area. One must wonder whether it had a special relationship to activities carried out primarily in or near the capital.[3] Several other factors influencing the appearance of Inka pottery are discussed below.

The strength of a local (non-Inka) building tradition affects the presence and/or amount of Inka architecture in an area. It is notable that for more than 1,000 km of the coastal area of north Peru there is little or no Inka architecture. Whereas buildings were certainly constructed there in Inka times, the absence of constructions with well-defined Inka building traits might lead one, if archaeological remains were our only source of information, to think that the North Coast was an area weakly controlled, or merely a zone influenced, by Tawantinsuyu (the Inka state). We know from the early historical sources (Rowe 1948) that such as not the case, and that the region was an integral part of the empire. We also know, primarily from archaeological investigations, that the North Coast was one of the most heavily developed and urbanized parts of the Andes prior to the Inka expansion. I suggest that the absence of Inka architecture there is due, in part, to

[2] The Inka horizon is expressed in many different media. Morris (n.d.b) discusses Inka style in several of them, including metal and textiles.

[3] Inasmuch as a long-necked bottle form is found on the near South Coast of Peru in pre-Inka times, one might speculate that it was a form "imported" to Cuzco from one of its conquered territories.

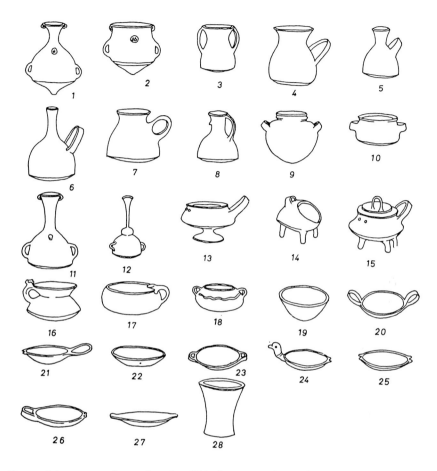

Fig. 2. Inka pottery forms found at Chinchero, an Inka settlement near Cuzco (from Rivera 1976: 29)

its local building tradition, which continued in Inka times. That is, Inka rulers decided to utilize existing buildings and roads, and, if new ones were built, capable local architects, engineers, and workmen were available for the task.

It is important not to define all areas with strong building traditions as those where Inka architecture will not occur. Certainly many factors came into play when Inka rulers needed new public works to carry out state activities. If we look at the area of the Lurin Valley and the near South Coast of Peru, another zone with a highly developed local building tradition, we find considerable amounts of architecture with well-defined Inka traits. Other factors (discussed below) had certainly come into play there.

The important point here for the archaeologist is the strength of Inka presence in a region must not be gauged automatically by the amount and quality of Inka artifacts and architecture. A more sophisticated approach must be used. It must consider all the related early historical sources, and detect Inka rearrangements in remains that exhibit primarily local traits.

MITMAQ AND STATE PRODUCTION SPECIALISTS

One of the most remarkable characteristics of the Inka state, and possibly of earlier Andean civilizations, was the movement of peoples, *mitmaq* (state colonists), from one zone to another (Murra 1980: 173–182). Many of the subject peoples were required to send groups to distant parts of the empire, sometimes as a reward for loyalty, and sometimes a punishment for disloyalty. Groups from Cuzco were sent to many regions, and performed many special, often privileged tasks. Of special interest to the archaeologist is the influence of state pottery specialists.

State potters capable of producing the very finest Inka pottery were sent to only a few zones of Tawantinsuyu.[4] In the areas of Quito and Cuenca of Ecuador, the near South Coast of Peru, and in the circum-lacustrine area of Lake Titicaca (Murra 1978) one can find substantial amounts of Inka pottery as finely made as in Cuzco. In these three zones, potters trained in Cuzco, or taught by experts trained there, produced large amounts of fine Inka ceramics. Potters capable of replicating state ceramics with extreme accuracy may have functioned in other areas, but solid evidence for this is still lacking.

Throughout most of Tawantinsuyu, Inka pottery was not produced by state potters who knew the Cuzco style well. Much appears to have been produced by local individuals performing the *mita* (rotational labor service). Such was the case at the administrative center Huanuco Pampa. One early historical source (Visitación . . . [1549] 1967: 306) relates that the Chupaychu ethnic group supplied the labor of forty individuals to make ceramic vessels for that center. Unfortunately, the historical record does not tell us what kind of pottery the Chupaychu produced. Archaeological research resolves the problem; investigations (Morris and Thompson 1985:1973–74) demonstrate that Inka pottery at Huanuco Pampa abounds to the near exclusion of local types. The Inka vessels are, however, of a rougher, generally undecorated sort than fine Cuzco pottery. In this case historical and archaeological data work together to indicate that Inka ceramics at Huanuco Pampa were made by non-Inka hands. I suspect that this was usually the case in most

---

[4] My inspections of Inka pottery collections throughout the Andes indicate that Inka pottery from the Cuzco region was rarely exported over long distances. Occasionally one finds a vessel in regional collections that may have had its origin in the Cuzco area, but absolute confirmation is usually lacking. One comparative study (D'Altroy and Bishop 1990) of the material composition of 173 sherds demonstrates that two sherds may have been exported from Cuzco into the Upper Mantaro and Lake Titicaca areas. In general, Inka pottery was made primarily in the zones where it was used.

parts of Tawantinsuyu. The potters expert in the Cuzco style were reserved for areas of very special administrative and/or ceremonial importance. Thus in most parts of Tawantinsuyu almost all Inka ceramics are imperfect imitations of pottery technology, forms, and designs used in Cuzco.

In still other areas it is now apparent that non-Inka *mitmaq* can be identified by their pottery in areas far from its place of origin. Their ceramics combine Inka and local traits and clearly are not the work of potters from Cuzco. From Bolivia south these types have a distribution well beyond their point of origin. Such is the case of the Inka-Diaguita pottery of the Norte Chico in Chile, the La Paya-Inka pottery originating in the Calchaqui Valley of Argentina, and the Inka-Pacaje (Saxamar) pottery originating just south of Lake Titicaca (Fig. 3). For example, the strong presence of Inka-Diaguita pottery in Inka sites in the Argentine provinces of San Juan and Mendoza suggests that Inkaized *mitmaq* from the western side of the Andes were moved to the eastern side (Schobinger 1971: 83).

INKA RULE IN AREAS OF LIMITED SOCIAL STRATIFICATION AND POPULATION

Only recently are we beginning to have a conception of the nature of Inka remains and rule in the area of Argentina and Chile, a vast territory ignored

Fig. 3. An Inka-Pacaje plate (left) and an Inka-Diaguita jar (right). Each vessel has an Inka ceramic shape, but some non-Inka design elements (photo: courtesy, American Museum of Natural History, New York. Catalog nos. B/8325 and 41.0/9666)

almost totally in nearly all syntheses of Inka history, economics, and architecture. The great number of Inka roads, sanctuaries, and *tampu* (roadside lodgings) in this zone make it increasingly difficult to define that region as it has been in the past—a marginal area (Hyslop 1984). There are, however, reasons it has been so viewed. For example, there is an absence of fine Inka stonework; Inka ceramics are generally imperfect imitations of Cuzco pottery; there is a lack of large administrative centers. The problems of interpreting what went on there in Inka times is compounded by a general scarcity of early historical sources.

Previously I too was willing to declare the region marginal, but now believe its "marginality" is in part a reflection of our imperfect understanding of the social and demographic context in which Inka cultural materials were produced. Crucial for understanding this large zone is its low population, now and in Inka times. The largest pre-Inka settlements are unplanned conglomerate villages numbering only hundreds of structures (Tarragó 1978). These are found only in the most productive areas such as in the Humahuaca, Santa Maria, and Calchaqui Valleys. It now appears that the Inkas dominated the areas with the same tactics and institutions as elsewhere in the state. However, the amount of available labor was far less. And since pre-Inka social structure was less stratified than in the central and south-central Andes, the establishment of full-time specialists for systematic creation of large amounts of state goods was more difficult to establish.

These factors influence Inka cultural materials in a way that superficially gives a concept of "marginality." For example, I now presume that the absence of fine stonework is in part a manifestation of the limited labor supply and that the "imperfect" Cuzco pottery is made by artisans, perhaps in great part not full-time specialists, who have seen models of Inka ceramics but had not been trained in Cuzco. The alleged absence of large Inka administrative centers is now better understood, for several sites have now been identified whose urban design is strikingly similar to the great centers of the central Andes (Fig. 4); that is, Inka administrative centers in the south are simply smaller, but they exist (Raffino 1981). In sum, the apparent "marginality" of the region's material remains is caused by factors that need not suggest it was less a part of the state than other, more populous areas.

Finally, there is not a total absence of the highest quality Cuzco architecture and artifacts in the southern part of the state. They occur, but only in areas of considerable ceremonial and/or administrative significance (Hyslop 1990). This brings us to the next factor that considers how the administrative and ceremonial importance of a zone or site influences the nature of Inka cultural materials.

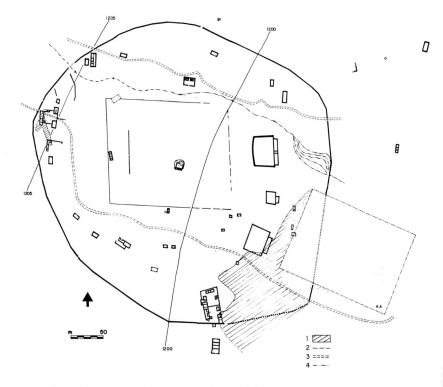

Fig. 4. The Inka center Chilecito (Tamberia del Inca) in La Rioja, Argentina. A central *ushnu* platform in a rectangular plaza is surrounded by buildings that face it (from Hyslop 1990: 208)

AREAS OF GREAT CEREMONIAL AND/OR ADMINISTRATIVE IMPORTANCE

There are at least three regions outside of the Cuzco area where the finest Inka pottery is found in combination with sophisticated Inka architecture: (1) the near South Coast of Peru, (2) the Lake Titicaca area (Fig. 5), and (3) the zones of Quito and Cuenca in Ecuador. Each of these corresponds to what we know from historical sources to be areas of great importance and priority. On the near South Coast we find the Pachacamac (Uhle 1903; Strong and Corbett 1943; Hyslop 1990: 255–261), the greatest coastal shrine and pilgrimage site, and Chincha (Uhle 1924; Menzel and Rowe 1966; Morris 1988), the coastal valley most closely allied to Inka interests. The Lake Titicaca region (Murra 1968; Hyslop 1979; Julien 1983) was the richest in the Andes in terms of manpower and herds and was the seat of an extremely important Inka sanctuary. Cuenca, known as Tomebamba (Uhle 1923; Idrovo n.d.), and Quito were used as secondary capitals of the state.

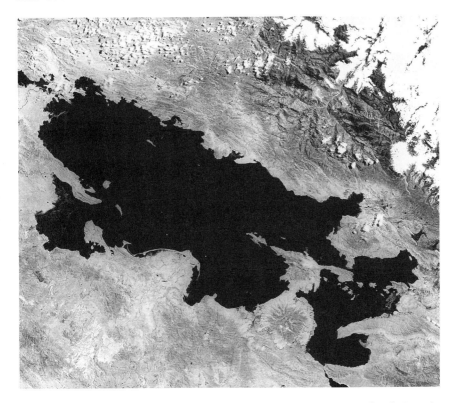

Fig. 5. Lake Titicaca as seen from a satellite. The region was integrated early into the expanding Inka state (photo: courtesy, NASA—Landsat)

In many respects the architectural and artifact evidence from these zones confirms the importance given these regions in the early historical sources. If we had no historical sources to guide us, the student of comparative Inka remains, after a thorough review of the archaeological literature, might well conclude that outside the Cuzco area, the Inka influence was strongest in these three regions. To reach this conclusion he or she must not be fooled into assigning great importance to areas or sites with large administrative centers or fortresses, which were built necessarily where no usable infrastructure existed. One aspect of these centers and forts is that they have little truly fine Inka pottery, a point suggesting that they do not equal in importance the above-mentioned three regions.

It was noted that some fine Inka artifacts are found in the empire's southern extreme. Limited but stunning examples of the finest Cuzco artifacts (Fig. 6) (textiles, shell and metal figurines, and so forth) are found in dozens of high-altitude sanctuaries (Schobinger 1966; Reinhard 1983; Beorchia 1987) as far south as Santiago, Chile, a point 3,000 km from the Inka capital.

John Hyslop

Fig. 6. Inka gold figurine and miniature textiles. The bag is 3.5 cm wide. Similar items are found in high altitude sanctuaries (photo: courtesy, American Museum of Natural History. Catalog nos. 41.2/902–905)

The ceremonial role of these objects is beyond dispute. They demonstrate that symbolic concerns can be a major force behind the long-distance distribution of artifacts. Whereas archaeologists will perhaps have little difficulty believing this, it is mentioned here as one of the best-documented cases where religious concerns are clearly responsible for the creation of part of a horizon that, in general, is considered the product of politics and warfare.

At this point I would like to consider in greater detail why fine examples of Inka architecture and Inka pottery do not necessarily go together. This is due to the different functional and symbolic role of each, a point that must be clarified if we are ever going to understand the Inka horizon, and others. The symbolic concepts behind Inka urban planning speak of control over nature, express cosmology, social organization, and spatial concepts (Morris n.d.a; Hyslop 1985, 1990). In several cases large Inka installations mirror an actual and mythological conception of Cuzco and in so doing are physical representations of an entire world view.

Inka architecture has symbolic content not only in site planning, but in the materials used for construction. Prime among these is fine Cuzco masonry (Hyslop 1990: 12–16) (Fig. 7). Such stonework is found most often in three categories of constructions: (1) royal and/or religious buildings, (2) waterworks, and (3) some terrace walls. The use of fine masonry in such diverse constructions suggests their related high significance. At Tomebamba, the secondary Inka capital destroyed in the Inka civil war, many fine masonry blocks have been hacked apart (Jaime Idrovo, personal communication, 1986; Hyslop 1990: 264–265), apparently by King Waskar's raiding army. The destruction of these stones is but one new indicator of their high symbolic importance.

346

Fig. 7. Fine Inka masonry at Limatambo near Cuzco

Pottery, as Craig Morris (1982) has discussed, is directly allied to the question of reciprocity, an element increasingly realized as central to labor management and the control of ethnic groups. The close relationship between hospitality and labor management may also explain why there are, as far as I know, no areas under the firm control of Tawantinsuyu where at least some Inka pottery has not been found. Here I am referring to all Inka pottery, not just the very fine examples found in a few regions. In some places the Inkas could, and did, run an empire without their fancy settlement layouts, but they could not do it without the state hospitality, which required pottery that symbolized the state (Morris n.d.b).

Finally, Inka pottery has a symbolic role, yet to be clarified, beyond that related to state hospitality. It was a symbol of the state control, high among the categories on *khipu* (knotted cords for record keeping). Some of the finest vessels were worthy of sacrifice in burial caches.

THE INFLUENCE OF MILITARY AND ECONOMIC ACTIVITIES

Whereas fine Inka architecture and pottery are found together in a few regions of greatest administrative and ceremonial importance within Tawantinsuyu, it appears that military and economic activities influence the nature of the mix of Inka and local non-Inka remans in other parts of Tawantinsuyu.

One of the Inka state's chief specialized activities was warfare. At perhaps no time during its brief existence was the state in peace. Military activities are clearly visible in the great number of fortresses (Hyslop 1990: 146–190) built where the state was expanding, such as in Pichincha and Imbabura in Ecuador (Plaza Schuler 1976), or protecting its territories from invaders, as in eastern Bolivia (Nordenskiöld 1924; González and Cravotto 1977) and northwest Argentina (Lange 1896). In general terms, one can say that forts and garrisons figure among the very largest Inka archaeological sites with pure, or nearly pure, Inka architecture. There are reasons for this. It was usually impossible to use preexisting (local) sites as forts either because there were none, or, if there were candidates, they were not strategically located. Although Inka military sites are often situated in isolated areas distant from dependable local sources of labor, it would appear that the state's military apparatus was able to import labor from distant areas to build them. I am impressed with the complex design of many of the fortresses and garrisons (Fig. 8). As with administrative centers, much care was taken to introduce many symbolic concepts into their layout. Such concepts found in the forts from Imbabura in the north to Catamarca far in the south suggest that Inka warfare was charged with high ceremonial content. The close relationship between Inka warfare and religious concerns was noted first by John Rowe (1946: 274) but has received little serious attention.

In recent years much has been said about the great importance of economic complementarity in the Andes (Murra 1972; Masuda, Shimada, and Morris 1985). That is, the mechanisms used to connect areas of different or varied economic production. It is clear that economic complementarity influences the distribution of artifacts in many parts of the Andes. Inka-related pottery types originating in the mountains or *altiplano* are found at lower altitudes on the Pacific Coast or eastern Andean slopes, areas known to be bound up economically with higher regions of denser populations. There may be more evidence of highland Inka artifacts in lower areas than vice versa. This may be due in part to the better preservation in coastal regions, and to the perishable nature of goods shipped from lower regions to the highlands. It may also be a reflection of the political supremacy of the highlands over the lowlands. In Inka times most major administrative and storage centers were in the *sierra,* and lowland areas were generally, with some exceptions, subordinate to them.

This highland–lowland distinction is most useful in the parts of Tawantin-suyu now occupied by Ecuador, Peru, and Bolivia. The large part of the Inka state in Chile and Argentina is not easily subject to this simplified dichotomy.

In general, I find the archaeological evidence from Inka times still contributes little to an understanding of economic complementarity. I suspect that we are just beginning to consider how certain types of Inka cultural material may supplement knowledge about it.

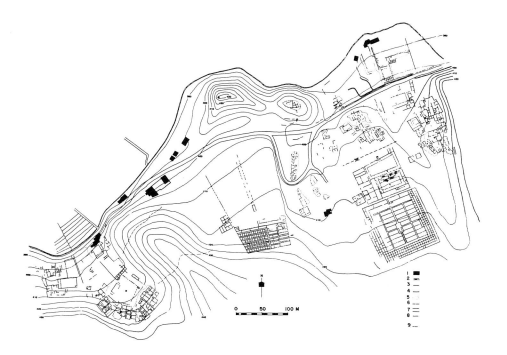

Fig. 8. The Inka garrison Inkawasi in the Cañete Valley, Peru. Its layout incorporates many Inka symbolic concepts. (1) Modern building; (2) irrigation channel; (3) building wall; (4) terrace; (5) indistinct buildings; (6) road or path; (7) modern road; (8) contour line; (9) platform edge or fallen wall (from Hyslop 1985: 137)

In many cases the special economic activities of a site or zone are clearly defined by the archaeological complexes. Stoneworking artifacts and finished products may define a lapidary workshop (Krapovikas 1958–59); spindle whorls, a textile complex (Morris and Thompson 1985: 70–71); metal debris and ovens, a foundry (Niemeyer, Cervellino, and Muñoz 1984); ceramic wasters (Hyslop n.d.: 409–411), a pottery production center. In areas where relatively detailed archaeological investigations have taken place, it generally appears state activities were usually more complex than those suggested by whatever early written sources are available.

THE USE OF INKA CULTURAL MATERIALS BY ELITE MEMBERS OF NON–INKA
GROUPS

Research in the last few decades with regional early historical sources in the Andes has allowed us to see more clearly how extensively Inka rule utilized the existing structure of local lords for the administration of the state

(Murra 1984: 78–82). This policy has important consequences for understanding the distribution and transmission of Inka cultural materials, since Inka materials tend to concentrate where local elites lived and were buried. This makes a certain amount of sense, since we know from the classic Andean chronicles that local lords were required to visit Cuzco and that their children were educated there. The use of Inka-influenced pottery and architecture by local, non-Inka elites cross-cuts the factors discussed above.

Manifestations of this phenomenon have now been revealed in several places. One example is the Titicaca area were local elites were buried in towers since well before the Inkas. After Inka domination, a considerable number of the towers were built with fine Inka masonry (Hyslop 1977). For me, this is a most visible demonstration of the "Inkaization" of local lords.

Elsewhere in the Andes, communities or towns where local lords lived in Inka times have been identified. Within those settlements (which are often composed of houses built with local non-rectangular architecture) one finds a house or compound, that of the local lord (Morris and Thompson 1985: 138–143; Gonzalez 1981), built on a rectangular plan adopted from Inka architecture (Hyslop 1990: 244–249).

Examples of local elites adopting and using Inka objects come from a number of cemeteries where people were buried during Inka domination. Whereas the graves of each burial area must be considered individually and in their context, it would appear that some tombs with Inka artifacts contain local people of importance (Menzel 1977: 8–18), not Inkas themselves. In short, Inka cultural materials are found not only where Inkas traveled and worked, but also where local elites lived and were buried.

TIME AND THE INKA HORIZON

The length of time a region or site was occupied has left its influence on the kinds and amounts of Inka pottery found, and thus affects the nature of the Inka horizon. The abrupt termination of the Inka state in the 1530s also has left its mark on some of the horizon's architectural remains.

There is ceramic evidence of the very short duration (perhaps only two or three decades) of the Inka state on some of its expanding frontiers (Salomon 1986). In most regions of Tawantinsuyu there is a tendency for at least some pottery of the Inka period to demonstrate a combination of Inka and local traits. Such is not the case in the frontier area north of Quito where pottery in Inka sites is either Inka, or local, but rarely if ever combines traits of both in the same vessels (Antonio Fresco, personal communication, 1986). Apparently the contact and acculturation of local populations there with Inkas was too short lived to result in hybrid Inka-local pottery so common throughout much of the state. Catherine Julien (1983: 111–241) documents the development of this hybridization with artifacts from her stratigraphy at Hatunquolla.

At the military site Inkawasi (Fig. 8) in the middle Cañete Valley we have a relatively unique example of an Inka garrison (Hyslop 1985) that was used only a few years and then abandoned (according to early written sources). The short temporal occupation of this site appears to be an important element in defining the nature of its pottery, the overwhelming proportion of which is local and non-Inka. It appears that Inka pottery production was not a high priority at a briefly used military installation.

The rapid demise of the Inka state has also left its archaeological indicators. Some of the big administrative centers have buildings or sectors that are not complete (Fig. 9). Some of the burial towers with Inka stonework still have construction ramps leading to their incomplete roofs (Fig. 10). The European invasion in 1532 cut short the massive reordering of the Andes. Nevertheless, it is quite amazing that the Inkas accomplished so much so briefly and left an indelible imprint of architecture and artifacts over such a large area.

This raises the classic question of how it was all possible in such a short time. One necessary response is that the Inkas assigned great priority to

Fig. 9. The Incomplete Temple at Huanuco Pampa, Peru. This building of fine masonry was under construction at the time of the Spanish Conquest and never completed (photo: courtesy, Craig Morris)

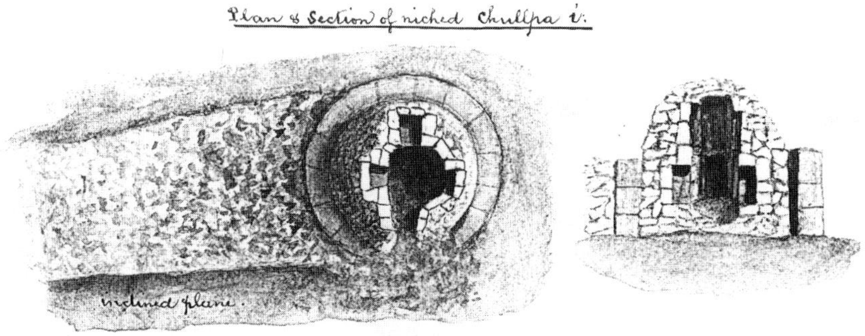

Fig. 10. A construction ramp leading to an unfinished burial tower or *chulpa* at Sillustani near Hatunqolla, Peru. Left: superior view; Right: lateral view. (drawing: A. Bandelier, courtesy, Anthropology Department, American Museum of Natural History, New York)

their monumental road system (Hyslop 1984), which bound together the Andes in such a way to make a state administrative, economic, and communication apparatus function over a very broad territory. In a more general sense, to understand the Inka horizon outside of the region of Cuzco, it is necessary to recognize that non-Inka populations did most of the work and that the role of the Inkas was one of ordering and management. The great public works—roads, cities, *tampu,* forts, and so forth—were created in great part with human and material resources that were traditionally non-Inka. In short, the Inka horizon must be viewed as the mobilization of pan-Andean resources, not just Inka ones from Cuzco. Also, the Inkas' success in reordering the Andes had a great deal to do with a profound understanding of traditional social orders, economic patterns, and religious practices. Where these, along with public works, could be utilized, they were often adapted to Inka needs, not ignorantly destroyed or ignored as was too often the case with their European successors. Much of the variation in the material remains of the Inka horizon is a reflection of that Inka adaptability.

In conclusion, the Inka state was probably overextended in its last years. Guarani peoples had overrun considerable segments of the eastern frontier. Military ventures south of Santiago had achieved little. Other military operations in northern Ecuador had succeeded with some territorial conquests but at tremendous cost to the state. Several years before the arrival of Pizarro, King Wayna Qhapaq decided to divide the empire. Although his decision was related to family and ethnic politics, I suspect it also reflected a knowledge that the state had achieved a size that was not easily managed by a central administration. It remains for us to wonder whether the Inka horizon was an aberration or evidence of a developing Andean capacity for unified rule.

BIBLIOGRAPHY

BEORCHIA NIGRIS, ANTONIO
    1987   *El enigma de los santuarios indígenas de alta montaña.* Centro de Investigaciones Arqueológicas de Alta Montaña, San Juan. *Revista del C.I.A.D.A.M.* 1985, 5. San Juan, Argentina.

D'ALTROY, TERENCE N., AND RONALD L. BISHOP
    1990   The Provincial Organization of Inka Ceramic Production. *American Antiquity* 55 (1): 120–137.

GONZÁLEZ, ALBERTO REX
    1981   La ciudad de Chicoana—Su importancia histórica y arqueológica. *Síntomas* 3: 15–21, Buenos Aires.

GONZÁLEZ, ALBERTO REX, AND ANTONIO CRAVOTTO
    1977   *Estudio arqueológico e inventario de las ruinas de Inkallajta.* UNESCO Informe Técnico PP/1975–76/3.411.6, Paris.

HYSLOP, JOHN
    1977   Chulpas of the Lupaca Zone of the Peruvian High Plateau. *Journal of Field Archaeology* 4: 149–170.
    1979   El área Lupaja Bajo el dominio Incaico—Un reconocimiento arqueológico. *Histórica* 3 (1): 53–79. Lima.
    1984   *The Inka Road System.* Academic Press, Orlando.
    1985   *Inkawasi—The New Cuzco,* BAR International Series 234. Oxford.
    1990   *Inka Settlement Planning,* University of Texas Press, Austin.
    n.d.   An Archaeological Investigation of the Lupaca Kingdom and Its Origins. Ph.D. dissertation, Anthropology Department, Columbia University, 1976.

IDROVO, JAIME
    n.d.   Prospection archeologique de la Vallée de Cuenca—Ecuador (Secteur sud; ou L'emplacement de la ville Inca de Tomebamba). Ph.D. dissertation, 2 vols. Université de Paris I, Panteon, Sorbonne, Paris, 1984.

JULIEN, CATHERINE J.
    1983   *Hatunqolla: A View of Inca Rule from the Lake Titicaca Region.* University of California Publications in Anthropology 15. Berkeley and Los Angeles.

KRAPOVIKAS, PEDRO
    1958–59   Un taller de lapidario en el Pucará de Tilcara. *Runa* 9 (1–2): 137–151. Buenos Aires.

LANGE, GUNARDO
    1896   Las ruinas de la fortaleza del Pucará. *Anales del Museo de la Plata,* Arqueología III. Universidad Nacional de La Plata, Argentina.

MASUDA, SHOZO, IZUMI SHIMADA, AND CRAIG MORRIS (EDS.)
    1985   *Andean Ecology and Civilization.* University of Tokyo Press, Japan.

John Hyslop

MENZEL, DOROTHY
1977   The Archaeology of Ancient Peru and the Work of Max Uhle. R. H. Lowie Museum of Anthropology, University of California, Berkeley.
MENZEL, DOROTHY, AND JOHN H. ROWE
1966   The Role of Chincha in Late Pre-Spanish Peru. Ñawpa Pacha 4: 63–76.
MORRIS, CRAIG, AND DONALD E. THOMPSON
1985   Huánuco Pampa—An Inka City and Its Hinterland. Thames and Hudson, London.
MORRIS, CRAIG
1982   The Infrastructure of Inka Control in the Peruvian Central Highlands. In The Inca and Aztec States, 1400–1800 (George A. Collier, Renato I. Rosaldo, and John D. Wirth, eds.): 153–171. Academic Press, New York.
1988   Más Allá de las Fronteras de Chincha. In La Frontera del Estado Inca (Tom D. Dillehay and Patricia Netherly, eds.) BAR International Series 442: 131–140. Oxford.
n.d.a   Architecture and the Structure of Space at Huanuco Pampa. Paper originally written in English in 1980. Courtesy of the author. In press in Spanish in Cuadernos del Instituto Nacional de Antropología, Buenos Aires.
n.d.b   Symbols to Power: Symbols and Media in the Inka State. In Style, Society and Power (Christopher Carr and Jill Neitzel, eds.). Cambridge University Press (in press).
MURRA, JOHN V.
1968   An Aymara Kingdom in 1567. Ethnohistory 15: 115–151.
1972   El "Control Vertical" de un máximo de pisos ecológicos en la economía de las sociedades andinas. In Visita de la Provincia de León de Huánuco en 1562 2 (John V. Murra, ed.): 429–476. Universidad Nacional Hermilio Valdizán, Huánuco, Perú.
1978   Los olleros del Inka: Hacia una historia y arqueología del Qollasuyu. In Historia, Problema, y Promesa: Homenaje a Jorge Basadre 1 (F. Miro Quesada C., F. Pease G. Y., and D. Sobrevilla A., eds.): 415–423. Pontificia Universidad Católica del Perú, Lima.
1980   The Economic Organization of the Inka State. JAI Press, Greenwich, Conn. [English version of 1955 Ph.D. dissertation].
1984   Andean Societies Before 1532. In The Cambridge History of Latin America I (Leslie Bethell, ed.): 59–90. Cambridge University Press, Cambridge.
NIEMEYER F., HANS, MIGUEL CERVELLINO G., AND EDUARDO MUÑOZ
1984   Viña del Cerro: Metalurgía Inka en Copiapó, Chile. Gaceta Arqueológica Andina 9: 6–7. Instituto Andino de Estudios Arqueológicos, Lima.
NORDENSKIÖLD, ERLAND VON
1924   Forschungen und Abenteuer in Südamerika. Stecker und Schroder Verlag, Stuttgart.
PLAZA SCHULER, FERNANDO
1976   La incursión Inca en el Septentrión Andino Ecuatoriano. Instituto Otavaleño de Antropología, Serie Arqueología 2. Otavalo.

RAFFINO, RUDOLFO A.
    1981   *Los Inkas del Kollasuyu,* 2nd ed. Ramos Americana Editora, La Plata.

REINHARD, JOHAN
    1983   Las montañas sagradas: Un estudio etnoarqueológico de ruinas en las altas cumbres andinas. *Cuadernos de Historia* 3: 27–62. Departamento de Ciencias Históricas, Universidad de Chile, Santiago.

RIVERA DORADO, MIGUEL
    1976   La cerámica Inca de Chinchero. In *Arqueología de Chinchero, 2— Cerámica y otros materiales* (José Alcina et al., eds.): 27–90. Ministerio de Asuntos Exteriores, Madrid.

ROWE, JOHN H.
    1946   Inka Culture at the Time of the Spanish Conquest. In *Handbook of South American Indians* 2 (Julian H. Steward, ed.): 183–330. Bureau of American Ethnology Bulletin 143. Smithsonian Institution, Washington, D.C.
    1948   The Kingdom of Chimor. *Acta Americana* 6: 26–59.
    1962   Stages and Periods in Archaeological Interpretation. *Southwestern Journal of Anthropology* 18: 40–54.

SALOMON, FRANK
    1986   Vertical Politics on the Inka Frontier. In *Anthropological History of Andean Polities* (John V. Murra, Nathan Wachtel, and Jacques Revel, eds.): 89–117. Cambridge University Press, Cambridge.

SCHOBINGER, JUAN
    1971   Arqueología del valle de Uspallata—Provincia de Mendoza. *Relaciones de la Sociedad Argentina de Antropología* n.s. 5: 71–84.

SCHOBINGER, JUAN (ED.)
    1966   *Anales de Arqueología y Etnología* (Volumen dedicado a la arqueología de alta montaña) 21. Universidad Nacional de Cuyo, Mendoza.

STRONG, WILLIAM D., AND JOHN M. CORBETT
    1943   A Ceramic Sequence at Pachacamac. In *Archaeological Studies in Peru— 1941–1942.* Columbia Studies in Archaeology and Ethnology 1: 27–124. Columbia University Press, New York.

TARRAGÓ, MYRIAM N.
    1978   Paleoecology of the Calchaquí Valley, Salta Province, Argentina. In *Advances in Andean Archaeology* (David L. Browman, ed.): 485–512. Mouton, La Haya.

UHLE, MAX
    1903   *Pachacamac: Report of the William Pepper, M.D., LL.D. Peruvian Expedition of 1896.* University of Pennsylvania, Philadelphia.
    1923   *Las ruinas de Tomebamba.* Imprenta Julio Sáenz Rebolledo, Quito.
    1924   *Explorations at Chincha.* University of California Publications in American Archaeology and Ethnology (A. L. Kroeber, ed.) 21 (2): 57–94. Berkeley.

John Hyslop

VISITACIÓN DE LOS PUEBLOS DE LOS CHUPACHU [1549]

    1967   In *Visita de la provincia de León de Huánuco en 1562* I (John V. Murra, ed.): 289–310. Documentos para la Historia y Etnología de Huánuco y la Selva Central, Universidad Nacional Hermilio Valdizán, Huánuco, Peru.

WILLEY, GORDON R., AND PHILIP PHILLIPS

    1958   *Method and Theory in American Archaeology.* University of Chicago Press, Chicago.

The Status of Latin American Horizons

DON STEPHEN RICE

SOUTHERN ILLINOIS UNIVERSITY AT CARBONDALE

THE CONTRIBUTORS TO THIS VOLUME have attempted to evaluate the content and utility of the "horizon" concept for archaeology and art history, for different regions and phases of Latin American prehistory, but they have approached this task from often divergent perspectives and with variable immediate goals. It would be very difficult, therefore, for anyone to review adequately more than a small portion of the range of methodological, substantive, and theoretical issues raised by these papers. Fortunately, however, some coherence and intelligibility are provided the volume by several themes that have occupied the authors' attention and recur from chapter to chapter. These are style, spatio-temporal relations, and cultural processes.

STYLE

One important methodological outcome of recent shifts in research emphasis and thinking in archaeology has been explicit debate on the nature of style and on the potential of stylistic studies for understanding human behavior (e.g., Conkey and Hastorf 1990). For many culture historians, the definition of style was intimately associated with the identification of types. Style was some residual formal characteristic by which one created artifact types, culture types, and evolutionary trajectories for use in historical inquiry.

Style is increasingly a basis for archaeological and art historical interpretation, however, and at various levels of cultural analysis. Style is now seen as having both functional and communicative roles that are context dependent. Style may be treated as formal variation that provides a measure of social processes: social interaction, social communication, social "marking," and social comparison. Style is also conceived of as a way of doing, a means by which humans make sense of their world and with which cultural meanings are always in production. In this latter sense, style is a way of knowing, visually rooted (Ong 1967, 1977), and it constitutes information about identity and boundaries (Wobst 1977).

The referent for style as communication can be the individual or the group, as can the level of social comparison or communication that it undertakes. Therefore, style can be studied at the level of the individual, group, or society, and at any of these levels, style can be functional or normative, active or passive, depending on context (Sackett 1977). A multivalent, multi-leveled view of style has obvious implications for the creation and interpretation of horizons. As Stephen Plog (1990) has indicated, as social systems evolve in complexity, so do the determinants of style, and with the realization that determinants of styles become more complex, stylistic studies break away from simplistic analyses involving one-to-one relations between style and chronology, culture, society, or history.

All of the authors' acknowledge a polythetic definition for their horizon styles, most agreeing in some way with Richard Schaedel's three classes of phenomena that can be diffused in any horizon—iconographic clusters, technologies, and systems (artifacts, technologies, and systemic relations). Richard Burger and Richard Diehl are careful to point out the distinction between art style and other archaeological evidence, however, noting that horizons like that of Chavin are marked not just by monumental arts, but by a suite of artifacts, attributes, and technological innovations. Although horizons in the abstract can be based on any phenomena, as Burger suggests, the majority of authors pay most attention to forms, decorative techniques, design motifs, and artifact types, particularly ceramics. Schaedel suggests that technology is a less explicit carrier of style, and perhaps for reasons of this sentiment there is generally less discussion of technological attributes.

Regardless of the materials or attributes that are brought to bear in the definition of horizon style, the authors' assumption of what Esther Pasztory calls a "materialistic" perspective on style dominates discussion. Styles are interpreted to recover cultural information on chronology, sources of origins, and interaction between social groups. Pasztory and others acknowledge that this materialistic view is not wrong, but incomplete, and most authors agree with Willey's earlier suggestion (1948, 1962) that the styles with which they are dealing carry ideological meanings. They do not, however, explore deeply the complex underpinnings of a maker's production or use of style, the degree of passive or active function, or the multiple levels of reference that are embedded in stylistic behavior. Most, in fact, express rather rigid ideas about the relationship of society to a style. That is, they tend to interpret style as active communication about ethnic geography and identity between groups, with style manipulated by the users for particular gains or ends.

TIME AND SPACE

The hallmark of horizons is the rather rapid and uniform distribution of stylistic traits over a broad area, and much functional interpretation of horizons is based on knowing the centers of origin for those attributes and their direction and rate of spread. Every author in this volume acknowledges greater diversity than uniformity in their horizons, with considerable geographic and temporal variability in the distribution of their defining characteristics. Such variability causes Burger to ponder the question, for example: "Is Chavin an illusion produced by conflating styles of different ages and origins?"

With improved absolute dating and more data, most horizons have been subdivided so that they can be seen as composed of transitions, rather than coherent systems. There are, for example, two such Olmec horizons and four Andean Middle Horizon divisions, and the Aztec horizon includes pre-imperial, imperial, and even post-imperial products. For some authors, heretofore "pure" horizon elements are now found to have existed well prior to (or after) their period of coalescence in a horizon construction. In some horizons, there were in fact multiple origins for products being brought together within the horizonal context, with different sources and modes of distribution.

What Arthur Demarest refers to as this "disturbing lack of chronological alignment" is exacerbated by the longevity of local traditions in many areas and the tendency of some groups to curate, reinterpret, reuse, and/or reintroduce older forms or styles. David Grove also notes the vexing problem that the diacritics of horizon styles—in the Olmec case pottery motifs and figurines—are easily borrowed and rapidly diffused symbols, which makes discussion of origins and rates of change difficult.

Another important conclusion of the papers is that horizonal phenomena do not necessarily occupy unbroken contiguous space. Emily Umberger and Cecelia Klein also make the point that different attributes respond to different processes and are not necessary coincident; there is not necessarily a co-occurrence of all defining attributes or materials at any given point. These disjunctions may be attributable, in part, to what George Kubler referred to as the fast and slow time of centers and peripheries, but John Hyslop and Umberger and Klein discuss some of the cultural processes that can bring about spatial variability including rearrangements of production by centralized authorities, differential stratification and population levels, variable symbolic value of manufactures, and differential levels of territorial control or imposition of one polity over others.

True to center-periphery distinctions that have long been implicit in horizonal definitions, there is a tendency for the complete assemblage of defining traits or materials to be found in centers of population and authority. It is important to note, however, that many distinguishing characteristics of horizons do not completely coincide in distribution with the boundaries of the social or political unit assumed to have been responsible for disseminating those features.

Discussions of the processes by which horizonal traits spread are invariably informed by notions of style and the diffusion of style, ethnographic or historical analogies (particularly to the known imperial Aztec and Inka), and/or processual considerations built into theoretical formulations on the origins and development of complex societies. The papers in this volume are no exception.

Every author acknowledges style as carrying information and equates the spread of style with the spread of some kind of ideology. Burger discusses the Chavin phenomenon as an expansive religious movement, regional cult, or revitalization movement. The vehicle of introduction is the establishment of branch oracles from a cult center, with kinship relations maintained between the branch and the center. The resulting arrangement is a religious archipelago of sorts, which in part explains the diversity of the Early Horizon and its distribution. Local ceramic production in Janabarriu style is a symbolic statement of a broadened social identity stimulated by shared religious ideology and associated with participation in a broadened network of economic activities that are presumably facilitated by the center-branch relationships.

Grove also sees the Olmec motif and figurine complex as a shared belief system, wherein motifs are associated with supernaturals, bloodletting rituals, and, through bloodletting ritual, rulership. Rulers are associated with supernaturals as nurturers of supernaturals, and the shared symbols serve as verification of rulership through display of power. Similarly, Demarest notes that ideological symbols legitimate the power of Maya kings in their roles as mediators of a cosmogram that involves solar elements and ancestor worship. Such symbols reinforce status and define internal social divisions.

Pasztory decries previous interpretations of Teotihuacan artifact distributions as manifestations of state-sponsored commerce and empire, a reconstruction that plays heavily on interpretations of the later Aztec, and suggests that trade exists between elites rather than as the product of a trading empire. She sees no singular power nor dominant art style from one center during the period. Rather, independent ethnic regions are in constant intensive contact through trade, gift exchange, dynastic alliance, war, religion, calendar, and ideology, creating Demarest's lattices of interaction.

In the Mesoamerican Middle Horizon, regions supposedly did their best to advertise their separateness and independence through their works of public art. Pasztory makes the point that concern for maintenance of boundaries and separation is relevant only in situations of considerable contact and cosmopolitanism, and she hypothesizes that during this period foreign art styles were symbols of the totality of the Mesoamerican world, and symbols of conquest, rather than "influence." Stylistic differences at places like Teotihuacan, then, were a major value, a value that would oppose the spread of a dominant art style or the establishment of a horizon.

While Alan Kolata acknowledges the ideological power and the social marking and comparison functions of styles, he relates the development of cultural horizons specifically to the political economy of states. For him, horizons result from shared participation in a single economic system. He proposes a model for the Andean Middle Horizon which sees Tiwanaku as the armature for an extensive network of producers, consumers, managers, and economic intermediaries, distributed over a relatively broad geographic area, with centralized control of production and a hierarchical set of administrative and productive settlements. The spread of style is related to the economic complementarity of this pluralistic and multi-ethnic empire, through caravans and clientage relationships between elites, who consume badges and symbols of patrons.

Although Schaedel disagrees with Kolata on the dynamics of Middle Horizon relations between Huari and Tiwanaku, he does agree that interregional hegemonies were responsible for major socioeconomic changes, ultimately reflected in material culture and iconography. His question is whether such hegemony should be defined traditionally as the state, or whether religious hegemony should be introduced. Ultimately, he opts for a systemic interpretation that focuses on economic factors, citing Willey's comment that the Middle Horizon "was a social, political, and religious turning point rather than a technological one . . . economic effects were probably the major ones . . . at this time state control of the distribution of foodstuffs on a territorial scale came into being" (1971: 64, cited in Schaedel, this volume).

Diehl's defense of the existence of a Toltec horizon lies in the broad distribution of locally produced household ritual items, which he feels indicate widespread ideas and beliefs. The religious bases for the diffusion of these ideas are not known, although he suggests the possibility of new cults or rituals, and Tula cannot be confirmed as a center for the ideas. Each class of object appears to have originated in a different part of Mesoamerica, and Diehl surmises that Toltec merchants are the most likely agents of diffusion, a model perhaps informed by long-standing notions of the behavior of Aztec *pochteca*. If this be the case, then Tula's commercial networks extended far beyond the political boundaries of a Toltec state.

Neither Hyslop, nor Umberger and Klein, spends much time discussing processual interpretations of the two Late Horizons, Aztec and Inka, because these systems are well-documented as militaristic empires. One of the important processual points made in each of these papers, however, is that the details of the written documents and the details of the material cultural record do not necessarily coincide. Likewise, it is not possible to equate empire and horizon. As Umberger and Klein point out, nuclear models, even when fully documented, do not always explain the complexity of interactions that contribute to the archaeological record.

In the case of the Aztec, the archaeological record does not suggest political domination by an external power, but we know this to be the case. The disjunction could, in part, be the result of disadvantaged preservation of the record or perhaps due to a relative lack of research. It is also likely, however, that Aztec modes of statecraft—alteration of political hierarchies and economic networks, strategic marriages and political alliances, suppression of dissidents and cooption of principal elites—did not find their way into materials. Unlike the Inka, the Aztec exercised little direct territorial control after conquest. Umberger and Klein suggest that religious and cultural imposition may have been limited to central provinces. They also point out that categories of objects distributed within the Aztec empire, prestige and ritual paraphernalia, were often perishable, but more importantly they were absorbed into the center rather than disseminated out.

The failure of the archaeological record to confirm completely the historically known facts of Aztec or Inka imperialism should give pause when the known ethnohistoric record is used as a basis for discussion of the cultural processes contributing to the distribution of horizon styles.

THE FUTURE OF LATIN AMERICAN HORIZONS

While Burger, Diehl, Kolata, and Hyslop find some justification for discussion of horizons, almost all authors believe that the concept has outlived its usefulness. Most agree with Burger that the concept of horizon style is out of step with processual archaeology and undermined by competing chronological methods. In particular, radiocarbon dating makes the horizon redundant and outmoded as a temporal index. Grove, Schaedel, and others also repeat Rowe's lament that the horizon confuses style and time with culture and the creation, evolution, and sharing of motifs with far different processes of evolution of the archaeological cultures that shared the symbol systems.

Pasztory points out that the horizon concept may have been useful when a certain quantity of material needed organizing, but once there is more complex and contradictory material available, it is too simple. She notes the difficulty of applying the horizon concept to situations where the makers' intended use of style is to emphasize regional uniqueness. For Pasztory the concept of horizon style does not help explain the nature of Mesoamerican art and style.

Demarest and others criticize the horizon concept as inappropriate to define processes of movement of elite subcomplexes between regional groups, given that such movement is traditionally conceptualized as a broad spread of ceramic or art style from a single center through rapid diffusion. As Demarest reiterates, *horizon* is not a neutral term; it imposes a structure that artificially forces consideration of "influence from particular centers and leads away from understanding of interrelated co-evolution to simplistic and dramatic forms of explanation."

In sum, the authors acknowledge the contributions of the horizon concept in the early history of archaeological studies in Latin America, as well as the legitimacy of chronological questions it was meant to solve. Chronology remains an issue in archaeology, but now on levels more specific than can be handled within the horizon structure. As many authors have implied, with the advent of radiocarbon dating, the vague processual attributes of horizons increasingly became the subject matter of study and speculation. These too are legitimate issues, but their resolution is not served well by the horizon concept.

All classification schemes have some utility to their makers, and there is always need for clear, distinct, and separate "periods," to teach students and to organize thoughts. As Rowe has long advocated, however, when it comes to chronological issues, these periods must be neutral in their cultural content As Umberger and Klein suggest, the horizon may have utility as a provisional analytical tool, to motivate and refine research, but it should no longer be indulged blindly as an organizing fixture of Latin American chronology.

Don Stephen Rice

BIBLIOGRAPHY

CONKEY, MARGARET W., AND CHRISTINE HASTORF (EDS.)

1990 *The Uses of Style in Archaeology*. Cambridge University Press, Cambridge.

ONG, WALTER J.

1967 *The Presence of the Word*. Yale University Press, New Haven.

1977 *Interfaces of the Word*. Cornell University Press, Ithaca.

PLOG, STEPHEN E.

1990 Sociopolitical Implications of Stylistic Variation in the American Southwest. In the *Uses of Style in Archaeology* (C. Hastorf and M. Conkey, eds.): 61–72. Cambridge University Press, Cambridge.

SACKETT, JAMES R.

1977 The Meaning of Style in Archaeology: A General Model. *American Antiquity* 32: 369–380.

WILLEY, GORDON R.

1948 A Functional Analysis of "Horizon Styles" in Peruvian Archaeology. In *A Reappraisal of Peruvian Archaeology* (W. C. Bennett, ed.). *Memoir* 4: 8–15. Society for American Archaeology, Menasha, Wisc.

1962 The Early Great Styles and the Rise of the Pre-Columbian Civilizations. *American Anthropologist* 64: 1–14.

1971 *An Introduction to American Archaeology. Volume II: South America*. Prentice-Hall, Englewood Cliffs, N.J.

WOBST, H. MARTIN

1977 Stylistic Behavior and Information Exchange. In *For the Director. Research Essays in Honor of James B. Griffin* (C. E. Cleland, ed.). University of Michigan Anthropological Papers: 317–342, Ann Arbor.

Index

An "f" following a page number indicates a figure.

Abaj Takalik, 100n
  sculpture, 148
Acacingo, 318, 319
Ahuitzotl, 303, 304
Alahuitzlan, 299
Altun Ha, 155
  green obsidian at, 163–164
Ancon, 42, 69, 250
Argentina, Inka empire in, 342–343,
  344f, 348
Arroyo Pesquero, 101n
Atalla, 60
Ayacucho, 62, 74, 200
Aymara kingdoms, 204
Azapa Valley, 202, 210, 213, 218
Azcapotzalco, 295, 318
Azoyu, Colonial painted manuscript
  from, 315
Aztec, 113–114, 117, 135, 139, 361–
  362. See also Mexica
  architecture: double temples, 307–
  309; general influence on Mesoamerica, 305–307; round temples,
  309–310, 311f; structures built by
  Aztecs, 302–305
  ceramics, 295, 298–302, 325
  Flowery Wars, 138
  horizon, 296–297
  mythology, solar fire serpent deity in,
  168
  painted murals and manuscripts, 312–
  316
  pochteca, 116
  relations with Maya, 301
  stone sculpture of, 316–324
  Triple Alliance, 295, 296, 303, 308

Balankanche cave, 276–277
Balberta, 151, 153, 154, 163, 164
Ballgame, Mesoamerican, 138
  ballcourts, Chichen Itza, 276
Balsas Valley, 299
Barbacoa, 44, 59
Batan Grande, 243
Bazan slab, 121–122, 122f, 129, 137
Becan, cache, 132, 132f, 133, 159–160
  Teotihuacan contact with, 155, 160;
  green obsidian, 163

Caballo Muerto, 59n, 60
Cacao, 151, 153, 162
Cacaxtla, 130, 134, 172, 173
Cahuachi, kero from, 234, 235f, 239
Cahyup, 308
Caiman. See Cayman motif
Cajabamba, 42
Cajamarca, 48, 55, 67
Calchaqui Valley, Inka in, 343
Callango, textiles from, 57
Callejon de Huaylas, 66, 71n, 252
Canta, 42
Cardal, 62, 68
Casma Valley, 49, 60, 67, 68, 69, 234,
  236, 251
Castillo de Teayo, 300, 302, 304, 305f,
  307, 312, 320, 321f, 322, 323
Catamarca, 348
Cawinal, 309
Cayalti, 73
Cayman motif
  Chavin, 57–58
  Olmec, 89f, 91, 92, 98

Cempoala, 300, 303, 309n, 310, 312, 313
Cerro Baul, 212
Cerro Blanco, 60
Cerro Cañocillo, 230
Cerro Corbacho, 72
Cerro Naranjo, pictograph, 315
Cerro Sechin, 54
Cerros, 151, 152, 153
Chaksinkin, 149
Chalcatzingo, 93, 95, 99n, 100–102
 monumental art, 100, 135
Chalchiuhtlicue, 318
Chalchuapa, 100n
 Olmecoid sculpture at, 148
Chancay, 242, 250
Chan Chan, 243
Chankillo, 240
 mural, 236, 237f
Chavin. *See also* Chavin de Huantar
 architectural characteristics, 54, 63. *See also* Chavin de Huantar: New Temple; Chavin de Huantar: Old Temple
 art style, 8
 ceramics, 42, 56f, 60–62, 61f, 67
 horizon (horizon style), 4, 6, 18, 27, 29, 41–74; history of, 41–47; presence on South Coast of Peru, 57, 60. *See also* Early Horizon
 preservation of artifacts, 57
 -related sites, 42
 spread of religious ideology, 63, 65, 68–69, 70, 360
Chavin de Huantar, 41–47
 ceramic sequence, 49
 dating, 49
 excavations at, 59
 New Temple, 55, 59, 70
 Old Temple, 54, 55, 60
 sculptural style and iconography, 47, 48, 51, 52f, 55, 56f, 60
Chen Chen, 212
Chiapas, 99, 100n, 102, 103, 301, 315
Chicama Valley, 42, 44, 59, 60, 230, 234
Chichen Itza, 265, 271, 288, 306
 chronology, 275, 276–277
 relations with Tula, 271, 273f, 274–275, 286; direction of influence, 278–279
 role of Putun at, 277–278

Chiclayo, 48
Chile, Inka empire in, 342–343, 345, 348
Chilecito (Tamberia del Inca), 344f
Chimu/Chimor, 45, 229, 242–244
Chimucapac, textiles, 230
Chincha, textiles, 57
 Valley, 344
Chinchero, Inka pottery at, 340f
Chiripa, 212
Cholula, 118, 299
Chongoyape, 42, 59, 62
 gold, 72, 72f
Chornancap, friezes, 251
Chotuna, reliefs, 236
Chronological charts, 2, 20–31
 Central Andes, 21f, 22f, 23f, 24f
 Central Mexico, 96
Chupaychu, 341
Cipactonal, 312n
Climate change, in Peru, 69–70
Coatetelco, 298, 320
Coatlan, 298, 318
Coatlinchan, 318
Cochabamba, 202, 210, 213, 218
Coixtlahuaca, 299, 302
Copacabana, 233
Copan, 96
 Middle Formative cemetery at, 149
 Teotihuacan influence at, 156
Cortés, Hernán, 315
Costa Rica, Aztec contact with, 301
Cotaxtla, 322
Courtyards, sunken, 54
Cozcatlan, 300
 Aztec-style sculpture, 322, 323f
Cuauhnahuac, 308
Cuauhtinchan, 299
Cuenca (Tomebamba), 341, 344, 346
Cuernavaca, 298, 303, 318, 319, 320
Cuetlaxtlan, 300, 315
Cupisnique, 44, 45, 59
 Tradition, 66
Curayacu, 62, 69
Cuzco, 339, 346, 349, 352
 potters of, 341–342

Danzantes, 135, 136f, 138
Dzibilchaltun
 double temple at, 309
 Teotihuacan influence at, 117, 155; ar-

chitecture, 164; green obsidian at, 163

Eagle motif, 51, 52f, 56f, 57, 58f, 59
Early Horizon, 7, 46, 47, 54n, 55, 59, 226
  in Mesoamerica, 88, 147–148, 174, 175
  on Peruvian North Coast, 67, 69. *See also* individual sites and valleys
  on Peruvian South Coast, 57, 69, 74
  religious iconography of, 60
  state development in, 74
  and trade, 69, 73–74
Early Postclassic horizon, artifactual indicators of, 279–286. *See also* Toltec(s), horizon
Edzna, 151, 152
El Baul, Herrera stela, 135, 136f
El Chile, 309
El Mirador, 152, 153
  dates of architecture, 152
El Niño event, 69
El Purgatorio, 240, 251
  mural, 236
Escuintla, 153, 154, 161, 167, 170, 171
  "hoards," 160, 161

Feline motifs. *See also* Jaguar motif, Chavin-related; Puma (chachapuma) motif; Were-jaguar motif
  Chavin, 42, 48
  Middle Horizon, 232–234
  Ocucaje, 57
  Preceramic, 51
Finca Toliman, 160
Fine Orange pottery, 270–271, 272f, 279, 286, 287, 288
  distribution, 273f

Garagay, 52, 53f, 54, 55
Gold
  Aztec, 324–325
  Chavin, 59, 70, 71, 72, 73
  Chongoyape, 72f
  Inka, 346f
Greenstone, 87, 95, 96–97, 99, 102, 135, 325
  exchange, 101
  use by elites, 103

Guerrero, 87, 90, 93, 100–101
  in Aztec times, 297, 325; and Aztec ceramics, 299, 301, 302
  Colonial painted manuscript from, 315
  sculpture of, 323–324n
  wheeled animal effigy figurines from, 281–282
Gulf Coast Olmec. *See* Olmec: Gulf Coast

Haldas, 68
Hatunqolla, 350, 352f
Hidalgo (Mexico), 114, 297, 315
Holmul, green obsidian at, 163–164
Horizon concept
  definition of, 1, 2, 15–16, 265, 337n; art historical vs. archaeological views of, 31–32; and spatial dimension, 1, 2, 16, 359; and time dimension, 1, 2, 4, 7, 8, 9, 16, 20–31, 41, 46, 359, 362, 363; through ceramic styles, 6, 9, 18
  history of, 3–9, 16–20, 102, 225, 337n
  use in Andes, 4–5, 19, 41. *See also* individual cultures and named horizons
  use in Mesoamerica, 18, 88, 116–117, 134, 139, 173, 176, 295. *See also* individual cultures and named horizons
Horizon marker, 2, 102, 103, 264
  for Chavin, 48
Horizon style, 1–2, 4, 7, 8, 15–16, 134, 139, 245, 264, 358, 362. *See also* Style, art
  attitudes toward, in North American archaeology, 41
  European parallels, 126
Horizons, interpretation. *See also* individual cultures and named horizons
  of creation and spread, 32–33, 285
  as distinct from tradition, 2, 4
  as (interregional) interaction, 33, 173–174, 176, 226; in relation to diffusion, 32–33, 173–174, 225, 245–247
  problems in, 103, 117, 173, 288, 362–363
  in relation to political economy, 203
  in relation to polity, 33, 247–248
  as revivals, 34–35

Huaca de los Chinos, 60
Huaca Cholope, 59
Huaca Dragon, 251
  mural, 235, 243
Huaca Guavalito, 59n, 60
Huaca Herederos Chica, 59n, 60
Huaca Lucia, 59
Huaca Prieta, textiles, 51, 52f
Huaca de los Reyes, 54, 59
Huaca del Sol, 230, 251
  kero, 234, 235f, 239
Huacachula, 318, 320
Huacaloma, 55
Huadca, mural, 236, 237f
Hualgayoc, 48
Huamachuco, 230
Huancavelica, 60, 73, 74
Huanuco, 51
Huanuco Pampa, 63, 341, 351f
Huari. *See also* Wari
  on Central Coast, 242, 243, 249
  on North Coast, 243, 244, 249, 251–
    252; corridors of diffusion, 230–
    231, 234. *See also* individual sites
    and valleys
  on South Coast, 242
  stone sculpture, 234
  styles, 242
Huaricoto, 65
Huarochiri, 42
Huaura, 51
Huascar. *See* Waskar
Huasteca, 268
Huatusco, 300, 301, 302, 304, 305f,
  312, 322
Huaxtepec, 318, 319
Huayna Capac. *See* Wayna Qhapaq
Huexotla, 310
Huexotzinco, 320
Huichapan, Colonial painted manu-
  script from, 315
Huitzilopochtli, 320
Humahuaca Valley, Inka in, 343

Ica Valley
  Chavin influence in, 54n, 59n; in tex-
    tiles from, 58, 66
  chronology, 7, 8, 19, 337n
  Huari-Tiahuanaco influence in, 228,
    242
Imbabura, 348

Inca. *See also* Inka
  conquest by, 45
  horizon, 4, 6, 17, 29; compared to
    Chavin, 63
Indigo dye, 35
Initial Period, 47, 51
  architecture, 53
  ceramic styles, 62
  conservatism of, 68
  decline, 68, 69
  transition to Early Horizon, 69, 74
Inka, 337–352. *See also* Inca;
    Tawantinsuyu
  architecture, 339–341, 346, 347; unfin-
    ished, 351–352
  ceramics, 339, 340f, 342, 346, 347
  horizon, 350, 352. *See also* Late Hori-
    zon: in Peru
  warfare, 348
Inkawasi, garrison, 349f, 351
Iximche, murals, 314, 315
Ixtapaluco Viejo, 310
Ixtepeque obsidian, 163
Izapa, 94
  art, 135

Jade, Olmec. *See* Greenstone
  cache in Peten, 149
Jaguar motif, Chavin-related, 57, 58f
Jargan Pata de Huamanga, 62
Jequetepeque Valley, 55, 59, 72, 230,
  234, 240, 251
Juxtlahuaca, 100n

Kalasasaya, 197f, 201f
Kaminaljuyu
  Olmecoid sculpture at, 148
  Teotihuacan influence at, 114, 116,
    117, 118
Karwa, textiles, 57, 58f, 59, 63, 65f, 73
Katun celebration, 155
Khonko Wankane, 207, 209, 210
Kotosh, 55
  Tradition, 65
Kroeber, Alfred
  and chronological charts, 20, 21f,
    26–27
  definition of horizon styles, 17; in
    Peru, 4
  evaluation of Julio Tello, 44
  on Tiahuanaco, 195

Kubler, George
chronological chart for Andes, 24f,
29–30
on style-based periodization, 9, 19–20
Kukulkan. *See* Quetzalcoatl
Kuntur Wasi, 48, 55, 66, 69, 72, 73, 74
gold, 73f

La Galgada
cache, 53
textiles, 51, 52f, 53
Lake Amatitlan, 161, 167
Lake Texcoco, 297
Lake Titicaca, 345f
agricultural systems in basin of, 206,
213
during Inka times; burial patterns
around, 350; pottery around, 341,
342f; wealth, 344
settlement distribution around, 196f,
202f, 204, 210, 217–218
Lamanai, 151, 152, 153
Lambayeque, 42, 59
Early Horizon at, 59
Chavin style at, 60
Middle Horizon at, 229, 230, 250
Larco Hoyle, Rafael, 44–45, 59, 227
La Venta, 84, 85, 86, 87, 94, 96–97, 98,
99, 100, 101, 102, 103, 138
Las Bocas, 90
Las Limas, 102n
Las Pilas, 135
Late Horizon
in Mesoamerica, 295, 296
in Peru, 7, 337n; on North Coast,
339. *See also* Inka: horizon
Lathrap, Donald, on Chavin horizon,
47
Leche Valley, 230, 243
Limatambo, Inka masonry at, 347f
Llamas
caravans, 206, 214–215; routes, 202f
consumption of, in Early Horizon,
69, 71
Locona horizon, 84n
Loreto Viejo, 212
Los Tuxtlas, 102n
Lukurmata, 207–209
Lumbreras, Luis, on Formative, 46
Lurin Valley, 62, 68, 242, 340

Malinalco, 298, 302, 303, 307, 310
mural painting at, 313, 314f
sculpture at, 318, 319
Mantaro Valley, 341
Matacapan, relation with Teotihuacan,
116, 117–118, 164–165, 170
Maya
architectural profile, 128
calendrical correlations, 286
dynastic ideology of, 153
Late Formative monumental architecture, 152
relation to Teotihuacan, 113–118,
151–172; in architecture, 164–166;
in art style, 123–124, 130, 132,
133, 135, 137; in iconography, 167–
170; Maya ceramics at
Teotihuacan, 162, 172; in state formation, 151–154
sacrificial complex, 167
state formation, 152, 154, 172
warfare cults, 168–169, 170,
176
Mayapan, 309
Mexica, 130, 133, 134, 295n
art, 35
Mezcala, 299
Middendorf, Ernst, 41–42
Middle Horizon
in Andes, 7, 22, 25, 205, 225–253,
361; cranial deformation, 239; engineering techniques, 240; iconographic clusters, 228, 229, 241,
242–243, 250, 251; mortuary patterns, 239; pottery, 236–237; stone
sculpture, 231–232; textiles, 238;
wood sculpture, 234, 235f, 239.
See also Huari
in Mesoamerica, 154, 155, 173, 175,
360–361
Mitla, 313
Mixco Viejo, 308, 309
Mixtec, manuscripts, 316
Mixteca Alta, 299, 301, 324
Mixteca-Puebla style, 264, 265–268,
301
ceramics, 296, 297, 315
on painted manuscripts, 313
reliefs, 316
Mixtequilla, 300
Mocachi, 210

Moche/Mochica, 27, 28, 45, 48, 240,
    242
  burial patterns, 239
  Valley, 60, 195, 230, 234
Mocupe friezes, 251
Mokan, 60
Monte Alban, 121, 122, 135, 138, 299
Moquegua Valley, 202, 210–214, 218
  Tiwanaku ceramics in, 212
Morelos, 90, 93, 100, 132, 297
  in Aztec times, 298, 299, 325
  green obsidian from, 163
  sculpture in, 318, 329
Morro de Eten, 59
Morropon, 48
Motecuhzoma, 299, 303, 315, 319
Moxeke, 49, 50, 51, 54
  sculpture, 50f, 51
Mural painting. *See also* individual sites
  Aztec, 312–316
  on public architecture in Peru, 55,
    235–236
  in Teotihuacan, 123–124, 123f

Nahuatl, language distribution, 114
Nakbe, 152
Natural disasters, in Peru, 69
Nayarit, 268, 301
Nepeña Valley, 51, 234
Nicaragua, Aztec contact with, 301
Nochixtlan, 299
Nohmul, 151, 152

Oaxaca, 91–92, 93, 172, 265
  architectural profile, 128
  in Aztec times, 297, 299, 301, 313,
    323–324n
Obsidian, 73
  green, 162–164, 287
  Orizaba mine, Aztec pottery at, 300
  at Teotihuacan, 116, 117, 118
Oceloapan, round structure at, 310
Olmec
  art style, 8, 84, 86
    architecture, public, 99
    of figurines, 89, 92, 95, 96, 98;
      baby-face figurines, 89, 95, 96
    of monumental art, 92, 95, 100,
      135; mutilation of, 94–95, 99,
      100
    motifs of, 89f, 90, 91–92, 95, 96,

      98, 99f; association with agricul-
      tural societies, 91, 102; elite asso-
      ciations, 98–99, 148; represent-
      ing lineage ancestors, 91–92
    on pottery, 90, 94, 95, 96, 98, 99,
      102; in Peten, 149, 150f
  culture, 84–86
  Gulf Coast, 83, 84, 85–86, 90–93, 94,
    100, 101, 103, 147, 175
  horizon, 83–103, 173; history of,
    86–87
  rulers, 93, 360
Omo, 212
Oxmoco, 312
Oxtotitlan, 100n
Oztuma, 299, 302, 304, 312

Pacatnamu, textiles, 230
Pachacamac, 41, 195, 230, 234, 236,
    242, 250, 344
  cult of, 63–65
Pacopampa, 51, 55, 65, 74
Padre Piedra, 100n
Pajaten, 236
Pajchiri, 207, 208–209
Palenque (Mexico), 129–130
Palenque (Peru), 44, 59
Pallasca, 231, 232f
Pallka, 60, 67, 69
Pampa de los Llamas, 49
Pampa Grande, 242
Pampa Koani, 207, 209, 212–213
Pampa Rosario, 67
Panama, Aztec contact with, 301
Pañamarca, *kero,* 239
Papantla, 321f
Paracas. *See also* Karwa
  Chavin style at, 60
  gourds, 57
  pottery, 42
Pashash, 232
Pichincha, 348
Piedras Negras, stela 12, 130–131f
Pijijiapan, 100n
Pipil, language distribution, 114, 115f
Piura, 48
  distribution of ceramic styles in, 231f
Plumbate pottery, 268, 269f, 270, 279,
    286, 287, 288
Pojoc, 71
Pomona, 130

Preceramic Period
  Cotton, 47
  Late, 51
Puebla, 90, 163, 265, 285
  in Aztec times, 297; sculpture in, 318, 320
Puente Yayes, 210
Pukara, 198, 200, 212, 217
Puma (chacha-puma) motif, 232, 233
Punkuri, 51
Puno, 210
Putun, 274, 277–278, 314
Puuc, 172
  architectural style, 275, 276

Quebrada Humahuaca, 214, 215
Quetzalcoatl, 274, 318, 321
Quiahuistlan, 300
Quiruvilca, 67
Quito, 341, 342, 350

Raimondi stone, 65
Raptorial bird motifs, 51. *See also* Eagle motif
Recuay, 71n, 234, 249
Regional cults, 63–64
  spread, 70
Rio Azul, 155, 159
Rio Seco, 160
Rio Zahuapan, 299
Rouse, Irving, on horizon styles, 19
Rowe, John
  on chronological implications of horizons, 5, 6–8, 19, 25, 46
  on Early Horizon, 46, 225–226

Samaca, 66
San Cristobal Ecatepec, cave, 312n
San Diego, 67
San Jose Mogote, 91–92, 93, 96
San Lorenzo Tenochtitlan, 84, 85, 87, 94, 96
San Miguel Amuco, 100n
San Pedro de Atacama oasis, 202, 214, 215
  textiles from, 215
Santa Cecelia Acatitlan, 307
Santa Maria Valley, Inka in, 343
Santa Rita, 265
  murals, 313, 314
Santa Valley, 234, 251

Sechin Bajo, 68
Seibal, jade cache from, 149
Shillacoto, 51
Sican, 229, 230, 240, 243, 244
Snake motifs
  Chavin, 51, 52f, 57, 58f
  in Mesoamerica: Olmec fire serpent, 89f, 91, 98; Teotihuacan fire serpent, 168–169; war serpent, 168
Soconusco, 132, 270
  in Aztec times, 297, 301
Solano, 151, 163, 164
"Staff god" motif, 57, 58f, 65, 200
Stages, historical-developmental, 6
Style, art, 357–358
  ideological meaning of, 120–121, 139
  juxtapositions, meaning of, 121–129, 130, 139
Supe, 42, 48, 250

Tabasco, 84
Tamazulapan, 299
Taukachi-Konkan, 68
Tawantinsuyu, 338f, 339, 341, 347. *See also* Inka
  economic complementarity in, 348
  southern extremes of, 342–343
Tazumal, 164, 306
Tecaxic-Calixtlahuaca, 298, 302, 303, 310, 311f, 318, 319
Tehuacan, 300, 322, 323
Tehuantepec, Isthmus of, 163, 301
Tello, Julio C.
  excavations at Moxeke, 49, 50f
  on spread of Chavin, 42, 43f, 44–45
Teloloapan, 299
Tenancingo, 319
Tenayuca, 307, 308, 312n, 318
Tenochtitlan, 130, 132, 138, 295, 303, 324–325
  architecture, 307, 308, 309, 310
  murals, 312n
  sculpture, 316, 317f, 318, 322n
Teopantecuanitlan, 93, 99n, 100–102
  monumental art, 100, 101
Teopanzalco, 303, 306, 308
Teotenango, 298, 319
Teotihuacan, 113–140, 151–172, 274, 285–286, 360, 361
  art and iconography of, 117, 122–123, 130, 134–135, 166–170

ceramics of, 118, 119f, 133f, 156f,
285; in Maya area, 155–162
history of archaeological research at,
113–117
Merchant's Barrio, 162
relation to Maya. *See* Maya: relation
to Teotihuacan
role of obsidian. *See* Obsidian: at
Teotihuacan
talud-tablero architecture, 128, 151,
164–166, 165f, 285
warrior cults, 169, 170, 175
Teotitlan, 322
Tepeaca, 320
Tepecoacuilco, 299
Tepexi el Viejo, 299
Tepotzlan, 302, 303, 307, 318, 319
Tetetla, 299
Tetitla, 123–124, 124f
Texcoco, 307
Textiles, Andean. *See also* individual
sites
Initial Period, 49
Late Preceramic Period, 51
Middle Horizon, 229–230, 238
technology, 35, 238
Tiahuanaco. *See also* Middle Horizon;
Tiwanaku
chacha-pumas, 232–233
horizon (style), 4, 6, 17, 248
relation to Huari, 227–228, 241, 248–
249, 361
stone sculpture, 232–234
Tikal, 116, 118, 155
ceramics, 168
iconography (Lintel 2), 169, 170, 173
Mundo Perdido complex, 151, 152,
158, 166
relation to Teotihuacan, 151, 155,
158, 170–171; architecture, 164–
166; green obsidian, 163, 164
relief from Central Acropolis, 130,
131f, 133
Stela 31, 118, 120f, 121–122, 155, 167
Tinyash, 236
Titicaca, Lake. *See* Lake Titicaca
Tiwanaku, 193–218, 361. *See also*
Tiahuanaco
Bennett monolith, 198f
ceramics, 195

colonization, 202, 206
habitation area of, 207, 209f
horizon, 218; history of investigations, 194–200; style, 203
political economy, 205–206, 217–218;
and agricultural production, 206,
209–210; expansion of, 213, 217;
zonal complementarity and, 215–
216, 361. *See also* Llamas, caravans
Ponce monolith, 197f
relation to Wari, 200
Tizapan, 312n
Tizatlan, 313, 320
Tlacopan, 307
Tlacotalpan, 322
Tlacotepec, 298, 319
Tlaloc, 155, 167, 168, 169
image: at Atlixco, 319f; on braziers,
279, 280f, 281, 282f, 284; at
Tenochtitlan, 312n
Tlamimilolpa, 118
Tlapacoya, pottery, 89f, 90, 91n
Tlatelolco, 307, 309
Tlatilco, 90
Tlaxcala, 138, 163, 285, 297, 313, 316,
318, 320
Tochtepec, 315, 322n
Tollan, 113, 114, 263
Toltec(s), 113, 114, 139
horizon, 264–279, 287–288, 361. *See
also* Early Postclassic horizon, arti-
factual indicators of
hybrid style with Maya, 275, 277
trade relations, 274, 277–278, 286–287
Toluca, 298, 303
Tomebamba. *See* Cuenca
Tonina, 129
Tres Zapotes, 94
Tula, 114, 134, 263, 268, 270, 271, 274,
276–281, 283, 285–288, 306, 310,
314, 315, 361
Aztec ceramics at, 298
Aztec sculpture at, 318
fall, 297
Tulancingo, 299
Tulum, 265
murals, 313, 314
Tupe, 42
Tuxpan, 300
Tzutzuculi, 100n

Uaxactun, 155, 163
  Stela 5, 167
  Teotihuacan ceramics at, 158f, 159
Uhle, Max, 3–4, 17, 41
Urcon, caryatid figure, 233–234
U-shaped architectural forms, 54
Utatlan, murals, 314, 315
Uxmal, 314–315

Ventanillas, 230
Venus
  imagery, 167
  wars, 170
Veracruz, 84, 102n, 173
  architecture, 128, 172
  in Aztec times, 297, 298, 300, 301,
    302, 304, 306, 310, 312, 322n; sculp-
    ture, 318, 320, 322, 323
  contacts with Pacific Coast, 171
  Mixteca-Puebla style in, 265
  relation to Teotihuacan, 118, 162,
    166, 285
  wheeled animal effigy figurines in,
    281–282, 283f, 286
Viru Valley, 240, 241, 250

Waman Wain, 71
Warfare, ritual
  in Andes, 138
  Maya, 167
Wari, 200, 205. *See also* Huari

horizon, 29
Waskar, 346
Wayna Qhapaq, 352
Were-jaguar motif, 89, 91
Willey, Gordon R.
  Andean chronological chart by, 22f,
    28
  on Chavin, 8, 46, 47, 48, 55
  on Mesoamerican horizon styles, 8–9
  on Olmec, 8
  on Peruvian horizon styles, 5, 8–9
World Systems theory, 175

Xicalanco, 301, 314
Xico Viejo, 312, 322
Xiuhcoatl, 168
Xoc, 100n
Xochicalco, 130, 134, 320
Xochipala, 90, 299
Xoconusco [Xoconochco]. *See*
  Soconusco

Yautepec, 298
Yauya, 48
Yaxha, 163
  Stela 11, 138
Ychma, 64

Zaculeu, 307
Zaña Valley, 59, 72, 230, 251